CW00952272

Mastering Executive Education

FINANCIAL TIMES

In an increasingly competitive world, we believe it's quality of thinking that gives you the edge – an idea that opens new doors, a technique that solves a problem, or an insight that simply makes sense of it all. The more you know, the smarter and faster you can go.

That's why we work with the best minds in business and finance to bring cutting-edge thinking and best learning practice to a global market.

Under a range of leading imprints, including *Financial Times Prentice Hall*, we create world-class print publications and electronic products bringing our readers knowledge, skills and understanding, which can be applied whether studying or at work.

To find out more about Pearson Education publications, or tell us about the books you'd like to find, you can visit us at **www.pearsoned.co.uk**

Mastering Executive Education

How to combine content with context and emotion

The IMD Guide

INTERNATIONAL

Real World. Real Learning®

Prentice Hall

FINANCIAL TIMES

An imprint of **Pearson Education**

Harlow, England • London • New York • Boston • San Francisco • Toronto • Sydney • Singapore • Hong Kong
Tokyo • Seoul • Taipei • New Delhi • Cape Town • Madrid • Mexico City • Amsterdam • Munich • Paris • Milan

PEARSON EDUCATION LIMITED

Edinburgh Gate
Harlow CM20 2JE
Tel: +44 (0)1279 623623
Fax: +44 (0)1279 431059
Website: www.pearsoned.co.uk

First published in Great Britain in 2005
© Pearson Education Limited 2005

ISBN-13: 978-0-27370-502-4
ISBN-10: 0-27370-502-4

British Library Cataloguing in Publication Data
A CIP catalogue record for this book can be obtained from the British Library

Library of Congress Cataloging-in-Publication Data
Mastering executive education: how to combine content with context and emotion—the IMD guide /
   Paul Strebel and Tracey Keys (editors).
      p. cm.
   Includes bibliographical references and index.
   ISBN 0-273-70502-4
      1. Executives—Training of. 2. Leadership—Study and teaching. 3. Management—Study
and teaching. 4. Organizational learning—Psychological aspects. 5. Executive coaching.
6. Active learning. I. Title: IMD guide. II. Strebel, Paul. III. Keys, Tracey. IV. IMD International
(Institute)

HD30.4.M373 2005
658.4'07124—dc22

                                                                                2005048454

In some instances we have been unable to trace the owners of copyright material, and we
would appreciate any information that would enable us to do so.

10 9 8 7 6 5 4 3 2 1
09 08 07 06 05

Typeset in 9pt Stone Serif by 70
Printed in Great Britain by Henry Ling Ltd., at the Dorset Press, Dorchester, Dorset

The Publisher's policy is to use paper manufactured from sustainable forests.

Contributors

Gordon Adler
Armande Boichat
Andrew Boynton
Henri Bourgeois
Gavin Brown
Bettina Büchel
Bala Chakravarthy
Robert S. Collins
Carlos Cordero
Carlos Cordón
Robert Crawford
Rhoda Davidson
Jean-Philippe Deschamps
Joseph J. DiStefano
James C. Ellert
William A. Fischer
Thierry Gachet
Xavier Gilbert
Georges Haour
Melanie Hammond
Robert Hooijberg

Kazuo Ichijo
Chris Jewell
Karsten Jonsen
Jean L. Kahwajy
Kamran Kashani
J.B.M. Kassarjian
Victoria Kemanian
J. Peter Killing
Jan Kubes
Nancy Lane
Petri Lehtivaara
Benoît F. Leleux
Beverley Lennox
Peter Lorange
Lindsay McTeague
Thomas W. Malnight
Donald A. Marchand
Martha Maznevski
Seán Meehan
Ivan Moss
Mopesola Ogunsulire

Elizabeth O'Halloran
Gianpiero Petriglieri
Vladimir Pucik
James Pulcrano
David Robertson
Adrian Ryans
Joachim Schwass
Ralf W. Seifert
Janet Shaner
Leif Sjöblom
Mike Stanford
Annie Tobias
Dominique Turpin
Els van Weering
Marianne Vandenbosch
Thomas E. Vollmann
John Walsh
John Ward
Ellie Weldon
Maria Wilhelmsson
Jack Denfeld Wood

Editors: Paul Strebel, Tracey Keys

Contents

Foreword

With the explosion of executive education, within companies, at business schools and elsewhere, it is time to ask: What are the hallmarks of a great executive education program? Of a great session? What distinguishes the good from the bad? What does it take to deliver executive education that will make a difference to organizations? That will stick with executives?

All too often, however, the answers to these questions are rather tentative. In this book we have tried to provide an explicit set of answers by bringing together key contributions from some of IMD's world-renowned faculty. We hope that this will be useful for you, as a business executive or business educator, and help you at least to come closer to deriving your own answers to the above questions. This book is about the drivers of great executive education, what you need to know or do to achieve learning experiences with high impact, learning that will be applied on the job to make a positive difference, in brief, learning that will stick.

I believe that our proximity to business is a key strength when it comes to creating this sort of cutting-edge experience. We have a real-world 'global meeting place' here, with over 5500 executives representing more than 70 different nationalities and from all continents of the world coming to IMD every year. We listen intently to our customers to tailor our programs to their needs. Our programs focus more on learning challenges and business dilemmas than on flat, one-dimensional problems and solutions. After all, being successful in the real world is a matter of understanding how to navigate global waters, benefiting from the multitude of cultures rather than advocating a narrower view dominated by one particular country or culture.

So, why should you read this book? We know that today people represent the key element in a firm's strategy. It is, therefore, critical to invest in one's key people when it comes to cutting-edge learning. And you can make a start by 'investing' in yourself, learning how to learn and how to help others learn. Everything revolves around learning and change these days – read on to discover the stimulating insights on what drives high-impact learning from the frontline of executive education.

Peter Lorange
IMD President and Nestlé Professor

Publisher's acknowledgements

We are grateful to the following for permission to reproduce copyright material:

'Business Life Business Education: The nitty-gritty of going solo' by Della Bradshaw, *Financial Times*, January 31 2005 reproduced with permission from the *Financial Times*; Figure 15.1 ©Ralph A. Clevenger/CORBIS; Figure 15.4 from Donald A. Marchand, William J. Kettinger and John D. Rollins, *Making the Invisible Visible: how companies win with the right information, people and IT* (London & Chichester, 2001). © John Wiley & Sons Limited. Reproduced with permission.

Microsoft, Microsoft Excel, Windows and Windows XP are either registered trademarks or trademarks of Microsoft Corporation in the United States and/or other countries.

In some instances we have been unable to trace the owners of copyright material, and we would appreciate any information that would enable us to do so.

Editors' acknowledgements

This book really is a team effort! What we have sought to capture is what makes an effective learning experience for executives and that is at the very heart of this institution. So while there are indeed many contributors, in effect it reflects the accumulated knowledge and experience of the IMD extended community: our Learning Network partners, our clients, executive participants, all the faculty and staff, alumni, and friends around the world. Thank you.

Such an ambitious project would not have got off the ground though without the energy and foresight of a number of key individuals. To them we offer special thanks. Peter Lorange, President of IMD, for his continued championing not only of the book project, but also of all IMD's thought leadership efforts. Derek Abell, who in the late 1980s was the Dean of IMEDE, one of the founding institutions of IMD, for challenging the faculty to look at scripts that go beyond the case method by using a wide range of learning materials. Andy Boynton, now Dean of Boston College's Business Faculty, and one of the initial leaders of this project, for his persuasiveness in getting colleagues on board and his creativity in pushing the thinking forward. Victoria Kemanian, for all her energy and ideas in helping put together the first two parts of the book, while juggling some other major commitments – namely the arrival of Nicole! Petri Lehtivaara, John Walsh, Benoît Leleux and the whole R&D team for all the support and help in drafting pieces and helping out when the pressure was on. Gordon Adler, Els van Weering, and the whole Marketing and Communications team for their creative input on examples and ideas throughout the process. Last, but by no means least, thanks to Richard, Linda, Laura and the team at FT Prentice Hall for their encouragement of the project and help in seeing it through.

A final thank you to our families for support and encouragement in what at times has seemed a huge mountain of a project, but has been a wonderfully rewarding one!

Paul Strebel and Tracey Keys

Why should you want to master executive education?

Because when you master it, you create lasting value. Take a look at these examples.

Executive EMBA: EMBA assignment leads to new Logitech product
IMD Webletter 23 February 2005

When Yves Karcher set about the 'Learning from your Customer' assignment as part of his IMD Executive MBA, he could hardly have imagined the impact it would have on him and his company.

Yves Karcher

Just 12 months down the line, his company – Logitech, the leading manufacturer of cordless PC peripherals – has just unveiled the first in a new generation of wireless presentation devices – a direct result of Yves' EMBA project.

The assignment introduced Yves to a novel approach that involved him (an engineering director and product unit manager for Retail Pointing Devices) carrying out intensive one-to-one interviews with customers and analyzing the feedback on their experience and needs.

In Yves' case, he selected nine representatives from the customer target base and spent two to three hours with each of them, in their own environment. He even asked them to demonstrate how they present, describing their fears and frustrations and their likes and dislikes as they went along.

Logitech's Cordless Presenter

The end result was the new 2.4 gigahertz Cordless Presenter – a product that addresses many of the concerns Yves had pinpointed, such as keeping to time (features a programmable timer with large LCD display and vibration feedback when five and two minutes remain) and the ability to redirect the audience's attention back to the person presenting (the user is able to turn the display to black – the equivalent of switching off an overhead projector).

Crediting IMD, Yves says, 'To say that this product would never have existed if not for this assignment is no exaggeration. We would have launched a new product at some point, but not this one.' His colleague, Ashish Arora, Logitech Director of Product Marketing, Retail Pointing Devices, agrees: 'If Yves had not been involved, we would not have done any additional research. Probably we would have just relaunched the Cordless Presenter at a cheaper price with little or no feature changes.'

That's not to say that getting the product to market was plain sailing. Yves first had to sell the idea to his marketing colleagues that an engineer could, or should, assume the role of a market researcher and – inevitably – there were times during the development of the product when tensions rose and compromises had to be made.

Yves comments, 'If I had not done the project for IMD, I would not be so passionate about the outcome. I felt a duty to improve the product for the customers based on what I had heard.' His long-term goal is to see the same research approach used for all future development projects: 'I want to redirect engineering – give them a challenge and keep them motivated and not have the expectation that what they want personally is what marketing will sell. Ideally, I would prefer that marketing and engineering conduct interviews together.'

Professor John Walsh is Director of the IMD Executive MBA Program and leads the 'Learning from your Customer' assignment. 'This is one of a series of five company-based assignments our Executive MBAs do throughout the program. Yves' experience is by no means an exception. These assignments get our executives deeply involved in parts of the business they may previously not have been familiar with. Not only are they delivering value to the company through the course of the assignment, as Yves clearly did, but each executive broadens his own knowledge of his company and becomes a more effective, execution-oriented contributor as a result. You can be sure that Yves will have lots of insights to offer Logitech from here on in – his contribution definitely won't end with this project.'

This innovative approach and the events leading up to the launch of Logitech's new 2.4 gigahertz Cordless Presenter are closely examined in a new case study by IMD. Prepared by Research Associate Michèle Barnett Berg under the supervision of Professor Jean-Philippe Deschamps, the case study will be used as a basis for class discussion in selected IMD programs.

Business life business education
The nitty-gritty of going solo: MANAGING CHANGE: Visa Europe turned to IMD for help when it wanted its managers to acquire a taste for project planning

DELLA BRADSHAW

With all the latest management jargon, from inspiration to innovation and creativity to cultural intelligence, it may seem at best humdrum and at worst distinctly boring for a company to engage some of the best business-school brains to help improve the way processes are carried out.

But for a company such as Visa Europe, the card payments organisation that represents some 5,000 European banks and financial institutions, the reputation of both it and its member banks depends on the quality of the management processes when it introduces change.

'The question is, how do you get it right first time, every time,' says David Joyce, head of customer services in Visa Europe's payment processing services department. The question has become particularly critical at Visa Europe over the past year.

On July 1 last year Visa Europe was incorporated as a separate organization from its parent, Visa, and the European company took control of its own information technology systems.

At the same time the organization had to roll out the chip-and-pin anti-fraud technology rapidly across its member institutions.

So Visa Europe turned to IMD in Lausanne, Switzerland, with which it had worked several times in the past, to help develop new processes for introducing change.

Dealing with the nitty-gritty of processes is not everyone's cup of tea, acknowledges Xavier Gilbert, professor of international business dynamics at IMD. 'Project planning is like whisky,' he says. 'It is an acquired taste.'

Some of the six Visa Europe managers charged with developing the change processes had already acquired the taste for it, some had not. But it was by mixing managers from IT, finance, human resources and marketing, and from several European countries that Visa Europe was hoping to get the best results. 'Two of the six will open it up; four will try and close it down,' predicted Mr Joyce.

The six people comprised one of seven project teams participating in last autumn's Booster program from IMD, a curious hybrid of an open enrolment and a customized program. (Visa Europe also had a second team participating in the Booster program.)

Each team was charged with working through a management issue at their organization with the help of IMD faculty and staff – much as organizations would do on a customized program. But for the plenary sessions, all the groups from different organizations worked together, as is customary on an open-enrolment project. As with many customized projects, interdepartmental communications was one of the goals, says Mr Joyce. 'One of the objectives is to get people from right across the organization working together.'

Although the biggest benefits to the Visa Europe team were in this 'custom' part of the course, there were some advantages in working with other companies in other sectors – in this case the food, construction and healthcare sectors – says Sarah Goodbody, the team leader. Their corporate culture and their input to the sessions were very different to that of Visa, she says. 'For our group it was quite an eye-opener . . . It made us appreciate our culture.'

The biggest advantage the Booster programme has over a traditional customised programme is the cost, says Thomas Malnight, professor of strategy and general management at IMD and director of the programme.

The Booster one-week programme comes in two formats. The basic variety – the Visa Europe experience – costs SFr100,000 (£45,000); the extended version, which includes more coaching in the company before and after the programme, costs SFr170,000. But as Prof Malnight points out, traditional in-company programmes are much, much more expensive. 'This is one common process, seven mini projects,' he says.

Even with the (non-extended) Booster programme, IMD has some input before the course. Prof Gilbert, for example, visited Visa Europe in London several weeks before the programme began to determine the aims and the organizational nuances of the project.

This preamble also helps IMD determine that the top management in the company supports the project and also that it is of adequate scope, says Prof Malnight. 'We would discourage someone from sending in a project which is not important.'

The sponsors in the company have to be involved at both the beginning and end of the programme. The directors sponsoring the Visa Europe programme flew to Lausanne as the week came to its conclusion to hear the team present its ideas. The bosses were 'very positive', says Ms Goodbody, and Prof Gilbert was 'incredibly insightful' in his comments.

At the beginning of the process Mr Joyce was reluctant to state too specifically what he wanted the project to achieve, for fear of stifling new ideas.

'Success looks like some sort of process aligned with some sort of organizational change,' he hazards. 'What we want are simple decision-making criteria.' The bottom line is that there would always be a financial benefit, he adds.

At the end of the day, this is what the team recommended – a 'mini department' through which all proposals above a certain cost, plus all changes that affected other departments, must be processed.

Since returning to their offices in mid November, the team has had weekly working sessions and each member of the Visa Europe group has spent between 30 and 40 per cent of their working week on the details of the project and on finalising the proposal.

Although all departments will be involved in the changes, it is the IT department that will be most affected, says Ms Goodbody.

For Mr Joyce, the initial aim of getting people to work together across departments was achieved. 'It's great to see a group of people working together as they did.'

Ms Goodbody also believes this was one big benefit from the programme. 'One comment I had (from one of the team) was: "I've learnt to trust people from other departments who speak a completely different language."'

The final proposal will go to the Visa Europe board next month. Only then will the team discover just how successful its project has been.

Financial Times, London Ed., 31 January 2005, p. 14. © 2005 The Financial Times Limited. All rights reserved.

1

High-impact learning

Paul Strebel and Tracey Keys

'*Learning is not compulsory . . . neither is survival.*'

W. Edwards Deming

Learning is difficult at the best of times. It usually occurs only at the worst of times. Most executives say that their best learning has occurred on the job in the school of hard knocks. By comparison, executive education – in the form of learning events and courses that take place off the job – rarely yields the promised fruits. At best, it provides some distance from the day-to-day hustle for reflection; more often it's a waste of time.

Yet people and their ability to rapidly apply continuous learning are increasingly critical levers of future success. In the face of fierce global competition, shrinking product life cycles, fragmenting but demanding customer segments, as well as radical terrorism, the difference between the winners and losers is small, in terms of both capabilities and time. Companies with great heritages, such as AT&T, Coca-Cola, Disney, Marks & Spencer, Swissair and Alstom, have found their dominant market positions rapidly reversed as they struggle with the new realities of this world.

Tweaking yesterday's business models will not work. To fuel imagination and innovation, learning must be continuous and applied creatively and rapidly. New ways of thinking, diverse perspectives, leadership courage and smart execution will characterize the next generation of successful organizations.

In order to win, tomorrow's successful executives will have to combine insight with the art and science of management. It won't do just to rely on chance for creative insight, to teach the skills that underpin the art of management in corporate training programs, or to look to consultants and business academics for the science that informs new concepts. Managers themselves have to be able to integrate and customize the relevant insight with the art and science of management for the particular business context they face. And they must manage their own emotions and those of their people in the process.

To meet these new challenges, the old approaches to executive development are not adequate. The market is demanding more for the increasing amounts it is spending. A much broader, holistic approach to developing the whole person is required to drive effective learning. Also, executive development has to integrate with the strategic learning needs of the company. One part of this new agenda has to be orchestrated on the job: the needs of the individual with a career development process, and the strategic needs of the company with an organizational implementation and learning process. The other part, the off-site learning experiences that are the focus of this book, clearly has to be customized to fit in with the on-the-job processes. More than that, to justify the expense of taking time out from the job, the off-site experience must provide learning with impact; learning that helps to shape the leaders and organizations that companies need not just to survive, but to prosper.

Rethinking executive education

What can be done to increase the return on executive education, so it delivers the value companies seek? The answer lies on the frontline, in radically rethinking and changing the way executive education is conceived and delivered.

Let's look briefly at some common characteristics of executive education. Much of it has evolved out of academic university courses. Good university courses are based on the rational logic of the latest thinking in the field, packaged into a series of lectures delivered to (usually) young students. But hard-bitten executives bring a career of intuitive experience to the table and are cynical about the fruits of 'pure logic.' Great lecturers can captivate them, but to do so they have to go well beyond logic and add passion and emotion.

The development of the case method at Harvard was a major step forward in making business education more relevant and interactive. But it is designed for MBA students who have recently completed their under-graduate degrees. Three cases a day for one or two years gives them an in-depth introduction to business life and hones their problem-solving skills. Experienced executives already know about business life as they bring their own case study, their accumulated experience, with them. They want less on problem-solving and skill-building, more on path-finding and execution. Plus, of course, they want a much more rapid exposure to new approaches and contexts, over days or weeks rather than years, faster than can possibly be provided by an exclusive MBA diet of three cases a day.

To increase the pace of concept and framework delivery, multimedia presentations have been added to the executive education agenda. So much so that successive PowerPoint presentations often comprise the whole agenda, especially on in-company training programs. But they are a pale substitute for passion and emotion, and overused to the point of overdose! As PowerPoint follows PowerPoint, participation declines and cynicism builds. To keep the boss or educator happy, 'learners' pay lip service to the latest slogans, sit there with zero emotional commitment and gradually become brain-dead.

Enter the guest speaker to liven things up and break the monotony! The better management gurus and business icons have mastered the art of a great lecture. They entertain and deliver concepts and frameworks in easily digestible packaging with passion. But they normally drop in on the learning event, with little understanding of the participants' context and are unwilling to customize their message, except in a cosmetic way. The result is some excitement and buzz after the talk, but little connection to the rest of the agenda and correspondingly little real learning.

While these innovations have improved the learning experience, they are not enough to deliver what business today needs to build solid advantages in people and learning. What's needed is executive education that 'sticks.' It is not just about learning facts. It is about content linked to context that is retained by the executive and applied outside the learning setting in the workplace, learning that generates changes in attitudes, beliefs and behaviors – in other words, high-impact learning.

What is high-impact learning?

Two streams of research point toward the characteristics of high-impact learning: recent neuro-scientific research on the brain and consciousness, and a longer tradition of psychological and sociological research on adult learning. The newer research on the brain[1] is especially important for this book. It points to four implications for adult learning that we found reflected in the characteristics of the best executive learning experiences at IMD:

- **Role of emotion:** Emotional states are the link between experience and memory – emotions allow people to recall experiences with greater clarity. Some research goes further to say that all action is driven by emotion.

- **Role of energy:** Rationality can be employed to analyze, reflect on and plan action, but not drive it. Since effective learning involves the active application of new knowledge, energized roles are central to high-impact learning.

- **Role of context:** Information that is contextually embedded is easier to learn. The brain is very quick to learn in situations that are true to real life. Learning involves the creation of meaning – assisting students in connecting learning experiences to their personal lives will help them to learn in ways that are relevant.

- **Role of the senses:** Employing multiple sensory experiences helps to activate learning – memory and learning are stimulated by experiences involving different senses and relationships. This supports the need for *multidimensional* learning activity to increase the range of multisensory experience. (In addition, work on learning preferences has reinforced the need to use a wide range of approaches, because people learn in different ways.)

The second stream of research on adult learning has been recognized as a distinct field for over 100 years. Early research differentiated the teaching of adults from that of children in a number of ways, in particular observing that adults are often self-directed in the learning process, and more interested in learning which they can immediately apply.

The constructivist theory pioneered by Piaget and other researchers[2,3] emphasizes two fundamental processes at work in learning – 'assimilation,' in which new information is mapped into the existing cognitive structure, and 'accommodation,' in which new information clashes or does not fit the existing structure, resulting in a modification of the structure itself. Transformational Learning[4,5,6] theories focus on two similar processes: 'Informative' learning, which adds additional knowledge or facts without disturbing the world view of the learner, and 'transformative' learning, which modifies the student's world view and fundamental assumptions. The social learning theory of Albert Bandura emphasizes the importance of learning from others and from the environment. The process of learning is held to have four fundamental steps, which include observation, retention, reproduction and motivation. An interesting feature of Bandura's theory, which has been most notably applied to criminology, is the importance of negative experiences and emotions (such as anger and frustration) in driving learning.[7]

Even if the terminology, sequences and some of the underlying rationale are different, the four learning phases cited by Bandura can be found in other theories as well, including a theory of organizational learning developed by our colleague Xavier Gilbert. In this book, we use a description of the four phases derived from the work of Reilly and Kort[8] which suggests links between different emotions and the different phases:

■ **Challenge:** *What's the issue?* Exposure to new information, new ways of doing things. *Why is this important?* A challenge to existing beliefs and/or behavior raises the tension and gets the participants involved. Common emotions involved in this phase are surprise, confusion and sometimes anger.

■ **Investigate:** *How does it work?* Analysis to understand what the challenge is really all about, and how key relationships will be impacted. *What should be done?* Choices and solutions, or more explicit articulation, of what might be done to deal with the challenge. Common emotions include anticipation, curiosity and determination.

■ **Construct:** *How can I use this?* Actual or simulated experience to see how the proposal, or solution, works in practice. *How can I build on it?* Constructing new mental models and approaches that integrate the learning. Common related emotions are hope, confidence and satisfaction.

■ **Change:** *How does this fit with my existing approach? What's similar and different to what I already know and do? What must I change?* Reflection on what this means for the participant's beliefs and behavior going forward. Common emotions are disappointment, fear and frustration.

These phases are not necessarily linear or sequential – the nature of learning is fluid and its exact mechanics remain obscure despite neurological break-throughs, because every person is unique. So, as an individual learns, some phases may be repeated or undertaken outside the learning setting. In particular, because fundamental change to beliefs and behaviors and construction of a new world view require active testing and experience, learning may only become truly embedded after the learning experience has been applied repeatedly.

What are the drivers of high-impact learning?

So how do you drive high-impact learning experiences? When you look at what's common across great, or high-impact, learning experiences for executives, what immediately stands out is an intense involvement and a certain tension or excitement just below the surface. When you dig deeper to see what is behind this, you find the same drivers again and again. Great learning experiences for executives avoid the pitfalls of existing practice mentioned earlier: Instead of an exclusively rational approach, they build up emotional tension and resolve it; instead of passive listening, they give participants energizing roles; instead of gurus out of context, they are grounded in relevant context; instead of a repetitive diet of cases, they use a mix of materials and learning activities.

Emotional highs

We have already said that it is important to engage at the emotional as well as the intellectual level. One participant remarked: 'It's common sense – people are 80 percent emotional and only 20 percent intellectual.' This driver is all about orchestrating emotional 'highs' (and 'lows' in some cases), as this is when participants are stretched and go beyond their comfort zone. Such stretching and opening often feels risky at first, but it is the foundation of 'learning that sticks.' 'Highs' may be realized when emotional tension has been built and resolved at any point through the class or program. Examples include: the 'aha' effect, when participants realize how things fit together or understand a new concept; a story that participants closely identify with; an argument or heated debate; seeing the world/situation through someone else's eyes in a role play. The key is to ensure the overall learning experience is associated with positive emotions ('highs'), because these make the learning far more likely to be applied, as we will discuss in Chapter 2.

Energizing roles

Learning requires interactions: sharing, engaging, debating, imagining, experimenting and reflecting. This driver focuses on how we structure and manage the relationships of the educators, learners, the peer group and others (e.g. guest speakers) to develop the interactions required for learning during sessions and programs. Here we think about the upfront agenda and who is playing what role, e.g. listener, discussant, leader, provocateur. It is also about how this agenda unfolds over time, how the roles evolve and how this evolution is managed, for example improvising where roles change; ensuring everyone is invited to actively participate; and how energy is created and shared to foster deeper learning. As Henry Mintzberg put it, '. . . deep managing and deep learning depend on personal engagement, not just on a detached expertise that "knows better."' [9]

Real-world context

All the theory and research agree on the importance of relevance and tapping into participants' wealth of experience. This driver is about designing and running sessions and programs that reflect the 'real' business challenges that executives are facing today, and the wealth of experiences they bring. Achieving this relevance requires a deep understanding of executives (their needs, objectives and experience), as well as the dynamics of the business environment. It means using examples and approaches that create situations in the class or program where participants can relate to the content effectively. Networks, in particular, are important for offering real-world challenge and support, for facilitating emotional engagement, providing relevance and suggesting new ways to turn learning into action. Networks also help educators understand their customers and vice versa; participants use networks to build and reinforce their own learning, even after the program is finished.

3-dimensional learning

As we suggested earlier, building 'hard,' primarily intellectual knowledge and skills is not sufficient to equip an executive for the demands of today's world and companies. In addition to intellectual awareness, they must build emotional intelligence and skills, to manage themselves and their relationships with the people and environment around them. But awareness alone is not enough, even on both the intellectual and emotional dimensions – a third dimension, action-based application, is critical to embed learning. How learning happens is as important as what it is about. Using many different ways and sensory stimuli to learn about a topic, or practice a new skill, helps to accelerate the learning.

What is a high-impact learning script?

If the drivers and the adult learning phases are the levers that the educator has in his or her toolbox to promote great learning, where's the roadmap for putting them together to meet specific learning objectives? Meet the *learning script*. This term, borrowed from the theater, describes the roadmap (plan) for orchestrating a high-impact learning session or program.

Great learning scripts resemble theatrical scripts. They comprise a series of major parts, or acts, each with specific learning content and activity that assigns different energizing roles to the participants in different scenes. Orchestration[10] and customization of these activities require a mix of insight, method and art. Insight into the context of the participants, method in the selection and design of the learning acts with a variety of content and activity, and art in the conducting of learning roles that energize and connect with emotion. In brief, great learning scripts for executives are where content meets context and emotion.

Sounds simple enough? In fact, a learning script is like putting together a complex puzzle. It needs to address multiple factors simultaneously. It is a sequence of content and learning activity for communicating that content over time, which draws participants into the stages of the adult learning process, while ensuring that the drivers of a high-impact experience are present.

Moreover, each learning script needs to be customized to reflect the context and objectives of the executives on several dimensions: their timeline (before, during and after the learning experience), place (the learning context and the dynamics of the world around us), relationships (groups and networks), individual experience and knowledge (conscious and unconscious).

How to use this book

This book is aimed at both executives and educators. For executives, the value is in understanding better what makes for an effective learning experience, so that you can cut through the wide array of learning choices to target your time (and spend) most efficiently, choosing learning experiences based on best practices as well as ways of learning that best suit your needs. Equally important, it provides insights and approaches that can be used in developing the learning of your teams and the learning processes in the organization more broadly.

For educators, both corporate development professionals and those in academia, we articulate the critical factors underpinning learning that sticks, as well as examples of effective scripts that work in practice.

Part I discusses the drivers of great learning sessions, and Part II the drivers of great learning programs. Parts III, IV and V of the book offer real examples of how this is done in practice, covering the development of learning materials, then scripts for successful sessions and programs. Figure 1.1 offers a schematic view: the navigation is designed to be straightforward, to allow you to dip in and out of the sections of most interest to you. In Chapters 2 to 7, we provide an overall guide with references to pertinent examples in Parts III, IV and V. In each chapter in Parts III, IV and V you will find summaries and key learning points.

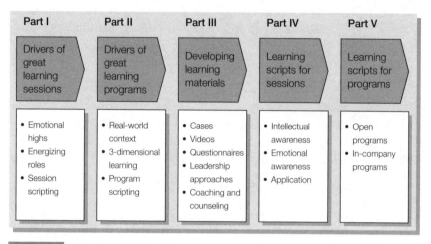

Figure 1.1 Structure of the book

As we move forward to discuss how to orchestrate great executive learning experiences, it is worth bearing this Chinese proverb in mind:

Teachers open the door. You enter by yourself.

Notes

1 See especially Hill, L.H. (2001) The Brain and Consciousness: Sources of Information for Understanding Adult Learning. *In*: Merriam, S. (ed.), *The New Update on Adult Learning Theory.* San Francisco: Jossey-Bass.

2 Fiddler, M., Marienau, C. and Taylor, K. (2000) *Developing Adult Learners: Strategies for Teachers and Trainers.* San Francisco: Jossey-Bass, pp. 17–20.

3 Doré, F. and Mercier, P. (1992) *Les fondements de l'apprentissage et de la cognition.* Morin, G. (ed.). Québec: Boucherville, pp. 11–13.

4 This discussion is by necessity somewhat simplified as dozens of books and articles have been written on transformative learning.

5 Kolb, D.A. (1984) *Experiential Learning: Experience on the source of learning and development.* Englewood Cliffs, NJ: Prentice-Hall.

6 Baumgartner, L.M. (2001) An Update on Transformational Learning. *In*: Merriam, S.B. (ed.) *The New Update on Adult Learning Theory.* San Francisco: Jossey-Bass.

7 Bandura, A. (1975) *Social Learning and Personality Development.* New Jersey: Holt, Rinehart & Winston.

8 Reilly, R. and Kort, B. (2003) The Science Behind the Art of Teaching Science: Emotional State and Learning. Boston: MIT (working paper).

9 Mintzberg, H. (2004) *Managers not MBAs*. Harlow: FT Prentice Hall.
10 It is no coincidence that one of our major programs (Orchestrating Winning Performance) also uses the orchestra analogy in its title: orchestras that perform outstanding music are a subtle mix of careful scripting and improvisation, held together by a common objective and leader. This combination of art, science and conducting closely reflects the domain of the teacher, faculty or facilitator.

1

Drivers of great learning sessions

2

Emotional highs

Contributions from: Jean L. Kahwajy, Victoria Kemanian, Tracey Keys, Paul Strebel

Let's not forget that the little emotions are the great captains of our lives and we obey them without realizing it.

Vincent Van Gogh, 1889

The board is waiting for you. You take a deep breath as you clutch the presentation in your slightly damp hands. It's the big one, the deal clincher. Fear and excitement make your heart race with adrenalin as you enter the boardroom. Sound familiar? Even when we are supposedly at the peak of our rationality, those 'little emotions' are driving how we think and behave, how our body sends messages to our brains and those around us. But to succeed in convincing the board, you have to manage your emotions and, if necessary, override them with rational thought.

What about another situation: your team is discussing a plan you have all agreed to with the CEO. Out of the blue, one of your colleagues turns around and says, 'Well, actually, I don't really agree with that plan now, I think I have a better way.' What do you do? Odds are that, before you can think the suggestion through and respond coherently, you are going to have to get your surprise and anger in check. Even then, you may feel defensive and have negative emotions towards this 'traitor,' which will color your response unless you manage your emotions.

Understand how emotions affect learning

Emotions describe the state of a person and include thoughts, feelings, physiological responses, cognitive responses and behavioral responses. While there is no one definitive list of emotions, Robert Plutchik's description of eight basic emotions[1] is widely used, and Book Two of Aristotle's *Rhetoric* offers another well-known list. [2]

Plutchik's basic emotions	Aristotle's emotions
From *Psychoevolutionary Theory:*	From Book Two of *Rhetoric:*
▦ Fear (or terror, shock, phobia).	▦ Anger vs. calmness.
▦ Anger (or rage, towards self or others).	▦ Friendship (or love) vs. enmity.
▦ Sorrow (or sadness, grief or depression).	▦ Fear vs. confidence.
▦ Joy (or happiness, gladness).	▦ Shame vs. shamelessness.
▦ Disgust.	▦ Kindness vs. unkindness.
▦ Acceptance.	▦ Pity.
▦ Anticipation.	▦ Indignation.
▦ Surprise.	▦ Envy.

Linking emotions and reason is not new. Formalized in disciplines of psychology and psychiatry, the study of mental processes and behavior was for many centuries built on the premise that there was a central control mechanism in the brain that oversees all the separate functions – the home of reason. In the late nineeenth century, the scholars Charles Darwin and William James sparked new scientific interest in human emotions,[3] making links between reason, emotion and how the body and brain function.

However, it has only been in the last 20 years that the understanding of these links has made giant leaps forward as the walls have come down between psychology and neuroscience. Remarkable discoveries about inter-connections in the brain have altered the way we understand how human reason and emotions interact. Scientists now know that there is no central processing center for cognitive functions – the brain acts as 'a committee without a chairman, in which rogue members may sometimes act alone or fail to show up for meetings.'[4] Many different sections of the brain work in parallel, for example different parts of speech, such as verbs, nouns and adjectives, are processed in different parts of the brain, but come together to create our understanding of language.

Building on these findings, Antonio Damasio,[5] a leading neurologist and neuroscientist, has done extensive work on the relationship between emotions and reason (cognitive functions). From practical studies, he concludes that the systems in the brain responsible for emotion are intimately intertwined with those that govern reason, stating: 'Reason may not be as pure as most of us think it is or wish it were' and that 'certain aspects of the process of emotion and feeling are indispensable for rationality.'[6] He demonstrates that reasoning draws on many different neural processing centers, including emotion centers. In particular, he suggests that the brain uses shortcuts for reasoning that rely on emotions embedded with experiences – these he calls somatic markers. Critically, these can both lock in and block learning. A good example of this is the 'gut feeling,' or intuition, that senior executives report is a critical part of how they make decisions.

Somatic markers

Damasio's hypothesis suggests that positive or negative emotions and the associated bodily feelings are stored as experiences or somatic markers in the brain. This complex bundle of feelings and emotions may be recalled as the processes of reasoning create scenarios that are similar to those that have been stored. For example, a plan or idea that triggers a somatic marker associated with negative feelings may cause the plan to be rejected outright, without full consideration. However, if the plan triggers positive responses, it may be accepted, even without thinking through all the implications.

The bottom line is that somatic markers are automatic biasing devices, generated by experience and stored in our brains. They explicitly link reason and emotion and may alter the probabilities of us making certain types of decisions or taking certain actions.

In later books[7] Damasio also argues that our view of the world and our place within it is constructed internally, in the brain, rather than by reference to some absolute external reality. Thus we make sense of the world around us subjectively through a continuous, highly complex process that combines emotions and reasoning.

So how do you manage emotions or override them with rational thought? In 1995, Daniel Goleman hit a chord with a huge audience with the concept of emotional intelligence.[8]

The domains of emotional intelligence

Adapted from *Primal Leadership* by Goleman, Boyatzis and McKee.

1 Self-awareness

Self-awareness is the foundation of emotional intelligence. The person who is self-aware recognizes how his feelings impact the way he acts, for example understanding that he is becoming angry and why, so he can defuse the emotions before they have a negative effect. Sensitivity to one's own emotions also helps a person empathize with the feelings of others. Such integration of their own feelings and knowledge (even unconsciously) makes people more comfortable and capable in using 'gut feel' to guide decisions – they know what matters most. Knowing one's own strengths and weaknesses also promotes a sound sense of self-confidence.

2 Self-management

This domain is all about managing our emotions rather than letting them control us. Mastering our own emotions is a critical part of leadership, because emotions are contagious. In particular, optimism, integrity, honesty and treating people and situations positively are important to creating a climate of trust and openness in an organization – positive and negative emotions have a trickle-down effect. Self-managers demonstrate initiative, coupled with adaptability and a drive for achievement, allowing them to seize new opportunities and overcome obstacles. They do not let disruptive emotions throw them off track.

3 Social awareness

Socially aware people build on their understanding of their own emotions, to be sensitive to the feelings and perspective of others. This is particularly important in multicultural settings. They show empathy and actively engage with others' interests and issues, both at an individual and organizational level. They read networks and decision flows effectively, managing rather than being hampered by 'politics.' The focus on relationships extends outside the organization to actively understanding and meeting customer needs to high standards.

4 Relationship management

Managing relationships skillfully boils down to handling other people's emotions. It involves being self-aware, demonstrating honesty and working empathetically with others in order to be able to influence them, collaborate and manage conflict. For leaders, it is about managing the collective emotional mood of an organization, inspiring people through a compelling vision that builds on the people's own values and motivations. It is about guiding, facilitating and developing others, firmly yet empathetically.

Importantly, from our perspective, Goleman *et al.* believe that the competencies underpinning emotional intelligence (EI) can be learned. Their suggested path for doing so (supported by case examples) involves intense self-reflection to understand who you are and what you really want to be so you can decide what aspects of yourself to change. They then recommend putting new leadership skills into practice consciously and, most importantly, involving others on this journey of change. This sort of training was precisely where a recent survey[9] suggests a lot of business schools and training programs are far behind where they should be. It is no longer enough to equip people with knowledge – they need the skills and attributes, for example integrity, judgment, intuition and self-awareness, to act upon their knowledge.

The implications of these neurological findings for executive learning and development, where emotions have traditionally been subjugated to the rational, are immense. Emotions are an inseparable part of reasoning: without emotion, reason is significantly diminished; without emotion, action is impaired; suppressing emotions could potentially impair judgment and action. The bottom line: for a high-impact learning experience that can be applied in practice – for individuals and organizations – emotions must be explicitly addressed. In particular:

- Establishing the right atmosphere for learning is critical:
  - New experiences are linked to previous experiences and knowledge in each person's internal construction of the world, so learning situations that resonate with previous experiences and/or are relevant to their current situation are more likely to promote rapid engagement and embedding of learning.
  - Actively addressing the potential blockers, promoting openness and experimentation and challenging existing mindsets to overcome blockers are essential.
- How the learning experience takes place is as important as the content; emotions strongly impact communications and relationships:
  - Active participation by learners will help embed the experience as it involves physiological and emotional functions actively, as well as cognitive functions.
  - Building shared experiences among the group of learners will help develop relationships and build bridges between individual 'mindmaps.'
  - Ensuring adequate time for reflection, alone and with others, is critical for behavior change.

To make this practical for the design of learning experiences, we can draw on the work by Reilly and Kort to associate emotions with the different stages of the participant learning cycle, as shown in Figure 2.1. Positive and negative emotions are associated with both the stimulation to learn and the integration of learning into the way we do things. With respect to the learning phases, Challenge and Change are associated often, but by no means always, with negative emotions, while Investigate and Construct are associated most frequently with positive emotions.

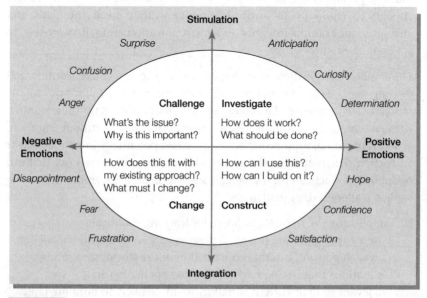

Figure 2.1 Emotions and the learning cycle

Source: Derived from Reilly, R. and Kort, B. (2003) The Science Behind the Art of Teaching Science: Emotional State and Learning. Boston: MIT (working paper).

As an educator, you should create an emotional high in at least one of the phases of the learning cycle, to ensure that the key learning points are retained as an integral experience that can be called on in future. We shall now discuss each of the phases in the learning cycle to see how this can be done from the participants' point of view.

Stimulate participants to learn through challenge

Unless it sneaks up on us in the form of fun, we are not naturally predisposed to learn. The natural response to a learning need is to try to avoid any discomfort by relating it to known beliefs and behavior, to deny the need for any change. The greater the discomfort involved, the less enthusiastic we are. The deepest learning that fundamentally changes the way we look at the world, or changes ingrained behavior, is by its very nature the least pleasant. Getting participants involved in a real learning experience cannot be taken for granted.

You have to earn the attention of the participants for every session by engaging their emotions. If you don't reach them emotionally, they will remain spectators, evaluating the proceedings, but not learning. The most common form of emotional engagement for learning is a challenge in the form of a provocative question (see below on surfacing learning blockers), a dilemma, new data or a new experience, which confronts participants with the questions:

■ What's the issue?

■ Why is this important?

The emotions triggered by these questions can range from surprise to confusion, even anger, depending on the degree of perceived provocation. Answering these questions pushes participants to address their emotions, to open up to new perspectives. Examples of emotional highs triggered by surprise include the following:

■ Being inspired by an educator: finding a role model in the passion, the personality, the energy and self-confidence of an instructor's approach.

■ Learning something unexpected from someone unexpected: when you learn something important from someone you did not expect to; sometimes the silent person surprises you with the deepest thought.

---

case study

Surfacing learning blockers: An example
Jean L. Kahwajy

To create a climate and attitude that invites learning as opposed to blocking it, you might ask this question: 'What does a great conversation look like?' This unravels a brainstorming of responses by participants, which when transferred to the blackboard for all to see, probably looks something like this:

■ There's **mutual interest** in adding value.
■ Greater than what you **expected**.
■ **Something I can remember** afterwards.

▶

- **Enriches** everyone involved.
- **Listening** took place.
- A **dialogue**, not a monologue.
- A **positive atmosphere** is created.
- **Energy** levels increase.

Focusing on the key words from their responses acts as a first-level 'unblocker' because participants have essentially arrived at the root of the problem: the blockers of learning.

But, be careful not to overprovoke. If the challenge is to fundamental beliefs, anger may take over as the dominant emotion. Anger can destroy any willingness to learn; hence, the importance of carefully calibrating the degree of provocation in the challenge. Once participants start to deal with the emotional challenge, they move on to one of the next phases in the learning cycle.

Stimulate participants to learn through investigation

Investigation of new models and exploration of problems, case studies and frameworks often take up most of the time in executive education. The questions to participants include:

- How does it work?
- What should be done?
- What's the solution?

Curiosity is one of the emotions that drive the answers to these questions, together with anticipation about what we might find. Once absorbed in the question at hand, determination to find out how it works or what can be done to find a solution often takes over. Use these positive emotions to orchestrate a high that will make the learning stick. Some examples of related emotional highs are the following:

- Stepping into someone else's shoes: understanding other people by putting yourself into the same situation and exploring how they feel.
- Having a stretching experience: when faced with an unknown topic or skill requirement, exploring what's involved.

▪ The 'aha' effect: understanding a topic in such a way that suddenly everything fits together and we can make sense of it. (This is often linked to gut feel, because we unconsciously recognize that the new pattern makes sense.)

Encourage participants to integrate learning by constructing a new reality

Constructing new meaning and integrating it into a new approach is key to locking in the benefits of a learning experience. This involves answering questions such as the following:

▪ How can I use this?

▪ How can I build on it?

Getting answers triggers emotions such as hope about what might be possible, satisfaction as the new approach takes shape and confidence in the new approach as the benefits become apparent. Emotional highs at this stage have the great advantage of being associated with both positive emotions and positive outcomes, the ideal basis for a somatic marker that will make the learning stick.

Following are some examples of emotional highs associated with constructing a new reality:

▪ A real-life story: when someone else's example gives us a new perspective on a familiar situation.

▪ Having a new experience: such as a project that represents a totally new opportunity requiring new attitudes and behaviors.

▪ Great teamwork and learning from peers: feeling deeply satisfied by successfully concluding a productive joint experience.

Encourage participants to integrate learning through personal change

We need a lifejacket to jump out of our old mental models and shift our paradigms to meet the changing context. You have to give participants the lifejackets they need to support them in the integration of learning through personal change.

During, or after, every session, give participants the opportunity to answer the following questions that address the need for change:

■ How does this fit in with my existing approach?

■ What must I change?

Grappling with things that don't fit into our normal way of doing things can be frustrating. Recognizing what we have been doing is no longer adequate may undermine our self-confidence; evoke feelings of disappointment, or failure. Contemplating the change needed may tap our deep fear of the unknown. These negative emotions don't make for a positive learning marker.

Moreover, since each individual learner brings along a unique set of personal experiences, he or she will experience the change required in a different way. All of this makes it difficult for the instructor to accompany a whole group through this phase of the learning cycle; hence, the importance of self-reflection exercises, either during or after formal learning sessions (see Chapter 6) and the growing recognition of the importance of personal coaching.

Managing our shifts in thinking

Changing our models may mean making a dramatic break with the past or slightly changing a perspective. While 'evolutionary' shifts may have less radical consequences in our lives, 'revolutionary' ones may cause strong resistance from old mental models.

To make a smooth transition between the old and new models, leaders recognize that it is not enough to switch models, but to provide the supporting structure that will facilitate changing actions accordingly. This means deploying resources to create systems of support such as follow-up sessions, individual coaching or group exercises that offer learners the tools to drive through change. Setting up these support mechanisms will be critical in effectively changing our models.

The negative emotions associated with unblocking one's preset ideas and behaviors and changing them are part of the learning cycle, but if that's all there is to it, people will simply avoid the issue altogether. To get change that sticks, the negative emotions have to be offset by positive emotions associated with a new, successful way of seeing or doing things. Examples of emotional highs associated with personal change include the following:

■ Learning from investigating failure: accepting failure as part of learning, understanding what went wrong and avoiding it.

■ Building on honest feedback: humbly receiving feedback, realizing our limitations and taking action to develop a new approach.

End with positive emotions

At the end of the session or program, learning should be associated with positive emotions (a special emotional high from either investigation or construction of a new reality) because such experiences are more likely to be put into practice in the future. Whatever the sequence of phases used in the learning cycle, as the process of building and resolving emotional tension unfolds, it is important to move towards aspiration and hopes, using empathy to build confidence in the learner and focus energy in support of his or her vision of the future and goals – both personal and organizational.[10]

Notes

1 Plutchik, R. (1980) A general psychoevolutionary theory of emotion. *In*: Plutchik, R. and Kellerman, H. (eds.) *Emotion: Theory, research, and experience: Vol. 1. Theories of emotion*. New York: Academic, pp. 3–33.

2 Fortenbaugh, W.W. (1975) *Aristotle on Emotion*. 2nd edn with new epilogue published 2003. London: Duckworth.

3 In *The Expression of Emotions in Man and Animals*, published in 1872, Darwin suggested a common evolutionary basis for emotions across human and animal species. In 1884, in his article 'What is an Emotion?' James proposed that bodily changes are triggered by external events, which in turn evoke an emotional response.

4 Suplee, C. (1994) Committee Without A Chairman: The Modular Theory of the Mind, *Washington Post*, 19 December.

5 M.W. Allen Distinguished Professor and Head of the Neurology Department at the University of Iowa College of Medicine; Adjunct Professor at the Salk Institute for Biological Studies in La Jolla, California.

6 Damasio, A. (1994) *Descartes' Error*. New York: Penguin Putnam.

7 Damasio, A. (1999) *The Feeling of What Happens: Body and Emotion in the Making of Consciousness*; and (2003) *Looking for Spinoza: Joy, Sorrow and the Feeling Brain*. London: Heinemann.

8 Goleman, D. (1996) *Emotional Intelligence*. London: Bloomsbury Publishing; the domains were updated in Goleman, D., Boyatzis, R. and McKee, A. (2002) *Primal Leadership*. Boston: Harvard Business School Publishing.

9 Andrews, N. and D'Andrea Tyson, L. (2004) The Upwardly Global MBA. *strategy+business*, Fall, Issue 36.

10 For an interesting discussion of focusing organizational energy and emotions on threats (slaying the dragon) versus vision (winning the princess), see Bruch, H. and Ghoshal, S. (2003) Unleashing Organizational Energy. *MIT Sloan Management Review*, Fall, Vol. 45, Issue 1.

3

Energizing roles

*Contributions from: Andrew Boynton, Carlos Cordón,
Elizabeth O'Halloran, Victoria Kemanian, Tracey Keys,
Paul Strebel, Ellie Weldon*

*'All the world's a stage, and all the men and women merely players. They have
their exits and their entrances, and one man in his time plays many parts.'*

William Shakespeare, *As You Like It*

How many roles do you play each day? Colleague, boss, parent, friend,
athlete, hunter-gatherer in the supermarket and so on. Our list is long and
that's just today! We each play many roles during the course of our lives.
'Parts' or roles are patterns of behavior that guide our thoughts and actions
in our interactions and relationships with the people and environments
around us. Some patterns may be hard-wired into our brains, e.g. the fight
or flight response; others may have been learned and refined over many
years, e.g. how to eat politely according to the rules of our culture. Essentially these patterns are the brain's autopilot. Our responses change almost
automatically as the situation around us does, unless we actively engage our
consciousness to think about whether we want to act differently.

Learning is about new ideas, information and people, so the process of
teaching demands that educators have the flexibility to play a number of
practiced roles, such as consultant, resource person or role model, as the
audience and the learning goals demand. And you have to switch between
them as the situation unfolds. The description 'educator' can therefore be
used as an umbrella term for many roles.[1]

Learners, however, are the principal actors in the learning experience. The
term 'participant' or 'learner' is a composite for many parts: from passive
listener, to group leader, to educator (of peers and faculty). As participants,
these roles may often be less practiced. They may need to learn a new role,
a new approach to thinking and interacting, which may or may not fit with

their previous experience. At worst, they may reject the new role as too threatening; at best, they will work through the discord to learn and expand their 'mind map' or repertoire of behaviors and knowledge. Whichever the case, the learner needs energy to actively engage with the new information and decide how to address it.

This chapter explores how roles interact and impact learning. We look at the elements that drive the dynamics: the types of educator and learner roles; how to create learning energy by varying the roles; how to manage your personal energy flow; and how to improvise to maintain relevance and energy.

Be aware of the roles you play

The paramount role of the educator is to create an environment in which participants consider themselves to be partners in learning as opposed to receptors of knowledge. Learning requires vulnerability; acknowledging the need to embrace new ideas or approaches, taking risks and rethinking existing knowledge and beliefs. It can be an uncomfortable situation, so developing a learning environment in which participants feel both safe and challenged is essential for high-impact learning.[2]

But participants must not feel too comfortable: they need to question their current assumptions and practices. What is the real reason they don't just stay at home and read a book or watch a video about marketing? It's the educator. The educator drives the energy, at least initially. She can push or pull, until the group assumes energy of its own and takes responsibility for its own learning. Once the audience comes on board, the dynamics will shift. One professor preferred to think of herself as a 'chariot driver' spurring the group on or reining them in, to stay on track towards her objectives.

However, even during a single session both the educator and participants will play several roles as the learning activity changes. This may be implicit as the session moves from plenary to small group work, or activities change. In others cases, it may be explicit, as participants are 'removed' from their original roles in order to take them out of their comfort zone and experience the learning from someone else's perspective, for example in customer or competitor role plays.

Different roles required for the stages in the learning cycle described in Chapter 2 are shown in Figure 3.1. Awareness of the different roles you and the learners play is the first step in varying the roles to further the learning process.

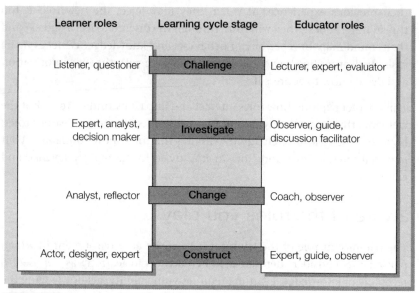

Learner roles	Learning cycle stage	Educator roles
Listener, questioner	Challenge	Lecturer, expert, evaluator
Expert, analyst, decision maker	Investigate	Observer, guide, discussion facilitator
Analyst, reflector	Change	Coach, observer
Actor, designer, expert	Construct	Expert, guide, observer

Figure 3.1 **Some roles associated with learning cycle stages**

Vary roles to create energy

Varying roles is important. First, it allows learners to look at things in new ways, through multiple 'lenses' (particularly important as learning styles differ). Second, it provides mechanisms to investigate new ideas and concepts and integrate these into new approaches. Third, it creates energy and momentum through a change of pace or perspective.

But the roles of the educator and learners interact. Adult learning theory[3] (see Chapter 1) suggests that learning is a three-way process between the educator, the individual learner and the learner's peers. Managing the learning process requires a delicate balance between each 'corner' of this 'triangle of learning.' Each party acts both as a teacher and as a learner, adopting different roles depending on its counterpart in a specific interaction. The flows of knowledge, experience[4] and learning are multidirectional and facilitated by everyone. These dynamics are at the heart of learning experiences.

To get the most out of such exchanges, guidance is important. Shaping roles and dynamics to ensure a learning experience has positive impact – is great – is one of the toughest challenges that educators face. The starting point is to think about the drivers of the energy flows: who owns the 'agenda' that forms the topic of the session and how the educator manages energy flows. The alternatives are illustrated in Figure 3.2.

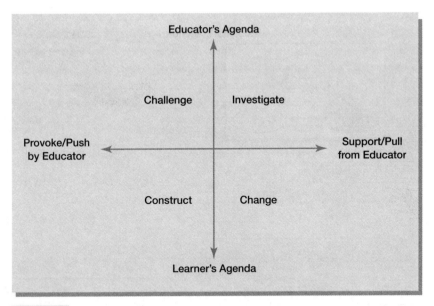

Figure 3.2 Energy drivers in different phases of the learning cycle

On the vertical axis, does the instructor set the agenda for the activity, or do the participants set the agenda for the activity? On the horizontal axis, does the instructor orchestrate the energy flow by provoking or by providing support? Each of the resulting combinations can be associated with a stage in the learning cycle, as shown in the figure.

Illustrating what this means in practice is best done with a relatively simple example, using the Zara video case on supply chain management taught by Carlos Cordón.[5] The stages he orchestrates in this session are briefly described in the paragraphs below, together with the related energy flows.

Educator as lecturer and expert setting up the topic and dilemmas (challenge)

The educator is driving, capturing attention by his enthusiasm for the subject he is introducing. He actively paces the classroom, making eye contact with each learner, challenging them, non-verbally as well as verbally, to start thinking about the issues the case presents. He drops in anecdotes about taking his daughter shopping, starting to engage emotions and build relevance. He is pushing out energy, with only limited flows back and among peers as yet (see Figure 3.3).

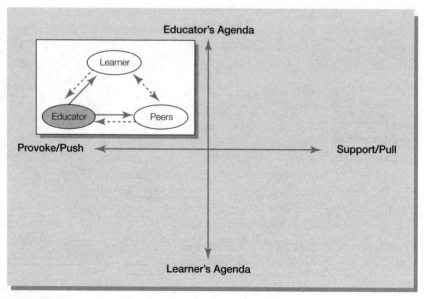

Figure 3.3 Energy flows with educator as lecturer and expert

Educator as discussion facilitator drawing the learners in through relevant experience (investigate)

Now it is time to pull the learners in, so they start to take ownership. The educator asks who else has taken their daughter shopping at Zara. He hones in on the learners who respond, 'pulling' out their stories and ideas about the company. He encourages discussion between peers who have had similar experiences, physically withdrawing a few steps so the learners have control of the flow. He steps back to draw in others who are quiet, asking about their experiences in other shopping situations, if they have not been to Zara. He starts to pull together the ideas that are being generated, defining the issues for discussion. The energy flows are greatest from learner to educator and picking up between peers (see Figure 3.4).

Educator as observer turning control over to participants (change)

It is time for the participants to act on their growing ownership of the problem. The group splits into study groups to discuss the issues that have been raised and what this means for them. From this discussion they prepare a short class presentation. They share their own experiences in dealing with similar situations, learning from each other. The educator puts

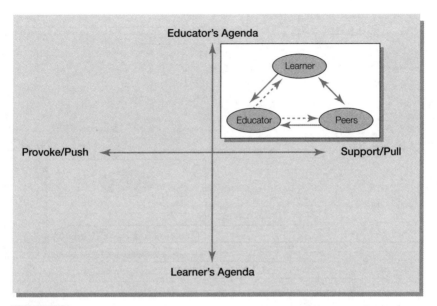

Figure 3.4 Energy flows with educator as discussion facilitator

his head around the doors of the study rooms intermittently, encouraging progress, using both verbal and non-verbal cues. The energy flows are almost entirely among participants (see Figure 3.5).

Educator as guide to participants applying the ideas (construct)

The final step is bringing together the learning as a group. The learners drive the presentations of their ideas, their peers challenge and build on these, with the educator hanging back to let conversations flow or intervening to challenge points or steer discussions back on track where needed. Talk flows freely between all corners of the learning triangle. The educator and the learners take joint responsibility for the take-aways from the session (see Figure 3.6).

Clearly you can choose to start from and end in different quadrants – this will depend on the learning objectives, the group of learners and the educator's preferred style. However, the message is clear: if you move around the quadrants you are more likely to create deep learner engagement and sustain energy. As you cede or retake control, recognize that energy is highest when participants feel that it is 'all about them.' If they drive the learning from their own thought processes, it will be deeper as a result.

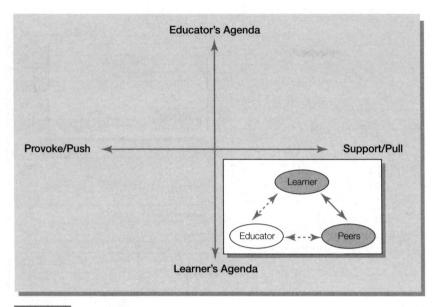

Figure 3.5   Energy flows with educator as observer

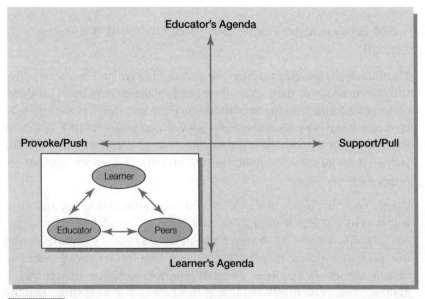

Figure 3.6   Energy flows with educator as guide

Manage your energy flow

Every educator has their own unique approach to creating energy, whether push or pull, largely based on experience. However, you can't take your own energy for granted. You have to manage your energy flow. To do so effectively follow some simple guidelines:

Show energy and empathy

Generating and dealing with emotions in the classroom is not an easy journey. It calls for a high level of personal involvement and putting on the table one's deepest fears and aspirations. One of the keys to success is your own attitude and passion, which plays a primary role in engaging emotions. As the leader of the learning process, your level of energy and demonstrated passion for teaching the subject matter are key motivators in the learning process.

The educator who demonstrates empathy will win the hearts of his participants. Hearts won are more likely to take in and believe what you are saying. Empathy can manifest itself in many ways. One educator makes a point of speaking to as many participants as possible on a one-to-one basis before the class starts and during breaks. Empathetic educators remember names and facts about students. They are not afraid to 'abandon the pedestal' and tell of their own experiences and learning processes. For example, the idea for scripting the Zara case came from a situation that the educator had not previously encountered – a shop that refused to stock an item again or for a prolonged period of time despite its selling out in no time.

Abandoning the pedestal can be done literally if the lecturer joins the back of the class as if he were becoming one of the participants and allows a discussion to carry on as if he were not there. Personalizing the session through the telling of stories related to the educator's own life can also engage learners' attention. Again in the Zara case, the professor used the story of his daughter's shopping expedition as a red thread for discussing supply chain management. Many participants identified with his situation and were thus more able to relate to the teaching points of the session. It made it real.

Establish credibility and respect

Participants are engaged and energized if they have faith in the professor and the message he is conveying. It is basically a question of establishing credibility and mutual respect, which is a two-way street as both are earned, not imposed. Today's world is no longer one where the educator is the unquestionable authority, the giver of knowledge that students must simply acquire, eliminating any prior knowledge they might have. An energetic classroom is a dynamic class in which the control passes from professor to participants in a sometimes planned but often unpredictable flow. So how do you establish credibility and respect?

- **Recognizing the experience learners bring**: A participant will respect a professor more if he recognizes the array of knowledge and ideas that the group brings, and builds upon it.

- **Demonstrating expertise with humility**: Participants expect professors to have an intimate knowledge of their subject matter. They will respect the professor who stops and deliberates over a challenging question rather than the one who glosses over it with broad statements. High-impact learning involves challenge and change, so if participants see the methodology in practice they will be more likely to take it on themselves.

- **Integrating the topic with the rest of the program and the outside world**: If the professor can relate an aspect of his lecture to another case or anecdote then his mastery of the subject will be confirmed. When discussing Zara, the educator related the case not only to other clothing manufacturers, but also to the car industry with regard to the question of who should evaluate new designs.

- **Knowing when to take and relinquish control**: The educator is the person to help summarize, communicate and keep the threads of logic going. As roles vary, she will cede or retake control of the thread, recognizing that energy is highest when participants drive the learning.

Communicate with body language

Gesture, facial expression, humor, movement and eye contact have a significant influence over participant energy.

- **Seeing the point as well as hearing it promotes understanding**: The energetic educator has lively hands and an expressive face. Sweeping hands in a circling motion may signify a two-week cycle. Resting one hand upon his chin may show that he is thinking about a comment a participant has made. A nod of the head, or lighting up like a neon sign, shows agreement with the direction of the answer. A head tilted to one side, or a blank look, indicates some doubt. He may scratch his head in wonderment or look pained at what the answer to the dilemma might be.

■ **Good humor in the classroom generates energy**: The professor's humor is most evident in his facial expressions. Energetic lecturers find humor in the learner group, often at their own expense, and they will laugh along with participants.

■ **Movement sends messages about the required energy level and who is in control**: More movement around the room will broaden engagement from different quarters. Honing in on a speaker encourages him to be more precise with his answer or could shut him down. Moving back as he speaks encourages expansion of the topic and invites contributions from the rest of the class. Agitated pacing of the classroom creates a vibrant energy, forcing participants to concentrate on the lecturer and imbuing them with his enthusiasm. If an argument erupts, the educator's physical withdrawal from the discussion will give it full latitude to continue. Once the points have been adequately made, the educator will then place himself, physically, between the factions to indicate the end of the discussion. To encourage reflection and calm he will move more slowly and deliberately or even adopt a passive pose, either sitting on the desk at the front of the room or taking a seat at the rear. This indicates that participants are to carry the class themselves for a while or if his arms are crossed then it might signify a moment's pause at the end of one discussion and the beginning of another.

■ **Eye contact engages the audience**: Energetic lecturers move from one participant to the next, willing them to believe what he is saying and to own the point he is making. The individual attention draws them into the action, engaging as many participants as possible, not just the handful that proffer their contributions willingly.

Modulate your voice

The way in which content is delivered strongly affects how it is absorbed. Educators must assume the right tone of voice at the right moment in the lecture. If they are explaining something detailed or difficult to grasp, they will be slow, clear and deliberate in their speech. For example, the educator who had to explain which form had to be filled out and in which order spoke slowly and repeated key points to ensure understanding. Slower speech is also used to calm down a class that has gone off track. Suppose an argument drags on too long. The educator might interject calmly to move the class on to the next point. Often lecturers raise their voices at these times so as to assert authority and regain control. Adjusting volume provides variation within the class and can help to shift between a high and low energy moment. The educator will speed up if he's telling a personal anecdote or giving a consequential piece of information. The excitement that can be transmitted in a voice is tangible and infectious. Speed of speech also manifests as energy as participants are forced to be attentive in order to keep up with the pace. All energetic lecturers use pause to great effect. One educator began a portion of his class by asking participants to consider how the protagonist would have felt after a particularly difficult meeting. He paused while the class reflected, and he allowed them to put themselves in the protagonist's shoes and consider his emotions. Another related the achievement of the case company under discussion to a similar activity within a participant's company. The difference was notable and again he paused to let that fact sink in.

case study

Getting great conversations going in class

Andrew Boynton

Great conversations require three central skills: the ability to ask, the ability to listen and the ability to redirect on the fly.

The starting point has to be an issue to discuss, and that can be a case, a lecture, a video, a framework or whatever. That starting point is the catalyst for the conversation and the more provocative, thoughtful and ultimately relevant to the participants it is, the better. Once the starting point is positioned, it is important to have the confidence to ask what people think about it, or how it relates to their job or company. The specific questions can vary, but it is key to have a series of questions available, and if one doesn't work, it is important to be relentless and keep asking questions until an answer is given that provides an opening for further conversation. To ask questions and persist takes confidence and attitude in the classroom. One cannot panic or give up – appearance is everything.

It is essential to listen to the answers being given. Each answer has to be listened to very carefully. A series of answers that appear unrelated might provide the opportunity for the instructor to link the opinions, summarize briefly and ask more questions. Listening is not just listening; it is really getting into the heads of the participants. Great teaching takes an ability to literally peer into the brains of the participants during the entire class and get their full commitment and energy into the learning process and conversation. Listening is essential to track not just the thoughts but the emotions of the participants.

Redirecting on the fly is probably the most difficult part of generating great conversations. First, the participant must believe that the conversation is 'their' conversation, not your conversation, so you really need to listen. The instructor must keep in mind all he or she knows about the participants, what has been said in that session (and in previous sessions if relevant) and instantly come up with provocative questions or probing summaries. The best questions are those that really challenge the participants: 'You said that, and so and so said this – how can both be true? What's going on?' 'Wait, a few minutes ago you said something entirely different; do you really think this? Does anyone agree? Disagree?'

The answers provided by participants become the fuel to drive the class. The material fades into the background. To do this, the instructor has to be able to ask, listen, quickly figure out what is going on and redirect the conversation towards specific objectives – all while appearing supremely self-confident the entire time – following the hearts and heads of those in the class. A major challenge is the parallel processing required – what to ask next, what is being said, what was said, and then how to redirect to increase the intensity and improve the conversation – the result is learning for those involved. The entire class (or program) has to be carefully scripted beforehand to make this work as well as it can.

Improvise to maintain relevance and energy

Energy is good, but too much of anything is not. Balance is critical, because people get tired if asked to sustain attention, or activity, at one level for too long. A 'monotone' activity also makes it hard to distinguish what is important and what is not. So a session or program needs to have both high and low energy periods.

Careful management of the energy level is key, because the combination of different roles and settings often creates tension and stress, due to situations like the following:[6] we have more than one role relationship to another person or group; we disagree on how a role should be played; others play their roles in ways that are incompatible with our own.

Improvisation is essential for dealing with these problems. For example, some delicate, on-the-spot discussion and redirection by the educator will often defuse many sources of tension. More generally, improvisation is a valuable skill for balancing the levels of energy in class, for re-engaging participants, for adding an additional challenge to the topic discussed or for creating a detour from the original plan to address newly emerged interests. Upfront preparation (and in some cases practice) determine how well and how much the educator can improvise during a session and/or program. But you will need to improvise, almost without fail, during every learning experience.

So what does improvisation entail? Are sessions highly scripted and, if so, do educators stick to these plans? Or is a session looser and more flexible? Is it enough to sketch out the topics to be addressed and then improvise around those topics? To find out the answers Ellie Weldon did a short survey.

Here's what she found. First, professors at IMD develop fairly detailed plans for their sessions, but most improvise to some extent. Second, for those who do improvise, the primary reason is to increase the relevance of the session to the participants. Third, faculty members rely on their intuition, accumulated knowledge and teaching experience to improvise effectively.

Although sessions are scripted, improvisation is important

All respondents said that they always develop plans for each classroom session. No one said that he or she would show up and try to 'wing it.' But most respondents also said that improvisation is an important part of their teaching – one said that it is 'absolutely essential.' Others estimated that anywhere from 25 to 50 per cent of what they say and do in the classroom is improvised.

Only two respondents preferred not to improvise. For example, one faculty member favored a well-scripted and well-structured session and tried to avoid improvisation. Another faculty member said that he almost never improvises.

Interestingly enough, improvisation doesn't seem to influence effectiveness in the classroom. But, the two professors who avoid improvisation are primarily case teachers. Those who improvise often facilitate other sorts of sessions.

Improvisation tends to focus the details, not the key points

Examples of how improvisation contributes to teaching showed that although the key points and primary activities for a session tend to be carefully scripted, the details and supporting material may be improvised. One faculty member explained that he sticks closely to his list of topics but is flexible during the discussion: 'I always come to class with a plan specifying major topics to be covered, an idea of how much time we will spend on each one, some leading questions, a few follow-up questions and usually a board plan. But because discussion-based teaching involves interaction between the faculty member and the participants, to some extent, I must follow where the class leads. To do that, I will improvise follow-up questions, and change my timing. But all of that is still within the structure of the session plan.'

Another faculty member scripts the key points to be addressed but improvises anecdotes and illustrations. Talking about a recent session, he said: 'In class yesterday evening, I intended to talk briefly about demographics, and I had examples in mind. But because there was an Italian woman in the class, and Italy has Europe's lowest fertility rate, we spent time talking specifically about Italian demographics. Then, because there was also a Brazilian present, I compared Italy to Brazil. I told the Brazilian that over the next twenty years the population of Brazil would grow by the equivalent of "one Italy," while the population of Italy would age and decrease by about 7 million. I pointed out that this has economic implications, but also implications for Italy's success in sports. In the future, how well will a geriatric Italy do against a youthful Brazil?'

In a similar vein, another professor is flexible about formal presentations. If the key points are covered in the discussion, he doesn't formally present his slides at the end.

Sometimes improvisation is used to change direction

Occasionally some faculty members will abandon their plans entirely and head off in new directions: 'I can remember two sessions when I completely dropped my lesson plan, and went off in an entirely new and totally unplanned direction. In one instance, I realized that the company had some pressing issues that were more important than the topic I had planned. We talked about these issues instead. In the other case, I realized that some background treatment of a topic was needed, so I made a big detour.' Several other faculty members told similar stories.

Most often, improvisation is used to increase relevance

The most common reason for improvisation – particularly when a new direction is pursued – is to follow the interests of the group. As one professor described: 'I do it because the material I improvise is more relevant for that audience at that moment. My new direction is spontaneous, based on the classroom flow, the energy in the room, reactions to my remarks, and the participants' particular issues. To focus on the new issues, I present new models or frameworks and ask a different set of questions.' He went on to say, 'Ideally, when I go into the classroom, I will know what the key issues are, but that doesn't always happen. Then I have to improvise.'

Focusing on 'real' issues in this way also fuels engagement: 'I improvise to engage the class. If they're not interested in the case, I have to depart from the script to link the issues more directly to their own situation. For example, I was starting to teach a case when a participant said, "I have a similar example in my company." I asked him to explain his situation, and then we dropped the assigned case and used the participant's case for the rest of the class. Subsequently, two more participants provided examples from their work, so we used all three cases to raise questions and create a new assignment for the group. All the issues that I had planned to cover were discussed, because I asked questions to lead the discussion in that direction. But other issues that I did not expect to cover were also discussed.'

This can lead to new frameworks, as well as emotional 'highs': 'Last week, I taught the new INTUIT case about Steve Bennett taking over as CEO. I had planned to focus on organization design, but the class started talking about his leadership. And they wanted to talk about Bennett's values. So, I improvised a framework about managerial values and how values drive behavior. Then I took the framework and asked the participants to examine their own assumptions and values – and link them to the decisions they made for the case. Then I asked them to consider how their values influence their own decisions and actions at work. They loved it and it was an important moment in the program. It gave them an opportunity to examine themselves in a natural way and link the material to their own work in a very personal way. When I selected the case, I never thought I would address these issues. But the class led me there, so I dove in, abandoned the script and spent an hour on the topic.'

Another professor told us that he uses improvisation to increase responsiveness in the classroom. He said, 'I have a problem with preparation: the more I prepare, the worse I deliver. If I overwrite the script, I end up delivering on automatic mode. For this reason, I do some preparation, but I assume that I will improvise. This makes me more responsive to the classroom situation.'

However, there are times when even the improvisational professor will stick to the script, even though participants might prefer to talk about something else. One told us: 'When I am teaching a model that they will use for an assignment, there is little improvisation.' Another said: 'Some clients want a specific topic covered. As a result, there would be little improvisation.' In these situations, faculty members stick to their plan.

Intuition, knowledge and experience are the keys to effective improvisation

When asked how to improvise effectively, several respondents said that they trust their intuition and they 'just do it.' For example, one told us: 'I just do it. I'll ask a different set of questions or present a new framework or introduce new issues into the discussion. I'll pause and say let's look at things differently. I'll have them buzz on something I didn't plan. I might have to run into my office to get the right overheads or whatever, but that's how I do it. And I have complete confidence that it will work. I've done it so many times that I trust my instincts completely.'

Other professors embrace the same willingness to improvise, but try to anticipate different directions the discussion might go and bring those materials with them to class so they can choose as they go.

Comments from other professors suggest that knowledge and teaching experience are also important. As one faculty member said, 'I didn't improvise early in my career, but now it's an integral part of my teaching. The knowledge I have accumulated throughout my career and my teaching experience make it possible to improvise. Now I can rely on my intuition to improvise effectively.' It seems that subject matter expertise and teaching experience work with intuition to make improvisation possible.

To do it again, and better, improvised material often becomes scripted

Finally, we discovered that improvised material often becomes scripted for future use. The professor who improvised while teaching the Intuit case ended his story with this comment: 'After class, I wrote copious notes about the session and put them in my teaching files. Now I know that the case is a great vehicle for discussing values and behavior, and I have another way to teach the case.'

Improvisation is also often a way to experiment with new material to see what works: 'When faced with presenting a new session, I'll usually over-prepare all the wrong stuff. When I get into class, I abandon the script and respond to what happens. After four to five trials like this, something workable usually emerges and the final product is almost always much less complicated than my original approach. I store that for future use.'

These findings show that improvisation is important for managing energy highs and lows. Although preparation is essential, the ability to assess the interests of the group quickly and change direction to follow their lead can contribute to a powerful learning experience – improving relevance, exploring new angles and, thereby, balancing energy ebbs and flows.

Dealing with energy ebbs and flows

Sometimes, even with the best professor and script, the group dives into passivity. They just cannot re-engage. Here are a 'top 10' of ideas we have found useful for re-igniting energy:

1 Move into buzz groups.
2 Make the discussion more relevant to participants – draw out their own examples.
3 Rephrase questions.
4 Take a break.
5 Change seats.
6 Cold-call.
7 Use video or different media.
8 Take a vote, plot an opinion line.
9 Role play the issue under discussion; change places.
10 Ask an expert among the participants.

Similarly, discussions and energy levels can get overheated and tempers can flare. A 'time out' is needed to get the session back on track and reflect on the critical learnings. Here again, some techniques to deal with energy highs:

1 Move into buzz or study groups.
2 Plot opinion lines and draw a line under the debate.
3 Exert (educator's) authority explicitly, e.g. 'We will come back to that issue later.'
4 Take a break.
5 Ask participants to summarize the arguments for and against the issue under discussion; move from emotional to rational analysis.
6 Drop the planned discussion; focus on the topic that is creating the debate, as it is clearly of importance to the participants.

Remember that generating energy surges is important at the start and the end of the session or program. In the first case, to capture attention and build energy that will create momentum for the rest of the time. At the end, to ensure participants take away their learnings on a high note. However, there should not be too many energy surges – these should be timed as far as possible to focus attention on the handful of session or program take-aways. And less collective energy is important too. This provides a respite for learners, allowing them time to pause and reflect, to regroup their thoughts and energies for the next challenge, just as athletes do between heats in the Olympics.

Notes

1   For more on this topic, see Grasha, A.F. (1996) *Teaching With Style*. Claremont, CA: Alliance Publishers.
2   Rogers, J. (1989) *Adults Learning*. 3rd ed. Maidenhead: Open University Press; and Vella, J. (1994) *Learning to Listen, Learning to Teach: The Power of Dialogue in Educating Adults*. San Francisco: Jossey Bass.
3   For example, Bandura, A. (1975) *Social Learning and Personality Development*. New Jersey: Holt, Rinehart & Winston.
4   Knowles posits that adults have a rich reservoir of experience that serves as a resource for learning, Knowles, M. (1984) *Andragogy In Action: Applying Modern Principles of Adult Education*. San Francisco: Jossey Bass.
5   *ZARA, The fashion retail billionaire* (2003) IMD Catalog No. 698. This case on Zara, part of the Inditex group, was developed by Gilles Delbos and illustrates the unique characteristics of the Zara business model, no advertisement, very fast product introduction, simplified decision processes and the internal network of companies that work within the group.
6   Grasha, A.F. (1996) *Teaching With Style*. Claremont, CA: Alliance Publishers.

4

Session scripting

Contributions from: Joe DiStefano, Victoria Kemanian, Tracey Keys, Paul Strebel

'You need three things in the theatre – the play, the actors and the audience, and each must give something.'

Kenneth Haigh, 1958

Some executive education experiences can be highly entertaining, even involve high-energy activity, and still leave you feeling empty at the end. You feel like you have been taken for a ride; you put energy and commitment in and get nothing out. There was no content. Emotions and energizing roles are not enough; there muset be relevant content.

High-impact learning scripts are about orchestrating both content and activity to help participants get answers that will stick, answers to the questions in the learning cycle: Why is this important? What's the issue? (Challenge); How does it work? What should be done? (Investigate); How can I apply this? How can I build on it? (Construct); How does it fit with my existing approach? What do I have to change? (Change). Not just any answers, but answers they internalize, because they are associated with energizing roles and emotional highs.

Developing a script to do this is tough. It is impossible to know exactly what experiences, beliefs, values, practices and learning styles a group of participants will bring. So, as the educator, you need to manage lots of interrelated factors, without knowing exactly what responses you will trigger. Understanding the group as much as possible upfront helps a lot, but every session will unfold in a unique way.

This is the conundrum of learning script design: can you design a script that incorporates energizing roles, emotional highs, scope for answers to the learning cycle questions and is tailored to your objectives and participants?

Will it provide a guide that can be useful for others (and yourself) as they (you) tackle similar situations in future? That's what this chapter will help you do, by integrating the learning drivers described in the previous chapters.

The key to successful integration is using lessons from the theater and theatrical scripting as a guide, keeping the participants in the center: in the sequence of learning acts and scenes, what will they be feeling; where will their energy come from; what roles will they be playing; how will they relate to the materials, how will they influence one another?

Use lessons from the theater

The world of storytelling and the theater provides inspiration for learning script design. Here, for millennia, people have passed on knowledge and new ways of thinking through stories with morals that are explicitly or implicitly scripted to grab our attention. Authors of every description – priests, philosophers, playwrights and novelists – have translated compelling stories into scripts that capture our emotions and feelings, offering dilemmas and actors we can identify with, so that the tales and the morals are brought to life and imprinted on our minds.

Many teachers use the analogy of themselves as actors performing a play in front of an audience that gradually becomes caught up in the 'drama.' Lowman[1] suggests that 'teaching is a performing art. Excellent teachers use their voices, gestures and movements to elicit and maintain attention and to stimulate students' emotions. Like other performers, teachers must convey a strong sense of presence, of highly focused energy.' However, professors are not comedians – their role is 'not just to make people happy in the hope that happy people will do the right things.'[2]

Use theatrical principles like those developed in the previous chapters to drive learning that sticks:

■ **Build and resolve dramatic tension over time**
Script the session like acts in a play. You capture attention in the first act, then build and resolve tension through the middle acts to arrive at the climax – the closure and key messages. In each act, different scenes can be used where necessary to introduce different activities and roles.

■ **Engage the whole person both emotionally and intellectually**
Sequence the intellectual content and learning points of the session in a logical way that makes sense to participants and can be easily

followed. At least one act in the session typically should be devoted to each major learning point to ensure that the latter is anchored with emotional intensity.

■ **Use a script that plays to your strengths as an educator**
Directors and scriptwriters interpret the same story and message, or moral, it aims to communicate, in very different ways, that play to their purpose and strength. The learning point 'story' suggests basic directions; you as the director and scriptwriter then interpret it as you see fit, e.g. in the theater a traditional *Romeo and Juliet* versus a modernized version such as *West Side Story*, to exploit the context.

Scripting the acts involves deciding not only what material and learning activity to use, but also what roles the educator and learners should play in the scenes making up an act. For example, as described in Chapter 3, in a first act designed to provoke, scene one often involves the educator getting the attention of participants by challenging them to react to an issue. Scene two might then involve the educator supporting the participation of more learners, thereby drawing them into the activity.

Each act needs to be opened, managed and closed, so the core messages are developed throughout the session. For example, an act might be built around discussing the core question of what should be the priorities for a new CEO, based on analyzing the challenges facing him. Scenes could involve debating the logic underlying each priority before the act is brought to a conclusion, with agreement on what priorities and why. This can then lead into the next act: how is the CEO going to be able to put these priorities into action?

However, keep in mind that learning scripts differ from theatrical scripts in two very important ways. First, the audience is not directly part of most theatrical scripts. By contrast, the participants are always part of a learning script. They need energizing roles. Second, the playwright mostly fixes the lines in a theatrical script in advance. By contrast, the responses of participants in a learning script are up to them. As the session evolves, each of the script elements may need to be adjusted to match or influence the dynamics of the situation, e.g. to maintain engagement, to increase or decrease energy levels, or to explore a different subject. These changes may or may not involve using options that the instructor had thought about in developing the original script (which is why improvisation is so critical for learning script instructors, as described in the previous chapter).

Figure 4.1 shows the main elements in the design of a half-day learning script, in which each of the acts is associated with one of the stages in the

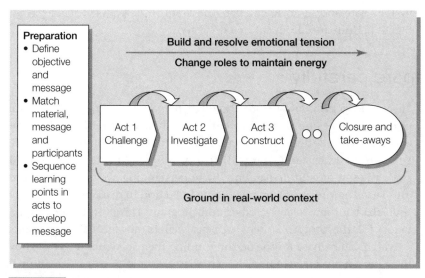

Figure 4.1 Session script design

learning cycle (as in the Zara example in Chapter 3). Another common, more traditional design is one in which several acts are associated with the investigation of a case situation, with the change and construct stages of the cycle being left to private reflection by the participants. More varied designs use a mix of cases, exercises, data and concepts, with the mix and duration of each component varying according to the learning objectives.[3]

The key to the success of any chosen design is the logic flow of the content and the way roles are changed to maintain energy, and build and resolve emotional tension. In the CEO example, you have to design a script that takes the participant through a series of dilemmas. Once the dilemma of what priorities has been resolved, there's a bigger one – how to implement these priorities. Assuming the participants have identified with the CEO's issues, they should feel some satisfaction at making the first decision, then some uncertainty about the implications and further decisions required.

It's important to engage the emotions, at least to some extent, in each act, but not to try to build in too many emotional highs, or you risk losing the plot. And remember, the acts will only connect emotionally with the participants and stick if the content is relevant, grounded in the real world. To see how all of this can be done, let us now look a little closer at each of the elements in the figure, with reference to an integrated session design used by Joe DiStefano in an in-company program to help global managers get higher performance from cultural diversity.

Prepare carefully

There's no getting away from thorough preparation. You need to think through from beginning to end what you wish to accomplish and how you will get there, starting with the group of participants you expect to have. You need to understand your participants well (see Chapter 5), as this will guide the rest of your preparation. By understanding, we mean more than 'this year's new recruits who need some induction in marketing 101' or the equivalent for an executive education program. However, because preparation for the program often happens well in advance of participants' arrival, it can be hard for the person running the experience to get to know them personally ahead of time. Nevertheless, in most cases, participants will have filled in an application form for the job or program, so please use it! Take the time to dip into the vast array of experience, cultures and expectations your participants will bring. If the program has run before, talk to colleagues who have taught on it. Get a feel for what sort of people come, how the group dynamics work and what teaching approaches have worked well or not. Finally, do not forget to talk to the recruitment or marketing teams who can tell you about the people they are trying to attract to the program.

In our example, the managers attending the in-company program, focused on developing leadership skills, are drawn from separate operating companies around the world. The forty or so participants have substantial experience and many have engineering or science backgrounds. While most have had little contact with their peers from other parts of the organization, they recognize that unless they work together more effectively it will be difficult to improve the company's overall performance.

Armed with an understanding of your prospective participants, it is time to design the program by defining the objective and message, matching the material to the message and the participants and sequencing the learning points in the message.

Define objective and message

Here the job is to identify the breadth and depth of content required in terms of subject matter, as well as initial thinking on framing the key learning points. Questions to ask yourself include:

■ From the participant's point of view, why is this session important? Where does this session fit in the overall module or program?

■ What's this session all about – what's the topic? What specific learning points and ways of thinking do I want participants to take away from it? Does the group already know enough – and know each other well enough – for these objectives to be appropriate? How will they react to the chosen approach?

■ How do I develop and frame the key messages and take-aways, e.g. do I let the participants figure it out for themselves as they go, or do I want to bring it all together for them? Will the session set them up effectively for how we want to develop the learning through the subsequent sessions?

In the cultural diversity session, the aim is to help the participants interpret and behave effectively in their own situation. The first objective is to provide a framework for using diversity to achieve higher performance. The participants have extensive experience but this tends to focus on technical aspects of the job, rather than the interpersonal relations critical for global leadership. So the second objective is to increase awareness among participants of themselves and the impact of differences. The final objective is to provide the opportunity for the group to test the applicability of the ideas to situations from their own experience and that of others.

Match material to message and participants

Given a reasonable idea of who your participants are, the objectives for the session and how the message will develop, you can start to tie all this together with appropriate materials and processes. Again, tap into the experience and ideas around you, asking:

■ What mix of materials and/or processes will be most useful in achieving my objectives and conveying the right messages to this audience (see Chapter 6 and Part III for some ideas)?

■ How will I achieve the sort of interactions that I require, e.g. through breakout sessions, buzz groups, plenary discussions, simulations, games, guest speakers, action learning?

■ Do I have the materials I would like available already? Are they really appropriate given the audience and the message – do I need to adapt them, supplement them or develop something completely new?

Back to the cultural diversity session: the educator chose a mix of concepts, cases, data and exercises to achieve the session objectives. This combination, while requiring significant upfront preparation, allowed the effective linking of concepts and behaviors to personal patterns of inter-action, as well as provoking personal application of the core framework to past experience and future improvement. The mix of learning techniques acknowledged the wide range of learning patterns typically found in a diverse group, while offering flexibility to respond to the emerging group dynamics.

Sequence learning points to develop message

The next challenge is to figure out the timing of the session – the acts in the play. What activity will happen when, with what expected result in terms of building up the overall message(s)? In our example, the 'Map-Bridge-Integrate' framework[4] described below is used to outline the session and intended take-aways. Such a framework or 'roadmap' should divide the session into the basic acts, the only fixed points being the first act of getting attention and the finale of closure and take-aways. We would suggest that you limit the total number of acts to between three and five, or you risk having too many activities and roles, as well as too many messages (diluting your primary ones) and not spending enough time developing each learning point in sufficient depth. Even the smartest people can only take away a handful of new learning points from one session.

As you work through each act or scene within an act, think about how to:

- Develop the message and key learning points, to build towards the expected take-aways.
- Ground the discussions in real-world context.
- Change roles to maintain energy.
- Build and resolve emotional tension.

Now it is time to design the actual learning experience. You will be on stage with the participants. How are you going to get through to the final curtain? The very first step is to get attention within the context that the participants come from.

Challenge: Why is this important? What's the issue?

A good challenge, one that grips the participants, typically has several scenes. How does this work? Put yourself in the shoes of the educator in our cultural diversity session example: **Act 1** has four short scenes, designed to engage and challenge participants, as well as to provide a clear roadmap for the session to which everyone can refer back as needed – important given that there will be a lot of different activities along the way.

In **Scene 1** you introduce the objectives of the session (described above) on how diversity helps – why are we participating in this session?

In **Scene 2** you change tack and declare that diversity gives synergy, asking for real examples to corroborate or refute this, which engages the participants by drawing on their own backgrounds. To help establish an atmosphere where individuals open up, you offer some stories from your own personal experiences to start the sharing process. It usually quickly becomes clear that there are differences of opinion and experience about the impact of diversity.

You then introduce data in **Scene 3**, showing that despite their potential, most diverse teams do not perform as well as homogeneous teams. But the best performers were diverse teams that were managed well. This kind of data is counter-intuitive to the widely held assumption that diversity offers greater potential for synergy. The questions for the group are: 'Why the gap? How can we close it?' Drawing examples from participants illustrates the reasons for failing to achieve synergies in practice and suggests ideas for enhancing the potential of diverse teams.

In **Scene 4** you wrap up the act with the introduction of the Map-Bridge-Integrate (M.B.I.) framework, which provides a framework for dealing with many of the issues that have been raised so far and a roadmap for the rest of the session. Briefly, mapping (M) is about understanding the differences between people in a diverse team; bridging (B) is about developing awareness and tools that will allow you to communicate effectively across the differences; and integrating (I) is about actively managing the differences to improve performance – valuing the differences because differences create value. In doing so, you outline the principle of 'decentering without blame,' which involves attributing problems and conflicts correctly and sending and receiving messages bearing in mind the meaning intended by the other party. You end this act with a direct challenge: 'You are all going to break this rule in the next half an hour, I'll bet $5 on it!'

As you think about framing your own scripts and attention-grabbing first acts, here are some questions we suggest you think through:

■ Given my objectives for the class, the type of participants and what they did just before my session, the materials and processes, what sort of opening would work best, e.g. an attention-grabber such as a controversial question or a guest speaker, or a gentle awakening to introduce the tools and frameworks they need for big challenges later?

- How do I make sure I introduce the dilemma or central theme and the key actors effectively?
- How do I position the participants' roles and my own vis-à-vis the situation or topic?
- How can I make sure the opening is relevant to the participants? How will they feel about it?
- Will the opening really engage their energy as well as attention, as I need to maintain this during the session?
- What are my opening lines and/or scene, so I set the right atmosphere? How will the dialogue start?

Investigate: How does it work? What should be done?

The participants' investigation and work with the material often is at the heart of the learning script for a single session. Several acts may be scripted for investigation and some of these can be quite elaborate. Going back to our group wrestling with the challenges of diversity, **Act 2** focuses on a hands-on (literally) investigation of the issues in managing diversity.

In **Scene 1** you introduce the Five Tricks card game to the group. Participants break into teams of two, with two teams per breakout room – where they find the rules of the game. Energy and spirits may be high as it sounds relatively simple and fun.

In **Scene 2**, participants play the first round of the game with the only communication permitted between team members and opposing teams being non-verbal. The winners then move along to play a new team in a new room. While all seems to go well, by the end of the second round, there are some slightly confused faces emerging. When the teams move on to the third round, you tell them to switch partners with the other team. Silence when playing is still mandatory, but this does not last long as it quickly becomes clear that in some rooms both teams think they have won a trick, while in others the two people in the same team disagree on whether they have won or not. Arguments erupt – 'You got it wrong; you didn't read the rules properly.' Others direct their annoyance at you, the faculty: 'That's not fair, everyone had different rules.' Emotions are high.

Time for **Scene 3**. The group has clearly lost their $5 bet. They reconvene to discuss what has just happened in the card game, and why they got so emotionally worked up over a trivial card game. As you organize the responses on the board using the M.B.I. framework, it quickly becomes clear that the different rules in each room are analogous to different rules and norms of behavior between different cultures. You voice what many are thinking: 'If we so quickly and vehemently blame others for being wrong, when in fact they are just operating by different rules and it is a simple game of no consequence, then how much more serious will be the conflicts when trying to communicate across much more complex and often unconscious cultural values and assumptions, about matters of major consequence?' The key learning point has been powerfully brought home to the group by their own behaviors – they need to actively be aware of different rules in order to be able to manage them. The question is: how?

Change: How does it fit my existing approach? What do I have to change?

Integration of learning into the manager's set of values, beliefs and behaviors is a personal process that requires self-reflection. Sometimes, self-reflection exercises are built into a session design, often followed by exchange between the members of a small group about what each has learned (e.g. see the example described in Chapter 3). More often, owing to the negative emotions often associated with recognition of the need for personal change, and the time required, instructors leave time for each participant to reflect alone after the session, or in networking with other participants. Good program designs explicitly set aside time for this (see Chapter 7).

In our diversity session example, the change element of learning was explicitly built into the design. After a simple game has metamorphosed into a high-impact experience for many, participants are normally much more open to thinking about the impact of their own behaviors – and want to get into the change element of the learning cycle.

Act 3, Scene 1, begins with each participant receiving their individual data from the cultural perspectives questionnaire (CPQ),[5] which maps the strength of a person's preferences for various cultural attributes. Individual scores are compared with those of the group, offering a view of the variance in cultural assumptions among participants – how big are the bridges we need to cross? You explain the context for the data and what the individual profiles mean, but defer questions, many of which started with 'does this mean I . . .' until the group has done some more work on the 'integrate' element of the M.B.I. framework.

In **Scene** 2, you again introduce data, this time showing the different distributions of scores for a group of Chinese and a group of US respondents on one of the questionnaire dimensions. The group is asked to describe the differences. A typical comment begins: *'The Americans have higher scores because they like to . . .'* Rather than just describing the differences, participants are interpreting and evaluating them against their own sets of rules. You bring them back to the need to describe the data first and look for different interpretations.

With this in mind, in **Scene** 3 the group breaks into buzz groups to reflect on their own cultural preferences and discuss how they have personally managed cultural differences. A few minutes later, everyone comes back together to share the examples – good and bad approaches and outcomes – and to discuss how to address such issues differently or change behaviors in future.

Construct: How can I use this? How can I build on it?

Participants have to move towards personal action, see how they can apply the message and develop something useful for their real-world context. Otherwise, the session is merely entertaining, interesting or a waste of time.

By the end of Act 3 in the cultural diversity session, participants have a deep awareness of if and how their own management of diversity needs to change and some ideas on how to go about this. **Act 4** is about moving beyond awareness to action, asking participants to play roles where they can practice managing diversity, make decisions that will help them to decide the best way to adapt their future behaviors.

Scene 1 focuses on a short case where two partners, in the same accounting firm, but in different countries, are clearly having some difficulties communicating effectively. In buzz groups, participants take first the role of one partner and then another, as they dissect the sources of frustration and behaviors which had led to the confrontation. Bringing it back to a plenary mode, and returning again to the M.B.I. framework as an anchor, you introduce data on the cultures of the people in the case (Mapping) and groups then suggest approaches to overcome the problem – to realize the synergy that should have existed (Bridging and Integrating). In such situations, the key is to sequence these contributions in a way that is not repetitive, but fleshes out the larger message.

Scene 2 offers another case vignette where participants can test out the decisions they would make about a situation where cultural differences were causing problems. Again you challenge them to find an appropriate solution, to put themselves in the shoes of the person managing the differences.

You take over in **Scene 3**, bringing the key learning points on integration together, ahead of closing the session.

Provide strong closure

Closing the session on a strong note is essential. The central question is whether to leave the learning points implicit for the participants to work out later, or whether to make your key message explicit. Here are some questions to help you frame your approach, as to what role you should take and should ask the participants to take in pulling things together:

- Is the participant group cohesive with a shared learning culture and experienced in drawing out learning points on their own, or do they need help? If so, what are the overall learning points that you want participants to take away?

- Is the emotional tension that built up during the session effectively resolved? Can the participants resolve it on their own, or do they need help? If they need help, you need to bring together your message, referring back to how the points were developed, using specific examples from the interactions and activities that went on during the session. This helps the participants to identify where the emotions have come from and how they contribute to the learning experience. If you can tie the emotional resolution to the central message of the session, implicitly or explicitly, the learning impact can be powerful.

- How will this session tie into the rest of the program or on-the-job training and is this clear? If not, what do you have to do to make the connection productive?

A summary of the key learning points is the obvious approach when you believe the participants need help. But you have to be careful how you do this, or you might destroy the whole experience. For example, if you have taken a facilitative or coaching role and built up excellent communication with the group and then close by suddenly reverting to a one-way lecturing style, you are likely to lose them right at the end. The participants, who are smart, feel they have been instrumental in developing the thinking to this point. They now feel cheated, as they think you knew the answer all along and have been 'holding out on them.' So, you have mental and emotional switch-off at the crucial point.

In the cultural diversity session, because the roadmap for the session, the M.B.I. framework, has been clear from the beginning and revisited frequently, there is no danger of losing the audience and it represents a useful way to reflect on the key learning points. It links back to the data introduced in Act 1 to reinforce the message that diversity, well-managed, can raise performance of teams and organizations. However, it is the group's hands-on experience of failing to manage differences effectively – or even recognizing them at first – that is typically the main subject of debate and reflection as the session closes.

Whichever way you choose to close a session, you want to promote reflection on new ways of thinking and behaving. At the end of the day there is no right or wrong approach to closure; the only imperative is that the message comes through strongly and the balance feels right in terms of how the session has run so far and the abilities and willingness of the group to integrate the message into their own learning.

Notes

1   Lowman, J. (1984) *Mastering the Techniques of Teaching*. San Francisco: Jossey-Bass, pp. 13–14.
2   Bruch, H. and Ghoshal, S. (2003) Unleashing Organizational Energy. *MIT Sloan Management Review*, Fall, Vol. 45 (Issue 1), p. 45.
3   For a full description of such a complete design, see DiStefano, J.J. and Maznevski, M.L. (2003) Developing Global Managers: Integrating Theory, Behavior, Data and Performance. *In:* Mobley, W.H. and Dorfman, P.W. (eds.) *Advances in Global Leadership, Volume 3*. Oxford: JAI Elsevier Science.
4   Maznevski, M.L. and DiStefano, J.J. (2004) Synergy from individual differences: map, bridge and integrate. *IMD Perspectives for Managers*, Issue 108, March.
5   The Cultural Perspectives Questionnaire, developed by Martha Maznevski and Joe DiStefano, measures individuals' expectations about 13 dimensions of cultural interaction. More information can be found at www.imd.ch/research/cpq.

Drivers of great learning programs

5

Real-world context

Contributions from: Gavin Brown, Kazuo Ichijo, Petri Lehtivaara, Victoria Kemanian, Tracey Keys, Martha Maznevski, Paul Strebel, Annie Tobias, John Walsh

'The teacher who is indeed wise does not bid you to enter the house of his wisdom but rather leads you to the threshold of your mind.'

Kalil Gibran

How many times have you sat looking at a screen full of words or numbers, thinking: so what, when am I ever going to use this? The presenter does his best to animate the discussion, but you don't feel involved. His voice begins to drone on, mirroring the sound of bees or traffic buzzing outside. You yawn; you switch off.

What's the disconnect? Much of the time it is relevance. Learning experiences should relate to real life, otherwise it is tough to make any impression, let alone deliver the sort of high-impact learning demanded today. New ideas need to resonate[1] with learners' existing experiences and the challenges they may be facing or anticipating. This does not mean merely confirming or building on what executives already know and think. Good learning experiences should challenge these premises. But they have to offer a legitimate and credible context for doing so, a situation that 'fits,' whether based on reason or research, or on an intuitive, unconscious and sometimes emotional connection.

Real-world relevance is critical. It must be built into every aspect of a program, from design (to cover the issues that face potential participants), through choice of materials, to delivery and, finally, it must prepare the participants for 're-entry.' The ultimate goal is learning what is tangible enough to answer the question: 'How can it be applied back home' – learning that will be demonstrated through real-world actions and behaviors in the future. This requires attention to the whole executive education value chain.

Address the whole executive education value chain

Looking at executive education as a value chain, its core output is learning about management that can be applied effectively on the job. The first activity in the value chain involves a deep understanding of the customer, followed by the development of relevant material (from management knowledge created through various forms of research, observation and analysis). This is then designed into an educational program comprised of sessions, and delivered to a specific audience, who will apply the learning on the job (see Figure 5.1).

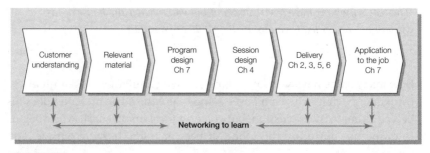

Figure 5.1 The executive education value chain

In 2001, UNICON, an international consortium of business schools that provide executive education, examined the value of programs delivered to their corporate customers.[2] The study measured feedback from participants on the value their educational experience delivered to them personally, as well as assessing the value delivered to the sponsoring corporations (for example, demonstrated improvement in management skills) via discussions with HR and line managers. In UNICON's words, 'Those programs that produce the best results seem to be best at managing the key elements and the linkages across the entire value chain.'

However, as the UNICON study showed, knowledge does not always make its way smoothly along the value chain from research to learning and especially to application. Executive education providers need to bridge the 'white spaces' you see in the diagram. This chapter looks at how to create a real-world context to bridge the white spaces, by putting in place the first pieces of the executive education value chain:

■ Customer understanding.

■ Relevant material.

■ Networking to learn.

Understand the customer deeply

The starting point is to understand where the learner is. Executive education deals with those most sensitive of topics: ourselves, our minds and our careers – so, customer insight is of paramount importance. The first step is to get out in the field to find out what is most important to customers. You should look at the two core constituencies: the organization and the individual.

The organization is the point of departure for company-specific programs, which must reflect the evolutionary stage of management development in the organization. Figure 5.2 shows four common stages in the evolution of the management development process.

Fast-growing smaller companies don't have the time or money for systematic management development. Individual executives, or business units, on an ad hoc basis, drive the little development they do.

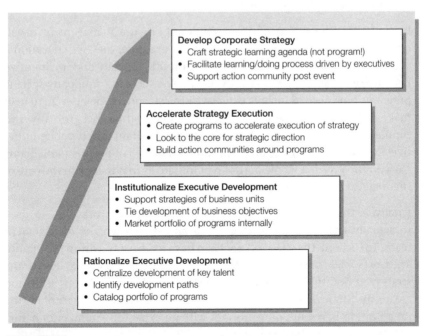

Develop Corporate Strategy
- Craft strategic learning agenda (not program!)
- Facilitate learning/doing process driven by executives
- Support action community post event

Accelerate Strategy Execution
- Create programs to accelerate execution of strategy
- Look to the core for strategic direction
- Build action communities around programs

Institutionalize Executive Development
- Support strategies of business units
- Tie development of business objectives
- Market portfolio of programs internally

Rationalize Executive Development
- Centralize development of key talent
- Identify development paths
- Catalog portfolio of programs

Figure 5.2 Typical evolution of management development

The first phase of systematic development is to rationalize what is going on around key talent. Companies typically start by pulling together and rationalizing existing processes and initiatives. They catalog what they have centrally and build their portfolio of favored options for nurturing talent. Since the development culture is focused on individuals, they might start sending selected executives to external open enrolment programs. It is very rare for companies, in this stage, to ask for company-specific programs. And if they do, the chances of a successful program are limited, unless the ground is very well prepared inside the company. Even if it is, you should expect a senior executive to try to derail the whole thing, because he or she isn't ready to have outsiders interfering with his or her managers!

In the second phase, management development becomes more closely linked to the organization's strategic objectives, e.g. developing managers with negotiation skills to oversee proposed acquisitions. Divisions start to request specific programs to support their own goals. The human resources department institutionalizes the development process by aligning it with the strategic challenges facing the company. Company-specific programs have to address the strategic challenges, but cannot move into action learning based on real problem solving. Top executives still see management development as a human resources issue, not one that should get mixed up with strategic implementation.

In the third phase, top management wants to use management development to accelerate strategy execution; for example, they see educational activities as a means to build cross-organizational networks to improve knowledge sharing and effectiveness. To succeed, company-specific programs now need to include extensive project work in their design to help make the strategy happen. These could be personal business initiatives to support the overall strategic implementation program, or corporate initiatives developed during the program and then carried out by the participants back on the job, or a whole portfolio of initiatives that makes up the core of the total execution program.

Finally, in the fourth phase, management development workshops are used to actually formulate the strategy itself and strengthen the management team. To succeed, the CEO and her team have to be ready, within the boundaries of some constraints, to let the workshop participants design the strategy; if not, the process becomes a charade. These workshops at the top create the strategic direction, which is then cascaded down through the organization in a series of workshops with an expanding number of participants to create the business unit plans.

The individual is the point of departure for open enrolment programs, which must be designed around the key learning needs and issues for the target audience. In the case of career development programs aimed at high-potential junior managers, the needs will be skills and knowledge to broaden their understanding of business functions, as well as develop their personal leadership skills. Mid-level managers need a large dose of people and relationship management skills with some retooling of functional skills and development of strategic thinking. Senior managers, on the other hand, need more attention to visioning and strategy, plus people management. The divisions within the horizontal bars in Figure 5.3 depict the variation in the appropriate mix of content with career level.

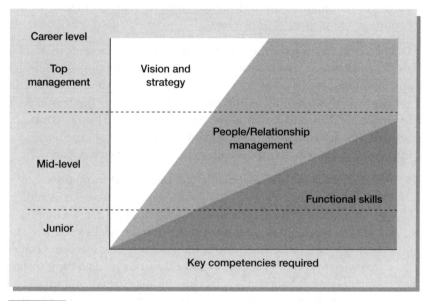

Figure 5.3   Career level versus importance of different competencies

The right mix of learning materials also changes with the career maturity of executives. Younger managers with little experience benefit most from detailed case studies of other companies, which provide not only a problem context, but also a sense for the twists, turns and challenges of managerial life. By contrast, more senior executives bring along an extensive case study of their own in the form of their personal experience. They benefit far less from third party cases and learn more from reflecting on what has worked and why in their own experience and relating new material to that experience, as well as from comparisons of different situations, or case vignettes, contrasted with the help of frameworks describing possible courses of action under different scenarios, and especially from action-based learning activities.

Develop relevant real-world material

The executives that attend a learning experience are living in the here and now, in a rapidly changing environment. They want to look forward and discuss the challenges that they are facing today and will face tomorrow, not engage overly in a backward reflection on history. Yet, history does teach us much and there are clear principles of management that are 'timeless' (e.g. cash-flow management or meeting customer needs). So the advantages of using recent examples must be balanced with the benefits of using the best examples of fundamental principles.

The need for executives to be able to apply learning, as well as to develop awareness of new ideas and approaches, favors the development of research and teaching materials that are practical. Top of mind should be not only content, but also how the insights can best be delivered. The best ideas or knowledge in the world is of little use if it is not translated into activities and content that actively engages participants in the learning experience. The following key principles help to achieve this 'dual' research mission:

1 **Focus research on practical challenges facing real companies**
   Executives from international companies want new ideas, tools and potential solutions for their issues. Research needs to address these challenges, offering insights and learning that can be taken back to the executive's real world. The identification of these practical issues comes from constant contact with the real world and deep understanding of customer needs. Methods for achieving this may include: direct networking and discussions with executives, companies or people that are part of the institution's broader network, in-class discussions and the latest world, business and academic news. Constant contact with the real world highlights practical questions that can then drive the research agenda.

2 **Translate insights into relevant output and materials**
   Research and development processes must be seamlessly integrated. Even if the original research question or hypothesis is relatively academic in nature, the work cannot stop when an answer has been established. Rather, the thinking must be taken to a more practical level, developing output and materials that can be used in the classroom. For example, a framework with supporting evidence may be developed during the research phase, which is then translated into a

range of materials to support a 'real-world' learning experience. This demands an output-focused culture, promoted through incentives both for the faculty and the research team. In addition to making sure that new ideas find their way into classroom, such an orientation makes the research effort more efficient and research cycles shorter.

3 Involve teaching faculty and executives
In general, teaching faculty and executives, rather than pure researchers, should drive the development agenda, because they are the ones involved in the learning experience. Although this can demand substantial resources in terms of faculty and research support time and opportunity cost, the benefits are substantial in terms of creating a high-impact learning experience. First, faculty members will know the subject intimately so can draw on a wide range of insights and materials – critical for effective improvisation. Second, with 'inside' knowledge of the research and the companies and people it is based upon, the faculty can bring richness to the discussions, engaging emotionally as well as intellectually with participants.

4 Use the 'live audience' and don't stop too soon!
A 'live audience' with a large amount of experience on the topics researched provides an excellent laboratory for testing new ideas and materials. If the ideas are not clear or not well communicated then the topic and/or materials may need further work. Conversely, the ideas and materials can spark new questions, deeper insights or another interesting direction to explore – again calling for further work, for example the development of additional cases on the topic of corporate entrepreneurship described in Chapter 10. Don't stop too soon with materials development, as there will often be another valuable iteration, or addition, that can enhance the learning experience.

The research interaction between educators and executives is but one of the networking activities that fill in the white spaces between the elements in the executive education value chain. There are many other networking opportunities.

Build in networking to learn

Networking has become a buzz word in the last decade, but in truth it is a concept that has been around for centuries – just think about Machiavelli's school of relationship philosophy. The somewhat cynical 'it's not what you know, but whom you know' approach with its implications of manipulation and power-broking are a shallow reflection of the importance of building interpersonal relationships. Because that's what networking is all about: building social capital.

In a learning context, nothing replaces the one-on-one interactions that networking promotes. The power of networking is threefold:

1 Offering new perspectives and ways of thinking, including novel approaches to solving common challenges.

2 Pushing thinking further than is possible by an individual alone: the sum is greater than the parts argument.

3 Providing mutual support to address the challenges of learning, including feedback, sounding boards for new ideas and ways of thinking and, in some cases, personal friendships.

The ability to reach out to potential participants before and after they attend a program is critical. First, get out into the field and bring the customer in. To do so, institutionalizing customer dialogue, for example through a learning network such as that at IMD, can be highly effective.

The IMD Learning Network

In a fast-changing world, companies realize that insularity is detrimental; they want access to the latest business trends that may impact them. At the same time, companies demand relevance: a combination of practical orientation and cutting-edge thinking.

IMD's Learning Network began over 30 years ago as an initiative to achieve strong, sustainable and mutually beneficial learning partnerships with our clients through a high-value, mutually crafted agenda. Today, it is comprised of 150 global companies with a shared passion for learning, and an overriding commitment to attract, develop and retain people. IMD works with these companies in open and customized activities on an ongoing basis, ensuring that our activities meet their learning and executive development demands.

Our relationship with partner companies takes place at multiple levels both at IMD and within the company, in independent efforts that meet different needs at each level. There is a continuous, coordinated communication between all the touch points internally at IMD and within our clients' companies. These multiple ties increase visibility and contribute to fostering the relationship. They also provide input to refine our value proposition, allowing us to understand rapidly what issues our customers are facing, so we can respond with the appropriate mix of content, programs and activities.

Networks, whether smaller or bigger learning communities, should also be fostered around programs to offer everything from support, advice and career counseling to friendship and further contacts long after the learning experience has ended. The key to creating the right environment to foster productive networking and interactions, both during and after a program, is for educators to provide tools, opportunities and encouragement for people who want to learn from each other, but to step back and allow the communities to develop their own paths and identities.

Companies may explicitly choose to send a group of executives to a program together (in-company or open enrolment) with the aim of helping them to build relationships that will be of benefit to all on their return, for example improving communications and cooperation across organizational bound-

Social networks and action learning among would-be leaders
Kazuo Ichijo

Action learning projects sponsored by senior executives are a very effective way to develop would-be leaders while facilitating knowledge management. Through action learning projects with global colleagues around the world, high-potential leaders can nurture cross-business and cross-functional friendships that can last a lifetime. Participating in a global taskforce with colleagues of different backgrounds, they gain precious experience of the difficulty and excitement of organizational knowledge creation and sharing. Would-be leaders get a better understanding of the company through the stories that current senior managers tell them face to face, together with a deeper grasp of the company's core competencies and its approach to knowledge creation.

Leaders can develop future leaders with this understanding and focus. But it only works if the senior executives themselves recognize the true importance of increasing knowledge by means of action learning. They too must experience the real value, difficulty and enablers of knowledge management. The focus must be on imparting the tacit aspects of knowledge more than the overt, while simultaneously creating an enabling infrastructure to facilitate knowledge management across geographical regions and business functions. Indeed, excellent companies such as Toyota and General Electric believe that top leaders should develop other leaders through shared action learning projects so that they gain leaders at every organizational level.[3] Nurturing new leaders and sharing knowledge is viewed as the foundation of competitive advantage in a global firm.

aries. In some cases these objectives are supported by explicit projects that may begin during a program, but continue back at the office.

One of the 'outputs' that organizations and individuals increasingly seek is an ongoing network after the program ends – a group of peers with some common interests and challenges that continue to stay in touch on a whole host of topics, from advice on business issues to moving house to raising children. Often this is informal, based on the relationships participants have established, but educational institutions are increasingly giving participants tools which will help both to establish and to reinforce the relationships. Examples include access to ongoing learning materials that encourage lifelong learning, alumni events and clubs, webletters offering content and news or simple tools such as email addresses that link a group.

There are several opportunities for virtual networking around a program that can help to integrate new learning with on-the-job realities, including:

- Before the program, executives can briefly communicate with each other regarding the topics of the program and share relevant experiences.

- During the program, executives can also communicate with a 'virtual buddy' back at work, sharing with them what they've learned at the program and setting up a context for bringing the learning back home; 'virtual buddies' can even have virtual access to some of the materials for the program and brief video clips for joint discussion after the program.

- After the program, a virtual follow-up with the whole group can reinforce lessons and help work against the inertia that makes it difficult to implement new ideas.

This isn't about doing projects virtually. This approach is about using communications technology to connect the learning to the executive's 'real world' in – ironically – a more tangible way.

Dynamic knowledge networks

Dynamic knowledge networks (DKNs), conceived as a tool to create communities of practice, bring together members of the IMD community to learn while creating knowledge and sharing best practices. The DKNs engage talented managers from around the world in an active learning community to build business knowledge and virtual leadership skills through seminars run by IMD faculty on various management and business topics.

Each dynamic knowledge network is a group of managers around the world, program participants, faculty and specially invited guests who collaborate virtually to create and share knowledge on a topic of common interest. The ultimate goal is to develop new principles, approaches and best practices that will improve and transform participants' businesses and companies. Each DKN works virtually over a period of 10 weeks, during which participants in each seminar run forum discussions, online chats and collaborate on advancing their topics. At the end of the project, the DKN members publish a 'white paper' on the knowledge created in their seminar.

Benefits to the individual and organization range from specific learning points around the seminar topic, e.g. learning to work with start-ups or developing trust in multinational teams, to general learning about how to build virtual networks for knowledge management. Depending on the initiative of the individual and the development of the community, there will be different kinds of opportunities to share best practices and get advice.

Networks build more networks. Flexibility and contact with the business world allows you to quickly transform ideas into content and effectively communicate them to your network. Research networks lead to client networks, which in turn lead to program networks, then to alumni and internal company networks. In brief, networks provide the foundation for the real-world context that is essential for high-impact learning.

Notes

1   In *Changing Minds, The Art and Science of Changing Our Own and Other People´s Minds* (2004, USA: Harvard Business School Press), Howard Gardner outlines seven levers that aid in changing minds, one of which is resonance. He defines resonance as impacting the affective component of the mind: a view, idea, or perspective resonates to the extent that it feels right to an individual, seems to fit the current situation, and convinces the person that further considerations are superfluous.
2   Sloan, E. (2001) The contribution of university based executive education to corporate talent management results. *Personnel Decisions International*/UNICON Study.
3   Tichy, N.M. with Cardwell, N. (2002) *The Cycle of Leadership: How Great Leaders Teach Their Companies to Win*. New York: HarperBusiness.

6

3-dimensional learning

Contributions from: Gordon Adler, Robert Hooijberg,
Victoria Kemanian, Tracey Keys, Nancy Lane, Paul Strebel

'The great aim of education is not knowledge but action.'

Herbert Spencer (1820–1903)

How many programs have you attended with two or three cases a day, in which private reading is followed by a group discussion, which is followed by a plenary session, day-in and day-out, until you can no longer remember the topic or day of the week? The typical management development diet of presentations, cases and study groups is not enough for high-impact learning. If well done, it stimulates executives to learn and investigate new approaches. But it does little, if anything, to help them change and apply the learning to their own situations. High-impact learning requires not only intellectual, but also emotional and application-based activity to promote a wide range of multisensory experiences, different ways of approaching or presenting topics that activate several of the human senses to reinforce and embed the learning.

In this chapter we explore the different dimensions of high-impact learning activity, and how we can use them effectively. 'How' is a big topic, so this chapter can provide only a snapshot: Chapter 7 on program design discusses in more detail how activities interact and can be combined effectively, while the chapters in Parts III, IV and V elaborate on the effective use of many of the types of activities outlined here.

Recognize the three dimensions of learning

What is ultimately important for designing a program or even a session is to creatively combine content and activity type in order to create high-impact learning that can be applied practically. In doing so, we distinguish between three types of learning activity: those that build intellectual ('I') awareness (knowledge and/or skills), those that develop emotional ('E') awareness (personal and social sensitivity) and those that involve actively applying intellectual and emotional learning:

1 **Intellectual awareness (knowledge and related skills)**
   This is by far the most developed of all three dimensions, and traditional business schools have explicitly focused on teaching or transferring knowledge and related skills (e.g. interpreting financial information) as a relevant means to management development. But while most executive education has long sustained this approach, recent research[1] on the attributes and skills demanded from globally minded managers revealed that (a) knowledge transfer is not sufficient, managers need to develop a set of higher-order skills (e.g. complex problem-solving) and personal qualities that enable them to effectively perform and (b) in order to successfully incorporate those skills and qualities, executive education has to provide a platform for practical application that prepares managers for the real-world challenges they will face at their companies. Intellectual awareness is an essential component of the learning puzzle, but not sufficient alone.

2 **Emotional awareness (personal and social capabilities)**
   Systems in the brain that manage the emotions are closely connected to those that govern reason, so: 'Certain aspects of the process of emotion and feeling are indispensable for rationality.'[2] Daniel Goleman's[3] articulation of 'emotional intelligence' offers a useful basis for thinking about the types of emotional sensitivity that leaders need to be more effective in today's world: self-awareness, and social awareness (see Chapter 2).

3 **Action-based application (intellectual and emotional)**
   But awareness, even on both the 'I' and 'E' dimensions, is still not enough. Learning that 'sticks' is promoted by opportunities for 'hands-on' application – trying it out for yourself to see what really works for you and what doesn't, and to begin constructing a new personal reality with new skills on the intellectual side and self-management and relationship management on the emotional side. For example, if you're teaching leadership, a lecture-format session will not be enough to get real learning; you'll need something hands-on, like an outdoor exercise, to internalize the learning. If you are teaching negotiation skills, you'll need something practical like a simulation or role-play exercises. Some application activities will focus more on I or E skills

and capabilities, others will allow action-based learning on both simultaneously.

Clearly there is some overlap between the dimensions when you think about different types of activity, e.g. a simulation can help you build personal and social awareness, as well as develop intellectual skills. Nevertheless, the dimensions offer useful guidance for thinking through the types of activity that can be used for different learning objectives. Figure 6.1 provides some examples of the range of learning activities that support each dimension of learning. It is not meant to be exhaustive, because there are ongoing innovations and experiments every day as we develop ideas; learn from participants, companies and other institutions and educators; or are challenged by new customer needs or see new challenges developing in the marketplace.

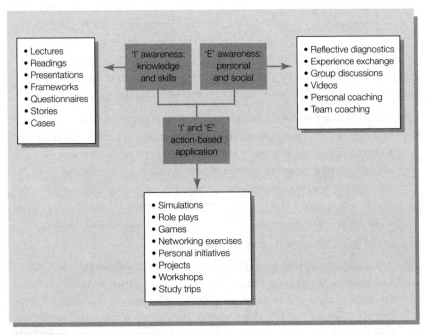

Figure 6.1   Linking learning dimensions and activities

Build intellectual awareness

This is the realm most of us are familiar with, as learners, from early school days onwards, whether learning the alphabet or how to master the 'jargon' of marketing plans and statistical models. The aim of many of these activities is to introduce new ideas, concepts and theories that challenge the learner's existing perspectives and stimulate them to investigate new approaches. Some investigative activities, such as cases, can also link to the other domains of 'E' awareness and application, but we discuss them here because they are generally focused more on building 'I' awareness.

Examples of the activities that fall on this dimension are the following:

Lectures with supporting data, practical real-world examples, energizing delivery and emotion, can still be one of the best ways to communicate a new concept, framework or theory. It can be especially powerful when combined, as a short lecture, with one of the other approaches listed above, as a way of clearing up any ambiguity and locking in the critical message. Experienced executives, in particular, appreciate a short lecture that summarizes the latest thinking on a topic and contrasts the advantages and disadvantages of different ways of looking at, and dealing with, a problem.

Readings prior to a session, can provide an attractive alternative to a lecture, especially if used to provoke complementary discussion or even as a lead-in to get attention and underline the importance of a topic. Similarly, it can be very useful in closing to give participants more information and show them where they might want to go to pursue the content further.

Presentations in the form of PowerPoint are so widely used in day-to-day business that they can easily backfire, especially when loaded with too many slides and concepts. Too often, one sees a manager draining an audience of its energy with so many slides that no one can follow the plot. If PowerPoint has to be used to get a point across, the rule of thumb should be 'less is more'; the fewer the number of slides, the greater the chances of getting the point across.

Frameworks developed by consultants and academics, for trying to determine what is right and wrong with a company or its leadership are also common. Understanding the issues is the usual starting point for deciding what kind of learning is needed. However, merely describing a framework is rarely enough for effective learning. Hands-on application to the participant's own context and seeing the results, especially in comparison to others, is what makes such diagnostic learning stick.

Questionnaires can be used to collect data on strategic, organizational and leadership practice, as well as perceptions of the business environment, in order to challenge, confirm or illustrate the application of a principle or framework. Questionnaire results naturally lead to questions like: What were the questions really about? What do the similarities and differences between our responses mean? What do the results tell us about who and where we are and what we might do?

Stories and vignettes, can add a touch of color and emotion, as well as create a change of pace in the overall learning process. The tighter the connection with the content and message of the session, the better are the chances of real impact. And an element of humor, lightening the atmosphere and making the learning more fun, helps participants take themselves less seriously and open up to the challenge of modifying their view of the world. The box on pages 80–82 offers some perspectives on the use of storytelling to promote learning.

Cases are the classic tool of executive education. But cases are not all equal. Only a few of those written become great learning vehicles. The successful ones tend to address frequently recurring issues, like the tension between head office and the field, and are centered on a few critical events in the case story, such as an adversarial meeting between the boss and the central character that brings the issue to life. In discussing these common issues and simulating the unfolding events, participants can bring their own experience to the table for comparison with others. However, not all case teachers are equal either. The best have mastered the art of using the case material to launch the discussions between the participants, allowing them, as much as possible, to discover the message in the case themselves. See Chapter 8 for more on writing a good case, and Chapter 16 on using a case to make participants experience the intensity of a fierce product battle.

As you consider learning activities that build intellectual awareness, it is worth bearing in mind some key principles:

- These activities are often most productive towards the start of a program (or session) to establish the challenges and issues that you want participants to focus on and investigate.

- Because many are educator-led, e.g. lectures, presentations or case introductions, roles need to be actively switched to ensure learners get fully engaged with the topic.

- A combination of the tools, e.g. lecture + case + video or experience exchange + small group discussion, is often more productive in engaging learners and keeping energy going than using a single approach throughout a session (or program).

Build emotional awareness

Building emotional awareness requires a great deal of sensitivity, as the activities often involve fundamental challenges to personal awareness of oneself and relationships with others. Such challenges can spark the realization that the learner will need to change in some way – both these areas potentially involve negative emotions (see Chapter 2). For the educator, the issue is how to move the learners forward from these realizations to investigating what can be done and constructing a new way of thinking or working. Oftentimes this means moving rapidly from awareness-building to application-based activities, where learners can explore and experiment in a relatively safe environment.

Activities that may be used to build emotional awareness include:

Reflective diagnostics challenge participants to review their own history to try to understand what has worked for them, why they have been successful, or failed, what is driving them, in terms of values, beliefs and behaviors, and how they can use this insight to better manage themselves, improve their leadership styles and increase the chances of business success. Touching, as it does, the very core of who we are as individuals, this can become very emotional. When it involves a business team trying to understand why it is not as effective as it would like, the emotion is not only personal, but can quickly become interpersonal and aggressive. Properly managed, these exercises result in defining moments; poorly managed, they can be very damaging. For more on this topic, see Chapter 18.

Exchange of experience in pairs, or a small group, can be very rewarding, especially for executives with lots of experience. The challenge is to keep the discussion focused. Hence, the need, always, for a well-defined mandate and sometimes for someone in the group to take the role of timekeeper to make sure that all of the group members can put their experience on the table when this is called for. When a group has been working together for a few days with sufficient trust and respect and the topic is not so much past experience, but, forward-looking action plans, the group can provide each member with invaluable counseling. Often one of the big surprises when they come from quite disparate industries is how many good questions and relevant suggestions managers can give each other. And this effect is not necessarily restricted to small groups.

Small group discussions are part of most learning scripts for executive education. In addition to a precise mandate, to make them work, you have to relinquish control and subsequently reconvene the group – and integrate the whole process seamlessly, even though you can manage neither the process nor the results of the group discussions directly. While usually guided by a simple assignment and constrained in time, discussion groups constitute intense learning and knowledge-sharing opportunities that require a substantial commitment from each participant, because no one can hide in a small group. While group work has its merits and is frequently employed, not every group assignment delivers what was intended! There is substantial risk of counterproductive outcomes, adverse group dynamics and participant frustration if the group effort produces lots of talk but little concrete learning. The best antidote is a carefully crafted assignment and periodic visits to the groups to make sure they are on track. See Chapter 17 for more on running effective study groups.

Videos fit today's media-drenched world. They can be used to complement written cases or, alternatively, as stand alone material, particularly to illustrate practice from settings that the participants are unfamiliar with, such as the leadership dilemmas in non-business organizations, like a space mission. When used with a case, it is typically the video that brings the case to life, triggering more 'points of touch' with participants, calling for a stronger sense of urgency, emotional engagement and exchange of experience. Through the video, participants can easily identify and sense attitudes, behaviors, conflicts and emotions present in the situation, information that is much harder to convey through a written piece. Videos alone are valuable when participants do not have enough preparation time or if there exists the need to break from a string of case-based classes. Videos alone, without written material, are a powerful way of contrasting different management behaviors, like leadership styles, or different organizational cultures. A 'video tour' of different corporate cultures, for example, can be the basis for a highly energized half-day session on organizational learning. See Chapter 9 for an in-depth exploration of *Real Video!*

Personal coaching has become popular of late, in the aftermath of the highly publicized management failures of the early 2000s, as managers try to avoid being blindsided by their own shortcomings. Coaches discuss the issues uppermost in the manager's mind, may even observe the manager in action (especially if the coach is a mentor in the same organization) and give feedback on how she's doing and advice on how to improve her leadership. Such soft data on personal performance over time is difficult to get in any other way and can make all the difference for leadership development. But, precisely because it's so personal, it all depends on the chemistry between the mentor and mentee. See Chapter 12 for more.

Team coaching, often outdoors, is a more collective approach. The team members give each other feedback on their personal performance during an exercise, with the help of videos of the exercises and under the guidance of professional facilitators. This is a less threatening environment than on the job coaching and less subject to the vagaries of personal chemistry. Yet, the video and team debriefing of personal behavior under the stress of the exercises provides the opportunity for real learning with strong emotional content. See Chapter 18 and also Chapter 26 on leadership training.

In using emotional awareness activities, the following principles are relevant:

■ Safety nets are critical and must be put in place, along with sufficient time to use them, when planning the activity: addressing personal competencies and relationships can be risky and damaging to the individual if there are not sufficient support mechanisms to help address issues and emotions, e.g. trained counselors to help work through the implications of a diagnostic exercise – see Chapter 12 for more on coaches, counselors, facilitators and behavioral consultants.

■ When awareness activities may create negative emotions, such as fear and uncertainty, it is often important to follow up with application-based activities so learners can explore what can be done to address the issues raised in a positive way.

Integrate with action-based application

So we have lots of new awareness, but will it stick? Not often, unless it can be personalized. 'But we have personalized it and made it relevant to the learners in the class,' some educators will argue – 'They have had the chance to tell their own stories and share their own issues; they know what the options are to tackle them.' OK, now ask the executives, 'When did you learn best?' Most times, they will tell you that it was through a particular experience – doing something new (e.g. tackling a tough challenge on a project). Direct action and application of thinking is where the learning markers that will guide our future actions really get embedded in our minds.

This is when we really move from investigation to change and constructing our new reality.

And it is where we must acknowledge a constraint with off-site education processes. Educators can indeed offer a rich range of action-based activities for applying knowledge, and frankly, the more the better. However, it is impossible to offer opportunities to try out every aspect of new learning, in every type of situation the learner can expect to meet in future. They are going to have to do a lot of the application themselves – take the person who only found a passion for cash flow when helping his friend finish the business plan. So with this in mind, here are some of the numerous activities that help learners to apply and internalize the learning, separated into two categories, simulations and real-world projects:

Simulations

Reflective simulations encourage participants to think through how a new theory might work out for them in practice. Learning from new theory only sticks once participants test the frameworks derived from the theory in practice. An initial test could be the simulated application of the new framework to the participant's situation, using a reflective exercise that is part of the learning session (think through what this means for you, describe and exchange perspectives with others).

Scenarios are a particular form of reflective simulation that challenge participants to come to grips with future uncertainty. Scenarios get participants to construct alternative futures and think through the consequences in each case. Depending on the exercise, these futures can range from different socio-political situations all the way to the future of a piece of the business. Keeping more than one future in mind together with the related contingency plans is key to the agility of mind and the repertoire of responses needed to deal with rapidly evolving environments.

In **decision simulations** based on computer programs, participants often compete in teams to maximize profits, based on a limited set of decisions, and sense how the different aspects of a firm or industry are interconnected and how decisions have lasting impacts over time (for example, how decisions up and down a supply chain can worsen shortages and overstocking). When combined with role plays, to deal with the reaction to the decisions of various stakeholders, like the press or unions, the games generate increased involvement and energy.

Much of the learning takes place during the debriefing on how the teams functioned as decision makers and how they managed the stakeholder relationships. One of the best ways of learning how large economic systems work can be a conceptual discussion of the rules underlying the decision game itself. See Chapter 32 for a discussion of using action-learning tools to help teams develop strategic marketing plans.

Organizational simulations challenge participants to confront unusual situations, especially those that have yet to occur. A well-known example is development exercises, which simulate the challenges of organizational life and are designed to improve behavior on the individual, group and organizational levels (see Kolb *et al.* on experiential learning in organizational behavior). But the possibilities for learning from simulation experiences go beyond organizational behavior.

With **role plays**, learning experiences come closest to actual theater. Participants play out roles in single scenes or in more elaborately scripted plays, like a negotiation exercise. See Chapter 19 for more on effective negotiation simulations. Role plays address behavior. They can be used to try out, practice or observe the impact of different behaviors. As part of case discussions, especially those involving interactions between people, they bring the situation to life and allow the participants to explore the impact of different behavioral tactics. Asking participants to make a taking charge speech, for example, and comparing the impact of their different styles can be highly illuminating. Having a professional actor help participants play roles in business vignettes, like an encounter between boss and subordinate at a coffee machine, is both fun and shows how control over our own mindset and behavior can dramatically change the impact we have in interpersonal relationships.

Games provide a fun but serious context for exploring how different roles play out in market, organizational, group or other settings. Management games come in many forms. The trick is to use a game that replicates an aspect of the participants' real-world context that is relevant for the educational objective, even though the game setting may be quite far from their working environment. Some of the most successful games look at leadership, or group effectiveness, in leisure, sporting or artistic contexts that appeal to managers. The box on Sewa Beats Leadership Drumming sessions at the end of this chapter illustrates one creative approach to developing leadership skills.

Networking exercises are powerful because they provide learners with numerous interactions (see Chapter 5 for further discussion of networking approaches). One example is the round robin exercise (see Chapter 7) where each group expands its knowledge of a topic by visiting other groups to pick their brains and, in turn, offers ideas on the other group's topic. Networking comes into its own in a program context. Even on short programs, there can be many opportunities for participants to get to know each other, not only professionally, but also personally. Often the intensity of the demands of the learning experience, which engage emotions as well as intellect, can quickly establish deep bonds among a group. For example, one participant told us of the deep connections his group had forged during an outdoor exercise: 'Working in my group on Monday, no one believed we had the ability to perform in the group, but by the end of the week we had become a really good team; it transformed our expectations and we achieved a good result.'

Real-world projects

Personal business initiatives fit when management development has reached the stage where it is designed to support the business strategy. These projects typically include a combination of activities, like diagnostic frameworks that challenge participants to identify high-impact initiatives for value creation and reflective exercises to identify the related leadership issues, as well as action planning, debriefing and follow-up to enhance execution.

Company projects fit once management development has reached the stage where it is designed to accelerate the implementation of the corporate strategy. This calls for learning projects with carefully chosen objectives. The projects usually involve group work, based on diagnostic frameworks and action planning, to identify solutions to implementation challenges. Their impact depends on how well the recommendations are integrated into the overall process of strategic implementation. Top management sponsorship and presence during the introduction and debriefing of these projects is essential for their credibility and effectiveness. See Chapter 24 on effective action learning projects, and Chapter 20 on client-initiated projects in company-specific programs.

Strategy workshops fit once management development has reached the stage where it plays a part in the process of strategy formulation. These workshops are designed not only as learning events, but also, more importantly, to be the vehicle for formulating the strategy itself, or for focusing execution by identifying and getting commitment to the critical implementation projects. To be effective, strategy formulation workshops have to go beyond the standard diagnostics for identifying what we could do (attractive opportunities), and what we can do (distinctive capabilities), to incorporate group exercises to surface what we want to do (managerial preferences) and balance that with what we should do (to satisfy the financial markets and stakeholders). To get commitment to critical projects, you have to go even further and align the projects with what 'I' want, that is, the personal agendas of the key players.

Third party projects with companies other than those of the participants can be deployed in open public programs, or in-company at any stage of the management development progression. For younger high fliers, these might involve formal consulting projects over several months, entrepreneurial start-up projects initiated by the participant teams, social responsibility projects in emerging markets, and so on, to develop leadership skills in challenging environments. For more senior executives, these projects only make sense if they are more closely tied to business objectives in the form of focused study trips. See Chapter 21 on projects with start-up companies and Chapter 22 on international consulting projects.

Study trips work best when tied to very specific objectives with tight activity scripts. In-company, this typically means building awareness and skills in an 'apprenticeship' mode, the discovery and acquisition of best practice at so-called 'best-in-class' business units or companies or learning how to manage relationships with supply chain partners or customers. In public programs, the study trips are typically to 'leading edge' companies in dynamic regions of the world, again with tight scripts, e.g. to acquire new perspectives on managing foreign joint ventures in Shanghai, or entrepreneurship in Silicon Valley. Chapter 23 explores this topic further.

Looking at the objectives of these types of learning activities, even with the broad range of possible approaches, there are some key principles to focus on:

▨ No matter how good the application activities educators can offer, the learner will need to create (or recognize) their own opportunities to test out and further integrate the learning after the formal program is completed.

- This means that the educator has a role in instilling the enthusiasm to seize and learn from such opportunities to apply new learning, while helping learners to prepare to return to their job and home life.

- Post-program opportunities to maintain networks with peers and to continue to learn will also be important in driving post-program application, as will promoting active links between company sponsors and learners.

Storytelling for high-impact learning
Gordon Adler

One way to orchestrate emotional highs, energize the people in your session, tap into various senses and put the session into a real-world context is to tell stories. Take a session for family business owners grappling with succession issues, where the educator tells of his own father's refusal to go into the family business in the 1930s, and the subsequent dissolution of the company. The brief tale strikes a chord with every person there: it taps into their own experiences, their conflicts and tensions, and is rich with detail which all will remember long after the session ends.

Research confirms this experience. When we hear a story, we are pulled into the scene and feel what the characters feel. Stories evoke visual images and emotions. A good story can touch something familiar in us, yet at the same time show us something new about our management challenges. Stories make information easier to remember. They often communicate values and ideas more powerfully than statistics or the ever-popular PowerPoint slides.

So what have we learned at IMD about the nitty gritty of storytelling for executive learning? First, let's look at the characteristics of a high-impact story. Effective stories are concrete: they tell about real people, describe real events and are set in a time and place with which participants can identify. The story must resonate with them: be new enough to capture their interest, but also feel like 'common knowledge.' Even if your story is about an unfamiliar organization, the participants must recognize the challenges, conflicts and characters – to feel that 'they've been there.' Without this element of believability, the learning won't stick.

Good stories come in many shapes and sizes, but all demonstrate common qualities. Like movies, they have a **setting**: time, place, players and context. They demand that we ask, 'If I were this manager in these circumstances, what would I do?' They have **build-up**, a series of events (or acts) that warn the listener of trouble coming up. This culminates in a **crisis** – it may be expected, but it can often be a surprise if the story takes a twist. Sometimes a new element is introduced here. Effective stories have learning: the 'moral' of the story, what the central character learned. Lastly, compelling stories have **lessons** about how and why life changes, the suspense of the 'struggle between expectation and reality in all its nastiness.'[4] A good story, in other words, can touch on the 'dark side' of management.

Although the research on storytelling as an educational medium is limited, bear these conclusions in mind as you develop your script.[5] A story told aloud is retained better than one told on television or on video. Stories told with rich visual imagery are retained longer than content learned by rote and drill. Learners asked to visualize the actions and content of a story remember its key ideas better than learners who memorize sentences from the story. Following a key teaching point with a humorous anecdote enhances retention and understanding.

So how do you use stories? Stories can serve a variety of teaching purposes in a learning script: they can entertain, evoke emotion, trigger visual memories and strengthen recall. Brief stories work well to launch a session – building context that frames the ensuing discussion. They raise questions and points that the participants can debate. A series of short stories – less than three minutes each – seems to work better than one long story unless you script your entire session around that long story. For high impact, first identify the point you want to frame. Is it about business priorities, or a certain view of leadership? Then make sure the story you choose will be interesting and relevant *for this audience*, so that the lessons they debate stick.

Educators who use stories well actively listen for good stories and recognize when they're in one. Spending a lot of time with managers means you hear potential teaching stories every day. Make your interest known. Once you've collected some, figure out which ones are most useful for certain scripts, and start trying them out.

Storytelling is not the educator's panacea. If you want to try it, follow a few rules of thumb. Recognize when the conditions are favorable for telling a story: the setting is right; the audience is receptive and the timing is spot on. Delivery is always a challenge. So remember the most important characteristic of a good story is authenticity. Your listeners will forgive you much as long as they believe you're being honest. Help the audience experience the feelings: describe your own or those of the characters. In the family business example, the participants suggested that the problems stemmed in part from a failure to communicate. The grandfather, they suggested, should have *engaged* the father. As you script your session, keep this advice in mind: try engaging the participants with a story.

Sewa Beats Leadeership Drumming sessions[6]

Nancy Lane and Robert Hooijberg

Boom-da-da-da-boom-boom, boom-da-da-boom, boom-da-da-da-boom-boom – not the sound you would expect to hear as you walk the halls of an international executive development institute. Nor would you expect to see senior executives huddled over a circle of African drums as you walk into the room for a leadership session. But this is not just fun! Sewa Beats Leadership Drumming sessions are an innovative way of developing leadership, encouraging learning while doing and infusing participants with renewed energy and enthusiasm – especially after demanding phases of their programs.

Before the drums are even touched, the lead drummer and two colleagues introduce participants to the concept of working in rhythm with each other, emphasizing that rhythm comes from the body – not the mind. It means bringing the whole self to the task, not just the mind and fingers (like firing off emails) but the body, heart and soul too. After learning to simply step to the right and left in time, the facilitator complicates things by asking participants to 'pass a clap' while keeping the rhythm – multitasking that demands concentration. It gets even harder when the clap has to be passed with eyes closed! However, participants quickly realize that listening is much more intense when they have to rely on their other senses.

Now it is time to get started on the music. Participants learn the four different elements that make up a piece of music – an introduction, the rhythm, call and response and an ending. To create music as a group, the leader uses a different non-verbal signal for each element to signal what should happen next. Call and response is the most complicated: the facilitator drums a particular rhythm, not necessarily one that was taught, and the participants must 'respond' by imitating it. They then continue to drum the rhythm, while listening to the next one, so they can change as soon as the next signal is given.

After practicing the four types of beat, the lead drummer shows the group how to create a unique piece of music. From the middle of the circle he 'conducts' the rest of the drummers, with the now familiar non-verbal signals. For example, he might signal a change in volume or tempo, or that the group should divide into two parts, each beating different rhythms.

Then it is time for the participants to step up: volunteers are called on to create music of their own. Despite initial reluctance, someone will normally take up the challenge. But the music is often not great! The facilitator guides the group to the realization that in order to lead successfully, and for the music to work, you need a vision of what you want and a plan for achieving it – very much like running an organization. In addition, the role of the leader is highlighted: when someone conducts a session, their structure must be respected and drummers should not drum whatever rhythm inspires them at the moment, as this destroys the group harmony. The keys for success (good music) are creative leadership rather than individual creativity, plus the conductor's enthusiasm.

By the end of the session, participants are able to lead the rest of the group in creating original music. More importantly, they have discovered in a truly hands-on way:

- How important non-verbal communication and active listening is to group success.

- What it is like to be in 'uncharted territory,' leading an activity when they are not an expert.

- How they personally approach risk, as leader or a follower, when invited to step up to lead the group.

- What it feels like when things do not go as planned and how they would respond in 'real time' – would they be able to lead the group back on track when needed?

Notes

1 Andrews, N. and D'Andrea Tyson, L. (2004) The Upwardly Mobile MBA. *strategy+business*, Issue 36.
2 Damasio, A. (1994) *Descartes' Error*. New York: Penguin Putnam.
3 Goleman, D. (1996) *Emotional Intelligence*. London: Bloomsbury Publishing; and Goleman, D., Boyatzis, R. and McKee, A. (2002) *Primal Leadership*. Boston: Harvard Business School Publishing.
4 McKee, R. (2003) Storytelling that moves people. *Harvard Business Review*, 81, pp. 51–56.
5 Zemke, R. (1990) Storytelling: back to basics. *Training Magazine*, 27, pp. 44–50; Martin, J., Feldman, M.S., Hatch, M.J. and Sitkin, S.B. (1983) The uniqueness paradox in organizational stories. *Administrative Science Quarterly*, 28, pp. 438–54; Wilkins, A. (1984) The creation of company cultures: the role of stories and human resource systems. *Human Resource Management*, 23, pp. 45–57.
6 Sewa Beats designs and facilitates interactive management training programs for organizations. They specialize in combining traditional African drumming with 21st century education techniques. The company is headquartered in Switzerland. For more information on Sewa Beats please see www.sewabeats.com.

7

Program scripting

*Contributions from: Carlos Cordero, Georges Haour, Jean L.
Kahwajy, Victoria Kemanian, Tracey Keys, Seán Meehan,
David Robertson, Leif Sjöblom, Paul Strebel, Thomas Vollmann*

*'I never teach my pupils; I only attempt to provide the conditions in which they
can learn.'*

Albert Einstein

Some programs raise expectations they never fulfill. Others start on a high
and then fizzle out. Many hit a low in the middle from which they never
recover. By contrast, great programs create a series of highs that end with
participants who can hardly wait to move into action back on the job.

Scripting a great program is about designing a whole learning experience. A
great script is one that generates a defining experience for the participants,
a series of emotional highs associated with relevant learning. This involves:

■ Sequencing program modules to address the learning objectives.

■ Clustering sessions in each module according to a design theme that
integrates the three learning dimensions of intellectual awareness,
emotional awareness and application.

To give participants the best learning experience, you should be creative and
innovative in designing content and learning activities. Your participants
will expect no less than that. Program scripting puts them at the beginning,
middle and end of the process – if you can't articulate why you are doing an
activity from the learner's perspective then it shouldn't be in the design.
Figure 7.1 illustrates the elements of a good program design, which are
described in the sections that follow.

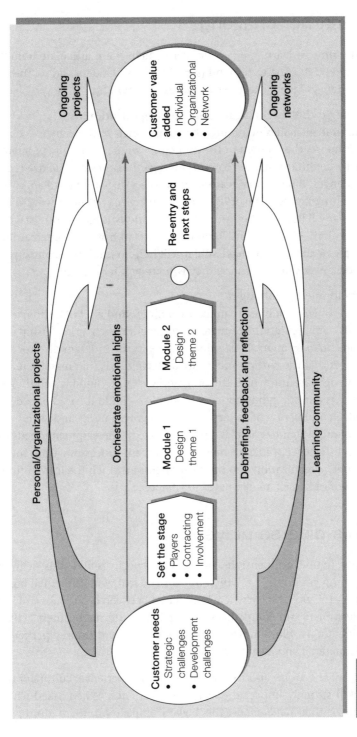

Figure 7.1 Program design framework

Identify learner challenges

Take the time to learn about your clients, help them articulate unfulfilled needs and be the first to respond (see Chapter 5). Understanding the needs and challenges facing executives requires attention to:

■ **Strategic challenges: individual and organizational**
The strategic issues determine the competencies needed by executives and, hence, the content of the program. Company-specific programs are by definition tailored towards an organization's unique needs and challenges. But some educators try to take a one-size-fits-all approach – 'This program design worked with company A, so it must work with company B because they are in the same industry/geography/stage of expansion.' Don't do this! Tempting as it is to trot out the same slides or case or simulation, make sure it will help to fulfill this company's specific needs first – because they will know if it does not.

■ **Development challenges**
Often, open or public programs are built around a set of customer needs, which might be termed more 'generic,' such as leadership or people management. This is fine, as long as the program director ensures that the participants really do have needs that match the challenges around which the program was built. 'Build it and they will come' is tempting, but not very productive. 'Build it based on a deep understanding of what a target market segment needs and then encourage them to come' is a bit more like it. Development needs that reflect the level of management development processes within the learner's organization and the career point at which the learner finds himself or herself are discussed in Chapter 5.

Assemble diverse players

Diversity, in all its dimensions, brings in perspectives and adds richness to the learning environment, which mirrors the real world in which business operates – the global stage where boundaries between economies and industries, customers and competitors, internal and external business activities, are increasingly blurred. Diversity can be created among participants, faculty, material and even location.

The size of the group and its diversity (e.g. in experience, culture or objectives) will strongly impact the learning experience. When asked what are the things that have made the biggest impact on them during their program, one of the things participants always say is 'the people' – the group dynamics, shared experiences, new perspectives, networks. The educator must consider what mix will work most effectively from the very design of a new program through its implementation and afterwards. Balancing sufficient diversity to bring in fresh perspectives and sufficient commonality of experience to allow dialogue to start is an ongoing challenge.

This is where close links between educators and their customers is critical, so open and honest dialogue can find the best approach to meet the organization's and individuals' needs. In some cases, this means advising that an executive attend a different program than the one he or she had originally planned, or that a company elects for an in-company rather than an open program approach. Spending time upfront on building shared understanding between participants, their home companies and educators is critical, as is ongoing dialogue during and after a program.

Even within the cohort from a single company, diverse participants can be drawn from different functional and hierarchical groups. To get the benefit from diversity, the program design has to build in multiple work and study groups, with frequent rotation of participants, as well as ongoing opportunities for networking. Rotating participant groups while maintaining diversity and forming new groups can be facilitated with software (see the box below on the team blender).

Team blender
Carlos Cordero

Every year, over 5500 executives, representing over 70 nationalities, attend IMD's open enrolment and company-specific programs. They come from virtually every industry, geography and cultural background, from young managers to seasoned board members, from family or entrepreneurial ventures to major multinationals.

However, the richness of this diversity could be lost in clusters or silos if we don't pay enough attention when arranging discussion groups, team projects, working meals, seating in the classroom or any other activity where diversity may play a role.

The dilemma is that managing the groups to exploit this potential is critical but time-consuming, particularly if you do it as often as we do. It can take anything from a couple of hours to a couple of days. With no off-the-shelf product for configuring groups based on multiple criteria, we built our own

> based on artificial intelligence algorithms – similar to those used for simulating chess, not an entirely inappropriate analogy! Criteria like industry sector, company, nationality, function, age, gender and whether two people had not met before can be easily taken into account.
>
> Today we can optimize the mix of participants, grouping or spreading people based on the number of groups and the overall profile of the class. The system is particularly helpful in programs of over a week, where we regularly rotate participants so they are grouped with people that they haven't worked with before. And we do all this about ten times faster and much more accurately than in the past – offering tremendous flexibility for the inevitable last-minute changes!

Invite, where possible, diverse faculty to participate in the program, though be aware that this demands a great deal of interaction, idea sharing and experience exchange. Visitors from other fields, orchestra conductors, actors, sports stars and the like can complement traditional management faculty and visiting CEOs. It is imperative that you communicate in advance the overall framework of the program and that you discuss how each session fits into that framework. That will allow individual faculty to come up with the best design for the session and you to maintain consistency across the program. Your role will be to push them to be creative and to come up with tailored solutions. In some cases, you may encounter faculty with a 'preferred' topic or type of activity that may conflict with another session. In other cases, different personalities and ways of handling problems may be a problem. Patience, open dialogue and joint preparation are crucial.

Beyond the faculty, diverse learning materials and activities (see Chapter 6) are essential to appeal to the different participant learning styles. And in longer programs, moving the participants to different locations for consulting, or study trips, or up to the mountains for self-reflection exercises, brings renewed energy into the learning process.

Develop the learning contract

No matter how clearly you communicate the program objectives and deliverables in the recruitment phase, there will be divergent expectations among participants. With a diverse group of learners it is important to set some ground rules for interactions from the start, to be mutually clear about the expectations of and objectives for the learning experience. Without these it is hard to establish an environment that fosters the individual change process required to incorporate new learning – the right mindset for learning to happen. To a great extent this environment is jointly constructed by participants and faculty – essentially forming a 'learning contract' (usually unwritten) for how the learning will take place.

Attitude is the starting point. Much of our interaction depends not on the content of our conversation, but on our attitude. Our attitudes influence how others interpret the information that we are giving them and, therefore, the learning process. So, how do we make someone want to learn? Commit to your participants and get them committed. Attitude runs both ways; your ability to create a supportive and challenging environment will generate confidence and open participants for better learning. Start by discussing attitudes and expectations with the participants, keeping the following in mind:

■ Participants on executive education programs come to be challenged in their ideas, views and beliefs, so we must encourage thought-provoking discussion and opinion sharing that enriches all.

■ We must be concerned not only with what they think, but also with what they feel. Learning is an emotional process as much as a cognitive one.

■ It is easier for the student to avoid the learning, because it requires the will to be transformed. The educator's role is to keep participants to the learning path whenever they risk leaving it.

■ Introducing the 'learning lens'[1] into participants' knowledge assimilation and reflection process involves an open and modifiable attitude.

■ Changing people's attitudes depends more on process than the content of interactions. It starts by accepting that our biases shape our thinking and that we make assumptions. With this understanding, we can block or be open to receiving new information and updating our beliefs.

Prepare participants to confront the 'pain.' High-impact learning involves addressing issues that may be hard to face (e.g. an inability to lead effectively or poor interpersonal relations) but unconsciously or consciously are part of a participant's agenda. Once these issues are confronted, the need to change becomes clear and participants will be ready to learn. If they simply avoid the 'pain' then there is no impact and, hence, no learning.

Yet, resistance to anything that involves pain and change is natural; the key is to channel it in a way that enhances learning. This starts with you, the educator, holding your opinions with humility and by acting as a role model for reflection. Humility shows we are ready to be affected by other individuals' ideas and that we are open to provide others with the right feedback for their behaviors. Reaching mutual agreement between educator and participants to this effect is at the heart of a learning contract that creates the best environment possible for learning.

An important part of establishing a contract is the discussion of the learning framework for the program at the first session and clearly explaining how each segment of the program fits together. To reinforce participants' understanding, reset expectations and wrap up themes frequently during the program. Starting each day or week by recapping what was achieved in previous sessions and how they all interconnect can provide a sense of direction and a clearer overview of how it all comes together.

Yet, all programs are not equal in terms of length, focus or group of participants. We need to recognize pragmatically that we cannot always reach the ideal contract of openness and a positive attitude to learning. In longer and open programs, reaching the appropriate 'norms' of behavior can be easier, because there is a longer period of reinforcement of the behaviors, plus equality of status among the participants. In week-long, in-company programs it can be harder. No matter how much you as faculty (or the head of the company team) try to promote openness, the guy in the back row will not voice his opinion until he has heard the view of his boss. But this does not mean you should not move towards wide-open dialogue – you just need to recognize the limitations you are working with, make sure the customer does too and screen the clients you work with (see the exhibit on handy hints).

When the unexpected happens: Handy hints for program directors
David Robertson

No matter how much accurate planning goes into the program, there are countless situations likely to confront you as program director: difficult decisions you will have to make on the spot or unexpected issues, situations or concerns that participants will raise. In an attempt to identify and find ways to deal with them, David Robertson surveyed faculty members on the most compelling situations they faced in programs and how they tackled them. Below, we describe some real (but disguised) situations:

1 **Participants ask to replace an educator because they did not like his session**
   Talk to participants and the faculty member to investigate where the problem really is. Sometimes the problem does not lie with the professor but with the topic or the approach chosen to address it. If that's the case, there is usually a way to correct the situation.

2 **A CEO asks for your opinion about a participant's performance**
   This situation puts the educator in a difficult spot, but as a rule, do not provide feedback about an employee's performance. In our view it would be unethical and, if known to occur, would compromise the learning process and could have serious implications on the participant's career development at the company.

3 **A staffing decision: Negotiation with a professor**
   Sometimes an educator is confirmed for a program and then needs to cancel as she is offered another assignment. Clients should come first, so the program has the priority. However, in a life-or-death case a replacement might have to be considered.

4 **A senior HR executive from the client side wants to sit in on an entire program**
   Accepting this proposal will depend on whether all educators involved agree and what the purpose of the request is. You need to make sure that the person will not attend in evaluation mode and that participants are aware of it. One way to handle this is to make him or her register as a participant and follow the program as the others do.

5 **Your program has a 'difficult' participant who challenges everything and everyone**
   One way to deal with this is to take an individual approach and talk to the person directly to surface his problem and try to solve it together. Another tactic would be to have the group give him a

Involve the participants upfront

How you start makes a world of difference to how the experience turns out – just think about an Olympic runner or even a new book someone has recommended to you. If you don't get off the blocks well or the book does not grab your attention in the first few pages, it's not going to be a great result. The learning experience is no different, so it's critical to break the ice and engage learners' interest fast.

How? Adults' readiness to learn is affected by their need to know or do something; they tend to have a problem-centered orientation to learning versus a subject-matter orientation.[2] One set of approaches for engaging learners upfront builds on this orientation, offering starting activities that require active participation, e.g. sharing a personal business challenge. A group-centered approach to sharing challenges that has been very effective in jump-starting interactions in programs is the round robin exercise (see below).

Jump-starting the process: The round robin
Thomas Vollmann

The basic objectives are to understand the collective thinking/ knowledge of a group about a set of specific issues – and for the group members to become acquainted much more rapidly than in a usual classroom setting.

The process starts by dividing the participants into teams, usually 4–6, with each team assigned a specific question. Each team then meets to discuss their question and think through the key issues it raises. They then conduct a series of interviews, asking the question individually to individual members of other teams, preferably choosing people the interviewer does not know well. The job of the interviewer is to listen and ask probing questions, but not to judge the response or agree/disagree. Instead the aim is to gather input/perceptions. The roles then switch, with the member of the other team becoming the interviewer and asking *their* question. This process is repeated several times (round robin), with each team always asking the same question. Finally, each team regroups to tabulate central themes in the responses (or perhaps opposing themes), and prepare a short presentation of these results for the overall group.

The key to success is carefully chosen questions. Ideally these will reflect the key issues to be addressed in the rest of the program. The questions allow sharing of opinions and practices (good and poor) and the initial formation of ideas that can be built on through the program. For example, in a manufacturing research program, each session addressed a different research issue. The round robin was an ideal way to rapidly share knowledge in the group – and establish the basis for the subsequent discussions. A typical set of questions was:

1 What is restructuring? How is it different from other kinds of change?

2 Why is restructuring necessary? What are the underlying forces, internal and external, which drive restructuring? Similarly, what are the constraints that impede it?

3 What are the specific aspects of restructuring? What are the action programs of restructuring with which you are familiar? What are the changes in the deployment of people, technology and information?

4 How is restructuring being implemented? What are the necessary managerial actions from the top down and the bottom up? What have you seen that are good and bad practice?

5 What are the key lessons for management? What should your company be thinking about in terms of restructuring?

Given the importance of context and emotion to high-impact learning, it is no surprise that a second 'family' of opening approaches emphasizes these factors. Techniques include asking a controversial question, posing a dilemma or inviting participants to take a position on a contentious issue.

External stimuli and provocative experiences are also useful in driving rapid engagement, for example bringing in a guest speaker (preferably fairly dynamic!) for an opening program dinner. Likewise, unusual settings can establish the foundation for conversations that are different: taking a top management team hiking up an alp has produced some important new dialogue and team commitments. However, at the end of the day, it is up to the educator to show empathy and engage the participants (see Chapter 3).

Sequence modules with appropriate design themes

Traditional programs are designed around the structure of intellectual content such as the functional areas of management followed by integrative topics like strategy and leadership. Great programs, however, continually link intellectual content with emotional awareness and both of these with application (see Chapter 6). There are two basic designs for linking intellectual and emotional awareness with application:

The **out-in design**: zooming in from the big picture to what it means for the individual, for example, from the macro environment, to the industry, to the company, to the team, to the manager and personal implementation.

And the **in-out design**: zooming out from the manager, to the team, the company and organizational execution.

Program scripting entails applying these themes to stage a coherent path for participants to follow in order to build the learning experience. It is important that this learning path considers the different energy flows in the group and paces the activities and the content so participants can follow the process smoothly.

A simple example of an **out-in design** for a company-specific program on strategic implementation is outlined below:

- Intellectual awareness of industry conditions.
- The application of industry analysis to identify opportunities and competitive battles.
- Then company analysis to identify business gaps.
- Focusing of the portfolio of strategic initiatives to identify priorities.
- Emotional awareness of team issues related to the priorities.
- Development of team management skills.
- Resolution of team issues.
- Awareness of personal emotional drivers.
- Skills for the mastery of self in dealing with the priorities.
- Development, debriefing and commitment to personal action plans to execute the priorities.

Programs often start with an in-out design to get the participants involved right away as individuals. They almost always end with an out-in theme that zeroes in on re-entry issues and individual next steps. A simple example of this is an **in-out-in design** that zooms out as follows:

- Individual emotional awareness.
- Team-related emotional awareness.
- Intellectual awareness of strategic issues.

And then zooms in on:

- Application of techniques to solve the strategic problems.
- Resolution of team-related issues.
- Individual emotional commitment to execute the strategic objectives.

In longer programs, the two design themes might be repeated on different types of content in different modules. In these programs, intellectual and emotional streams can run in parallel or in sequence:

■ First **in-out-in** from emotional awareness to broader functional knowledge and back in to personal leadership.

■ Then **out-in** from broad integrating themes to personal organizational leadership.

■ Finally, **out-in** from high level action-based problem solving to personal project execution.

Drive to application

To close the learning cycle and give participants the opportunity to construct a new reality and change their approach, action-learning projects should be part of the program design, wherever possible, as a hands-on tool to apply skills learned.

Personal and organizational projects

Personal projects involve the commitment of an individual executive, typically, to a business initiative and/or personal leadership improvement (see Chapter 6). An example of the latter is the 'Personal and Professional Identity Statement' or PPIS (see also Chapter 26). The PPIS is a confidential 10–page autobiography that participants create before coming to the program. This exercise provides a first level of personal reflection about their careers and their lives and prepares them to better engage with their own personal development. During the program, participants are assigned a coach, who follows up on their personal development process, referring back to and providing feedback on the PPIS. Support is a significant dimension in individual projects, as they make participants face aspects of themselves they may not feel fully comfortable with and find difficult to overcome.

Organizational projects vary according to the participants' stage of management development. In public programs these can be consulting or entrepreneurship projects, which provide opportunities for on-the-job learning while addressing a critical challenge for a specific company. In in-company programs, company projects or strategy workshops can be used, especially at higher levels of management development, to support the strategy formulation process or to roll out the implementation of strategy (see Chapter 6).

The learning community

But projects can't succeed in a vacuum. They must be embedded in a learning community; in other words, surrounded by a mutually supportive network of participants learning from one another. Each new program creates a potential new learning network and a unique source of learning. The program design must build in opportunities that encourage networking among the participants and motivate them to learn from one another (see Chapter 5 and the box below). Include social or other events in the program design to nurture the network. Some effective ways of fostering relationships and networks include cosmopolitan dinners to enhance cultural awareness, theatrical presentations to illustrate the central themes in a program module and exercises that combine fun, networking and learning.

Participant-led sessions to build a learning community
Leif Sjöblom

The objective of participant-led sessions is to tap into the specific expertise of the participants. It is also an excellent way of breaking the routine in a longer program, as long as the topics complement the program design. In these sessions, the learners take center stage. The educator's role is to guide preparation, act as timekeeper during the presentations (anyone who has tried to control a person talking about his favorite topic knows what we mean!) and to facilitate the discussion that should link the topics to the content of the program.

A simple version is to ask participants to make presentations – normally about two hours in length – on one of two alternative types of topic. The first type is a topic that is of great interest to a large number of participants, for example 'SAP implementation,' which is an issue for many companies and one with which a fair number of participants have experience. The second type is a 'mind broadening' topic. This topic will not be of immediate use on Monday morning, but is nevertheless educational and many times fascinating. An example is a session on 'Islamic Banking.' Many participants are surprised to find that it is the fastest growing segment in banking, and it is a topic few participants would otherwise get an opportunity to explore.

A more ambitious version of this exercise is a knowledge fair. This involves four steps:

1 Participants are asked to volunteer (either individually or in groups) to prepare and discuss a topic on which they are 'experts.'

2 The number of topics is narrowed down by voting.

3 Participants can sign up for a few sessions (typically two to three).

4 Each volunteer prepares a 'knowledge booth' – typically posters with information and a short presentation. But most of the time spent in each knowledge booth should be devoted to questions and answers.

The value of such learning is illustrated by a group of participants from the financial services industry who presented their industry. They showed how the core topics and concepts covered in the program applied to their specific issues – which served as a great review. It was also a good opportunity to compare how issues such as segmentation, distribution channels, operational efficiency, innovation and motivation and leadership apply to banking and other industries.

Orchestrate emotional highs

Individual sessions tend to produce emotional highs associated with provocation/challenge or investigation of problems, issues and the way things really work, but mainly the instructor drives them. By contrast, the program design should include sessions or events driven mainly by the participants, aiming at emotional highs associated with constructing new realities or changing oneself. With participants in the driver's seat, the emotional highs can get really high. These events become the program learning points that stick.

Examples include end-of-module exercises during which participants simulate a consulting assignment and report to the management on an ailing company or, even better, an actual consulting assignment carried out over several months. Often more emotional are outdoor exercises or weekend mountain trips for personal development and coaching that explore the ultimate questions: Who am I? Where am I going? Where do I want to go? How can I get there? More fun, but no less memorable, are social and module-closing events which challenge participants to explore new activities like singing an opera chorus or putting on a self-scripted play.

However, remember to control the quantity and intensity of intended emotional highs in the program design, so as not to generate a sensory or emotional overload. A balanced sequence of activities and content must allow time for informal interaction with peers and personal reflection.

Debrief, provide feedback and time for reflection

Recognize that emotional highs are of little use if they do not lead to long-term change. Provide opportunities in the program design for debriefing, feedback and reflection on 'what this means for me.' After meaningful experiences this helps to incorporate learning successfully into participants' behaviors and attitudes.

Debriefing, feedback and reflection are not only often central to the change phase of the learning cycle, but also valuable for participants to gauge their learning and their contribution to the program relative to their peers. While all the program steps fuel learning, it is in the debriefing and reflection phase that participants begin identifying and articulating new learning.

Regardless of which model of debriefing is adopted – individual or collective, driven by participants or by faculty – it becomes essential to allocate the necessary time and carefully plan the approach that will prompt the reflection phase. Reflection should naturally roll in tandem with each session, but deliberately planning reflection instances will push participants to reflect on their experience early on and change gears if needed.

One of the simplest ways of doing this is to encourage participants to maintain a learning diary in which they record the most important personal learning points that emerged out of the day's experience. This can be supported by the participants sharing their learning points from yesterday at the start of each day, first in small groups and then in pointed discussion with the whole group.

To complement the internal process of reflection, external feedback from faculty and peers will bring closure and meaning to the individual learning process. Feedback is a powerful tool to support participants' reflection; it is a mirror that helps them match their own impressions with that of their peers and faculty members. For feedback to act as such, it is important that it is closely related to concrete skills or topics discussed within the program and that it provides hints for participants on how to improve a behavior or an approach. The box on coaching teams for business development illus-trates one approach to helping teams in this phase of the learning cycle.

Coaching teams for business development
Georges Haour

The everyday learning experience of managers can be powerfully complemented by occasional booster courses that include a 'coaching' activity. Different working modes and objectives may be used, depending upon whether it is addressed to an individual or to a team. Here we describe a team-based approach and example.

The 'Booster' program has the ambitious aim of helping corporations substantially accelerate the development and profitable growth of one of their new business segments (see 'Why should you want to master executive education?' at the start of this book for another example). The 'leverage' of such an activity can be very large: imagine the impact of taking a new venture from an uncertain outcome and launching it on a path of success as a result of the advisory, catalytic process provided by the booster program!

The way it works is as follows: a team of four to nine persons involved in a new business venture attends the one-week booster program. Four to five different teams from non-competing companies participate in the same program. During the week, the mornings are plenary sessions allowing participants to discuss general management topics. In the afternoons and evenings, each team intensively works on the business issues of their venture, led by one educator. The latter has the dual role of asking the difficult business questions, while coaching the team so that the conversations progress fruitfully.

Let us take the example of a very large company which wanted to rapidly enhance its business of serving the pharmaceutical and life-science sector. The mission of the team was to prepare a compelling business plan for an activity that would leverage the company's considerable set of activities in the areas of medical analytical equipment, genetic engineering and bio-informatics.

The team worked long hours on this large task, sometimes splitting into two sub-groups to address different issues in parallel. Three days into the one-week program, the team completed a compelling plan for the business development of the activity, with timelines and figures, segment by segment. It had been a long day of work and it was 22:00. The team burst into applause: 'We did it!' Many other substantive issues, such as distribution channels, organizational aspects, still needed to be discussed, but the breakthrough was reached. The comprehensive business plan, produced at the end of the week, was widely communicated and accepted within the company. Regularly updated, it still serves now as a blueprint for the development of the activity.

Support re-entry and next steps

Ensuring that learning is used on the job is key to getting the value out of executive education. After participants have been involved in an intense learning experience during a program, facing the routine in their companies and lives is not always an easy transition. This is particularly true after long, highly intense or catalytic programs that demand an extra level of commitment and where involvement with peers, faculty and the overall program becomes deep. The commitment and engagement developed during the program makes participants want to implement the ideas and new approaches they have absorbed. But their organizations were not part of the learning experience and are not ready for this. Thus, the transition from learning off-site to back on the job needs to be facilitated.

To different degrees, both open and custom-made programs need to provide an opportunity for participants to address re-entry. In particular, they need to think through how they intend to debrief their boss on what happened during the program and, most importantly, whether the psychological contract with their boss should be put on the table and renewed. The more senior the executives, the more critical the psychological contract, because so much of what they do is not laid out in any formal way. Hence, there is a strong need to have a plan for renewing the contract and other important relationships on return.

To support re-entry, the program design should include an integrative portion that pulls together all the experiences and learning and prepares executives to address the challenges they may encounter going back to the 'real world.' For example, in one program, participants break into small groups to discuss their 'must-win battles':[3] the key actions they needed to take to achieve their business and personal objectives. The groups quickly became self-reliant, challenging and supporting each other in developing plans to realize their goals beyond the program – as well as building a network of mutual support that would likely continue well after the end of the program.

Another approach is to dedicate the last module of the program to the execution of change. All the sessions in the module focus on change and implementation. The renewal of critical relationships can be acted out in vignettes with other participants, who play the role of those back home. To support the transition to home and family, spouses or partners can be invited to social events and even some program sessions. A closing dinner for all, organized by participants, far from being a merely fun event, can close the program on an emotional high: it becomes a celebration of the learning network the participants have created.

Lock in customer value

Locking in the value of executive education for participants and their companies is more easily done after company-specific rather than open-enrolment programs. After the former, project work done during the program can be integrated into the company's ongoing management system. To make this happen, the integration process should be discussed with the client company during the program design, to ensure that the action learning can be easily absorbed into the management system when the participants return. Make sure that action learning intended for transfer supports the management system and doesn't complicate it. Too many companies are already suffering from project pollution!

For individual executives with personal initiatives, the challenge is even greater, because they have to convert their colleagues to their cause. This is no easy matter, because everyone is already over-occupied with their own agendas. Again, a large part of the solution is in the choice of the initiatives up front: compatibility with the existing portfolio of business initiatives, in terms of resources needed, implementation risk and value-creating potential, is a must. Build an appropriate framework for the selection of initiatives into the program design. The re-entry tactics discussed above are also essential, especially anticipating how to mobilize support and deal with resistance.

The deep value of a great learning experience will emerge gradually over time as the participants pursue their managerial careers, especially for those without ongoing projects. If the learning 'sticks' then, even if it is not relevant to the executive's immediate challenges, it will be there when needed. As one participant put it, 'I think every day about what I learned and how I can use it in my company. I realize I will probably not face some of the topics and situations I am learning about in the short term, but I will certainly face them at some point in my career.'

Participation in an active alumni network that maintains at least part of the learning community developed during the program can be a great support for the ongoing exchange of advice and experience as it unfolds. Follow-up events can also play a role, although it's important to realize that these can never replicate the atmosphere of the original experience, but should be designed as separate new learning experiences.

The final element of the program script is how you assess whether the learning objectives were accomplished. The two key dimensions will be the individual and the organizational; you have to make sure that the experience met participants' individual goals, as much as the organizational goals for which your client has chosen the program. In addition to traditional techniques such as evaluation forms and surveys, corporate clients should be debriefed in some depth, via a formal post-program review and informal dialogue with the customer at different levels to exchange honest feedback. With this input and the observations of your team, you will need an after-action review to detail improvements and, some three to six months later, a follow-up survey of participants to see how they changed and what part of the learning stuck.

Notes

1 Collins, J. (1997) The Learning Executive. *Inc. Magazine*, August.
2 Knowles, M.S. and Associates (1984) *Andragogy in Action: Applying Modern Principles of Adult Education*. San Francisco: Jossey-Bass.
3 Killing, P. and Malnight, T. with Keys, T. (2005) *Must-Win Battles*. FT Prentice Hall, (forthcoming publication); and *IMD Perspectives for Managers* (2004), Issue 106, January.

part

3

Developing learning materials and methodologies

8

Writing an effective case for executive programs

J.B. Kassarjian and Kamran Kashani

Summary

Cases are an important tool in bringing the realities of complex business issues into the classroom. They offer executives the opportunity to immerse themselves in the decision-making process and to extrapolate from the case issues to personal experience as well as to the business realities they face in their own company. The topics must therefore be relevant and compelling. Development of cases can be driven by need, to illustrate a particular issue in class, or lead, inspired by research or simply by learning about someone or something that might generate an interesting debate. Often the latter sources prove richer learning contexts, because the situations are more 'natural.'

To produce an effective case, the authors outline a systematic approach, together with deep insights on common case-writing challenges:

- Generating 'leads' that pose real decision dilemmas and present complex and compelling issues.
- Grounding the work in the teaching objectives and the analysis required on the part of participants to address those issues.
- Developing multiple iterations to produce a tool that will effectively guide executives in the learning experience.

However, they conclude that a 'good case' is not just a well-written document and a teaching tool, or even simply an engaging story about a compelling management issue. It is an opportunity to embark on a personal journey of discovery, for the case writer, for the teacher, for the participant, and sometimes for the company. It opens horizons instead of closing them; it raises new questions instead of merely answering them, and it provides a rich forum for personal development and growth.

Case writing is a subtle craft: It should provoke rigorous thinking, challenge comfortable assumptions, stimulate engaging discussion, and jolt executives into real learning that matters in the real world. Like any demanding craft, it requires knowledge of materials, mastery of tools, a plan of what is to be produced, a carefully calibrated process, and the skills necessary to combine these into an effective learning script that can be used by a variety of teachers to carry groups of managers on journeys of discovery.

The objective: Is it teaching or learning goals?

An effective case study is more than simply a gripping business story or a way to demonstrate one or more currently fashionable management theories. And the case itself is not the final goal.

The real destination is to provide the setting and central metaphor that encourage teachers and participants to explore with excitement, to reflect in depth, and to discover personal insights that can enrich their independent judgment. A realistic measure of success is the response of participants at the end of the case discussion, when asked to think and write down their *own* most significant insights from the class. Another measure may be how readily teachers (other than the authors) adopt the case and enjoy teaching it in different executive programs.

> **❝ The real destination is to provide the setting and the central metaphor that encourage teachers and participants to explore with excitement, to reflect in depth, and to discover personal insights that can enrich their independent judgment. ❞**

Even though most cases carry the familiar disclaimer on the first page, 'Cases are not designed to illustrate either effective or ineffective ways of handling management situations,' in fact many cases are written to illustrate the author's thoughts and current conclusions; predictably, such cases have a rather short shelf life. If your goal is to underscore 'the eight key steps for an effective change program,' you would be better advised to deliver these as *your ideas*, rather than trying to place participants in a case discussion so you can pull these points from them. In our experience, astute executives in class often point this out, to the merriment of the class and the loss of credibility of the professor.

The route to independent judgment is more often self-discovered, rather than directed by others. It is discovered through immersion in the decision-making process, by identifying with key managers in real-world situations, by formulating and defending a point of view in response to provocative questions, and by learning through a dialectic process, where discussion and reasoning – coupled with active reflection – provide the fuel for learning.

Identifying opportunities: Driven by need or lead?

Like most entrepreneurial ventures, case 'leads' come from many sources, but in most instances the good ones turn out to be opportunity-driven. It may appear more logical to start the search with your *program needs* in mind, but often *exploring leads* that pose real decision dilemmas, and present complex and compelling issues, reshapes your view of program needs. For example, a decisive action by an articulate executive, in response to a complex set of interacting competitive and internal forces that are producing counter-intuitive outcomes, could represent such a promising lead.

In recent years, most widely adopted and effectively used cases have accompanying videos of key players, either elaborating on critical decisions or providing an epilogue of ensuing events. While a colorful character alone does not provide effective learning in a case, an interesting business situation in which a colorful character faces a critical decision goes a long way toward that. Through repeated experience with carefully edited videos, we have been increasingly convinced that the storyteller *is* part of the story.

> ❝ We have been increasingly convinced that the storyteller *is* part of the story. ❞

For example, we discovered the lead for the widely used IMD case *Shaping Spaarbeleg*[1] in an executive program. When the professor asked the class if anyone was taking a significant risk at their job whose outcome was not yet clear, Johan van der Werf (at the time General Manager of the Spaarbeleg Division of Aegon, NL) responded boldly: 'Yes, I want to run some exciting ads in the paper, but many at headquarters are upset about ruining our reputation as "the agents' company." I think they are afraid of such advertising. But I am convinced we should try direct marketing, and I am willing to put my job on the line to do it!' His comments carried real conviction – he was the only person in that program who was willing to openly contradict his senior management, and he was certainly articulate. Johan's willingness to go against company conventional wisdom turned out to be the start of a major transformation at his division. We followed this lead and got the case.

Case writing is often an iterative process, where you may have to navigate around sensitive company issues while taking detours to explore new areas – you need to negotiate with the host company the specific case-writing mandate at the start. Nonetheless, the time and effort to be invested can only be justified if you have found a willing organization, one that finds the prospect of exploration equally fascinating.

Getting started: The early imperatives

At the beginning of the process, it is useful to thoroughly scan the territory:

- What are the critical issues in the company now? How are they likely to evolve?

- Who are the key players: those with formal power *and* those who have informal sources of influence?

- What are likely to be the most serious roadblocks to the case effort?

- Who is most likely to be the 'sponsor' for this case, who would be willing and in the position to release the case? An alternative?

On the basis of what you turn up in this process, you can begin to focus on one or a few key executives to establish a certain level of trust. If a key player feels vulnerable about opening company records, or sensitive actions, you are likely to produce a shallow case. You should be trusted to handle sensitive data responsibly, and be willing to balance case integrity with company needs.

> **If your case involves an ongoing situation, you may well discover new lenses that reveal the landscape in a new light.**

As you become familiar with the territory, you can begin to conceptualize the case, to visualize ways in which such a case can be taught. This is a delicate balance of clarity regarding how case issues can be discussed and the openness to include emerging data that modifies that vision. If your case involves an ongoing situation, you may well discover new lenses that reveal the landscape in a new light.

Despite the caution about being openminded, it is essential to have a working outline, one that anticipates the building blocks of the final case. Based on this outline, and the trust you develop with identified sponsors, it is advisable for all concerned to get a written authorization to proceed.

Sony's European operation provides an example that touches on most of these points. For some years, while IMD had been conducting a custom-designed program for Sony in Europe, we had become quite familiar with the challenges Sony was facing there. When Chairman and CEO Jack Schmuckli launched a major strategic and organizational change in Europe, and chose Dr Ron Sommer to spearhead the effort, we asked if we could develop a case series about it. While we had already developed a certain level of trust with many of the executives through teaching in the Sony program, we still had to negotiate about the inclusion and form of certain events that were unfolding. Through numerous iterations, this effort resulted in the three-part Sony Europa[2] case series, which includes a three-part video featuring the three key players who were driving the change.

Field interviews and data collection

This chapter is on field-researched cases, where hard facts are woven together with the opinions, perceptions and feelings of key players in a way that focuses on a critical decision faced by a particular company at a point in time. But the choice of a setting and the questions at issue are also guided by the kind of new light this case can shed on similar dilemmas faced by many organizations.

In choosing executives to interview, we have found it useful to identify three types that can help us to allocate effort judiciously:

■ **Drivers**: Key decision makers who own the problem or decision and who will appear at the start and end the case with their dilemma.

■ **Passengers**: Managers who can provide additional context, filling in the blanks of facts and figures, as well as an alternative perspective on what really goes on backstage.

■ **Bystanders**: Outsiders to the decision-making locus of responsibility who can also provide 'objective' external points of view, and certain insights that are not shared by those directly involved.

A conversation with a passenger or bystander could help shape your interviews with drivers. It could also fill in gaps.

A critical task at the start of a first interview is to put the person at ease by explaining the educational objective of the venture and by clarifying that all the content of the case is subject to review and final release. For example, in convincing Jack Schmuckli of Sony Europa to let us proceed with the case, we presented evidence that companies which had been open to case writing and had many cases written about their operations – such as GE, IBM,

Johnson & Johnson and Hewlett-Packard – were more successful over time than those who had always refused. He bought the argument!

Whether to tape-record interviews is a question of personal preference. Some prefer to record every interview, listen multiple times while taking notes, and mark direct quotes. Others find tape recorders distracting and take detailed notes to capture actual words and expressions to be used in the case. The technique used is less important than a determination to question all central premises, and to capture – as closely as possible – what each key player has to say about the issues. What may sound peripheral at the time of the interview could well become a salient point later on, as the case writer develops a deeper understanding into pivotal issues.

> **" The technique used is less important than a determination to question all central premises, and to capture – as closely as possible – what each key player has to say about the issues. "**

In addition to interviews, data can be collected from company records (usually the most efficient source, though sometimes biased), industry studies and databases, consulting reports, or even earlier cases on the company (a particularly efficient source of data for history and background). Whatever the source, it is crucially important to be selective rather than exhaustive: 'data dump' should be avoided at all cost. The inclusion of marginally useful charts and tables can be a serious distraction, especially for executive audiences who lose interest when the material gets away from what they regard as the real business issues in the case.

Writing the first draft: Probably the first of many

Having first immersed yourself in the interview data and picked some memorable quotations, but before you start writing, ask yourself: How would I go about teaching this case? A first cut at a teaching strategy is a far better guide for the first draft than a detailed outline that exhausts all the data gathered or that merely follows the original case outline. You must resist the temptation to find ways to include everything you found: you are not trying to prove your diligence at data collection, but trying to compose a learning script, one that has clear focus and can hold the interest of the reader.

> **" Before you start writing, ask yourself: How would I go about teaching this case? A first cut at a teaching strategy is a far better guide for the first draft than a detailed outline that exhausts all the data. "**

❝ Should readers sense that you are peddling your own diagnosis, they will inevitably focus on shooting holes in your argument – a battle you cannot win. ❞

By this time, you know too much about the company. You have most likely formed a large body of 'informed judgments' about the competitive prospects of the company and the current pitfalls they face – but these almost certainly don't belong in the case. The case writer should maintain strict neutrality at all times, citing in a fair and balanced way the conflicting opinions of different players but never taking sides. Should readers sense that you are peddling your own diagnosis, they will inevitably focus on shooting holes in your argument – a battle you cannot win.

Personal writing styles vary a great deal, and you may resist being told how to proceed. But experience suggests that it is safe to start with a central dilemma, one faced by the key driver in the case, and one about which sensible people could have contrasting opinions. In the first two paragraphs you must interest the reader in the eventual outcome, triggering a readiness to take sides on the issue; without this interest, you are unlikely to hold their attention. Then get out of their way and let central case characters express their logic and their emotions in their own words.

Writing multiple drafts of a case is like pruning a tree: each cutting reveals the underlying design and overall shape of the case as the random abundance of branches is pared away. It is probably a useful discipline to cut the case by 50 percent on the second draft, as a way to focus on certain dilemmas as well as make critical choices about the essential issues. When we were working on the Sony Europa (A)[3] case, the version that was released (and in fact won a peer-evaluated prize) was 18 pages. Later we wanted to feature the case in a large IMD program, where participants had limited time to read, so we cut it down to an eight-page 'abridged' version, which worked just fine. Some time later, for a different setting and use, the case was cut down to five pages, and it worked just as well again! The authors, who had to cut out so much precious content, including many favorite phrases and funny quotes, felt the only pain associated with these iterations. Nonetheless, it has become clear to us that readers appreciate the brevity and the greater clarity of focus.

Case outline: Is there a magic format?

The evidence from the most widely used cases would suggest that they typically follow a sequence like the following:

1 Introduction: a dilemma, a problem, an action called for . . .

2 Company background.

3 External context: market, industry, etc.

4 Company context: the evolution of the case problem.

5 Drilling down: issues and actions that have a bearing on the decision.

6 Conclusion: decision points.

We consider this a 'suggested' outline, rather than a fixed blueprint. It forces the writer to consider what should be the dilemma being faced by the central player in the situation with which to open the case. The essential issue is not the detailed sequence proposed above, but the need to start and end the case with a compelling question, one with options that most executives would find interesting enough to consider how they would resolve it.

Section 2 is intended to remind the case writer that some company background is needed to provide a context for the decision at hand. Similarly, sections 3 and 4 cover, respectively, external competitive realities as well as internal organizational culture issues. Often, in the crossfire of conflicting perspectives about a current issue at a specific company, protagonists place exclusive emphasis on one or the other.

As a respected colleague put it many years ago, section 5 is designed to make sure 'the onion has enough layers to peel,' that is, that all the contributing factors have been presented, and presented impartially.

> **❝ Any good case is a story: it has a punchy opening, a middle that paints the background and puts the action in context, and a dramatic ending. ❞**

In the sense that human experience is most likely to be conveyed through stories,[4] any good case is a story: it has a punchy opening, a middle that paints the background and puts the action in context, and a dramatic ending. In writing a case for an executive audience, the added challenge is to compose a compelling story that engages their interest, requires a stretch for analysis, and demands action.

Case release: Reassuring closure or a losing battle?

One of the well-kept secrets of case-writing and case-teaching institutions is that many completed cases, about current and compelling business issues at reputable companies, are never formally released. These cases represent a large sunk cost for the institution, as well as the dashed hopes of aspiring faculty and research staff. Therefore, ideas and steps to carry a case all the way to formal release deserve serious attention.

In an earlier section we talked about the need to identify and develop a trusting relationship with a powerful and willing sponsor. Ironically, this sponsor is perhaps the most frequent cause that kills the case: the stronger your relationship with this key sponsor, the more devastating for you when this executive departs the scene, for whatever reason. (Unanticipated events include: transfer to another unit, promotion to a different job, being head-hunted out to another company, or some personal situation.) Because you invest heavily in this one relationship, you are less likely to develop an alternative sponsor. The lesson is simple in retrospect: throughout the case-writing process, keep your primary sponsor in the loop on progress, and don't forget to develop an alternative.

ff Fifteen minutes of defusing an issue can save you months of anguish. 🢖🢖

Part of the process of keeping sponsors in the loop is to defuse concerns before they become magnified; as a wise colleague once commented, 'Fifteen minutes of defusing an issue can save you months of anguish.' As events unfold, you can reiterate the case focus and your writing objectives. You can check and verify facts and figures, which are cleared to be included in the case. After there is sufficient mutual trust and respect, you should be willing to negotiate hard to safeguard the essence of the case.

The actual signing of the case release card, by an authorized executive, does not have to wait for the final edit of the case. It may be prudent to have a release card ready earlier in the process, in case the sponsor feels comfortable to approve it. We had one instance where the (A) case had been more or less accepted, the (B) case was not finished and the (C) had not yet been started and the CEO offered to sign the release cards of all three parts of the case. He must have felt confident that we would not violate his trust. Whatever you do, get the case formally released at the earliest date.

ff Whatever you do, get the case formally released at the earliest date. 🢖🢖

The learning script: No case is complete without one

Many case-producing institutions adopt the policy that, without a teaching note, a case is not considered fully completed. Instead of considering a teaching note an added burden, think about it as a learning script. If you start by asking 'How would I go about teaching this case,' including what roles you and the learners need to play and what emotions you expect to evoke, you will have a number of different approaches in mind once the case is completed. Starting with early formulations of a teaching strategy and building on these as the case takes final shape, you can challenge yourself to outline at least two very different ways of teaching the case; this can help you stretch beyond earlier conceptions as well as stimulate different sets of questions.

Our experiences with case teaching, and observing others teach, suggest that the most critical skill revolves around: how questions are shaped and formed; the sequence and timing of when they are asked; and the tone in which they are asked. These are craft skills, but they can be elevated to a personal art. Legendary case teachers (indeed possibly all great teachers) come in many guises, but they all have one thing in common: the way they compose and ask questions, and the intensity with which they listen to the answers.

> ❝ [In] case teaching . . . the most critical skill revolves around: how questions are shaped and formed; the sequence and timing of when they are asked; and the tone in which they are asked. ❞

A good learning script offers more than one way to tackle a case. It also has explicit objectives for each segment of class time (the acts of the script), specifies questions in sufficient detail, and supplements each section with what we have come to call 'professor stories.' Since these are based on actual class experience (and they reflect the ebb and flow of questions asked and responses given), an effective learning script is seldom finished before the case is taught multiple times, preferably by more than one person.

We could cite a longer list of items to be included, but a script can best be judged by how readily it entices a new faculty member to try to teach it. We have seen colleagues who, having read and reflected on a teaching note, are not only ready to try the case, but are eager to try a different approach of their own invention. It helps to have additional conceptual materials that can support the analysis; clear pointers for a crisp wrap-up; and an informed epilogue to provide a sense of closure. But the way you describe the paths of discussion, and how certain questions could act as pivots for exploring new directions, should be designed to increase the confidence of the novice. Sometimes a good walking stick is better suited to exploring new terrain than a detailed survey map.

> ❝ Sometimes a good walking stick is better suited to exploring new terrain than a detailed survey map. ❞

So what is a really good case? Some final thoughts

Experienced managers attend executive education programs primarily because they are sent. They may arrive with resentment or indifference, but seldom with the enthusiastic expectation of being provoked, challenged or stretched. Whatever the HRD manager promised, or however the CEO tried to inspire participants on opening night, deep down most managers come to class on Monday morning with a secret hope that, apart from all this hype, they might find a few tools and techniques that would enhance their chances of promotion. The last thing most of them want is to be jolted out of their cherished assumptions. Initially, they are even uncomfortable to be asked for their judgment on a strange case, and then have that judgment directly confronted with an opposing view.

> **❝ In a very real sense teaching cases to experienced managers could be viewed as a subversive activity. ❞**

Burdened with such misgivings, the first test of a good case is whether it can engage the interest of the skeptical reader, sort of get under their skin; hence the critical importance of the opening paragraphs. This first part of the case, which describes a vital dilemma faced by a 'recognizable' executive, together with the assignment questions, should be sufficiently intriguing to pull the reader into the territory of the case. This brings to mind a book published many years ago with the remarkable title *Teaching As a Subversive Activity*;[5] in a very real sense, teaching cases to experienced managers could be viewed as a subversive activity. In addition to acquiring tools and techniques, they are primarily interested in discussing their own company situation.

But we know that the most effective way for them to gain a better, or deeper, perspective into their own company situation is to be willing to climb up the branches of the story, and to struggle with the data in the case at hand. No bullets and pointers provided by the teacher at the end of class could substitute for the personal effort that this demands. In this sense, composing a case that engages their interest and stretches their thinking could be viewed as a subversive activity: the case and the class are daring them to challenge their view of their own situation.

Recently, one of the authors was stopped on a campus path by a barely familiar colleague, with the remark, 'You know, I re-read that long teaching note you wrote on Spaarbeleg; I think I finally figured out how to teach it, because I realized that it has changed the way I look at . . .!' This may be a humbling experience, but before long we realize that we too have been changed by teaching someone else's case.

Teaching the Alto Chemicals[6] case significantly impressed one person about the centrality of shocking managers as a necessary step in any difficult organizational change effort. For another colleague, writing and teaching the Tetra Pak[7] case convinced him that the metaphor of a burning platform represented a crucial means to challenge the complacency bred by world market leadership. And the Sony Europa case has revised the thinking of many colleagues about the pace of change and role of the leader, on both sides of the Atlantic. Yes, a good case taught well can shake perspectives; it can transform minds and models.

> **❝ Yes, a good case taught well can shake perspectives; it can transform minds and models. ❞**

It is in this spirit that we close this chapter with the following final thoughts:

A 'good case' is not just a well-written document and a teaching tool, or even simply an engaging story about a compelling management issue. It is an opportunity to embark on a personal journey of discovery, for the case writer, for the teacher, for the participant, and sometimes for the company.

It opens horizons instead of closing them; it raises new questions instead of merely answering them, and it provides a rich forum for personal development and growth.

That's what a good case is all about.

Key take-aways

- A good case is a story that encourages executives to open perspectives, reflect in depth and discover personal insights that can enrich their judgment.

- This journey is most often self-discovered not directed by others, so the educator and case writer serve as guides along the path. The critical skill in this role is to shape and ask questions that drive progress.

- To engage executives in such exploration, cases must center on real and compelling people and challenges, offering the opportunity for immersion in the decision-making process, stretching analyses and action. The storyteller is an integral part of the story.

■ While the subject of cases may be identified by need or lead, the case outline should be driven by a central question that links clearly to the teaching objectives and provides interesting options for debate – it is not a vehicle to expound a theory or a 'data dump.'

■ Case writing is an iterative process; like pruning a tree, focus on the core dilemmas comes as branches are cut away. Executives much appreciate brevity and clarity – teaching impact is not generally affected by reducing the length of the case.

■ The development of good relationships with the people who can provide the necessary perspectives for a full and rounded story is critical: drivers, passengers and bystanders. This is also important to ensure the case release is signed as early as possible.

Notes

1   Kassarjian, J.B.M. (1992) *Shaping Spaarlbeleg: Real and Unreal.* IMD Case number IMD-3–0537.
2   Kashani, K. and Kassarjian, J.B.M. (1998): *Sony Europa (A)*, IMD-5–0488; *Sony Europa (B)*, IMD-5–0489; *Sony Europa (C)*, IMD-5–0490; and the Sony Europa case video (1995), IMD Catalog number 449.
3   Kashani, K. and Kassarjian, J.B.M. (1998): *Sony Europa (A)*, IMD-5–0488
4   In the old mainframe computer era joke (which in recent years has become a mantra for learning-theorists and AI types), the computer is asked: *Can you think like a human being?* After many blips and blinks it answers: *That reminds me of a story!*
5   Postman, N. and Weingartner, C. (1973) *Teaching as a Subversive Activity.* New York: Delacorte Press.
6   Kashani, K. (1995): *Alto Chemicals Europe (AR)*, IMD-5–0484; *Alto Chemicals Europe (BR)*, IMD-5–0485; *Alto Chemicals Europe (CR)*, IMD-5–0486.
7   Kashani, K. and Shaner, J. (2002): *Tetra Pak (A): The Challenge of Intimacy with a Key Customer*, IMD-5–0604; *Tetra Pak (B): The Customer Satisfaction Initiative*, IMD-5–0605; *Tetra Pak (C): Implementing New Initiatives*, IMD-5–0606; *Tetra Pak (D): Results Achieved (and the Remaining Issues)*, IMD-5–0607.

9

Real world. Real learning. Real video!

J. Peter Killing

Summary

Videos bring cases to life and offer the opportunity for much richer class discussions. In addition, they help executives to move beyond extracting the 'key issues' from cases and focus on the dynamics of assessing and managing people, a core skill for business success. This chapter discusses principles for making and using case-based videos.

Good planning upfront and flexibility as new facts emerge from the interviews are critical. Planning involves matching the material to the intended audience and building a relationship of trust with the subjects of the video. Location of taping is also important. Videos shot in class often elicit greater engagement and openness from the executives featured in the case – and so learning – than more formal settings. New insights and facts from tapes mean revising the original case, alongside the tapes, to ensure a cohesive package. This is often a juggling act, as the third dimension in editing is making sure the finished products drive an effective learning experience. So, for each video segment and part of the case, it is important to work through how it will be used as part of the session script.

Commonly, case-based videos are used to confirm class discussion, driving home the fact that the issues under discussion are real and important. Educators can also challenge the group on issues which may be less obvious, but which the upcoming video will reveal as critical – or as a tool to offer insights into issues that have not been raised as yet. Such tape segments also offer the opportunity to move the story forward, setting up the next discussion topic. Further uses include providing the basis for assessing managers, and concluding the story.

Creating a winning combination of case, video and lecture materials is a big job – and requires creativity. But it is important not to stop editing too soon. The key is to build on class reaction to make refinements that will improve the overall learning experience in future.

Because you never know exactly what an executive will say while being taped, you cannot completely design a case and video combination in advance. Of course, at a certain point you will have more video footage and case information than you can use. The challenge is to create the best possible learning experience with the least amount of material.

Many business schools feed their participants a relentless diet of case studies over a period of weeks or even years. It should come as no surprise that participants become adept at extracting the 'key issues' from 20-page summaries of interesting situations. But any CEO will tell you that success in business is largely about selecting, promoting and trusting the right people, and giving them space to 'get on with it.' While the ability to extract the essence of documents may be a useful business skill, it is certainly not at the top of the list of abilities that lead to managerial success.

A partial solution to this problem is to write shorter case studies and augment them with what we call *real video!* This is videotape of the key players in a given case study that functions as an integral part of the partic-ipants' learning process – not just a 'here is what happened' wrap-up at the end of class.

In this chapter I will illustrate how we both make and use such videos, and why we think they are a vital ingredient in today's approach to executive learning. Today we are in fact using a DVD format as often as videotape, but for convenience I will use the terms 'video' and 'videotape' throughout this chapter.

Case-based video

There are many ways that you can use videotape in a class session. The most fundamental choice is whether the video is to be integrated with a case study or stand alone, which means that the video itself is the basis for class discussion rather than a supplement to a text. A stand-alone video can be particularly valuable when there is no time for participants to read a case before class, or if one of the objectives of the class is to provide a break from a steady diet of case-based classes. Either format can work well, but in this chapter I will focus on videos that are created to be integrated with case studies, within a broader learning script.

The greatest power of case-based video is that, by bringing the case to life, it dramatically increases the interest level of the class participants. An effective video also provides information that one cannot convey through the written word. Making correct judgments about people, for example, is a key element of business success and asking participants to make judgments about executives they see on tape can lead to a much richer class discussion than if you were to carry out the same exercise based only on written material.

Participants are frequently surprised by what their peers conclude from a segment of tape. They may disagree on both what they have observed and its significance. For example, I have reproduced below a portion of a typical conversation between participants who have been asked to play the role of board members of a newly formed joint venture; they are trying to decide if they have chosen the right manager to be its CEO. They have just seen the CEO on videotape.

> *Participant A*: He is a poor leader. He has been in this job six months and has still not learned the technology that lies at the heart of the business. His focus is completely wrong – in fact I would say he has no focus.

> *Participant B*: A CEO does not have to understand the technology. But I do agree with you that he is not the right person for the job. He completely lacks charisma. I would not want him as my boss.

> *Participant A*: Charisma? What is that? Whatever it is, it certainly has nothing to do with business success. But in a company of this size – a few hundred employees – he certainly must understand the technology. How else can he play a role in the key decisions that need to be made?

> *Participant C*: You two are both focused on the wrong things. This executive avoids conflict. And he cannot continue to do that if the JV is to be successful. There are important and fundamental conflicts between his subordinates, and if he does not deal with them, the venture will fail. That is the real issue. And the question that we need to deal with as board members is whether or not we can lead him to deal with and resolve these conflicts.

From this beginning the conversation becomes increasingly rich. What characteristics and knowledge does one require to be an effective CEO? Can they be learned? How quickly? As board members, what action should we take? Should we coach the CEO? Replace him? Give him another six months? And so on. The richness of the discussion is driven almost entirely by the video of the CEO – the written case simply provides the necessary background information.

Planning the package

If you want to create a case- and video-teaching package, you need to decide at the outset approximately how the combination is going to work in the classroom, but your initial ideas will probably change as you learn more about the situation and the people involved. The critical act of creativity comes near the end, when you have more tape and case material than you can use and have to decide what to keep and what to cut.

There is no 'single way' to create a winning case and video combination, but I have presented below some guidelines that we use when planning a new package.

1 Match material and participants

You will achieve best results with a video and case combination when your group of participants can identify with the key actor(s) because they have approximately the same level of responsibility and deal with similar issues. If the case and video feature managers who are one level above your participants, that will also work well. However, choosing case protagonists who are one level below participants is often less effective. Thus the joint venture general manager videotape described previously works best with participants who are or have been board members and/or business unit CEOs, and possibly have worked in joint ventures.

2 Ensure company cooperation at the outset

Case packages that are going to include video need to be based on interviews with company managers – you cannot write them solely from public sources, such as newspaper articles. During your first interview at the company, which we recommend be with the most senior person involved in the situation you want to document, you should outline the scope of what you want to do and find out how comfortable the company is with your plans.

If, for example, the company is willing to let you write the case, but wants it disguised in some way, you need to give the matter some thought. Changing a few numbers is not a serious problem, but a request that you change the company name, characteristics, or even its industry should give you pause. I have videotaped two executives in a class session discussing a disguised case study written on their company. It was a little tricky for the managers to remember the altered case facts as they were answering questions from class participants, but by using the managers' real first names in the case, and not changing the industry or the key facts of the situation, it worked. Clearly these two managers did not mind if anyone participating in the class or subsequently watching the tape happened to recognize them and thus 'saw through' the disguise.

3 Decide whom you want to interview, and when

You need to decide if you want to videotape key case protagonists as part of the case-writing process or much later during your class session, after they have listened to a group of students or executives discussing the newly created case. Either process can work well, but my preference is to bring the executives to class. I find that after listening to a room full of senior managers discuss their situations, the case principals become very engaged and when they come to the front of the room to address the group they are extremely lucid and clear, often saying things that they would not say in their offices. They are also likely to field some very perceptive questions from the participants, especially those who have been in similar situations themselves. In short, I believe that you will get better videotape if you shoot it in class. My favorite format is to create A and B cases, and to bring the case protagonists to the front of the room twice: say for 45 minutes after the A case discussion and an hour after the B case. Each session is videotaped.

If there are several key managers in the case that you want to tape, it is best to bring them to different classes. If you bring them together, hierarchy tends to get in the way, as one defers to the other; even without hierarchical issues, appearing together they may for obvious reasons avoid sensitive issues. The better plan is to let each be the star of his or her own day in class and blend the edited tapes together after the fact.

In the interest of full disclosure I must add that one of the most successful pieces of videotape ever created at IMD – the Sony Europa video[1] – was not made in class but at Sony's European headquarters in Cologne. The reason this tape is so powerful is that the executives on tape are disagreeing about the speed and direction of change required of Sony in Europe. You are very lucky if you get executives to disagree with one another while they are being taped – especially if one is the other's boss! In this case one of the executives was leaving the company for a very senior job elsewhere, and the more junior manager knew this – hence his willingness to publicly (and, as it was captured on tape, permanently) disagree with his boss.

4 Plan to revise the case as you edit the videotape

If you bring case protagonists to class the first time you teach your new case and videotape them, you will then probably want to revise the case. This allows you to incorporate new facts that you learned during the taping into the case and, more importantly, to 'fit' the case to the edited video you are creating.

At this point you will find yourself juggling three things simultaneously: (1) your recently made videotape which you are trying to edit; (2) the case itself; and (3) your learning script. To finalize the learning script, you need to decide which parts of the class conversation will be driven by the case, and which parts by the video. Typically, your classroom experience (with the case protagonist present) should help you to create your script, as you will have been able to see which topics generated energy. However, a session with a case protagonist is not a reliable indicator of how the video-based class would be conducted. (For further elaboration on this point, see the comments at the end of the chapter regarding the Astra + Zeneca videotape edits.) You really need to think it through carefully, bearing in mind what you have on tape and in your case(s).

Here are a few pointers on editing videotape that we have developed over the years:

■ If you have been using a case writer, make sure you get personally involved in the videotape editing process. The trade-offs you will be making will directly impact what happens in the classroom and are too important to be left to others.

■ For best results, your final tape should consist of short segments (no more than 10 minutes each), which you can show at different points during your class. Too long a tape segment will dilute the participants' attention, and may get them into an evaluation mode. In most situations you want to keep the emphasis on what the participants think and would do; less on what the person on the tape thinks and did.

■ In a four-hour session that could include A and B cases, study group time and perhaps a lecture, the total time for all videotape segments should not normally exceed 30–45 minutes. Any longer and you risk reducing the level of group engagement, because there is reduced interactivity.

■ Be sure that you understand how you will use each segment of tape. What do you want your participants to be thinking, assessing or learning as they watch each piece of tape? If you are not sure about a segment, you might try it once with a class to gauge whether it adds value. If not, remove it.

■ If your tape segments seem too long, consider putting some of the information into the case. Sometimes two sentences can replace a lot of verbiage.

Four ways to teach with case-based video

There are four essential ways in which we use case-based video: (1) to confirm class discussion; (2) to move the story forward; (3) to ask participants to assess the person on the tape; and (4) to tell what happened.

1 Confirming class discussion

This is the most commonly used type of video at IMD. In a typical situation, we might start class with the questions, 'What are the most important issues facing this manager, and why do you think so?' These questions could drive discussion for, say, half an hour, with various members of the class arguing their points of view. Then, we would show a videotape segment in which the manager explains what he or she believed the principal issues to be. This first piece of video adds immensely to the credibility of the case, as the group sees the manager in the flesh and the point is driven home that this is not just a case study that someone made up – this is real.

A good example of videotape confirmation is the first piece of tape that we use when teaching the Quest case.[2] This case, which deals with change management, features Paul Drechsler, the CEO of Quest, a business recently acquired by ICI. On the tape, Paul uses the 'language' of change management to describe the challenges he faced, employing such terms as urgency, creating readiness for change and so on. His choice of language subtly legitimizes a lot of things that class is debating and even some of the subsequent lecture content. This piece of tape supports not only the discussion that has just taken place, but also the general topic under investigation.

We created a variation on the 'confirming class discussion' theme with the Nestlé Rowntree acquisition case.[3] In this, class participants take on the roles of Nestlé executives and Rowntree executives to negotiate the terms of the acquisition. After the role play, we show videotape of two executives who were actually part of that negotiation, one from Rowntree and one from Nestlé. These videos are well received, as each half of the class is particularly interested to learn how 'their' company executive saw the situation and handled the negotiation, in comparison to their own approach.

Sometimes the video content allows you to 'teach to the upcoming video' because you know precisely what is going to be said on the tape. For example, a case study on Ballarpur Industries Limited (BILT) is about a family controlled Indian company in crisis.[4] The case focuses on Gautam Thapar, the young family member who is brought in to try to turn the company around. One of the issues that he has to decide on is whether or not to try to preserve good relationships with other family members in the business as he attempts his rescue of the company. Most class members are not sensitive to this issue and focus only on the 'business aspects' of the situation. However, with the knowledge that on tape the manager is going to say that one of his biggest issues was how to deal with various family members, the professor can push this issue hard and trigger a class debate as to whether the manager should try to 'save the business' or 'save the family' or both.

Another technique is to lead the class into a discussion of action options faced by the manager in the case, with foreknowledge of what the manager actually did – and which he describes clearly on tape. Thus at one point in the Nestlé GLOBE video,[5] the manager who is the principal focus of the case, a 39-year-old American named Chris Johnson, says that he will resign unless he gets his way. He adds that he had never before made such an ultimatum in his career and hated it when subordinates did it to him. But he felt so strongly about the issue that this was the stand he had to take. Knowing that this video footage is coming, I can with confidence lead the class into a discussion of Chris's three options: (a) go along with what your boss wants, (b) negotiate a compromise, or (c) be uncompromising and insist that you must do it your way. Because Chris's answer is on the tape, it becomes a very powerful session.

For variety, you can also create a video segment related to an issue that you do not raise yourself in class questions. The issue, however, should be something that perceptive participants will raise. And when they do so, you can say something to the effect of 'let's hear our case protagonist on that very topic' and then show the segment. The participants who identify such issues feel rewarded for raising the topic that a senior executive felt compelled to address. A good example of this is our segment of videotape of Sir Tom McKillop, in which he talked about the merger of equals that led to the creation of AstraZeneca.[6] We divide the class – half as Astra and half as

Zeneca – in order to discuss the terms of the merger; it usually gets quite acrimonious. However, at least one participant often says, 'We are going about this all wrong, we should be cooperating, this is a merger, not a hostile takeover.' McKillop makes this point on videotape, and you can use it at the appropriate moment. If no one raises that issue, you can use the segment anyway, and it will provide food for thought for the whole class.

2 Moving the story forward

Very often the same segment of tape can be used to confirm a discussion and then to move the story forward. Or it can be done with sequential segments. We begin the BILT class, for example, by identifying the major issues that Gautam is going to face and what challenges they will present. That discussion is followed by the 'confirming the discussion' tape segment during which Gautam outlines the challenges as he saw them. Then in study groups the participants must formulate an action plan for Gautam. 'What,' we ask, 'should he do on the first day?' After we discuss it, we play videotape of Gautam stating exactly what he did on that first day. But to move the story forward, we then show the videotaped reaction to the actions that he took. Now the participants have new and, in this case, unexpected information. So we now break into 'buzz groups' (meaning that the participants discuss the question at their seats in groups of four or five) to determine what action he should take. The same process could be orchestrated by using a one-page B case – but the tape is more interesting, as Gautam tells the story better himself than we could write it.

3 Assessing managers

Participants always assess the managers that you show them on videotape, even if you do not explicitly ask them to do so. However, there are situations in which such an assessment becomes the most important point of showing the tape – and you can preface the tape segment by saying, 'I am showing you this tape because I want you to make a judgment about this manager.'

Our favorite managerial evaluation videotape accompanies the Sony Europa case; in it, participants see three executives on tape: the CEO of Sony Europe, the COO, and the head of Sony's operations in the UK. The question is whether or not the COO should promote the head of Sony UK. His CV is provided in the case study. Based on the CV alone, most participants would say yes, offer him the promotion. However, after viewing the tape they feel less certain, and we very often get a near 50–50 split when we ask for a class vote. The issue gets more complex when some participants say that they are happy with the head of the UK on his own merits, but are not sure that he and the COO would be able to work together effectively. The ensuing very rich discussion could only be driven by videotape – the written word alone could not provide enough of a base.

The most famous and widely used business school videotapes are undoubtedly those made of Jack Welch at the Harvard Business School over a period of almost 20 years.[7] These tapes are of great interest to participants because they have read so much about this man and seen the outstanding performance of General Electric under his leadership. They are eager to see him 'in person' and make their own judgments about him. However, we find many European managers dismiss Jack Welch as 'too American,' arguing that his style would 'never work here.' That is debatable but, rather than hitting the issue head on, we change the focus from an assessment of Welch to an assessment of the initiatives that he has introduced over two decades. Are 'work out' and 'number one, number two: fix, close, or sell,' to pick only two examples, initiatives that could provide value in your company? These questions are powerful. Thus the Welch videotapes, which could be used as the basis for an assessment of Jack, are instead primarily used to enhance participants' understanding of his various initiatives at GE and to provide a point of departure for reflection on their own organizations. Like most videotapes, the GE tapes can be used for more than one purpose.

4 Concluding the story

If you have been using segments of videotape throughout your class, it usually makes sense to create a final segment in which the principal actor tells the end of the story. This is generally quite straightforward and should not be too long. If, however, there is a lot of detail involved in the follow-up, it might be better to create a short B case that you do not teach, but simply hand out at the end of class.

A final note: Don't stop too soon

Creating a combination of case study, videotape and lecture materials that can be integrated into a learning script to drive a four-hour class discussion is a big job. By the time you have used the package once, the temptation is to stop working on it. But in our experience, there is usually room for significant improvement through fine-tuning, as chances are that you will not get it 100 percent right the first time. So, while we spoke earlier of the need to revise the case while you are editing the videotape, you will probably have to do the same to the videotape after you have used it a few times.

Editing several hours of videotape down to, say, 15–20 minutes requires a lot of judgment, as you are trying to anticipate how the class will react to each segment of tape. I did not get the original version of our new Astra + Zeneca case right. The class went very well the first time we taught it, when Sir Tom McKillop, the CEO of AstraZeneca came to IMD and talked to the class. However, when I later taught the case using the tape I had created of Sir Tom, the results were mediocre. My frustration increased over the next few months as I failed to find ways to improve it. Finally I went back to the raw videotape of Sir Tom and watched it again. I realized that I was very impressed by material on the tape that I had not used, and decided to have more of Sir Tom and less of me towards the end of class. In the end, I approximately doubled the amount of tape I was using (up to almost half an hour) and it worked.

As a final point, let me emphasize that putting together case and video packages is a creative art. There are few hard and fast rules. The best way to learn to do it is to try it, and then try it again. The only rule I would emphasize is: Do not fall in love with your own creation. Keep editing. Whether you are talking of a case or a videotape, shorter is always better.

Key take-aways

- Videos integrated with cases offer the potential to drive much richer class discussions, moving beyond the normal case-only focus on key business issues to enhance learners' skills in assessing people, a critical business skill.

- Making an effective case and video combination requires good matching of the material to the intended participants, close relationships with the company and principals involved, a location where the principals will be fully engaged, plus flexibility and creativity in editing the materials within the context of the desired learning experience.

- Case-based video can be used in a number of ways including: confirming class discussions, moving the story forward, providing the basis for assessment of managers, and concluding the story.

- Driving a rich, effective learning experience is the ultimate aim of creating such packages, so it is important not to stop editing too soon. Using feedback from teaching can enhance the future impact of the material.

Notes

1   See Kashani, K. and Kassarjian, J.B.M. (1998): *Sony Europa (A)*, IMD-5–0488; *Sony Europa (B)*, IMD-5–0489; *Sony Europa (C)*, IMD-5–0490; and the Sony Europa case video (1995), IMD Catalog number 449.

2   Killing, P. (2001) *Quest International*, IMD-3–0925; and Quest International case video, IMD Catalog number 642.

3   Killing, P. and Ellert, J.C. (1989): *Nestlé Rowntree (A)*, IMD-3–0423; *Nestlé Rowntree (B)*, IMD-3–0424; *Nestlé Rowntree (C)*, IMD-3–0425; and Nestlé Rowntree 'B' (the negotiation) case video, IMD Catalog number 95.

4   Killing, P. (2002): *Ballarpur Industries Limited (A)*, IMD-3–1133; *Ballarpur Industries Limited (B)*, IMD-3–1233; and Ballarpur Industries Limited case video (2003), IMD Catalog number 709.

5   Killing, P. (2003): *Nestlé's GLOBE Program (A): The Early Months*, IMD-3–1334; *Nestlé's GLOBE Program (B): July Executive Board Meeting*, IMD-3–1335; *Nestlé's GLOBE Program (C): 'GLOBE Day,'* IMD-3–1336; and Nestlé's GLOBA project (A), (B) and (C) case video, IMD Catalog number 721.

6   Killing, P. (2002): *Astra + Zeneca (A): 'Merger of Equals,'* IMD-3–1088; *Astra + Zeneca (B): Forming a New Company*, IMD-2–1089; and Astra + Zeneca: Forming a New Company case video (2003), IMD Catalog number 722.

7   Bartlett, C.A. (2000) *GE's Two-Decade Transformation: Interview With Jack Welch, November 1999*, Harvard Business School Case Video, Product Number 9–300–508; and Bartlett, C.A. (2000) *GE Compilation: Jack Welch – 1981–1999*, Harvard Business School Case Video, Product Number 9–300–511. Complete information on ordering Harvard HBSP material can be found at the following webpage: www.hbsp.harvard.edu/b01/en/academic/edu_orderserv.jhtml

10

Developing a suite of cases for nurturing corporate entrepreneurship

Bala Chakravarthy and Peter Lorange

Summary

In terms of content, learning materials have to cover the different aspects of a topic. This chapter examines the challenges that arise in developing materials for corporate entrepreneurship in the form of four different cases. The Nestlé case focuses on the ability to leverage a business unit's existing competency and considers the conditions that are needed to support corporate entrepreneurship. In the Freymont case, participants are encouraged to discuss and reflect on the profile and key behaviors of a successful corporate entrepreneur. The crucial role that a sponsor plays in shaping an entrepreneurial venture is explored in the Dow Chemical story. Finally, the Best Buy case addresses the importance that support from top management plays in ensuring the long-term viability of corporate entre-preneurship within an organization.

Our research and teaching at IMD brings us close to the inner workings of leading companies around the world. Some are national or regional leaders busily transforming themselves into global contenders. Others already face the challenges that globalization can bring: commoditization pressures for their products and the accelerating pace of innovation in their industries. They too are engaged in a metamorphosis that will restructure their manufacturing, migrate their presence up the value chain, and redouble their commitment to innovation. Though these companies may differ in their goals, size, industry focus and geographic scope, they are all similar in one respect: while enjoying profitable growth in their current business niches, they are now transforming themselves proactively in order to sustain this performance well into the future.

The CEOs of these companies, several of whom we have talked to, describe their challenge in graphic metaphors such as changing wheels on a fast-moving train or erecting a new mast on a boat that is racing at full clip. In other words, they strive to exploit the current competence base and opportunities available to their firms even as they seek to develop new competencies and market opportunities in order to ensure their firms' long-term success. This latter task is what we define as corporate entrepreneurship.

We have been actively researching corporate entrepreneurship for the past four years and applying our insights to help partner companies. In the process, we have developed a number of cases that address various aspects of corporate entrepreneurship. We list a few of them below:

1 *Managing Internal Growth at Nestlé: The Story of LC$_1$*
   Peter Lorange / IMD-3-0840 copyright 2000.

2 *Freymont: A Successful Internal Entrepreneur (A) (Expanded)*
   Peter Lorange / Bettina Büchel / IMD-3-1107 copyright 2000

3 *Freymont: A Successful Internal Entrepreneur (B)*
   Peter Lorange / IMD-3-0951 copyright 2003.

4 *Internal Entrepreneurship at the Dow Chemical Company*
   Bala Chakravarthy / IMD-3-1117 copyright 2003.

5 *Best Buy: Staying at the Top*
   Bala Chakravarthy / IMD-3-1430 copyright 2004.

In this brief chapter, we will not have the space to describe each case in detail or how it is used in the classroom. Instead we will provide a brief synopsis of each case and outline for the reader how it can help 'teach' corporate entrepreneurship.

---

case study

Understanding corporate entrepreneurship: The Nestlé LC$_1$ case

This case is about the creation of a new competence platform within Nestlé, the global food giant. Nestlé's yoghurt business, then headed by James Gallagher, faced a tough competitive environment in Europe. Its market share was stagnating. Traditional approaches, such as increasing the advertising budget, improving product features, introducing new flavors and new packaging, etc., had not helped to reverse the decline.   ▶

> Then, in a routine briefing at Nestlé's research laboratories, Gallagher was introduced to the company's leading-edge research on pro-biotic bacteria. These bacteria had the potential to help strengthen the human immune system. Gallagher saw in this research not only an immediate solution to his problems in the yoghurt market, but also the beginnings of an entirely new competence platform for the firm. He decided to introduce the pro-biotic bacteria in yoghurt and launched it as LC_1, a health product in the French market. This initially failed. Consumers seemed to place more emphasis on taste rather than on the health benefits from eating this yoghurt. The product was then relaunched in the German market and, based on what was learned from the French market failure, it was repositioned as a health/pleasure product. This proved to be a success and the product was soon launched in other international markets with equal success. Subsequently, Nestlé has used pro-biotic bacteria in other food and beverage products and in pet foods as well. The LC_1 bacterium has provided a distinctive competence base for the company to build a portfolio of novel nutritional products.

The case is a good illustration of what we mean by corporate entrepreneurship. Our definition is intentionally restrictive (the shaded areas in Figure 10.1). We do not see the task of protecting or extending the firm's current franchise as necessarily entrepreneurial. It is an important task, but

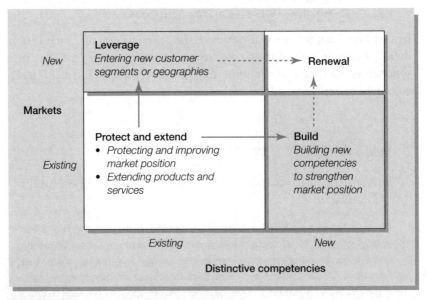

Figure 10.1 Defining corporate entrepreneurship

one which should be handled in the routine running of a business. However, diversifying the business horizon of a firm and/or its competence platform is a distinct task. This task gets neglected in many firms, given the pressing preoccupation with producing short-term business results.

The case also lends itself to a good discussion of the conditions that support corporate entrepreneurship:

1 With the impersonal and fast-paced nature of business today, conducted primarily through emails, faxes, mobile phones and videoconferences, informal face-to-face meetings are a rarity. In the Nestlé LC_1 case there were two executives: the one with the 'problem' (Gallagher) had a chance to meet another with a possible 'solution' (Pfeiffer from Nestlé's R&D group). It was their brainstorming that transformed LC_1 into a distinctive competence platform for the company. Providing a place and time to meet informally is key to sparking new business ideas.

2 Nestlé had been producing yoghurt for a long time. Therefore, it was a bold move to dramatically change its composition, by adding the LC_1 bacteria to it. Often, corporate entrepreneurship requires challenging the status quo.

3 Not getting bogged down in organizational silos and taking an enterprise-wide perspective is another key to successful corporate entrepreneurship. Various parts of Nestlé came together around the LC_1 product, notably the chilled products group and the R&D group, as well as the country organizations in France, Germany and then around the world.

4 The LC_1 campaign initially failed in France, but Gallagher learned from this trial.

5 Equally important was the support and persistence that Nestlé's top management gave Gallagher.

What was fascinating to us when we discussed the LC_1 case with executives was the intense interest in the personality and behavior of Gallagher and in the support that he got (or did not get) from senior management. We developed other cases to deal with these issues. The second case that we wrote was on a corporate entrepreneur who had found repeated success in a major European multinational company (disguised case Freymont).

The corporate entrepreneur: The Freymont case

The Freymont case is about another kind of entrepreneurship – discovering new business opportunities by leveraging the firm's (not only the business unit's) existing competencies. It raises issues about the process of identifying customer needs and mobilizing company resources, in particular when such needs fall between traditional business units. The key player in the case is the corporate entrepreneur who drove this project to success. When participants watch him on video and read about him in the case, it immediately reminds them of their own experiences. In praising or criticizing the entrepreneur, they share their tacit knowledge on what made a corporate entrepreneur successful.

There are many executives who are outstanding business analysts, indeed able to spot new business opportunities. But they can also be self-centered and lack the 'team focus' that effective corporate entrepreneurs must develop. At the other extreme, we might also have leaders with excellent people skills but lacking in business aptitude. The Freymont case allows the following profile of the corporate entrepreneur to emerge through the class discussion:

Profile of the corporate entrepreneur

Personality traits

- Integrity.
- Political savvy.
- Honest about mistakes.
- Shares credit.
- Breaks rules but always stays true to the corporate vision and values.

Experience

- Established track record. Brings credibility.
- Long tenure helps.
- General manager, not a narrow expert. Ability to think laterally.

Behaviors

- Ability to discover a profitable value proposition.

▪ Ability to communicate and market the value proposition.

▪ Ability to mobilize resources (networking ability – borrow with pride).

▪ Ability to assemble and motivate a team of experts. Energy and inner fire.

▪ Ability to deliver results.

▪ Ability to take informed risks, speedy decisions. Unafraid.

▪ Ability to ramp up or pull the plug.

In particular there are three key behaviors that a corporate entrepreneur must excel at (see Figure 10.2).

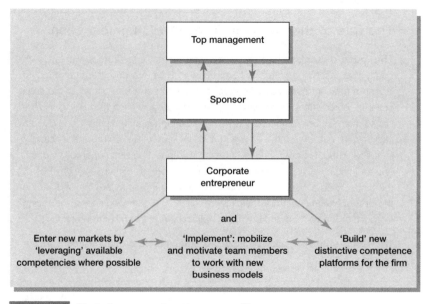

Figure 10.2 Nurturing corporate entrepreneurship

1 'See' new markets before they are obvious to everyone else. In addition, the corporate entrepreneur must try to leverage all of the firm's available competencies (not just those available in his/her business unit) to exploit this opportunity. Like the corporate entrepreneur in the Freymont case, he/she must borrow with pride.

2 Understand the overall competence base of the firm, and try to build through his/her venture a competence platform that is of future value to the entire firm.

3 'Lead' his/her colleagues as a team in a flat, project-based organization. Distinct from the lone geniuses, whom we celebrate as successful external entrepreneurs, internal entrepreneurs are essentially team players. They must mobilize the required team and motivate it to work on a risky venture. They must be trustworthy.

Having focused on the corporate entrepreneur in the Freymont case, we developed the next case at Dow Chemical, the leading chemical and plastics company in the world, to showcase the critical role of the sponsor – the second actor in the multi-actor process sketched in Figure 10.2.

---

case study

The role of the sponsor: The Dow Chemical case

This case describes Ian Telford, the sales director for Europe within Dow's epoxy business, who, with his boss Philippe Reynaud de Fitte, attempted to launch a new entrepreneurial venture for the company. The 'story' of the case covers a corporate entrepreneur and his creative approach to building a web-based channel for selling epoxy resins. It also highlights how this creativity can easily spin out of control. Even a brilliant corporate entrepreneur cannot succeed without a courageous sponsor. Through two accompanying videos, one an interview with Reynaud de Fitte and the other an interview with Telford, the case allows a discussion of the crucial role that a sponsor plays in shaping the entrepreneurial venture, helping to sell it to top management, mobilizing support for the venture and providing political cover for the entrepreneur.

The discussion that follows helps elaborate the following desired sponsor behaviors:

Sponsor behaviors

- Spot the entrepreneur.
- Provide the right assignment.
- Empower.
- Ensure integrity of mission.
- Believe in the concept.
- Set tough goals.
- Demand results.
- Sell upwards.

■ Help access resources: finance, people, time.

■ Provide political cover.

■ Tolerate 'idea' failures.

■ Coach/mentor.

■ Plan personal development of the entrepreneur.

The Dow case also points to the important role that top management plays in creating a context for entrepreneurship. To discuss this topic more fully, we developed the case on Best Buy.

---

case study

Setting the corporate context: The Best Buy case

This case is about the largest North American retailer in consumer electronics. It describes the issues facing the company's current CEO, Brad Anderson, who recently took over from Best Buy's legendary founder. Anderson is seeking to make the company more customer-centric, but without hurting the superb operating efficiency that the previous product-centric approach had given the company. He sees entrepreneurship as a key to transforming the company in this manner. But to empower the company's employees, he would have to change its structure and processes, and even its culture. In three videos that accompany the case, Anderson talks candidly about the strategic, organizational and leadership challenges that he faced in making Best Buy more entrepreneurial. While an exceptional entrepreneur and sponsor can on occasion compensate for the lack of organizational support, corporate entrepreneurship cannot be sustained over the long term without top management providing a conducive context.

The Best Buy case points to the following critical roles that top management plays in setting such a context:

■ The CEO must function as the voice of the customer, 'representing' them to the rest of the organization. It is the customer who will point the firm to new market opportunities. Anderson knew that customer-centricity would not succeed if he did not champion it personally. He worked with an external consultant to give shape to the new strategy. He then sent clear signals that there would be no discussion of the 'why' and 'what' of customer-centricity, but that he would always welcome contributions on the 'how.'

■ While the CEO is typically seen as the custodian of the budget process, where he/she typically 'asks for more performance with fewer resources,' it is important that, when it comes to key entrepreneurial ventures, he/she actually 'pushes' resources on to these projects and helps speed them up. In the case of Best Buy, Anderson created 'laboratory stores' to protect the new initiative from naysayers in the rest of the organization, staffed these with specially selected executives and gave these stores an additional expense budget.

■ The CEO must deal with resistance to change, often from members of his own executive team. Anderson handed overall charge for the laboratory stores to a member of his senior executive team who had initially been a staunch opponent. It was important to Anderson to sell this individual on the new concept and solicit his support for leading the implementation. Converting that executive, Anderson reasoned, was a useful first step to convert the entire tribe.

■ Top management must also demonstrate a strong willingness to protect the corporate entrepreneur against both occasional setbacks and political interference from the rest of the organization. In the case of Best Buy, Anderson knew that customer-centricity would shift power to the retail stores and away from the corporate headquarters. He chose to use his middle managers as key change agents and gave them protection and support.

■ Anderson also supported the introduction of a strength-based human resource management system, where employees were given a chance to work on tasks that best leveraged their individual strengths rather than by assigning tasks through a personnel plan. But there was strict accountability. Empowerment was directed at those who could deliver against their promised targets.

Teaching considerations

In using the above cases the reader may wish to consider the following:

1 We do not try to provide a common synthesis at the end of case discussions. We use each of the four cases as a vehicle to tap into the participant's own experiences with corporate entrepreneurship. The learning in each group varies. The live examples that fellow participants provide have a far better take-home value than PowerPoint wrap-up presentations by the instructor.

2 We seldom use more than one case with the same group. Our selection is based on the level of the group that we are working with. We tend to use the LC_1 and Freymont cases when working with business unit managers, the Dow case with sponsors and the Best Buy case with senior executives. The participant must identify with the key actor in the case. Only then are they motivated to dig into their own experiences.

3 We find videotaped interviews with key actors to be invaluable tools in the classroom. No matter how well a case is written, visual stimulation is important for identifying with a case character.

Parting observation

There is a seamless link between research on corporate entrepreneurship and teaching it to executives. Each class is a learning laboratory. Prior notions get challenged and new hunches are developed. This prompts us to develop new teaching materials that can shed further light on these hunches. This step-by-step process of knowledge building and diffusion is indeed a hallmark of the way IMD lives up to its credo of Real World, Real Learning.

Key take-aways

■ Cases serve as a starting point for class discussion, which prompts participants to share their own experiences and challenge conventions.

■ Participants will be motivated to make contributions only when they can relate to the case; materials must be matched to the relevant career level of the participants.

■ Video interviews with the central figures of the cases are particularly effective in helping participants relate to the case.

■ 'Real life' examples from participants in the classroom provide valuable contributions in terms of furthering research in this area.

11

Learning for leadership: The 'engineering' and 'clinical' approaches

Gianpiero Petriglieri and Jack Denfeld Wood

Summary

Meaningful leadership development requires a deeper and more fundamental approach than is usually deployed in university classrooms and
corporate training centers. It needs to incorporate difficult emotions and
unconscious forces, and provide a safe place for their investigation and
integration. While the typical 'engineering' approach has a valuable contribution to make in leadership development, it is limited by the heavy
reliance placed on a rational and cognitive view. In contrast, a 'clinical'
approach emphasizes working with the individual's existing natural
patterns of behavior, with the aim of understanding and managing the
multiple forces that motivate individual and collective behavior. A real-life
example from a leadership program highlights the substantially different
approaches and the different results that can be produced depending on
the method employed.

Beneath the merchandising of leadership

Leadership makes money. Consider the economic situation over the past
several years: despite a severe business downturn and a reduced demand for
general management programs, the demand for leadership training has
grown markedly. Why? Some argue that empowerment is 'in' and autocracy
is 'out,' that enlightened management has grudgingly acknowledged
leadership as part of everyone's job, and that it no longer views leadership
as the preserve of the executive suite. Others contend that the leadership
trend is simply the most recent management fad. In either case, companies
flood business school classrooms with managers seeking 'leadership' – but

what is it that they are really looking for? Overtly, the purpose of leadership training is the acquisition of tools and techniques to facilitate corporate goals. Covertly, the appeal of leadership training appears to be coming from somewhere else.

The dismantling of formal corporate structures and the disappearance of job stability has left today's manager with an acute sense of anxiety and insecurity.[1] Traditional hierarchies, stable organizations and life-long employment, however unfashionable and inefficient for the pace of modern business, used to satisfy the human need for structure[2] and provided a sense of security. The psychological function of much organizational structure, as scholars at the British Tavistock Institute have pointed out, is to provide social defenses against unavoidable feelings of anxiety.[3] The 'contract' was clear: individuals joining an organization relinquished some of their freedom in exchange for protection. No longer. When we ask executives what they want from a leadership program – what they are *really* looking for – the answer is unequivocal: tools to influence and manipulate others in order to regain some degree of control, over their direct reports, their bosses, their organizations, their careers and their lives.[4]

Looking for leader

Every group, no matter how large, needs leadership. And hope for a better future. Ambitious leaders owe their ascension less to their desire for power and visibility than to their ability to capitalize on the followers' needs for reassurance, and to create a vaguely plausible plan of action rather than one that reflects an objective appraisal of the situation at hand.[5]

Social scientists and depth psychologists have long known that anxiety and uncertainty drive groups to select leaders who provide a simple and reassuring picture of reality, and within that 'reality,' a simple vision of a goal and the means for achieving it. To remain in power, leaders and followers collude in denying the 'chaotic complexity in which so much of human life is lived.'[6] They insulate themselves from the dissonance of discordant views, in the process concealing or suppressing alternative perceptions of reality. Reality, however, has a habit of imposing itself on even the most creative collective fictions.

Few leaders, especially in difficult historical moments, can build a fiction solid enough to last, and so they inevitably are found inadequate. When the gap between the shared fiction and the complexity of the real world becomes too wide, leaders fall from grace. At that point, their followers seldom engage in serious collective soul-searching about what went wrong, and instead take the simple way out – adopting a new leader who offers an alternative fiction. The 'rise and fall of leaders' follows an archetypal template that repeats itself, from dependency and deification to disillusionment, demonization and, finally, replacement. With few exceptions, things only change on the surface.

If we temporarily lose our fascination with great leaders, we can never abandon our deep-seated need for the shared fictions that help us deal with the complexity and distress of contemporary life. Today, the idea of 'leadership' has replaced the search for 'great leaders' and 'great corporations' that are no longer viewed as dependable or as offering sufficient protection against the anxiety of modern economic life.[7] Managers feel increasingly vulnerable and seek 'leadership skills' as a new means of protection. In other words, they are looking for hope – on the 'leadership market.' And there's no shortage of dealers in hope.

Recently, the sales vice-president of a privately held conglomerate that distributes a wildly successful weight-loss product in the US put it this way:

When I train sales-people, I say to them, "Do you know what people are calling you for? It isn't the pill. They are calling you for hope. That is really what they want from you."[8]

The company that produces the pill has no offices and no labs. The conglomerate's marketing team created its name because it sounded scientific.[9] It's not about testing chemicals, nor even about selling products that work – it's about marketing hope.

From a psychological standpoint, the leadership industry also markets hope. It caters to the human tendency to invest in gifted individuals and seek magical solutions that offer the illusion that we can control our anxieties and our destiny. This tendency is the driver of the leadership industry's main 'product lines' – the glorification of celebrity chief executives, the merchandising of 'Great Leader' books and the teaching of leadership 'models' and 'toolkits.'[10] Merchandising leadership includes mass-market 'autobiographies,' one-minute cookbooks, leadership fables, inspirational lectures, and 'fun and games' outdoor exercises of various sorts.[11] These products are seductive – and remarkably simplistic.

If managers seek to protect themselves against emotional uncertainty, corporations, in turn, try to manage their employees' turmoil by outsourcing the responsibility for emotional support to executive 'coaches' and leadership programs. Once a kind of surrogate mother, organizations now hire business schools to function as surrogate nannies.

Today's business schools tackle the market demand for 'leadership programs' – to help manage the pressing emotional demands of their participants – with one of two approaches: engineering or clinical. In the engineering case, leadership faculty deploy an array of tools and techniques to fortify executives' defenses, so that their anxiety and emotional stress can be held at bay and their company's primary task can be accomplished. In the clinical case, leadership faculty provide a space where emotions can be explored and integrated, so that anxious energy can be transformed into energy for individual learning and personal and professional development. Both approaches are useful, but they are based on radically different psychological assumptions about human development (see Table 11.1 for summary).

The engineering approach to leadership training

According to Edgar Schein's pioneering work on corporate cultures, the basic assumptions of the 'engineering culture' are the following: engineers are proactively optimistic and assume that they can and should master nature. They are stimulated by puzzles and problems. They are pragmatic perfectionists who prefer 'people free' solutions; their ideal world is one of elegant machines and processes working in perfect precision and harmony without human intervention. 'Engineers' are concerned with safety, and over-design for it; and they prefer linear, quantitative thinking with simple cause-and-effect solutions.[12] While the majority of management professors might not have engineering degrees, their approach to research and teaching leadership works from the same set of assumptions:

1 What makes us tick

The engineering approach to leadership training rests heavily on a rational and cognitive view. Leadership, in this view, is a collection of individual attributes or a set of skills; it is modern and changes with culture, century and civilization. Support for the engineering approach stems from the assumptions embedded in basic economics and cognitive psychology: people tend to behave in ways they associate with rewards, and avoid behaving in ways they associate with punishments. For example, if research indicated that certain behaviors would enhance their career advancement prospects, managers would naturally be motivated to learn and apply those behaviors to get ahead.

2 Learning to lead

Within this framework, leadership skills can be identified and learned through practice and emulation. The engineering approach describes a set of desirable leadership behaviors and provides the related theories, models and tools to 'train' participants through study, imitation, practice and feedback. For the individual, the effort to change and improve needs to be sustained by a conscious resolution to keep applying oneself and improving.

3 The value of self-reflection

The engineering approach encourages self-reflection for *diagnostic* purposes – to compare and contrast oneself with desired (or 'correct') behaviors and with others. Self-reflection clarifies individual beliefs and values, increases awareness of one's dominant leadership 'style,' assesses one's key strengths and weaknesses, focuses on desired areas for change, and identifies potential internal and external obstacles to that change. After this initial 'gap-analysis,' self-reflection becomes just a part of the review and feedback process as executives practice and gain proficiency in applying the necessary leadership 'tools.' Executives are encouraged to reflect before and after they act, both to respond to their present context appropriately and to spot potential areas for further improvement.

4 The use of theory

Engineering-minded management faculty value theories more to solve practical problems than as explanations of reality. For them, theory tends to be 'normative' and 'prescriptive' – the former in the sense that 'this is the way things are' and the latter as in 'this is what you should do about it.' For example, the recognition that storytelling and 'mythic themes' inspire people more than spreadsheets and bar charts led a popular screenwriter to dispense advice on how to construct management stories with a mytho-logical flavor.[13] Similarly, a finding that many 'accomplished leaders' suffered a major failure early in their career prompted some academics to suggest that young and arrogant executives with promising career prospects ought to be denied a promotion, in order to humble them and pre-empt some 'future failure' – an application of a 'fail now, succeed later' strategy.[14]

5 Learning methods

Leadership faculty make every effort to maximize the *impact* of their courses – they have to be entertaining, inspirational and motivating. A central space is given to motivational speeches of former athletes and retired CEOs, breathtaking views on mountaintop walks, the thrill of helicopter rides, camps in the wilderness, and similar amenities.

Role-playing and experiential activities provide a means to measure relative 'success' and practice 'new ways of behaving.' The emphasis is on the emulation of others. Smoothly enacted planned behavioral routines and the attempt to keep distressing feelings hidden and under control is viewed as a clear sign of progress. The quicker one appears to change, the better.

6 Faculty attitude

The engineering approach underpins the overwhelming majority of leadership programs. The underlying issue, of course, is control. Ideally, there is a tool for every problem, and the more tools one masters, the more control one should attain. The more control one believes one has, the more reassured both professor and participant should feel.

7 Managers' reactions

Most managers exposed to this type of leadership training first experience great enthusiasm, only to lapse into disappointment later. Once back home, they sometimes feel worse than they did before – if nothing has fundamentally changed despite their expensive training, they think something must be wrong with them. Nothing is. In our view, the reason for this mood-reversal is the same as the reason for the programs' initial popularity. The 'engineering' approach promises to rid participants and faculty of discomfort. Convincingly, but only for a moment, it tries to leave the unconscious and emotional factors behind.

The engineering approach will always be needed and it will always have a central place in management education. Executives cannot hope to exercise leadership effectively without a grasp of their organization's primary task, and a solid base of knowledge and skill, both technical and strategic. When thoughtfully done, the engineering approach works brilliantly to enhance technical skills, even very complex ones, such as flying fighter aircraft, performing surgery or playing a good game of golf. These endeavors require dedicated study, strong focus, constant practice, good feedback and frequent performance review. Leadership, however, is not quite like a perfect golf swing.

The clinical approach to leadership development

By employing the word 'clinical,' we are not invoking emotionless doctors in white coats scribbling on clipboards – quite the opposite. The focus of the clinical approach is our humanity in all its emotional complexity. While the engineering approach focuses on assessment and judgment as a means for improvement, and provides strategies, techniques and tools to cope with, and control, behavior, the clinical approach focuses on exploring and deepening our working knowledge of natural human behavior so as to permit more autonomous, better informed, decisions.[15] Working with a clinical approach means using *both* accumulated knowledge and present experience to understand what's *really* going on, at a given moment, in the social system in which we find ourselves – or that we are trying to change. It involves addressing situations facing us without excessive reliance on prescribed procedure and technique, working collaboratively with colleagues and clients, and considering the influence of elusive, emotional and unconscious aspects of human behavior.

1 What makes us tick

Individuals and groups are not simply manipulated by rewards and punishments presented by others in an overt social context. Covert unconscious forces play a central role in motivating individual and collective behavior. Leadership in this view is an interaction of psychological 'energy' that includes both domains – conscious and unconscious – within any social system. Learning to recognize, understand and work with these unconscious influences is the only way to avoid being inadvertently surprised, disturbed or unwittingly controlled by them.

2 Learning to lead

Leadership is a universal human phenomenon, and its essence has not changed over millennia. The leadership *training* of the engineering approach is not the same as leadership *development* of the clinical one. Within a clinical framework, managers are not complex machines in need of fixing and upgrading – they are human beings naturally seeking growth and integration. *Training* is about acquiring and practicing something new.

Development is about exploring and dealing with things that we already have with us – growth works 'from the inside out.' The integration of one's 'thinking' and 'feeling,' for example, is an invaluable instrument for leading responsibly.

Leadership can't be taught, but the capacity to lead can be learned and developed – less from academic study and imitation than from the experience of leading and following. Meaningful behavioral learning occurs only as a result of a strongly felt need and a personal decision. It is impossible to coerce somebody into leading. It would be equally impossible to develop leadership if executives were not truly allowed to be curious, experiment, and make mistakes – i.e. if they were prevented from taking the lead in their own development.

3 The value of self-reflection

The clinical approach encourages the manager to reflect *as* they act, to develop what we call *reflective spontaneity* – the capacity to be oneself and use one's experience as data while engaged in action. To do so, this approach provides a space where one can explore and experiment in a relatively safe environment. One can learn, for example, that difficult feelings might not be as harmful as we often believe – on the contrary, they provide us with invaluable information. We measure success by the capacity to let ourselves experience, and then make sense of, an increasingly full range of emotions, behaviors and reactions.

4 Use of theories

The clinical approach is more 'pragmatic' and 'descriptive' than it is normative and prescriptive. Rather than state 'this is what you should do,' it suggests that 'this is how to understand what is happening, and here are some choices about what to do.' It uses whatever theory in a given case might provide a reasonable framework for understanding the meaning of people's actions, so that one can choose how to act – or whether to act at all.

5 Learning methods

The clinical approach does not rely on inspiring stories or the emulation of celebrity executives for reassurance and comfort. Rather than practicing 'new behaviors' and acquiring control tools, executives are encouraged to be themselves, experience what is happening, and reflect upon the complex and conflicting emotions that they usually avoid. Role plays and experiential activities are not used to demonstrate proficiency in imitating 'how to do it right' but as data collection opportunities for later reflection on 'how you do it.' The more naturally and spontaneously participants behave, the more learning material emerges. However, this is not a prescription for their behavior. Reluctance and defensiveness are as natural and spontaneous as are openness and enthusiasm. As long as one is willing to explore what provokes one's behavior, one can learn from the program and further one's leadership development.

6 Faculty attitude

The clinical approach strives to bring the unconscious back into play in the corporate classroom, in an effort to enhance the relevance, depth and meaning of leadership education. A central assumption is that the *primary responsibility* to learn is with the client. Whereas the engineering approach is centered on its models, the clinical approach is centered on its clients, and it does not assume that the faculty knows best what managers should know in order to exercise leadership. Clinically minded management faculty tend to be more curious about what participants will learn within the context provided. Their approach fosters interdependence between participant and faculty, but it is the participants who remain firmly in charge of their learning.

7 Managers' reactions

Unlike those exposed to the engineering approach, who often move from enthusiasm to disappointment, participants in a clinical program usually go through a different sequence – from an initial mixture of anxiety, suspicion and impatience with the faculty for lack of both clear-cut solutions and directive teaching, through a feeling of relief for not having to 'fake it,' to a realization that they are already equipped to exercise leadership responsibly and wisely, and already have a sense of how to lead others in ways that increase health and foster growth for all concerned.

Which unconscious?

Some detractors of the clinical approach reject the concept of the unconscious altogether. Other critics, while not denying the unconscious, argue that working with it might open up 'a can of worms' that is best left to the psychotherapist. This discomfort, argues Insead's psychoanalyst Manfred Kets de Vries, is a defense against the idea that our behavior will always elude our best intentions – the existence of an active unconscious sweeps away the illusion of being fully in control.[16] However, depictions of the unconscious as a hidden puppeteer lend it a somewhat sinister character that keeps us imprisoned in a repetitive loop of childhood behavioral patterns.[17]

Those either hostile or sympathetic to the reality of the unconscious both tend to pathologize it. We have come to see it differently. Our experience has made us somewhat skeptical of such a gloomy view. We put less emphasis on the unconscious as an obstacle that constantly threatens us than as a source of richness and vitality.

The unconscious that animates human life is not just the Freudian container of repressed memories and irrational wishes. To be sure, some psychic wounds are always present when one explores an individual's psychology, but the unconscious with which we are mostly concerned is the Jungian one of collective images and living archetypes. If we are scuba diving in the images of the unconscious, it is less to uncover emotional shipwrecks and more to explore the natural aquatic flora and fauna hidden from the surface. We assume that the enrichment of individual and collective experience comes from seriously engaging and playing with image and metaphor. Our goal is neither to harness unconscious processes to gain influence and control over the external environment, nor even to reduce immediate distress. Instead, it is to experience and become more familiar with archetypal images and patterns of behavior in an effort to gain a measure of lasting integration with our deeper selves – so that we can lead from our psychological center.

Working with feelings

Whereas both the engineering and clinical approaches acknowledge the primary importance of emotion in the exercise of leadership, their attitudes towards emotions are radically different. The engineering approach is geared to assess and adjust to a norm; the clinical approach is geared to understanding and developing uniquely individual capabilities.

A concrete example can illustrate the differences between the two approaches. Not long ago, during the debriefing of an inter-group competition in an IMD leadership program, one of the participants expressed extreme disappointment and anger at the behavior of the leader of another group, who had publicly dismissed and humiliated him. The participant candidly admitted that he felt mounting aggression towards the leader, which reminded him of how he felt immediately before a fistfight, years before.

Working from an engineering approach, one of our colleagues instantly remarked, 'Aggression is a primitive instinct . . . an animal reaction.' His air of disapproval was proportionate to his poise and self-righteousness. He then launched into a dual attempt to 'help' the upset manager understand how 'dysfunctional' his reaction was, and to 'coach' him to explore 'more appropriate' ways to respond. Shamed and disappointed with himself, the participant nodded and listened dispiritedly to the defensive strategies that he should employ to suppress his aggressive impulses. From an engineering standpoint, the participant had exhibited a personal inadequacy that he needed to overcome through hard work, so that it wouldn't happen again.

In contrast, from a clinical standpoint, a great learning opportunity was slipping by. The participant's verbal expression of deeply rooted anger was an invitation for an extended exploration of authentic feelings, a chance to learn how to understand and resourcefully manage the complexity of all our reactions to everyday organizational behavior.

The clinical response was: 'Aggression has helped humans survive for millennia, and I doubt we'll eradicate it from our nature in a couple of weeks. So let's try to understand *why* it manifested itself *in this particular occasion* . . .' As we de-pathologized aggressive feelings and legitimized their exploration, we were able to examine what happened. Archaic impulses have their own integrity and can be used diagnostically to reveal what is really going on within and between groups. An initial angry reaction is a natural response to being treated unfairly. In this case, its emergence was a strong signal that the interaction between the groups had turned into a confrontation; the anger wasn't one participant's personal failure, but rather a clue to managing an unconscious 'power play' at work in the larger social system. In the debriefing, the class experimented with how to express feelings, reflect on them, and wonder about their purpose at the same time. Later, another participant applied the same skill in a similarly heated exchange by pausing and asking herself, 'I am noticing myself getting aggressive. I wonder if this negotiation is becoming a fight. Why would that be?' – a transaction that neither required suppression of her feelings, nor an attack on another individual, nor placing a fake smile on one's face.

Conclusion

More than ever before, executives turn to schools of business administration for help in dealing with the mounting pressures of contemporary managerial life. The difficulty of modern corporations to satisfy dependency needs, and the failure of publicly acclaimed leaders to hold at bay the discomfort of reality, has led managers to invest their desires for reassurance, direction and structure in the acquisition of 'leadership skills.' In the midst of overwhelming uncertainty, they turn to 'leadership training' to regain some control and restore hope. The promise of hope abounds in the leadership mass market. However, the selling of 'leadership as a happy pill' by educational and consulting organizations is questionable at best and irresponsible at worst.

Taken together, the engineering approach's lure of reassurance, reliance on crude models for emulation, and illusion of control undermine the goal of developing deeper leadership skills. Easy reassurance and superficial morale boosts are counterproductive when it comes to serious personal development and lasting behavioral change. If we are to provide conditions that help executives develop the capacity to lead effectively and responsibly in turbulent times, such simplistic expedients are best avoided.

Leadership is a *social-psychological* phenomenon, and its roots reach deeply into individual and collective psychological terrain. Meaningful leadership development – whether individual or organizational – requires a deeper and more fundamental approach than is usually employed in university classrooms and corporate training centers. It needs to incorporate difficult emotions and unconscious forces, and provide a safe space for their exploration and integration. Uncertainty, discomfort and anxiety can be unpleasant but they are necessary and useful; the effort to control or suppress them, via the engineering approach, is a diversion from genuine development.

In order to foster leadership development, the clinical approach creates a safe space to take risks and switches focus from action to reflection, from short-term reassurance to long-term change, from emulation to experimentation, and from self-control to self-discovery. A shift in attitude from avoidance and rationalization to engagement and integration of emotions requires a willingness to accept them, recognize their value, and explore their implications – for the individual, the group and the organization. With a more generous acceptance, ambivalent feelings are useful and reliable aids for leadership development. Welcoming their exploration is not easy. Nor is it meant to be. But it can be immensely rewarding.

Key take-aways

■ An 'engineering' approach to leadership training relies on teaching individuals tools and techniques for influencing others and controlling individual behavior.

■ The engineering approach gives the illusion of control but is ultimately ineffective in developing deeper leadership skills.

■ A 'clinical' approach focuses on leadership *development*, where emotions and the unconscious aspects of human behavior are explored and integrated.

■ Meaningful leadership development is a process of self-discovery and development and requires elements such as risk taking, reflection, recognition and acceptance of one's own feelings.

■ Those exposed to a clinical program are more likely to develop authentic and responsible leadership.

Table 11.1 An 'engineering' versus a 'clinical' approach to leadership development

Engineering approach	Clinical approach
Prescriptive – normative use of theories	Descriptive – pragmatic use of theories
Focuses primarily on visible behavior and external reality	Focuses primarily on the interaction between external and internal reality
Works well for technical and cognitive skills	Works well for behavioral and emotional skills
Orientation is on 'performance'	Orientation is on 'meaning'
Focus is on adding skills	Focus is on making sense of things
Primary reliance on *training* cognitive and rational analytical skills	Primary reliance on *development* and integration of rational and emotional capacities
Individuals are motivated by external rewards and punishments	Individuals are motivated by instinctual drives and socialized desires
Operating metaphor is electro-mechanical: the individual is like a networked computer	Operating metaphor is ecological: the individual is a living organism in a fluid system
One 'upgrades' by fixing or adding	One 'upgrades' by exploring and integrating
Learning is a teaching process that happens from the 'outside in'	Learning is a developmental process that happens from the 'inside out'

Table 11.1 continued	
Engineering approach	*Clinical approach*
Encourages emulation of role models and smoother enactment of 'appropriate' feelings and behaviors	Encourages 'reflective spontaneity' and familiarity with a range of feelings and behaviors
Leaves the unconscious out of the dialogue	Includes the unconscious as part of the dialogue
Pathologizes 'bad' emotions	Accepts all emotions as normal
Learning is the acquisition and application of objective tools	Learning is the recognition and calibration of the 'self-as-instrument'
Aim is 'progressive' and future-oriented	Aim is the integration of past, present and future
Leadership is a collection of individual attributes or a set of skills	Leadership is an interaction of psychological 'energy' that occurs within a larger social system
Leadership is modern and changes with culture, century and civilization	Leadership is a timeless and universal human phenomenon
Leadership can be taught and imitated – process is 'teacher-centric'	Leadership can be learned and developed – process is 'learner-centric'
Fosters dependent and counter-dependent relations with authority	Fosters interdependent and independent relations with authority
Programs need to demonstrate immediate impact and boost participant morale	Programs need to provide opportunity for long-term relevance and lasting personal change

Notes

1 Miller, E.J. (1999) Dependency, Alienation, or Partnership? The changing relatedness of the individual to the enterprise. *In*: French, R. and Vince, R. *Group Relations, Management and Organization*. Oxford: Oxford University Press, pp. 98–111.
2 Berne, E. (1964) *Games People Play*. New York: Grove Press.
3 Jaques, E. (1953) On the dynamics of social structure. *Human Relations*, 6 (1), pp. 3–24; Menzies, I.E.P. (1960) A case study in the functioning of social systems as a defense against anxiety. *Human Relations*, 13 (1), pp. 95–121.
4 Hirschhorn, L. (1988) *The workplace within: psychodynamics of organizational life*. Cambridge, MA: MIT Press.
5 Le Bon, G. (2002) *The crowd: a study of the popular mind*. Mineola, NY: Dover Publications; original work published 1895.
6 Rice, A.K. (1999) *Learning for leadership: interpersonal and group relating*. London: Karnac books; original work published 1965, p. 87.
7 Gemmill, G. and Oakley, J. (1992) Leadership: An alienating social myth? *Human Relations*, 45 (2), pp. 113–129.
8 Specter, M. (2004) Miracle in a bottle. *The New Yorker*. February 2, pp. 64–75.

9 Specter, M. (2004) op. cit., p. 69.

10 Krantz, J. and Gilmore, T. (1989) The splitting of leadership and management as a social defence. *Human Relations*, 43 (2), pp. 183–204.

11 Wood, J.D. and Petriglieri, G. (2004) The merchandising of leadership. *In*: Chowdhury, S. (ed.) *Next Generation Business Handbook*. Hoboken, NJ: John Wiley & Sons.

12 Schein, E.H. (1996) Three cultures of management: the key to organizational learning. *MIT Sloan Management Review*, Fall, pp. 9–20.

13 McKee, R. (2003) Storytelling that moves people. *Harvard Business Review*, June, pp. 51–5.

14 Bunker, K.A., Kram, K.E. and Ting, S. (2002) The young and the clueless. *Harvard Business Review*, March, pp. 80–7.

15 Miller, E.J. (1993) Values and concepts. *From dependency to autonomy: studies in organization and change*. London: Free Association Books, pp. 3–23; Campbell Quick, J. and Gavin Johanne, H. (interviewers) (2000) The next frontier: Edgar Schein on organizational therapy. *Academy of Management Executive*, 14 (1), pp. 31–49; van de Loo, E. (interviewer) (2000) The clinical paradigm: Manfred Kets de Vries's reflections on organizational therapy. An interview by Eric van de Loo. *European Management Journal*, 18 (1), pp. 2–22; Kets de Vries, M. (2004) Organizations on the couch: a clinical perspective on organizational dynamics. *European Management Journal*, 22 (2), pp. 183–200.

16 Coutu, D.L. (2004) Putting leaders on the couch: a conversation with Manfred Kets de Vries. *Harvard Business Review*, January, pp. 64–71.

17 Kets de Vries, M. (1994) The leadership mystique. *Academy of Management Executive*, 8 (3), pp. 73–89.

12

On coaches, counselors, facilitators and behavioral consultants

Jack Denfeld Wood and Gianpiero Petriglieri

Summary

Executive coaches, career counselors, psychotherapists, group facilitators and behavioral consultants all have overlapping, yet different areas of expertise. To make an informed decision about the kind of long-term leadership development program you want, it is crucial that you understand these differences and limitations. In individual sessions, coaches, counselors and psychotherapists work with very different aims and at varying psychological depth. In group work, the contribution that experienced behavioral consultants make to the process of learning from the group's experience can make the difference between success and failure.

In recent years, the trend in executive education has turned increasingly toward behavioral topics. Corporations come to business schools seeking faculty skilled in one-on-one coaching sessions and intensive small group work. Beyond the traditional business school curricula of readings, lectures and case discussions on the topics of general management, most programs now include behavioral sessions dedicated to personality questionnaires, 360° feedback inventories, business simulations, and outdoor leadership activities of various sorts.

However, because full-time faculty members seldom have either the time or the behavioral background to fulfill these demands, business schools hire independent practitioners from outside to do much of the intensive one-on-one and group work. But these practitioners – 'coaches,' 'counselors,' 'facilitators' and 'behavioral consultants' – come from different backgrounds and have different abilities and expertise. Prospective clients need to know what those differences are. This chapter will outline the principal differences among the backgrounds and roles of executive coaches, career counselors, group facilitators and behavioral consultants.

Working with individuals

Single-session coaching

One can approach human behavior in a number of ways. One can work, for example, with off-the-shelf questionnaires as a basis for a one-on-one discussion. This is the domain of 'single-session coaching.' Questionnaires such as the Myers-Briggs Type Indicator (MBTI), a personality inventory based on the psychological thinking of Carl Jung, or any of several commercially available 360° feedback inventories[1] are popular. Anyone with a good feel for people, one or two days training and a familiarity with the specific questionnaire can become an effective single-session coach. This style of coaching involves listening well, explaining unclear aspects of the questionnaire, identifying trends and patterns in the results, and occasionally dispensing advice for action. In other words, it all boils down to helping managers make sense of pages of summary data as well as encouraging them to do something about the results. This is different from longer-term 'executive coaching.'

Executive coaching

In the last two decades, executive coaching has become a flourishing segment of the 'leadership industry.' Individuals who market themselves as 'executive coaches' usually sell a variety of services that go beyond elucidating questionnaire results. Their services are typically delivered in the executive's office, over the telephone or via the internet.

Most executive coaches work from a base of contractual cognitive psychology, that is, at a conscious, overt and rational level. Advice, support and encouragement are the cornerstones of their methods. They invite managers to identify personal strengths and weaknesses, set measurable goals and prepare action plans for 'improvement.' Structured exercises are suggested for practice of desired behaviors, as well as to provide feedback and measure progress over time. Executive coaches may give explicit, straightforward advice on surviving office politics, strategies for promotion and 'good career moves.' They may also dispense tactical advice on how to work with difficult bosses, peers, subordinates and customers.

The sponsoring company and the individual manager are usually the executive coaches' primary 'clients.' It's not uncommon for executive coaching to be imposed on talented managers to smooth their 'rough edges.' Occasionally, executive coaches market new and different services than the traditional career-related ones. For example, within the wider mandate of increasing managerial productivity by restoring stressed-out executives to equanimity over lunch breaks, many different types of 'coaches' are now offering nutritional advice, meditation techniques, work–life balance guidance, security coaching and all sorts of New Age practices.

The majority of executive coaches are former managers who, often as a result of a mid-life transition, decided to pursue an independent career, helping other managers achieve their personal and professional goals. The most popular ones can easily charge thousands of dollars for an hour of advice. A smaller segment of the executive coach supply comes from other walks of life – they are former athletes, sport coaches, members of military Special Forces, actors, and health workers of various sorts. Most 'qualified' executive coaches have completed some training over several months or years. These courses are often based on management models popularized by pop-psychology bestsellers – *Seven Habits of Highly Effective People*,[2] *Primal Leadership*,[3] *Fish!*[4] – and represent a cottage industry by themselves.

But are such qualifications enough to work with the long-term development of business executives? Psychologist Steven Berglas warns that executive coaches are frequently 'purveyors of simple answers and quick solutions' and simply make matters worse. Berglas spent 25 years working in the department of psychiatry of Harvard Medical School and, though an executive coach himself, is deeply skeptical about the qualifications of its many practitioners. 'To best help their executives,' he wrote, 'companies need to draw on the expertise of both psychotherapists and executive coaches with legitimate skills.'[5] The 'expertise' and 'legitimate skills' to which Berglas refers include some form of intensive, full-time clinical training in psychology.

Coaches, counselors and psychotherapists work at different levels of psychological depth. One can work at the conscious, overt and rational level mentioned above, or one can work at a deeper psychological level with the unconscious, covert and irrational influences in human behavior. We can use the image of the iceberg to illustrate these distinctions. Executive coaching involves addressing the visible part of the iceberg, the part clearly above the surface and in plain sight. Executive coaches occupy themselves with their clients' present situation to improve their business performance and future career advancement. If a rocketing career trajectory is the measure of performance, there is much less concern for the impact of that career trajectory on the executive's personal and family life. Career counseling can go a little bit deeper.

Career counseling

Career counselors also work at the level of conscious intention and rational decision making. However, unlike those executive coaches who are concerned mainly with present and future business performance, career counselors explore the individual client's personal history and have a sense of their life situation as a whole. In fact, the 'client' for the executive counselor may be less the company paying the bill than the individual who sits in the chair across from them. Their interventions can include suggestions for alternative jobs in other companies or even different professions altogether. To extend the iceberg metaphor, competent counselors operate in the visible portion staked out by executive coaches, as well as just below the water line where the overt influences of the corporate environment meet the covert influences of the executive's personal history and family life.

Psychotherapy

Aimed at examining the experience and meaning of a person's life – with an eye to the development of an individual who has a unique history and destiny – psychotherapy reaches much farther into the depths below the water's surface. Psychotherapy is an internally directed learning process aimed at personal exploration, integration and growth. Such an endeavor involves accessing one's feelings and thinking creatively about one's experience. It entails reconnecting with the past to discover its meaning in the present as well as shaping the future. Effective therapy alternates between triggering and experiencing feelings, followed by the analysis and integration of those feelings.[6] Work-related concerns are discussed in therapy as one of many important elements in the client's past and present experience. Seeing a therapist is usually a personal choice, and for the psychotherapist the individual is the primary client – no one else. Psychotherapists are usually professionals with advanced degrees in medicine or psychology who have spent several additional years in training, supervision and personal therapy themselves.[7]

Working with groups: Facilitation and behavioral consultation

Working with managers in a group setting requires different skills than working with an individual alone. Whereas individual coaching and counseling are interpersonally oriented (i.e. on the relationship with a boss, the relationship with an assistant, etc.), group 'facilitation' and 'behavioral consultation' *also* focus on the complexity of group and organizational dynamics (e.g. team decision making, interdepartmental conflict and similar issues). To expand into the group domain, business schools sometimes use group facilitators for business games and negotiation simulations. IMD uses group facilitators or behavioral consultants primarily in the outdoor portion of leadership development programs.[8]

We prefer employing the term *behavioral consultant* rather than *group facilitator* in order to emphasize their depth of expertise and multidimensional professional role. The word *facilitator* suggests an intention to 'facilitate' – which literally means 'to make things easier.' We have found that making things easier, smoother and more efficient for executives engaged in leadership activities does not necessarily optimize their learning experience – on the contrary. We believe the word *consultant* better captures the actual function of this role in a group of managers.

The word 'consultant' can easily bring to mind images of the 'Big Five' business consulting firms recommending off-the-shelf models as solutions to complex corporate problems. In fact, the attitude and approach of most 'group facilitators' clearly resembles those of a typical business consultant working with a large corporation. Similarly, facilitators work with groups in a manner analogous to executive coaches' work with individuals – relying on prescribed models and tools to indoctrinate participants in 'appropriate' leadership behaviors. Their background and training also resemble that of 'executive coaches' and, in practice, many of them use the terms 'group facilitator' and 'group coach' interchangeably. However, a *behavioral consultant* represents a different kind of 'consulting' – more akin to a therapist's clinical consultation.[9]

Behavioral consultants work with a collaborative clinical approach, which relies on their own and group members' immediate experience as a means to explore and understand what is happening in the group.[10] In short, if facilitators are concerned with what the group *should* be doing, consultants are concerned with what the group *is* doing – and work to discover *why*. Whereas both facilitators and consultants are concerned with the success of their groups, their definition of *success* is very different. For facilitators, success is mostly concerned with participants' accomplishment of a particular exercise and getting a good rating for themselves at the end of the program. Consultants are concerned with achieving the primary task of maximizing the learning of the participants – not with the completion of a particular exercise, with 'feeling good together,' with 'working well as a team' or with getting a good end-of-program evaluation.

Competent behavioral professionals do not avoid the uncomfortable nature of their work. We strongly believe that 'coaching' a group to operate smoothly, or working to maximize the group's feeling of self-satisfaction, does a great disservice to the group's learning. Consultants are neither there to make things easier, nor more difficult – they are there to support the group's effort to explore its own behavior and to learn from it. Where a facilitator might attempt to reduce discomfort and smooth over controversy, consultants might do the opposite if it serves the group's learning. While consultants do not intentionally provoke tension and controversy as an end in itself, they expose existing, though covert, tensions, invite the group to look at them, provide hypotheses to understand them and, finally, support individual and group efforts to explore what might be done about them. This is a set of skills that few business school faculty members or freelance business consultants have. It is an aptitude for working with subtle psychological variables that is enhanced by rigorous professional training and serious personal work.

Professionals for world-class leadership development

After a decade of doing outdoor leadership exercises at IMD, it became apparent that there was a terrible loss in depth of learning using facilitators who were unable or unwilling to work among themselves as a staff team in the same way they demanded of the participant groups – studying their own behavior rigorously, honestly and collaboratively in the service of collective learning. If the aim of doing this kind of work is to provide individual and corporate clients with a world-class leadership development experience – one that fosters meaningful and long-lasting behavioral learning – a staff of competent professionals is not just desirable, it is absolutely necessary. We found that executive coaches, counselors and facilitators without a clinical background are simply incapable of dealing professionally with the full range of behavior that occurs in serious leadership development. Unfortunately, the qualities required to do behavioral work well are difficult both to find and to develop.

After much experimentation, we found that doing outdoor leadership work well requires familiarity and comfort in three domains: (a) the technical exercise procedures, (b) the ambience of corporate business organizations, and (c) the psychological terrain on which one is working. The strategies for putting in place competent individuals to do the work took time.

Mountain guide strategy

Because trained behavioral faculty were not immediately available for our work, we initially used company employees whom we had trained to set up the technical aspects – they were primarily mountain guides with an interest in working with people. It didn't work. Viewing the work as technical in nature, they learned the exercises we had given them, but were unfamiliar with both the language of business and the behavioral complexity of this kind of work.

Facilitator strategy

We then searched for individuals with backgrounds in human resources or corporate training and development. Though none of the individuals we found had faculty backgrounds with doctorates, they did have some experience as facilitators of indoor business simulations and exercises. Furthermore, they understood the corporate preference for concrete questionnaires and results. We hoped that they would develop more 'behavioral' depth during the work.

While this 'facilitator' strategy represented a modest improvement over the mountain guide strategy, it didn't work very well either. They learned the technical aspects of the exercises, but their 'training,' 'coaching' or 'counseling' backgrounds proved inadequate to the task of operating at a clinical psychological level. Unlike the mountain guides, the facilitators did have a sense of the corporate world – but they played to it. They were constantly colluding with their groups, usually to keep participants 'happy' and thereby bolster their popularity and ratings. To our surprise, some facilitators were even more resistant to working in depth than the program participants.

By 'collusion' we mean a situation where the consultant influences, and is influenced by, the group without being aware of it. A related way to describe collusion is as an unconscious agreement between the group's and the consultant's defenses with the indirect aim of avoiding discomfort. Collusion might be a normal occurrence in any group and it could even help us to understand what is going on. But in order to put it to good use, consultants need to be honest, reflective enough to 'catch' themselves, and at least willing to be challenged by their colleagues.[11] Unfortunately, with rare exceptions, most facilitators colluded as a *modus operandi*, ran their groups without sharing much with staff colleagues, and resented questions.

We have seen facilitators collude with their groups in innumerable ways, usually to allow participants to avoid being penalized, complete the assigned tasks and experience a superficial sense of accomplishment. The collusion included: (a) warning the participants not to touch a simulated electrified fence; (b) letting them repeat a failed exercise; (c) secretly prolonging the allocated time for an exercise; (d) observing a rules infraction yet not calling attention to it; and (e) lobbying another facilitator in charge of a competition on behalf of their own group. At other times, collusion is more subtle – enacted in those 'little ways' in which facilitators attempt to rescue individual participants, the whole group and themselves from discomfort during debriefings or social events. This kind of insidious collusion, if allowed or unobserved, can damage the learning experience even further. Apart from a few gifted individuals, facilitators with a corporate background retreated to their formal role as a 'friendly' instructor, and were unable to bring themselves and their own emotions forward as an integral part of the learning process.

The examples of collusion mentioned above are basically patronizing and imply that the group needs to be 'taken care of' as one would take care of children. In our view, this conceals a lack of faith in the capacity of adults to learn as a group from their own experience, and it undermines the integrity of the learning environment. Finally, facilitators had great difficulty working with more competent clinical staff members at the behavioral depth and sophistication that we were aiming for. By 1998, we again sought to improve the quality of our behavioral work, in order to deliver the quality of learning our clients deserved.

Psychotherapist strategy

Since we had failed to train corporate facilitators to conduct outdoor exercises and acquire a clinical sense, perhaps we could train the clinicians to work with business groups for leadership development. First, we tried using individuals with a psychotherapy background. Unfortunately, while the therapists could work competently with individuals, most felt overwhelmed when facing a group of demanding business executives during several days of tightly choreographed leadership exercises. Many retreated into confusing psychobabble to cope and, when challenged by the participants or even queried by their more experienced colleagues, became defensive and insecure.

Behavioral consultant strategy

We desperately needed a staff composed of professionals comfortable working not only with the 'visible top of the iceberg' but also with the 'invisible bottom' as well. They had to understand and intervene concurrently and competently at several 'levels of analysis' – at the individual level, at the interpersonal level of two-person conflicts, at the level of the three- to twelve-person small group, at the inter-group level of complex relations among groups competing and cooperating, and even at the level of the larger social system.

We finally began to select consultants who had significant experience in the psychological professions, but who also had a familiarity with how organizations really work. These were PhDs or MDs specializing in psychology or psychiatry, or individuals with a social science Master's degree who had worked in business, had a depth of clinical experience in group and organizational consultation, and had experience in individual therapy. In other words, we sought those able to cover the entire 'iceberg,' from the overt and visible concerns in managers' rational career plans, to the covert and invisible forces that influence their lives and eventually determine their ultimate destiny. With such behavioral consultants, training in the methods and procedures of outdoor leadership activities has proved relatively straightforward.

The work of behavioral consultants

In an outdoor leadership development program, the behavioral consultant occupies several distinct roles: observer/cameraman, technician, referee/rule interpreter, collaborative debriefer and, at the end of the program, one-on-one coach. During the activities, the consultant observes and films the group in action with minimal interference in the group's process, penalizes participants for rule transgressions, intervenes when necessary, and calls an end to the formal exercise. During the subsequent 'debriefing' session – which is a crucial learning opportunity – the consultant joins the group to reflect on the events and explore the systematic behavioral dynamics at play.

Technically speaking, the consultant's principal function is to contribute to the creation of favorable conditions within which meaningful behavioral learning can take place. Individually and as a staff, they provide a holding environment for participants, with two main features: *containment* and *interpretation*.[12] *Containment* refers to a reliable presence that conveys the message: 'Here, it is possible to look at whatever happens, pleasant or not. We can express our emotions and articulate our experiences, work them through, and learn from them together.' This stance provides a suitable vessel for learning from one's experiences, and a means for accelerating personal development. *Interpretation* helps the group to put its experience in context and then integrate it within a framework for application to similar situations later on. Briefly, the function of consultants is to provide two kinds of learning opportunities: *situations* and *interventions*. They must also master the art of advancing the most useful *hypotheses* and overcome the natural *resistance* that emerges in groups during the learning process.

Situations

Situations that provide an opportunity for learning set the *frame* of the event, including the boundaries of time, method and place – for example, start and finish times, formal participant roles, rules and penalties, and the space where consultant and group debrief their work and explore their behavior. In addition, given the complex reactions, moods and behaviors that the consultant provokes among different participants, his or her *presence* provides an opportunity to explore individual and group relations with formal authority – if the consultant is competent and does not shy away from making his or her role the subject of discussion when necessary.

Interventions

Consultants tend to intervene at specific input points, providing observations, descriptions, emotional reactions and provisional hypotheses. In addition, they occasionally intervene to encourage group members to express their thoughts and feelings, to talk to each other directly, and to remain in the 'here and now.' Helpful interventions are aimed at stimulating an open and productive dialogue on a group's behavior.

We find that there are three kinds of interventions. The worst ones are those that tell the group what they *should* be doing, either overtly by judging their behavior and giving advice on how to 'improve'; or covertly by continuously telling the group what it seems to be avoiding – and therefore, indirectly, what in the consultant's opinion it should be talking about or doing. More useful interventions cast some light on what the group *is* actually doing without realizing it, i.e. pointing out behaviors that suggest what the group might unconsciously be aiming at. Nonetheless, the best interventions are those that not only raise awareness of potential unconscious dynamics, but also illustrate both defensive and adaptive purposes of behavior – what it hides and what it reveals – and encourage further exploration and dialogue.

For such an open and productive dialogue to occur, a helpful practice for both consultant and participants is to share and discuss: (a) observations on the overall behavior of the group ('This is what I saw happening . . .'); (b) simple, clear and direct descriptions of specific sequences of events and repeating patterns ('And each time you, Fred, take leadership . . .'); (c) emotional reactions to those events ('And so I felt angry/frustrated/left out/ignored/happy . . .'); (d) hypotheses about what the group seems to be doing *overtly* and more or less *consciously* ('It seems as if the group is avoiding conflict . . .'); and finally (e) some provisional observations as to what the group may be up to more or less covertly or unconsciously ('. . . to protect certain shared fictions – like we're all the same . . .').

Let us give you a concrete example: a consultant observes that a group believes its exercise is 'impossible' to complete successfully – even though it has discarded half a dozen viable solutions. While the group is still half-heartedly engaged in the exercise, the consultant might interject a comment such as, 'It appears that the group favors failure over the risk of developing one person's idea at the expense of someone else's idea.' Usually this is ignored. Later on, as they debrief the event, the consultant might follow up a participant's complaint that the group gave up and 'threw in the towel' too soon, by offering the hypothesis that the group might unconsciously prefer to fail and feel depressed *because* that lets them circumvent an uncomfortable fight for alternative ideas – and for power – among several individuals, all of whom made good contributions, any of which would have worked if picked up by the group and developed. Such interventions are usually met with initial irritation before leading to a collaborative exploration of why the group is avoiding the discomfort of internal discrimination, competition and the exercise of leadership.

Hypotheses

Hypotheses such as the one above can be aimed at identifying possible *causes* for the group's current behavior ('Perhaps we are avoiding conflict *because* there is a "protection racket" among the macho guys in the group . . .') as well as its possible *purposes* ('Perhaps we are avoiding conflict *in order to* feel comfortable by pretending to be the same . . . and operate *as if* there are no differences among us . . . so we don't have to compete or look at who is taking over leadership and how'). Of course, human behavior never lends itself to simple, single explanations.

In truth, countless hypotheses could be developed about the covert dynamics occurring in a group. Perhaps what distinguishes excellent consultants from mediocre ones is the intuitive capacity to: (a) select the hypotheses that best promote the group's learning at any given moment, rather than merely the ones that by default fit the consultant's theoretical framework; and (b) deliver the hypothesis in a *clear, simple* and *timely* manner so that it can be heard. Nonetheless, when consultants offer a working hypothesis, the purpose is never to discover and announce 'the one and only true reason' for what the group is doing. Hypotheses are *always* provisional and never claim to be ultimate truths – they are simply pragmatic heuristic devices to stimulate understanding and encourage further exploration. This kind of exploration is not always welcome by a group.

Resistance

Resistance is a natural occurrence during serious behavioral work. Behavioral hypotheses, especially when they ring true, are usually met with resistance and controversy – with either polite disregard or heated denial. The closer to a sensitive spot and the more accurate the hypothesis, the more provocative it is. And the more it is resisted. The consultants' work, if done well, upsets and comforts at the same time. Therefore their position is a delicate and often lonely one. Helping group members to uncover what lies beneath the surface of their visible behavior can evoke significant resistance and the consultant can become the lightning rod of a group's tension and anger. It represents a learning opportunity if – and only if – it can be talked about and understood. When this is avoided by either consultant or participants, the learning process pays a heavy price. Consultants that fear such unpleasant moments of isolation and attempt to please the group, as well as groups that prefer to hold a grudge and refuse to examine their feelings towards the consultant, deprive themselves of a unique opportunity.

A balanced reaction of some defensiveness as well as sudden insight ('Aha, so *that's* what we are up to!') is usually a promising indication that group and consultant are working well together. Learning proceeds most swiftly when they work through the initial feelings of remoteness and inequality, and become fellow explorers who are curious about 'what might be going on in the group now' – of the intricate underpinnings of group behavior.

The staff as a team

A grouping of competent behavioral professionals is not necessarily the same as a competent and cohesive *team* of behavioral professionals. To do good behavioral work, the staff of a leadership program needs to operate as a coordinated unit. If the staff is not familiar with each other's style and approaches, this is impossible. To bring continuity to our work together, we limit the core staff to around a dozen individuals. While the team members are diverse in many ways, they share a clinical approach towards behavioral work, a willingness to question themselves, a certain psychological eclecticism, and a playfulness and willingness to experiment.

Unlike most other program staffs, ours shares responsibility for all aspects of the work. Beyond work with their designated group, each consultant participates in the management of the program as a whole. Their collaboration ranges from client contact to pre-planning and program design, staffing, remuneration, evaluations, paper grading, and taking various upfront roles with the class. Furthermore, for quality control and staff development, we try to use at least a few co-consulting pairs in each program. In order to operate as a team, familiarity and co-consulting are helpful, but they certainly aren't enough. Long and frequent clinical meetings before, during and after the program are necessary as well.

Staff members need to demonstrate the same commitment to explore and reflect upon their own behavior that they demand from participant groups. Therefore, continuous *clinical meetings* are an essential part of their work. During the meetings the team discusses what is happening in the participant and staff groups. These meetings release accumulated stress and restore psychological availability, which are necessary to create the least contaminated learning environment possible. They are a prerequisite for experimentation, reciprocal learning and feedback.

We always remind participants of the importance of continuing development. It is no less true for the staff members. Beyond active participation in the clinical meetings, the staff needs commitment to continuing development of the team as a whole and of its individual members. The former is helped through one or two annual retreats, where the team as a whole reflects on its work and discusses potential improvements. The latter requires that individuals regularly pursue personal psychological work and attend group relations and group dynamics programs, to enhance their professional skills, and to remind themselves of *what it feels like* to be in the participant's role.

Conclusion

A company seeking leadership development can choose coaches, counselors, facilitators or clinically trained behavioral consultants for the task. It is crucial to consider what you really want. If you are serious about the development of your managers and their ability to lead, it is probably preferable to have them work with a professional who has the capacity to engage them at whatever level is necessary for their personal and professional growth. To do so, one must ask for behavioral depth and sophistication from practitioners who have the background and skills to deliver it.

Key take-aways

- Coaches, counselors and psychotherapists have different abilities, expertise and approaches to working with individuals.

- In the context of group work, the behavioral consultant's primary function is to provide a holding environment within which meaningful learning can take place.

- Competent behavioral consultants have the skills to work at several 'levels of analysis,' the ability to select and deliver hypotheses that elucidate covert group dynamics, and the willingness to work with group resistance, in order to promote learning.

- Effective behavioral work requires the staff of the leadership program to operate as a team, participating in the management of the program as a whole, and engaging in frequent clinical staff meetings.

Notes

1 In 360° feedback inventories, managers rate themselves and are rated by their supervisors, peers, and subordinates on behaviors categorized as managerial 'competencies'.
2 Covey, S.R. (1990) *Seven Habits of Highly Effective People*. New York: Simon & Schuster.
3 Goleman, D., McKee, A. and Boyatzis, R.E. (2002) *Primal Leadership*. Cambridge, MA: Harvard Business School Press.
4 Lundin, S.C., Paul, H. and Christensen, J. (2000) *Fish! A Remarkable Way to Boost Morale and Improve Results*. New York: Hyperion Press.
5 Berglas, S. (2002) The very real dangers of executive coaching. *Harvard Business Review*, 80 (6), pp. 86–92.
6 Yalom, I.D. (2003) *The Gift of Therapy*. New York: Harper Collins, p. 71.
7 Wood, J.D. and Petriglieri, G. (2004) Behind the mask: the MBA personal development elective (unpublished manuscript).
8 See this book, Chapter 18.

9 For different approaches to consulting see: Schein, E. (1999) *Process Consultation Revisited: Building The Helping Relationship*. Reading, MA: Addison Wesley; Block, P. (2000) *Flawless Consulting: A Guide To Getting Your Expertise Used*. 2nd ed. San Francisco: Jossey Bass Pfeiffer.
10 See this book, Chapter 11.
11 Petriglieri, G. and Wood, J.D. (2003) The Invisible Revealed: Collusion as an Entry to the Group Unconscious. *Transactional Analysis Journal*, 33 (4), pp. 332–343.
12 Winnicott, D.W. (1990) *The Maturational Processes and the Facilitating Environment: Studies in the Theory of Emotional Development*. London: Karnac; Shapiro, E.R. and Carr, A.W. (1991) *Lost in familiar places*. New Haven, CT: Yale University Press.

13

The hidden agenda of management development: Coaching managers on project teams

Xavier Gilbert

Summary

Business projects provide a rich opportunity to address the hidden agenda of management development: enhancing the manager's cognitive capability to build viable mental roadmaps to address complex business situations. The more viable mental roadmaps are the more encompassing ones. This chapter describes the seven building blocks of this hidden agenda: stimulating an emotional commitment, applying prior knowledge, broadening the relevance bandwidth, building overview mental patterns, challenging the mental patterns, mental rehearsal and after-action review.

Management development pursues a three-tier agenda. The most tangible tier addresses the acquisition of tools and techniques. Tools and techniques can be taught; learning when and how to use them, however, cannot. Developing this ability to adapt the tool or technique to a specific business context is a second, less tangible tier that can be facilitated by guided practice. Then, there is a third, higher level of learning that involves developing the ability to map a business context in a viable way, allowing implementation of the first two tiers. We have all witnessed intervention approaches that seemed to ignore the territory where they were executed. Because their cognitive capabilities have remained insufficiently addressed through their educational curricula, or because they have been atrophied through professional and organizational specialization, or simply because of limited experience, many managers lack this ability to construct viable maps of complex business situations.

There lies the hidden agenda of management development. We cannot really tell managers 'We will help you enhance your cognitive capabilities!' Yet, this has to be the dominant part of the learning agenda, without which the rest of the curriculum remains irrelevant.

Business projects provide a unique opportunity to address this hidden agenda against the background of achieving relevant business objectives. Coaching is an effective way to do so and yields improved cognitive capabilities. This chapter discusses coaching approaches to do so.

Learning and knowledge

Epistemologists and neurologists alike generally agree that learning has its roots in survival. Jean Piaget and other *constructivist* thinkers[1] provided empirical support for the idea that knowledge consists in viable approaches that are actively built by the learner by leveraging prior knowledge, to adapt and respond to experiential feedback, and survive in his context. This perspective differs radically from earlier views of learning, which are in fact still wide spread, according to which learning would consist of passively absorbing (being taught) the right answers that allow one to perform in the real world.

Neurologists confirm that there is a survival motivation in learning. Mental patterns are formed by connected neurons; when the brain receives new information, which it does whenever we are awake and even during phases of our sleep, it tries innumerable possible neuronal connections to find a place for it in a response-oriented pattern. If such connections can be found, the information is retained as relevant. Making and organizing these connections is a trial-and-error process, rather than a linear one; mental connections must prove viable, i.e. serve the purpose of dealing effectively with the environment. But there is never any confirmation that a mental pattern is 'right'; it remains viable as long as it is not proven ineffective. The tentative nature of mental patterns makes it vitally important to test them all the time and use the experiential feedback information to reinforce them, redirect them or discard them.

The more durable patterns seem to be those that reflect the more encompassing overviews, referred to by the epistemologists as the 'structure of the subject matter' or the 'fundamental ideas of a field.'[2] They are broad problem-solving maps that allow one to respond effectively to a wider range of experienced situations and can be deployed to unfamiliar problems. When these patterns grow broad enough, they increase the ability to process new experiential information; but when they remain narrow, they prevent one from 'seeing' information that is too difficult to fit; 'out of the box' information is often deemed irrelevant. Overall, the more mental maps one has accumulated, the more encompassing they can become, the more effective the processing of new information becomes – this is experience. So, learning is also learning to learn – making learning more and more effective. There is a flywheel analogy in learning.

Emotion is often referred to as being linked to effective learning. Everyone has experienced that emotionally loaded events are more likely to be remembered. But it is still unclear whether emotion is the cause of better learning, a circumstantial phenomenon or a consequence. Establishing such a relationship is complicated by the sociological and cultural dimensions in emotions: emotions have different behavioral effects in different contexts. It is not even clear which emotions, with which intensities, and in which mixes, at which times, induce either tackling the environment or withdrawal from the environment. A dose of enthusiasm for the subject will support learning, but too much enthusiasm will be distracting; a dose of interest will help focus the attention, but too much interest can lead to confusion.

Neurologists confirm that the observable relationships between emotion and cognition are still far from building up to a scientifically established and widely applicable overview. For complex neurochemical reasons, the neuronal connections, and the type, level and mix of concomitant emotions, vary considerably across individuals and, individually, over time, making it difficult to determine, also from a neurological perspective, which is the cause, which is the effect, and what the ultimate outcome of their interplay might be.

Overall, referring to the survival roots of learning is probably the safest way to approach the relationship between learning and emotions. The prospect of a positive outcome from building a viable roadmap to tackle the environment supports learning. Positive outcomes such as expectations of self-respect, pride, joy, in 'reasonable' doses and mixes, are fairly generic motivators. If the environment is so hostile that only negative outcomes may be expected, such as loss of personal integrity, humiliation, distress and anxiety, withdrawal will be seen as the only viable strategy. Yet, even these dreadful prospects could trigger the inventiveness of some individuals – definitely a risky manipulation.

The hidden agenda

Leveraging these findings on learning and knowledge, we would like to propose seven building blocks that we have found helpful in designing and steering the learning 'hidden agenda':

1 Stimulating an emotional commitment
The learner actively builds knowledge in order to operate effectively in her environment. Making a commitment to learning something vital, or at least something that will allow one to remain in relative control of one's destiny, enhances learning.

2 Applying prior knowledge to construct new knowledge
Stretching prior knowledge to address new problems, as uncomfortable as it may feel, will in fact enhance the learning by leveraging existing mental patterns, consolidating them, redirecting them or even discarding them.

3 Broadening the 'relevance bandwidth'
Relevance choices define the scope of learning. Building more connections, to address more dimensions of a complex problem, requires that these unexpected or unknown dimensions enter the radar screen.

4 Building overview mental patterns
Overview, more encompassing mental patterns, provide more connection opportunities for new information and enhance the ability to give meaning to this new information.

5 Challenging the mental patterns
Seeking opportunities to challenge and test mental patterns, to generate feedback information, particularly through discussion, enhances the robustness of mental patterns.

6 Mental rehearsing
Mental rehearsal is a strategy the brain uses to verify the connections of a mental pattern. Communicating mental patterns provides effective mental-rehearsal opportunities.

7 After-action review
Revisiting the pathways that led to the formation of mental patterns is another form of mental rehearsal. After-action review provides opportunities to consolidate connections.

Similar to learning in general, managerial learning seeks to develop the manager's ability to retain some control over the business environment by constructing mental patterns to act effectively within it, rather than by seeking to master the universal rules governing an ultimate external managerial reality. Even if such a thing existed, it would be so complex and elusive that managers would soon realize that a more viable approach is to learn to adapt.

Coaching managers through managerial situations, like business projects, provides a rich context for applying these building blocks, not only to construct knowledge that is managerially relevant, but more importantly to develop the manager's fitness for mastering complex environments. This learning can be deployed beyond the context of project work; many business situations can indeed be construed as projects. The huge advantage of coaching a manager on a project team, rather than individually, is that it provides an even richer learning context, where individual mental patterns have to adjust to each other, yielding more varied feedback.

Stimulating an emotional commitment

As discussed, leveraging emotions to enhance learning should acknowledge social, cultural and individual idiosyncrasies. 'This is a very good question!' generally meant to make the author of the question feel good, will work with some, leave others indifferent to that form of politeness, and turn others off as a display of contempt. The coach can play an important role in ensuring that, at least, emotions that assist in tackling the environment are engaged. But what these emotions are, and how they interact, will vary considerably across individuals, so it requires a lot of personal attention and listening.

Emotional commitment seems to be the most generalizable condition that induces learning. It relates again to a form of survival in a situation perceived as having substantial personal consequences. While it varies considerably across individuals, in a business-project context it is easier to find commonalities. A great deal of emotional commitment will come from the fact that it makes strong sense for the manager to undertake the proposed project. The outcome of the project must make a difference for him or her. For example, some companies make project work part of the normal development path of their high potential managers. The project should be important enough to legitimate an explicit recognition of the achievement.

Challenge also creates emotional commitment. Challenge may come from the recognized difficulty of the project. An easy project will not only get little recognition within the company, it will not produce much learning; easy tasks do not enhance mental patterns. Creating challenge for oneself, by seeking feedback, is a way to raise one's emotional commitment; seeking feedback is an attitude that is recognized as powerful in boosting learning. Emotion-creating challenge may also come from being challenged, which is sometimes less appreciated. Challenging through open-ended questioning, or challenging by stating a different opinion as a point of departure for a discussion, will create more energy to push the exploration of ideas than yes-no questions or judgmental feedback.

Applying prior knowledge

The coach should generally recommend that the team or individual 'Go as far as you can with what you know.' There are several reasons why this is helpful. The first one is that prior knowledge provides the neuronal blueprint for new knowledge: it is by reference to prior knowledge that new experiential information will be deemed relevant, and grafted to that prior knowledge.

The second one is that it signals the emphasis on learning, rather than on being taught. How much the coach should 'teach' is a matter of debate in which the constructivists' answer (supported by empirical evidence) tends to be rather on the side of 'as little as possible.'

The third reason is that it gives the learner the confidence that prior knowledge, acquired in previous jobs, can be deployed to new issues, that is, to unknown issues. It addresses several misconceptions that get in the way of learning: 'Learning should come before doing' or 'There is a real world out there and I first need the tools to tackle it.' Managers will develop more learning autonomy by developing their own, good enough, viable roadmaps, stretching past experience to address the situation at hand.

The fear of being incompetent in addressing a situation will often result in requests for more tools and for more information. Unless the request is for some base tools that are indeed best rote taught, acquiescing will only save time by doing away with the learning altogether. Providing the tools first can result in an overflow of 'just-in-case' information that will clog the cortex with short-lived connections looking for a purpose.

Helping the manager to explore all the opportunities provided by his existing maps can be done through open-ended questioning, such as 'What are you trying to do?' 'What are you missing to do it?' 'How about trying this or that?' Beyond this questioning, the inputs from the coach should consist of 'fundamental ideas,' like generally applicable information, the general topology of a strategy roadmap, or, at a more mundane level, why the time value of money matters. These general frameworks, when immediately tested in practice, help the learner see broader, and consider a wider range of, experiential information as useful in constructing more generally applicable knowledge.

The coach may also support mental risk taking. Some managers may be reluctant to use their prior knowledge publicly because, in their company, either one is 'right' – an illusion that generally requires the support of hierarchical structures – or one shuts up; being wrong can indeed be fatal. Managers must realize that tentative maps are the foundation for learning and that the more experimental maps they explore, the more robust the learning – it will indeed be supported by many more viable neuron connections.

Such realizations are assisted by open-ended questioning; this helps to make explicit the reasoning and underlying hypotheses drawn from previous experiences. Revisiting how a conclusion was arrived at will also help legitimize the application of prior knowledge to unknown situations and the perceived risk this represents.

The coach must also encourage the manager to broaden her scope. Rather than pushing the limits of their own knowledge, some managers may narrow the scope of their project. Rather than applying their existing maps to unknown territories, they may try to reframe these new territories as known territory. To leverage its learning opportunities, the scope of a project must stretch the manager's perspective, for example from a business-unit level to the strategic level, or from one function to several functions, or from working within a closed context to working with several stakeholders. The coach should remember that the purpose of the exercise is not merely to answer a project question, but to provide a rich learning agenda. This learning agenda must be explicit in the mind of the coach so that the variety of perspectives required to stretch existing knowledge are not curtailed to ensure that something gets done. Insisting on tangible results is fine, but not at the expense of learning.

Broadening the 'relevance bandwidth'

Constructivists and neurologists have similar theories on how relevance decisions are made. A neuron loaded with a new piece of information immediately seeks to connect with other neurons. If it finds existing mental patterns to connect to, the new information is deemed relevant. The more connections that already exist that can connect to the new piece of information, the more it will be connected, and the more likely that it will become knowledge. Experts, like expert chess players, have multitudes of such mental patterns that help them see the relevance of more information than can novices because the latter have fewer of these connections already wired. This very simplified scenario suggests that relevance decisions, which are essential for learning and building experience, should be facilitated for the less experienced learners.

Some individuals have a natural curiosity that makes them 'generous' with respect to their relevance criteria. They are often referred to as 'broad categorizers,' meaning that their mental categories are very accommodating. Broad categorizers have also developed conceptual capabilities that help them deal effectively with the larger volume of information that will result from their openness. For them, learning potential is high.

For the narrow-categorizers, new information must meet very narrow and precise specifications to be deemed relevant. Their limited information intake limits their learning potential. In addition, when confronted with large volumes of information, their brain panics and becomes very digital, ruling out any 'maybes,' and limiting further the possible connections that a new piece of information may make with already scarce prior patterns. We have seen narrow categorizers select irrelevant information with a higher probability than if information had been selected randomly. Helping learners broaden their relevance bandwidth is thus helpful to most of them.

In doing so, the challenge is not to see more details; it is to see 'outside the box.' A helpful approach is, with questioning, to guide the manager through broader, more-encompassing perspectives. For example, a global business-unit manager was experiencing great difficulty in getting one of the country teams to commit to higher sales targets, comparable to those that other country units had agreed. Their argument was that there was only limited market growth, so their target was already ambitious. In a way, it was, and these people were hard working. Rather than pushing further the rationale for growth, perspective-expanding questioning helped the business-unit manager explore the incentive system in place in that country, which he believed to be beyond his scope. For all practical purposes, this system punished risk taking and encouraged predictability. This was not showing up on this manager's radar screen.

Helping managers during this process requires some tact. Often, they feel vulnerable when they go through the process of exploring unfamiliar ground and try not to reveal their hesitations. One of their strategies is to ignore the coach until they have made up their mind. It should generally be interpreted as 'help!' and a good way to start the conversation is to ask whether this is a good time to share where they are. Other managers may simply try to completely hand over to the coach their dilemmas from these difficult choices about relevance. It is then fair to answer their questions with more open-ended, guiding questions that point at a few hypotheses to be tested. In some instances, the coach may leave more space for the manager's trial-and-error process of assimilating new information, resisting the temptation of providing immediate guidance, and merely suggest deadlines for reviewing progress.

When the manager does take the mental risk of venturing beyond familiar ground, it is important that the coach provides some reasonable degree of protection. The coach must allow organization taboos to be challenged, mandates to be expanded, and higher-level issues to be addressed.

Building overview mental patterns

Potentially, there seems to be a risk of information overflow. Here again, the constructivists and the neurologists appear to converge. It seems that the way the brain deals with these masses of mental connections is by regrouping them into hierarchical classifications, like outline formats, in patterns that point at viable meanings. More-encompassing, high-level patterns are known to facilitate the integration of new information by making it add up to a more meaningful whole. The process is not one of adding details to the map, but of making the map more-encompassing, of mapping at a higher level.

These overview perspectives may range from generic classifications – like relating a factual observation to a management function: 'This is a marketing issue' – to solution-oriented classifications – like 'These facts point to a need to grow our market share.' The solution-pointing clusters are believed to be more robust because they can be tested, thus providing usable confirmations or refutations that enrich further the cluster of mental connections.

The ability to form overview patterns is not uniform among managers. Some easily get lost in details and end up 'shooting from the hip.' For them, learning to construct overview patterns needs to be facilitated.

Steering the thinking process from the general to the specific, rather than the other way around, helps build overview patterns in which experiential information will more easily build up to a meaning. For example, a manager can be asked to position his or her project on the company's overall strategy roadmap; then to explain how it addresses those strategic priorities. In some instances, this may lead to a reformulation of the project scope. Another approach is to ask the manager to provide regular overviews of what the project is all about. Frequent references to this overview, as a working hypothesis, will be made through the analysis, either to organize new information, or to update it to incorporate new, relevant information. As a result, the project scope may get revised several times, each time 'going back to the drawing board,' i.e. going back to the overview and its link to the strategy.

The formation of overview patterns is also facilitated by trial-and-error testing of the mental pathways that support them. The coach can ask for the implicit assumptions behind the proposed patterns and challenge the solidity of these assumptions by asking for the supporting information. Verifying these logical links will help the formation of mental connections across point observations. Similarly, reasoning inconsistencies may be surfaced. Action-oriented managers easily jump to a conclusion without a fully thought-out path from their observations to that conclusion. Giving the benefit of the doubt that this logical path exists and asking them to make it explicit also helps build the missing connections for an overview pattern to take shape. The conceptual complexity of most business initiatives will easily provide such learning opportunities.

It seems that huge numbers of concurrent patterns get formed in parallel by the brain. Perhaps this is part of a survival strategy, as it decreases the risk of being very wrong. It also allows cross-checking: the patterns that can make most connections with each other carry higher-level meaning and are more robust. Building several concurrent patterns is thus helpful in enriching and probably confirming this meaning, particularly as they eventually get included in overall, more-encompassing patterns. We have observed from decision-making simulations with managers that testing alternative patterns concurrently, looking selectively for confirming information, provides more accurate conclusions than the early, random accumulation of data points. The latter led quite systematically to the least likely conclusions, as a result of information overflow with no pattern context to make it meaningful.

Action-oriented managers also easily jump to solutions by resorting instinctively to one known pattern. Helping them keep their mental options open will help them form higher-level patterns that will, in fact, enhance the accuracy of their decisions. When you ask managers to provide you with a list of issues, they will generally come back with a list of solutions. It is then natural to ask them which issues their solutions are addressing. The famous 'Why? Why? Why?' questioning, asking at least three times 'Why?' in response to 'because . . .' is an effective approach to surface the root causes of a problem, rather than merely addressing its symptoms. Similarly, separating causes from effects, independent variables from dependent variables, same (i.e. duplicate) information from similar (i.e. groupable) information, points to patterns to be further confirmed. Business initiatives naturally lend themselves to running several options in parallel and to comparing their respective merits on the basis of the issues they really address.

The formation of rich overview patterns is also facilitated by the diversity of the information at hand. This diversity is inherently present in most business projects and it should be leveraged, rather than diminished for the well-intended purpose of making the scope of the project more manageable. We guide the manager through a sequence of different perspectives: starting from the strategy context, deciding on the project scope and its deliverables, cascading the tasks to be performed down to the level of execution, assessing the required resources and capabilities, measuring its financial impact, aligning individual performance, and establishing a mobilization plan, a communication plan and a follow-up plan. At each step, the focus on the project fundamentals, the adjustment of the project overview, the prioritization of the execution drivers, and what the project is really aiming to achieve, get revisited to shape progressively an overview roadmap that gets detailed in the execution plan.

Challenging the mental patterns

Mental patterns are tentative; they are viable only until proven unviable. The brain uses different strategies to test them. One of these strategies is to look for overlaps with mental patterns of other individuals through discussion. In discussion, there is an attempt to confirm one's own exploratory views. When the manager's project requires teamwork, discussion is a necessity. When the manager is on her own the illusion of being more effective by being able to avoid discussions should be dismissed. Ultimately, other individuals will have to buy-in for execution to follow.

Discussion provides early testing of the viability of the manager's mental roadmaps, and a chance to enrich them before roll out.

A discussion process starts as if team members were mentally rehearsing patterns relevant to the situation at hand, using the other members of the team as the audience. The purpose of sharing one's views with the other team members is twofold: it is to present a pattern to oneself, in addition to presenting it to the other team members for feedback. The first purpose can be compared to a musician imagining a tune and then trying it out on an instrument for oneself. This 'listening to oneself' part of a discussion – when people say 'I guess what I mean is . . .' – probably plays a role in checking for oneself the electrical circuitry of the mental pattern. As painful as it may be for the other team members, it needs to be given some time. At times, it may sound like a 'House of Lords' debate because not everything said is perceived as relevant by everyone: 'What are we talking about?' But making everyone's perspectives as explicit for the others as possible lays the foundations on which learning can be built. Teams may need help in this process; for example, having a team member repeat what someone else has just been saying.

Identifying or building overlaps across the mental patterns held by the team members is the other important purpose of the discussion. One difficulty with this process is the difference between the broad categorizers, who have generous relevance bandwidths and broad overview patterns, and the narrow categorizers, who are on the opposite side of the spectrum. Conflicts easily arise due to differences in relevance bandwidth. Broad overview patterns should easily overlap with narrower ones, but this is not always the case: broad categorizers are perceived to be traveling at too high an altitude, while narrow categorizers are derided as 'nitpickers.' Some are happy to let a broader mental pattern cover their perspective; others will insist on giving airtime to their narrow perspective. The latter see the former as 'fuzzy thinkers,' the former see the latter as narrow-minded and slowing down the process.

The challenge for the coach is to find the right balance between letting the team struggle with reconciling its mental differences, and intervening to help the team out, without making winners and losers. In general, the process does take time which is stressful for the coach, and some teams prefer to go through it without witness, particularly without a coach keen to surface embarrassing undercurrent conflicts. However, we find that looking at this process as a learning process, rather than as a team problem, does help.

There are ways to help this learning process. The simplest is to give team members time to accommodate to each other's patterns and to make meaningful connections across them, while also imposing reasonable deadlines for producing deliverables. Other strategies include helping the team members to see the merits of each other's mental patterns and to integrate them at a higher level of overview, which can again be done through open-ended questioning: 'What do you find wrong with Jane's perspective? Putting it next to yours, what could it add up to? How would that take care of Joe's point?'

In this process, as with relevance decisions, teams will look for strategies to deal with the coach because the coach represents another part of the challenge. Not even acknowledging the coach's presence and making him feel uncomfortable is one of them; the aim is to discourage witnesses of mental work in process that exposes the team's weaknesses. The other frequently used strategy is to see the coach as an opportunity to get rid of the challenge; she is surreptitiously brought into the conversation and within minutes finds herself in charge of reconciling the diverse perspectives. Whichever way the team behaves, it is communicating that its major challenge is learning from each other. It is important to sense where the team is in its learning process and, if timely, to guide it through open-ended questioning. Telling, rather than questioning, is generally the most effective way for the coach to be taken as hostage – which some coaches have an urge to be; but it is better to resist the temptation. In this process, managers need to listen and synthesize, to integrate different mental maps into a more-encompassing, higher-level and more viable one. They may even recognize a leadership attribute in this capability.

Mental rehearsing

Another strategy to test mental patterns is mental rehearsal: mentally going through the steps of execution to convince an audience – and oneself – that the roadmap is viable. Communicating the proposed course of action reinforces the mental patterns that underlie it. Neurological research has shown that the neuronal pathways used through the mental rehearsal are essentially the same as those that will be used during execution.

The communication format that supports mental rehearsing is not the usual business presentation. The purpose is to share the thinking and walk the audience through it, rather than 'take it down the garden path' to an inescapable conclusion. This is best done by reviewing the key milestones along the mental pathway, the key decision points, the key underlying frameworks, as representative artifacts of this journey. To communicate trustworthiness, the material presented must communicate the overview perspective, while also providing evidence that thorough analysis has been performed, such as the execution Gantt chart, the drivers of financial performance, and the detailed execution follow-up plan.

At this stage, the coach should assemble an audience of committed senior managers. While they have a stake in the success of the project, they also have the 'neutrality' of not having gone through the cognitive iterations that the manager, his team members, and possibly the coach, went through. They represent a useful bridge between the learning process and execution.

If the manager and his team have used a 'war room,' it provides an effective context for this communication, going through milestone flipcharts displayed on its walls. The audience should be seated in a meeting-like manner, or standing around the flipcharts displayed on the walls. The approach should be interactive discussions rather than one-way presentations: walking through the reasoning, looking inside it and seeking feedback, rather than imposing conclusions.

After-action review

After-action review is comparable to mental rehearsal in that it confirms and consolidates the mental connections and patterns that led to a course of action. The purpose of after-action review is to make explicit for the manager the learning 'hidden agenda' covered while working on his or her business project: 'This is how I can build viable mental roadmaps, moving forward.' After-action review supports learning how to learn.

After-action review is a continuous improvement and learning procedure routinely practiced in some contexts, especially when learning is vital. It has long been part of military procedures in many countries. But it is relatively less practiced in corporate contexts; in particular, the closer to the top, the less it is done. Indeed, at these levels, learning is not always seen as vital; knowledge may be perceived as an inherent part of the position, a belief sometimes supported by a sense of invulnerability. So, like the other building blocks of learning, after-action review often also needs facilitation.

There are many opportunities to revisit the mental roadmaps followed in the course of a business project. The coach does not need to wait for the completion of the project. Throughout the planning and execution milestones, frequent opportunities exist. Whenever it is performed, the process remains the same. An initial comparison between the actual and intended outcomes sets the scene for assessing how the mental roadmaps that were followed led to the difference. It is helpful to provide a factual structure to this process. The manager conceptualized her way through a series of planning and execution steps, the key steps in preparing the execution plan, the key phases in the execution itself. These provide the framework to review which mental roadmaps proved viable, which didn't, and how to improve them moving forward.

More important in addressing the learning 'hidden-agenda' are the questions to be raised by the coach on each of the above steps. These questions are those that have been proposed in this chapter:

- What was our level of emotional commitment to this task?
- How far were we able to go with our prior knowledge?
- Was our relevance bandwidth broad enough?
- Did our roadmaps reflect a sufficiently broad overview?
- Did we have our roadmaps sufficiently challenged? How did it help?
- Did we rehearse our roadmaps with enough audiences? How did it help?

The role of the coach is important in making the after-action review an effective opportunity to enhance the ability of the manager to build viable mental roadmaps. First, as in the previous phases of this process, the coach steers the learning with open-ended questions that trigger further thinking, rather than with questions that dictate an answer. The coach also helps to ensure that the involvement of all team members provides rich mental rehearsal by challenging different individual mental roadmaps. The simple rules to facilitate such participation are well known: being factual, refraining from finger pointing, looking at issues from different points of view.

The coach can also help the manager become aware of some mental roadmaps he or she seemed to apply, by acting as a mirror of the different roles and behaviors adopted: 'At this particular point, I saw you withdraw; what was going through your mind?' Or: 'While you were going through this task and I walked in, I sensed that you were trying to signal something; what was it?' These questions should be asked without looking for a confirmation, rather in the vein of exploring the consequences of a hypothesis.

Finally, the coach may also play the role of a 'confessor.' Some team members may feel anxious or guilty for behaviors that they have adopted which are not normally supported by the norms of the company. For example, one team changed its leader for judicious reasons, and in a fairly professional way. This change did help the team move ahead and get to tangible results. Yet, some team members felt quite guilty because this was normally not done in their company. After-action review helped them legitimize the mental roadmaps that had led them to act, in fact, in a fairly professional way, rather than dismissing them as risky.

Conclusion

Coaching managers on project teams provides a very effective way to address our learning agenda: helping managers enhance their ability to build viable mental roadmaps to address complex business situations. The most viable mental roadmaps are the more-encompassing ones. They allow the manager to address a wider range of management situations, to deem as relevant and process more diverse information, to give it richer meaning, and to develop more effective approaches to taking on his environment, thus retaining control of his destiny.

Key take-aways

To address the hidden agenda of action learning:

■ Find what can stimulate the emotional commitment to the task at hand.

■ Stretch the application of prior knowledge and experience.

■ Help broaden the manager's relevance bandwidth, notably through open questioning.

■ Help the manager build more-encompassing mental roadmaps, primarily through multidimensional tasks.

■ Challenge the manager's mental roadmaps, in particular through discussion.

■ Encourage mental rehearsal of the manager's mental roadmaps, especially by providing opportunities to communicate them.

■ Make sure that after-action review revisits how mental roadmaps were built and made more viable at each action step.

Notes

1   von Glasersfeld, E. (1995) Radical Constructivism, A Way of Knowing and Learning. *Studies in Mathematics Education, Series no. 6.* London: Falmer Press.
2   Brunner, J. (1960, 1977) *The Process of Education.* Boston: Harvard University Press (see in particular Chapter 2 – The importance of structure).

Learning scripts for sessions

Building intellectual and emotional awareness

Driving into action-based application

14

Scripting approaches for cross-cultural effectiveness

Martha Maznevski and Karsten Jonsen

Summary

What kind of thinking goes into scripting a session on cross-cultural effectiveness? Cross-cultural effectiveness involves both dynamic knowledge and sophisticated behavioral skills. In this chapter, we discuss scripting for cross-cultural effectiveness with a variety of materials and experiences, including a cultural profiling questionnaire. We address how to engage managers in learning about a 'soft' subject, including preparing appropriately, getting key messages across to participants, creating a lasting impact that translates into action back at the office, and managing the challenges that come with teaching a complex and abstract subject.

The thinking for scripting has to be both logical and creative. We present this chapter as an interview by one of us (Karsten Jonsen) with the other (Martha Maznevski) to capture the dynamic of balancing multiple elements of teaching, including content, process and connection with the material. We start with the first question from Karsten to Martha:

Thinking about your most successful teaching experiences – where you felt that there was a great rapport with the group, or that the feedback was particularly good afterwards – what made them great?

Those moments don't have as much to do with the content as they do with connecting with the class. In the best experiences, I really felt like I *connected* and *contributed* something. It could be about culture, personality or leadership. Success comes when you have really connected with the group and provided something that they need.

For cross-cultural analysis to be effective, it is important to make sure that the group needs it. In the past I have taught cross-cultural interaction because somebody thought it was a good thing for the group to know about, but the participants did not actually have a need for it. Then it's much more difficult to connect with them. They are not learning something relevant about managing themselves or other people, so they cannot get excited about how to use it.

Scripting for a 'soft subject'

Let's look at culture as a 'soft subject.' Some people coming here are hard number crunchers or results-driven. How do you 'sell culture' to them?

I usually start off by framing this as 'something different,' rather than trying to justify it within the framework of hard results. You lose something if you do that. There are two helpful ways to position 'soft subjects.'

First, by pointing out the importance of implementation and innovation. For example, you may have a good strategy but you can't implement it in the same way everywhere. How should you execute? Or, how can you create a culture of innovation where everybody's ideas can contribute to the company's operations?

Second, almost every company we work with acknowledges that people leadership is one of their weaknesses. Often it's best to say this is in a straightforward way: 'This is addressing people leadership, which we all find difficult. We may be going out of your comfort zone.'

The story of Hari Seldon from Isaac Asimov's *Foundation*[1] is sometimes a good starting point. Seldon's goal in life was to develop a science called 'psychohistory,' predicting human behavior with 100 percent certainty using mathematical equations. He develops enormously complex equations. The series of books then explores the principles and implications of psychohistory. For example, you can *never* predict the behavior of one person at a single point in time with any certainty. But, with extensive knowledge about humans, you *can* predict the behavior of groups of people over time with high probability, you can predict the behavior of an individual over time with some certainty, and you can use your knowledge to influence that behavior. Seldon figured out that humanity was headed for a 30,000-year dark age. He told the Emperor, who replied, 'Well, change it!' Seldon said, 'I can't, it's too late. However, I can play with the variables to understand the conditions under which the dark ages can be shortened.' He found a way to shorten the dark ages from 30,000 to 1,000 years, and also to create a healthier society than before.

Managers need to be like Hari Seldon. If you are a manager, you can't predict one person's behavior at one point in time. But, with good knowledge, you can predict the behavior of one person over time and a group of people over time. The role of a manager, then, is to set up the conditions under which those people are most likely to perform well over time, by understanding and managing certain variables.

Does the concept of predictability appeal more to these 'hard core' managers?

It does. Especially if you separate it from rationality. Predictability is not the same as rationality. We are trying to understand and predict people's behavior and influence it. But we accept that it is not always rational.

Sometimes, I tell the Hari Seldon story to illustrate the role of predictability, challenging the group to take on the role of Hari Seldon: 'Your job is to take all of these understandings of humans and set up the environment so they perform better.' This promotes a lot of curiosity. It tends to take away much of the resistance to a soft subject, which is usually rooted in the belief that we cannot study people systematically because they are not rational. The Seldon story separates rationality from predictability, and opens people to moving forward.

Preparing the script

How do you script and prepare for a session on culture?

The most important part of scripting is to determine the objectives. It is important always to have a discussion with the program director, whether it is an in-company or a public program, to understand: 'Why are we teaching this? Why is this part of the program?' There may be a very specific need. A typical situation is a company that has grown through acquisition, and until now has not had to work a lot across country units or across business units. Now it is trying to grow internally, which means much more integration and collaboration across units, and management is discovering that it is difficult to get those conversations going.

Sometimes in an open program, different individuals in the class have very different needs. In that case it's important to prepare the participants by framing the need explicitly, for example: 'This is the set of situations that we are going to talk about. Even if you don't have these, here are some ways you can relate to it.'

Do you ever come to class with a 'menu' and then choose a few of the items, after talking with the class about what is most interesting for them? Or do you have the script totally prepared, with a framework that you stick to?

I generally prepare the session script ahead of time. If you go into class and ask participants what they want, there is always a danger that they choose something you aren't prepared to do. That happened once – not on cross-cultural issues, but on getting breakthroughs in cost cutting by working creatively with people. The program director asked me to run a session about using broad networks of people to innovate. When I got there I asked, 'What ways of exploring this subject would be most meaningful to you?' In fact, they wanted a session on managing layoffs!

'Menu selection' is best done ahead of time. Interviews with future participants, others from the company, or past participants can help in selecting the applications and activities that are most likely to be important for a particular group. In terms of more specific preparation, I analyze the data from the Cultural Perspectives Questionnaire (CPQ).[2] Looking at the country and demographic profile, the variance in the class, the distribution of countries, and the scores within country and out of country, determines the highlights that can be discussed in class.

Getting the message across

What's the key to getting the message across?

The main message to convey is that cross-cultural effectiveness comes from a blend of deep knowledge about cultures and sophisticated skills for communicating across cultures. This message is easy on the surface, but the details can be quite challenging.

In an old but very relevant study, Indrei Ratiu[3] asked experienced managers to identify which among them was the most cross-culturally effective and which the least effective, dividing them into two groups. He posed the question, 'When you go into a new culture, what kind of mindset do you take in with you?' One group said, 'We go in with a completely open mind.' The other replied, 'We go in with some expectations about what the other culture is going to be like.'

After describing the study, I ask the participants, 'Which group is the most culturally competent – the group that went in with an open mind or the group that went in with some expectations?' Most people say, 'The most competent group, of course, went in with a completely open mind.' Actually it's the opposite! The less competent group went in with an open mind – or said they did. The more competent group went in with expectations.

Then we discuss the psychology of what an expectation really means. You simply cannot go in with an open mind. A set of expectations *as a starting point* is more effective than a belief that you have an open mind.

So a map that is not very detailed is better than having no map?

It is. Emphasizing the map metaphor is very useful, because everyone can understand it. When you first go to a new country, you get a handful of maps. Say you're there for six months. How long do you need the maps? A week? Two weeks? At some point, your picture of the territory becomes much better than the maps. But when you're first there, the maps are invaluable. You can't function without them.

Individual understanding in cultural groups

You teach culture, which is a collective construct, but participants are obviously individuals. This means communicating and managing ideas and actions across levels, all the way from individuals to teams, groups, organizations and nations for that matter. How do you differentiate these levels in class?

With great difficulty. The notion that people behave like individuals *and* according to multiple cultural expectations at the same time is complex and abstract.

To address this, I start by having people deeply explore the notion of what culture is, asking them, in groups of two to three people, to brainstorm a list of as many cultures as they can. Providing a few examples – the Canadian culture, the Swiss culture, the IMD culture – helps them to begin generating lists. Some groups always have a long list, including everything from religious cultures, to generational and sports and hobby cultures.

After they have generated these lists, I ask people to define culture. It's easy to identify culture when you see it, but harder to define. We look at the lists of cultures and develop a definition together. One of the first things to come out is that culture is shared. It is a group set of norms, beliefs, values and so on. This leads naturally to the question: 'What does culture do? What is the function of culture?' Culture makes things efficient, it makes things easy, it gives a sense of identity, it gives a sense of safety, and it creates boundaries inside and outside, things like that. All of this becomes evident from the lists of cultures.

This in-depth discussion helps later when we come to the relationship between individual and group levels. The group has a culture, but individuals are different within the culture. And each individual belongs to many cultures. Cultures tend not to be completely homogeneous. In fact, cultures that are too homogeneous die, because the individual variation within a culture gives the culture the ability to adapt.

Having that discussion upfront and then being able to refer back to the lists of cultures and the definition provides a useful frame of reference for handling multiple levels at the same time.

How do you avoid spending too much time on the individual?

We do spend time on the individuals. But what is most difficult for people to understand is 'How can I have individual results when this is still about culture?'

We use the Cultural Orientations Framework and the CPQ, which measures the dimensions of the framework, together to go back and forth between the levels. The framework outlines a set of questions that every culture has to find answers to, and agree on those answers *as a group*. The CPQ measures individuals' assumptions about those answers. When we put together an aggregate of individual answers about a group, we get a profile of the group but we also get to see the individual variance within the group.

Engaging people

Why, apart from 'having empathy,' is it important to engage people?

You have to engage people. Culture is very abstract, and it is difficult to get below the superficial level. The 'kiss, bow and shake hands' – here are the dos and don'ts in different countries – is a lot of fun. But we know from research that this is not the most helpful perspective for managers who are working in many different cultures. If you are Swiss and going to work in Japan, then by all means take a course on working in Japan. But if you are going to work in a global, multinational environment, then cross-cultural intelligence is required. This cannot be superficial; it is much deeper and more difficult to acquire. Participants who are not engaged are not likely to make the effort to take the necessary steps to achieve it.

Does using a mix of materials engage people? Is that why you mix methods?

Mixing content and methods serves two purposes. Of course, it helps to keep people engaged, but it is also a useful mechanism to switch between the abstract and the real. People need real experiences upon which they can reflect at the abstract level, to build deeper cultural intelligence.

We often start with the Five Tricks card game (see also Chapter 4), which is a game played in groups of four with two sets of partners. Each group starts in a different room, and learns the card game. It is fairly easy, using just 20 cards. During the tournament, pairs play against each other, under the constraint of complete silence. After each round, the winners rotate to the next room. The information we hold back is that each room starts with its own set of rules. We set it up saying, 'Cultures are like card games . . . you've got a set of arbitrary rules that people follow in order to make the game happen. There are winners and losers. We are going to learn a card game to have an experience in learning about new cultures.' Most people do not suspect that there are different rules in different rooms. In the second round of the tournament when the winners rotate to the next room, the two pairs in the room are playing – in silence – with different rules. At some point, two people reach out to grab the cards at the same time because they both think they've won. Then the fun begins! The immediate reaction is very emotional, something like 'they're stupid,' 'they're cheating,' 'they didn't understand the rules,' or even 'we didn't understand the rules.' That single moment is fundamental to learning and engaging. Before that moment, the experience is a predictable card game. At that moment, it becomes an engaging life experience. We spend a lot of time analyzing that moment, because it is a typical cross-cultural incident and it is very, very emotional.

How does this game accelerate participants' experience?

The game gives participants a 'feel and touch' of cultural differences which they never forget, including the confusion that happens afterwards. They ask: 'What do we do with this?'

During the debriefing we discuss the fact that the moment is created by just 15 minutes of playing a game. People learn a set of rules, and assume these are constant. When they encounter another set of rules, they assume the people are in error, not the rules. This helps people to understand the much deeper impact of culture. Creating this effect in 15 minutes with intelligent adults where the outcome is unimportant brings home powerfully the impact on behaviors and assumptions of years of growing up or working in one cultural setting.

The learning continues with the question – what do you do about it? Which rules are you going to play by? In this part of the discussion, we find that different groups negotiate how to play in different ways. We get into the skills of cross-cultural communication, an understanding of power dynamics, and other elements of cross-cultural effectiveness.

The game also provides a useful parallel to the dimensions of the CPQ. There are some general rules by which card games differ. If you're a good card player, you know that ace is sometimes high and sometimes low; sometimes there are trumps and sometimes not; trump may be diamonds or spades; and so on. If you have a good map for card games – an understanding of how card games differ – it is easier for you to analyze and predict what the next set of rules could be. The CPQ does the same thing for cultures. It gives you a map of how cultures differ from each other. And if you know that map, then you're better at going into these situations and predicting the basic elements.

Talking about games and role play, OB (organizational behavior) educators are famous for doing 'fun stuff' – is this expected?

Many people think, if it's not fun, it's not OB! OB is, in fact, all about people learning from their behavior. Most concepts are not very difficult to understand, but putting them into context, into action, is where the important learning happens. By doing an exercise, people create a case study of their own experiences, which provides much deeper learning than simply discussing the pros and cons of the concept.

The key, though, is in the debrief. It is important to spend at least equal time on debrief as on the exercise itself. The real point of the exercises is the debrief, the learning points that come afterwards. The exercises should be structured to bring out the patterns that you expect to discuss.

How you run that debrief is critical. For example, in the Five Tricks card game debrief, the cultural frameworks are linked to the memories of the games. The games are etched indelibly on memories because of the emotional engagement. Remembering the game triggers a memory of the framework. The debrief is vital because it makes that link explicit.

What other learning activities do you use?

We use a lot of mini cases and examples. Within very short cases there can be a lot of richness about all kinds of different cultural dimensions.

We also use many examples from past experiences. We don't present them as cases, more as puzzles and situations we have seen – 'Here's a company that did this; here's a company that has these kinds of profile; here's an example of this kind of situation . . .'

Then we get the participants to develop their own examples as well, often in smaller groups or buzz groups. Because it is so difficult for people to move from abstract to concrete and back again, we frequently use small groups for exploratory dialogue. Primed with an abstract concept and examples, people quickly begin to share their own examples.

Making it stick

How do you manage the ongoing session to engage participants throughout, while still moving towards your teaching goals? You mentioned it is important to connect with them, and it is important to get them emotionally engaged. What is the best way to do that, to involve them emotionally?

A lot of emotional involvement comes through telling stories and hearing participants' stories about how the situation is relevant or meaningful for them. It is different for every professor, but for me a critical part is being personal and very engaged myself. Modeling the behavior that I want from them. I share stories from my own experience, from previous participants, or observations of others in companies. The aim is to give them something of myself, bring my enthusiasm and passion about the topic. It is also about listening to what they have to say and helping them to connect with each other, to work through examples and see patterns.

Participants also become personally engaged when they receive their own individual feedback, their cultural profiles from the scores on the survey. People like hearing about themselves, and getting information about their profiles is very engaging.

Don't participants want some kind of 'good/bad' assessment?

Often they do, but that's the opposite of what we measure with the CPQ. The CPQ dimensions are descriptive, not evaluative. There is no good score and no bad score, just implications based on what the scores are. This is often difficult for people to come to terms with, because cultures often evaluate each other.

To overcome this issue, ideally it is better to teach personality – such as the Myers-Briggs Type Indicator (MBTI) – to a group first, to introduce the notions of predictability and non-evaluative dimensions. Personality is much closer to the surface than culture, so personality differences tend to be more visible in the classroom than cultural differences and much easier to discuss. Again, the MBTI dimensions are not evaluative. Introverts and extraverts are equally valuable to a team or company; they just contribute in different ways. Most people have little difficulty understanding the impact of personality.

These ideas of predictability and non-evaluation can then be applied to the more difficult discussion on culture. Culture is so deeply buried that we do not always see it in the classroom. It is all about norms and expectations around social behavior, and the 'executive education culture' of the classroom often determines the norms more than people's 'home' cultures do. It is only through telling stories and discussing examples that the impact of culture can be seen.

Once the nature of culture is better understood, the individual CPQ feedback can be introduced. Then people become engaged with the potential in their own profiles, moving away from the instinctive evaluation of cultural differences.

Let's talk about change, and how people apply new learning when they come home. How do you make them receptive to change?

Transferring new behavior back home is the biggest challenge in executive education, and one that often remains hidden to us. Nonetheless, there are some important ways we can facilitate this transfer. First, by connecting the ideas to participants' home situations as much as possible, throughout the session. For example, as we discuss the CPQ dimensions before people have received their profiles, you can ask them to guess what their profile will look like, and also to guess the profiles of other people and groups they work with. While they cannot check these other profiles against data, it encourages them to have conversations about these dimensions when they return home, to test their hypotheses and discuss the implications. Having participants give examples from their own experiences to link the abstract to the concrete is also important here.

The other critical activity is explicitly linking the concepts to behaviors, so that people go home not just with knowledge and awareness, but knowing what to do with it. This is why I teach the CPQ as mapping culture, which is only the first part of the Map-Bridge-Integrate[4] sequence for achieving synergy from diversity. As we go through the mapping discussions in class, we also explicitly practice Bridging skills, which are about communicating effectively across cultures. We discuss how those specific behaviors can be translated into the participants' work environments and real-world situations that they may encounter. The behavioral skills transfer fairly easily, and the mapping knowledge gets associated with them so it is also transferred. So when managers find themselves in a situation with cultural dimensions, they can move pretty quickly into Mapping and Bridging, because they know the tools are useful.

Creating change means constantly connecting the session script and activities back to the work environment. It's not . . . 'We are setting this aside as a separate session, and now you take it to work' . . . but the whole time we are exploring culture, we are relating the ideas to how you would use it. Therefore, the knowledge and skills are always linked with the practice in participants' minds.

Managing difficult situations

How do you avoid some groups or cultures dominating the session, perhaps because they are more extraverted or simply louder?

Cold calling is not something that I really use when running sessions about culture. The professor must be culturally sensitive, and asking people to explain their own culture in a large group is not always culturally sensitive. At the same time, the rest of the group does need to hear from a wide variety of people who have different preferences for contributing.

To reconcile these goals, one approach is to vary the activities, for example using buzz or study groups. The groups are instructed: 'Make sure you hear from everybody. Not everybody feels comfortable sharing with a large group, and that's fine. But share your thoughts in a small group, and then make sure the small group shares these with the large group.'

In addition, it is helpful to talk to individuals from cultures that do not normally speak up in large groups, to ask them if they will share with the class. For example, I've interviewed a lot of Muslims to try to understand their cultural assumptions better along with the implications for business practices and for management. While I can explain Islam to Westerners, I'm not Muslim and my descriptions are not adequate. So if there is a Muslim in the class it is far better to have them explain the culture, although it is not appropriate to put the person on the spot in 'defending' their culture to the Western world, especially with current political events. Talking with the person one-on-one ahead of time can encourage them to share with the group. The professor can then give the person opportunities to volunteer, and if they don't, try to pull them out a bit.

How do you deal with 'destructive' dynamics in the class?

First you try to head them off even before they happen. You find out from the program director whether there are challenging individuals or sensitive issues in the class. Also, during the introductory discussions and exercises it is important to feel people out – to get a sense of the types of question and initial expectations people bring in at the beginning.

No matter how difficult the situation is, it is important to remember that if somebody has a contrary perspective, for them, it is valid. By taking this view, I try to do whatever I can to turn negative into positive. However, a big part of dealing with destructive dynamics comes from experience. There are two common challenges when teaching culture, and after many experiences I have learned how to deal with them most of the time.

The first – and simpler one – is about the methodology of the questionnaire. 'How can this really be measuring culture?' 'When I filled out the question-naire, I thought these questions were stupid, I could never answer them consistently, and now you've taken them and put them in this profile!' And so on. Sometimes people really are concerned about the methodology, but more often they are avoiding the results for some reason and the method-ology is a useful sidetrack. Either way, they cannot move into learning mode until the methodology questions are closed for them. My first response is to say, without emotion: 'We've been using this survey for fifteen years in research and in team and company situations. It is measuring what it says it's measuring. It's been applied in a lot of contexts and it has been very helpful.'

Then I'll answer a few methods questions, but if a person keeps going down that road, I'll say, 'You caught me in my academic mode! I would *love* to have this conversation, because this really gets my heart going. You wouldn't believe how much controversy there is around these issues! But can we do that after class? I think it's something that probably not everybody is interested in.' The aim is to turn the stream of challenges into a positive, but to move the session forward: 'You've made me excited . . . this is something that I'd love to talk about, but it's not taking us towards our learning objectives.'

The other dynamic is more complicated to manage: 'Isn't this stereotyping? We shouldn't be measuring cultures. You are talking about cultures as if everybody in the culture is the same. The way you're talking about Italians and Germans is really offensive. This is wrong.' The issue for the educator is that the participant making the challenge is, in fact, right. This *is* precisely the danger of talking about culture. But avoiding the discussion is worse, because then it gets suppressed. The discussion *must* happen, and if no one brings up the issue then I always do myself, before the class is about three-quarters over, starting by confirming the problem. 'This is one of the main dangers of discussing culture, and we need a sophisticated understanding of it. Let's stop right here and tackle that.' It is useful to get a feel of the room as the debate starts, to get other participants to comment and reflect. Usually there is a balance of views – some people agree that measuring culture is unhealthy; others say, 'No, I can see that this is useful under certain conditions.'

Then we discuss the notion of stereotypes versus generalizations. Stereotypes are evaluative shorthand summaries of other cultures, often developed without good information, and assumed to hold true for everyone in the culture. Generalizations are non-evaluative expectations of other cultures, developed with objective information and changed with new information, and assumed *not* to hold true for everyone in the culture. Generalizations are helpful starting points in cross-cultural effectiveness and important foundations for cross-cultural intelligence; stereotypes are destructive judgments that get in the way of understanding and action. Fortunately our perspective on teaching culture allows for a good discussion of this. For example, the CPQ measures individuals, so we can show distributions and demonstrate with data that not everybody from the same culture has the same profile.

Cultural understanding, therefore, can be a dangerous tool. But just because it's dangerous, it does not mean it is not important. In fact, all the tools that we use are dangerous if they are used wrongly. Used correctly, they can help substantially.

The future

Looking out ten or even thirty years, how will learning about culture differ from today?

People's understanding of the role of culture in the global economy will be different. Now it is in transition. On the one hand, there is a sense that cultures are converging, for example in consumer markets. On the other, when you look at political and economic situations, it looks like cultures are diverging. It's a complex picture and hard to see a pattern. My sense is that ten or thirty years from now, we will have had enough of a pattern that we can answer that question more clearly. Cultures will no longer be simply converging or diverging, but we will be able to say more about how: 'In these ways it's converging and in these ways it's diverging.'

The type of cultural understanding required by managers is also changing, and will continue to do so. This is in large part because organizational structures are shifting towards greater global integration. Ten years ago, culture was taught mostly to help somebody move from one location to another. Now, the emphasis is much more on operating in multicultural situations everywhere. There are still expatriates, but most people operating internationally today work in multiple cultures simultaneously, with travel or short assignments, or bringing a global team together. 'Average' managers have much more opportunity to work with people from different cultures, so need more sophisticated multicultural skills.

These trends – cultural and organizational dynamics *plus* increased diversity in classrooms – are going to change how we teach culture and it will be a much richer learning environment. You will have a lot of examples and stories without going further than the room itself. Teaching about culture and cross-cultural effectiveness will provide participants with tools to talk about what is already there. People will have a better sense of the impact of culture around the world. Or at least more data about cultural dynamics in a mixed-up cultural world than we have now.

Individuals coming into a session or program are going to be more sophisticated in their cross-cultural skills – so teaching will need to become more sophisticated too. The simple dos and don'ts of each country will certainly be outdated. With some colleagues, I am working on a project to define and measure cultural intelligence beyond what we know today. One core aspect of this is 'mindfulness.' In the past the 'cultural chameleon' – when in Rome do as the Romans – was viewed as the most sophisticated person. But with increased multicultural interaction we recognize the importance of being yourself and having personal integrity, in multiple situations and in ways that are acceptable to many cultures. This requires a great deal of knowledge and skills, plus a meta-capability of mindfulness that directs you how to use these effectively. These are ideas we were not even thinking about ten years ago. Now we are talking about it, but we are still not sure how to measure it, see it, and train people to do it. But it will come, and certainly ten years from now we will be good at learning and teaching these ideas.

Key take-aways

■ Managers need to know about *deep* levels of culture. Superficial numbers or practices about how to do things in different countries are deceptively useful. They give a false sense of security, unless they represent knowledge in a broader context of deep assumptions and cross-cultural effectiveness skills.

■ Culture is not a static, homogeneous whole, but is constantly changing. The *CPQ map* of culture is an excellent starting point to capture a snapshot of culture but it is also important to develop *communications skills* to quickly go beyond that map.

■ Vary the methods of teaching and the kinds of materials used – both to keep people emotionally engaged, and to constantly move between the abstract and the concrete.

■ Enjoy it all and appreciate the impact. The immense diversity of humanity is what we're working with here, and we can help unleash its potential and point it towards the most difficult challenges society faces. It's worth trying to get it right.

Notes

1 Asimov, I. (1951, 1991) *Foundation*. Tega Clay, SC: Spectra Publishers.
2 The Cultural Perspectives Questionnaire, developed by Martha Maznevski and Joe DiStefano, measures individuals' expectations about 13 dimensions of cultural interaction. More information can be found at www.imd.ch/research/cpq.
3 Ratiu, I. (1983) Thinking internationally: A comparison of how international executives learn. *International Studies of Management and Organization*, 13 (1–2), pp. 139–150.
4 See also Chapter 4 for discussion of this framework.

15

Teaching general managers about the business value of IT: Making the invisible visible!

Don Marchand

Summary

Only a small percentage of business managers really understand the role of information management and IT in their business. Many fear the subject, have no confidence in dealing with it and some senior executives hope to 'retire' before they have to deal with it in their everyday business lives! However, they are competitive necessities today in virtually every company – and in some cases even the source of strategic advantage. The challenge is how to transform a subject that many managers fear, loathe or find boring into a positive experience, relevant to general managers as a vital part of their mindset and toolkit to leverage value. The chapter offers lessons learned in the design, development and delivery of learning sessions in ways that build confidence and interest in the design, deployment and use of information and IT.

How does one teach a topic that, to many business managers, is frightening, imponderable and boring? How can you approach it so that managers understand the value of IT and information management in their approach to career and company? How can you enable managers to build confidence in making judgments about business strategy and capabilities that are inclusive of, yet realistic about, what IT and information resources can do for their company and business success?

When I arrived at IMD in 1994, my principal responsibility was to anchor the topics of 'IT' and 'information management' (IM) in the executive programs of IMD. During the previous 20 years, I had taught, researched, managed and consulted at the intersection of general management and information/IT management. What was new for me was the diversity of my new environment, where there were public and in-company programs with participants ranging from middle to senior management, from early 30s to late 50s in age, representing industries from cement to high technology and from many cultures.

However, the diversity did not extend to opinions about IT and IM. There were some widely held beliefs (what we called 'basic realities') that needed to be addressed. First, business managers did not want to be taught about IT, the IT function or the use of IT personnel. Second, fearful yet curious, they wanted to know about IT and IM business opportunities, but not about the nitty-gritty of deploying the technology. Third, in their experience, failure and disappointment with IT projects were far more common than successes – it was risky and most business managers had a healthy, almost intuitive, skepticism about IT.[1] Even in the late 1990s at the height of the dot.com bubble and Y2K scare, most business managers wanted to probe the reality behind the 'hype,' though many suspected that their companies lacked the information capabilities and experience to really leverage the internet and e-business as did Dell, Cisco and Amazon. Fourth, because these 'best practice' examples were exclusively American or Anglo-Saxon, the cases and teaching approach would have to be more diverse, representing various countries and regions as well as developed and emerging markets.

Based on these realities, the challenge was to get inside the minds of business managers and focus on how to extract business value from IT and IM. Executing this challenge required me to focus my research, publication and teaching materials on this topic and move away from a CIO (Chief Information Officer) and IT functional perspective, which 95 percent of the existing business school thinking and publications covered in the US and the UK.[2]

The objectives of this chapter are to share my insight and experience in this topic from over ten years of program direction and teaching as well as seven years of research. I will begin with a discussion of the executive learning process, then cover the style of learning and teaching, and conclude with a section on designing programs and sessions for business managers.

The approach and process of executive learning about IT and IM

In this section, let's focus on five key questions that define my approach to the process of executive education about IT and IM.[3]

1 Are business managers spending their attention and time on the right management challenges?

How do they allocate their scarce time and attention on IT and IM? Usually, business managers spend about 90 percent of their available time and attention on IT investments and deployment issues, i.e. hard, measurable and visible factors. They plan IT projects, align IT with the business, budget and invest in IT and deal with the IT function and external suppliers. In some cases, business managers naively seek to solve business problems with ill-defined 'IT solutions.' For example, in the last five years some companies have invested in Customer Relationship Management (CRM) systems to improve the 'customer orientation' of their company. However, to be effective, CRM systems must be accompanied by significant behavioral and cultural changes in the sales, marketing and servicing areas – most business managers did not foresee that![4]

In contrast to managerial perceptions, business research indicates that only 20–25 percent of the business value of IT is linked to deployment and investments, while 75–80 percent of the business value of IT and IM is associated with the so-called 'soft factors' of information usage by managers and employees as well as by external customers, suppliers and partners (see Figure 15.1).[5] This is an important disconnect in the perceptions of business managers. Many devote 90 percent of their time and attention to IT investments and deployment that only account for 20–25 percent of the business value of IT and IM in a company! As such, by failing to focus on how effectively information and IT are used by themselves and their people in their

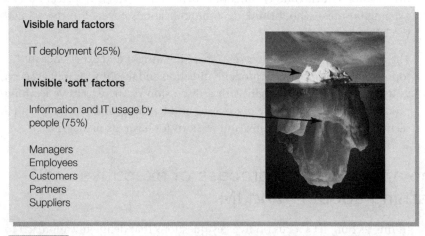

Figure 15.1 The business value of IT is greater than the deployment of IT

companies, business managers may be overlooking the largest potential pay-off from IT.

2 What is the difference between IT deployment and usage?

Many business managers have never really considered the difference between IT deployment and how it might be used to create business value. They fail to recognize that these aspects require differing managerial perspectives, mindsets and measures of performance, as Figure 15.2 illustrates.

Many business managers understand that IT deployment focuses on functional issues and is the CIO's domain, but not that the responsibility for usage of IT and IM rests with business managers. Focusing on *both* of these concerns as two sides of the same coin provides a more holistic view of what a company must do to exploit the full business value of IT.

Deployment focuses on:
- IT governance
- IT services and processes
- IT infrastructure
- IT applications and data management
- IT resources (people and expertise)
- IT investments

Usage focuses on:
- Organization and governance of decision rights in a business
- Usage of IT and information processes for management decision making
- Usage of information and IT in operational and business process management
- The behaviors and values of people that lead them to use IT and information in their work

IT deployment measures focus on:
- IT availability and access
- Quality of IT services
- User satisfaction
- Cost reduction and standardization
- Efficiency of IT
- IT ROI for projects
- IT organization maturity (e.g. Gartner Model)

IT usage measures focus on:
- Information and IT usage in the business
- Effectiveness of information use by people (Information Orientation Maturity)
- Contribution to top line growth relative to:
  – Profitability
  – Market share
  – EBIT
  – EVA
  – Innovation in products and services
  – Company reputation

Figure 15.2 IT deployment differs from IT usage

3 What are the strategic choices for exploiting the business value of IT?

If strategy is choice, then general managers must make decisions that leverage both the use and deployment of information and IT for **value creation** rather than **value destruction**, as Figure 15.3 suggests.

Deployment	?	Usage	=	Business Value ?
Deployment	–	Usage	=	Dilutes Value
Deployment	+	Usage	=	OK return
Deployment	X	Usage	=	Multiplier Effect

Deployment of IT inside and outside the business	Usage of IT by managers, employees, suppliers, customers and partners	For driving business performance

Figure 15.3 Key strategic choices about achieving the business value of IT

First, do business managers really care to understand the deployment, usage and business value relationship in their business? How important are these concerns to the business strategy of the company and its execution?

Second, the relationship between IT deployment and usage may dilute business value, because neither is the direct focus of managerial attention or they are poorly executed. Business managers may remove themselves from IT decisions to such an extent that the IT function drives IT deployment and, indirectly, usage. In other cases, IT deployment may be done well, but business managers pay scant attention to usage, which diminishes or even ruins its business impact.

Third, IT deployment and usage may add to each other with OK results, which is better than the prior alternatives. Business managers may have low expectations, either due to past failure or mixed results.

Fourth, because deployment of IT can leverage excellent usage, the relationship can be a multiplier of value. How can companies achieve the multiplier effect? What are examples of companies that strive to do so?

4 Under what circumstances do IT and IM contribute to 'competitive necessity' versus 'competitive advantage'?

Despite the frequent claims that IT investments offer 'competitive advantages' to companies, many business managers suspect that IT only maintains their 'competitive necessity,' that is, the operational efficiency that a minimal technological investment requires. The real question is 'under what conditions can IT contribute to a firm's "competitive advantage," that is, achieve a multiplier effect on business value?'

According to our research, successful senior managers value IT and IM far beyond their simple deployment, and thus view them as knowledge embedded in their people and organization; we refer to this as the Information Orientation (IO) of a company (see Figure 15.4). With this approach, business managers consider the effectiveness, behavior and values of the people who use information and IT in their execution of the basic business

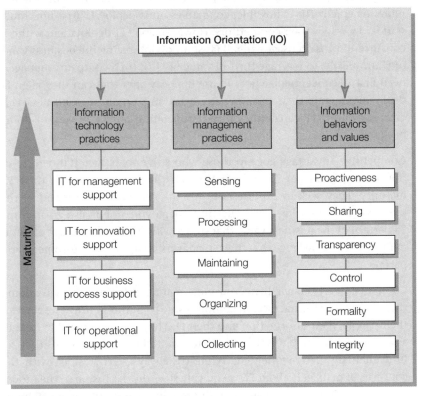

Figure 15.4 The Information Orientation Maturity Model

Source: Marchand, D.A., Kettinger, W.J. and Rollins, J.D. (2001), *Making the Invisible Visible: How companies win with the right information, people and IT.* New York and London: John Wiley & Sons.

capabilities and purpose, rather than some magic bullet that confers instant competitive advantage. We call the process of building this capacity the 'Information Orientation Maturity' of a company.[6] In addition, because the IO maturity of a company can be measured and benchmarked, corporate managers can track their progress in developing their company's information capabilities in order to enhance company value.[7]

Thus, IT deployment can enable, but not drive, the usage of information and IT in a company. Creating value via effective usage of information, people and IT in a company is the multiplier IT effect that propels a company beyond competitive necessity to the creation of true competitive advantage.

5 How should managers focus their attention and time to extract the most business value from IT?

IT deployment matters, but how people use IT and information matters more! As efficiently as possible, companies must deploy IT to a minimum standard vis-à-vis their competitors. However, good IT deployment without concurrent focus on usage can fall far short of optimizing the business value of IT. Ironically, to leverage the full value of IT in their company, managers need first to conceptualize how to use it – only after that can they align IT deployment with their business strategies and unique capabilities. This change embeds IT capabilities into its operating model or way of doing business.

Competitive advantage goes to those who strive to extract 100 percent of the business value of IT and IM through the improvement of their IO maturity. They seek to capture not only the customary 25 percent of the business value resulting from efficient IT deployment, but also go after the 75 percent of the business value that comes with the effective usage of information and knowledge by their managers, employees, customers and partners.

These five questions challenge business managers to think about leading their company to extract the maximum value from three critical resources – their people, their information and their IT. They are encouraged to treat IT as a powerful 'tool,' but not as the 'solution' to business problems that are fundamentally people-oriented. While we always start sessions with the concerns of managers about IT, we quickly steer the discussion to the fundamental questions about creating business value. We should avoid IT hype, though some business managers will want to discuss it, and focus instead on how effective use of information, people and IT capabilities can accelerate and boost the performance of the company's operating business model and strategy. Once these strategic choices are *visible* to managers, they can consider how they should approach this topic with the right mindset, values and emphasis in their company to maximize its business impact.

The style of executive learning about IT and IM

There are some basic principles that influence my personal style of executive teaching. These 'dos and don'ts' help to create 'face value validity' and credibility with business managers. Business managers will evaluate the content and dialogue during the sessions based on their sense of whether the session leader has a realistic and credible grasp of the topic and knows how to discuss it with them.

1 Avoid 'point in time' views – it's IT's evolution that counts!

At any given moment, IT use can be seen as 'leading edge' or as a 'breakthrough' in the industry.[8] In the late 1990s, it was popular to highlight 'pioneering' examples of internet use as the means of strategic transformation. One could identify a company's deployment of internet portals at a specific point in time and tout its 'innovative' use. Thus, without reference to the actual history of IT deployment and use in the company, isolated uses of 'new technology' were spotlighted as the sources of success. It was impossible to evaluate whether the point in time reference was an isolated example or an aberration. Most experienced business managers are keenly aware that 'what goes up must come down' and so expect disillusionment with some new technology. Session leaders must provide a credible view of these cycles and where IT innovations may be positioned so that managers can properly interpret the business context at any point in time.

2 IT deployment is not a destination, it's part of the business journey

Many managers believe that the deployment of IT projects, such as ERP (Enterprise Resource Planning) or CRM (Customer Relationship Management), is enough to achieve business value. They see the successful 'go live' of a large-scale project as the final destination rather than a single step in the journey. Others get so involved in the complexity of the undertaking that they confuse 'end' (use) with the 'means' (deployment). Still others believe deployment drives organizational change rather than the other way around.

When deeper cultural changes fail to occur in their companies, managers blame IT rather than their own naive views of IT and organizational change. In sum, the session leader must clearly understand this diversity of views of IT and business change and then focus the discussion on the business-change journey rather than IT deployment.

3 Know the difference between an IT innovation in the business and a business innovation that uses IT

Most managers know that innovating with IT for its own sake often leads to disappointing business results. However, the lure of 'new technology' regularly leads to ill-considered projects with little or no business justification. For fear of falling behind – or merely to be 'fashionable' – managers advocate IT innovations before they understand their potential use from a business perspective, in the hope that one will be found. In all these cases, session leaders must understand the difference between a business project using IT for a clear business purpose and an IT project 'searching' for a mission.

4 Build the confidence of business managers that they really can 'manage' IT!

In contrast to other business capabilities, many managers lack confidence in their IT judgment. With its complex and dynamic language, general managers often delegate IT business decisions related to others 'down the line.' In some companies, IT managers purposefully convince general managers that IT is so 'different' that decisions should be left to IT specialists. In other companies, senior managers in their 50s and 60s are only 'lite' users of IT, though working knowledge of IT is moving up the experience curve.

Thus, through examples and cases, session leaders must nurture their confidence that they too can manage IT without being 'experts.' To managers in their late 40s and 50s, it is important to point out that 'they cannot retire without knowing about this subject!'

5 Show managers how to make a 'boring' subject like IT and IM 'exciting' for their company

Many business managers, bored with topics in IT and IM, prefer to delegate them to others. This 'out of sight, out of mind' view implies that there is little or no direct business value in them. As such, the challenge facing session leaders is to inspire managers, under certain business conditions, to focus their attention on managing information and IT in their search for a significant business payback. Why is information collection and maintenance by people in sales and services critical for cross-selling products to customers? How can IT and IM lead to faster and better decision making? Why is it critical for your company to know more about your competitors than they do about you? Why do managers like Michael Dell believe that it all comes down to being customer focused and executing his famous direct model of business, 'information is everything'?[9]

6 Focus on how effective IT and IM deployment and usage are 'essential' to lead a business

The best way to make this point for business managers is a counter-intuitive example. My favorite case for this purpose is CEMEX.[10] Most business managers believe that the cement industry is boring, commoditized, low tech and low growth. However, CEMEX is the third-largest producer of cement in the world and a pioneer in the use of information and IT to drive a branded, customer-driven and process-oriented business model. With the session leader's guidance, business managers come to 'see' the links between IT and IM with a business strategy for growth, the design of global processes with local flexibility and leadership commitment in its execution excellence, with superior business results over 20-plus years. Which, of course, prompts the question, 'If CEMEX can do all this in the cement industry, why can't you do it in yours?'

7 To stimulate debate about the business consequences of information and IT practices, use company examples of successes and failures

Business school cases invariably highlight the best practices of one company. For obvious reasons, companies rarely offer their experiences as 'ineffective business managers.' My favorite case is a side-by-side comparison of the experience of two retail banks over the same five-year period, one effective and one ineffective in using IT and IM as a tool to grow their businesses.[11] This case idea derived from a four-year research project that involved over 100 companies globally, in which we identified wildly contrasting scores on IO maturity. Over the past four years, these cases have been successful in helping to build managerial understanding about effective and ineffective information practices and their impact on cross-selling capabilities and organic growth. In these sessions, teams of managers are also asked to evaluate and score their own companies on IO maturity and performance, with the two banks as anchors for good and poor IO practices.

8 Use historical examples of information/IT deployment and uses that demonstrate their business relevance in the creation of sustainable competitive advantage

Many business managers believe that the topic of competing with information capabilities is a twenty-first-century concern, without much historical precedent. However, while the IT tools have changed, the ability to use information, people and available IT as a key business capability in a company's operating business model has not.

To remind managers of historical precedents and how certain companies achieved sustainable competitive advantage through superior information capabilities, we use video cases of Frito-Lay and Pioneer-Hybred Seed.[12] Each was an information-oriented company that sensed, collected and used customer and market intelligence better than their competitors to develop long-term customer loyalty and repeat sales. I also point out that companies like Wal-Mart, USAA and other market leaders developed similar information-oriented business models going back 15–20 years. In each case, these companies chose information orientation as a key part of their business strategy and execution focus.

The most important point is to provide business managers with a clear view of the information-oriented business model and its link to business results and sustainable advantage. While IT evolves and changes, an information-oriented business model (which uses customer, market, product and operational information better than their rivals) can create and sustain competitive advantage, whether locally or globally.

9 Walk the talk – combine relevant research with business practice

Credibility in executive programs requires that the session leader have *both* academic independence and practitioner experience. Managers respect academic independence: they assume that an educator has seriously studied developments in his field over time and across industries and companies. On the other hand, they also expect educators to have tested the relevance of their ideas and research in the real world, by work with managers and companies. In addition, managers respect educators who have served in executive roles or founded their own companies.[13]

Combining real-world experience with rigorous, but relevant, scientific research provides the credibility to address controversial issues and challenge skeptical managers. For example, at the start of my sessions, many managers disagree with my view that, without a focus on effective use, IT investments and deployment alone will fail to optimize business performance. Exploring contentious issues requires that the session leader combine academic research findings with practical cases, in which managers have addressed usage with deployment successfully, and real-world experience. Managers must feel – not just think – that the session leader 'has been there before' and brings a more objective and broader perspective as well. In executive education, achieving this emotional engagement is as important as marshalling credible arguments and evidence.

Designing programs and sessions on the business value of information and IT

In this section, I will apply the executive learning approach and style guidelines discussed earlier to the design and delivery of an actual company program. The program in Figure 15.5 was developed in 2003 and offered seven times in 2004 to the top executives of a global specialty chemical company. The CIO sponsored the program with a managing board member, who heads a business-oriented IT management committee across the company. The objectives were to develop a common mindset and approach to extract better business value from IT deployment and usage across the company in line with the company's growth objectives.

The company is organized into four product divisions, with 16 lines of business and varied operational models. During the 1990s, it transformed itself from a bulk chemical company into a specialty chemical company with over 40 divestitures and acquisitions. Over the last three years, the challenge has been to create a more homogeneous management style and approach across the company, while recognizing the diversity of past organizational cultures within it. The program participants were senior executives from the division and business units, including their DIOs (Division Information Officers) and BIOs (Business Information Officers). The program was designed to raise the level of awareness of how to extract better business value from not just IT deployment, but also information usage in the company's diverse businesses. For the first time, both senior managers and the CIO, DIOs and BIOs had to develop a shared mindset and approach for IT and IM.

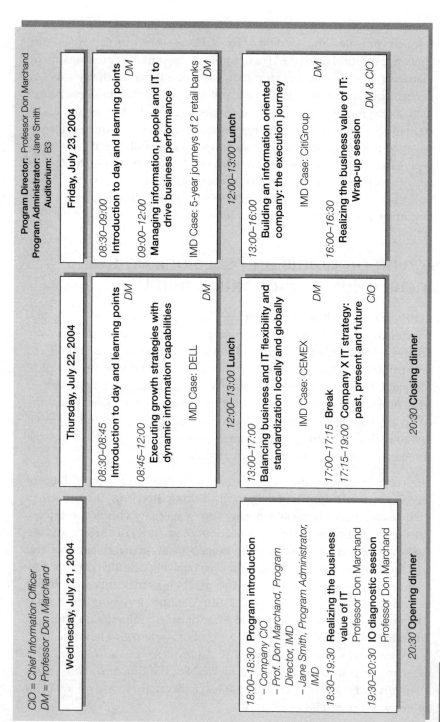

Figure 15.5 Business value of IT program for senior managers, 21–23 July 2004

After the program introduction by the CIO and IMD program director, the first session explores the five key questions set out above. This challenges prevailing management views and concerns, and initiates a dialogue to answer these questions during the next two days. During the first evening, the executive participants complete the Information Orientation (IO) Diagnostic online.[14] The IO Diagnostic results are used in the third day of the program, but the experience of completing the IO Diagnostic sets the tone – to focus on business issues and practices rather than solely on IT deployment concerns.

Day two focuses on the relationship between business growth, customer focus and a company's capabilities to effectively use information and knowledge. The intent of this session is to discuss the link between being information-oriented and successfully executing a business operating model that is customer-focused, multi-channel and both local and global. The Dell case illustrates how over 20 years Michael Dell learned to deploy and use information, people and IT practices to execute his 'direct' model.[15] It focuses on Dell's obsession with customers, service, execution and information capabilities. The executive dialogue zeros in on the role of information, people and IT capabilities to execute growth strategies in specialty chemicals. The session leader asks managers to focus on their business unit's operating model for value creation with customers. How can improvements in information capabilities drive organic growth?

In the afternoon session, the session leader exposes the business managers to various approaches of company organization, from a multi-local to a global enterprise; then the session leader asks them to assess their company's progress in balancing business flexibility and standardization on a local, regional *and* global basis.[16] The CEMEX case is used to show CEMEX's journey from a local, then regional, and finally global company, which required the continual re-balancing of business flexibility and standardization to lower the costs of operating the business while growing. Regarding these concerns, the session leader invites managers to consider where the company needs to be in the next three to five years.

This session sets the stage for the CIO to present the past, present and future of the company's IT deployment and to raise questions regarding the company's use of IT and its capability to enhance the different business models of the company. The CIO is completely candid about the IT strategy and focus of the company and is open to discuss relevant concerns with senior managers. Typically, the CIO is joined by a managing board member, who emphasizes his support of the program and the IT/business discussion.

The board member's presence re-enforces senior management support for a change in mindset and approach across the company.

On day three, the sessions focus on the Information Orientation Maturity approach and the interpretation of individual and group results of the company's IO Diagnostic. The IMD Two Bank case illustrates the impact of high and low IO Maturity on business performance.[17] With their IO Maturity results in hand, they discuss the strengths and weaknesses of *their* company. The afternoon session uses the IMD Citigroup case to focus on what a business unit manager and their team can do to improve the information, people and IT practices without necessarily waiting for the group to change.[18] The session leader challenges each manager to identify a strategic improvement initiative that he or she should advocate for their business unit or function.

Finally, the program ends with a call to action by the participants with each other and the CIO as a 'team expression' of commitment and concern with the learning points of the program.

The success of the program design has been in managers recognizing that it is all about 'business,' not just IT, and success depends on *their* under-standing, support and involvement with *both* deployment and usage improvements to optimize business impact. Most importantly, the business management approach to deployment and usage of information and IT is being disseminated and implemented throughout the company. In sum, the program takes the seemingly 'boring' subject of IT and IM, and engages senior managers to accept ownership of their mindsets and actions to improve information capabilities for competitive advantage.

Conclusion: The business value of IT is all about management mindset

Over the last ten years in management education, research and learning, I have concluded that, to fully realize the business value of IT, management must understand and feel confident and motivated to deal with the deployment and use of information, people and IT in their companies in ways that impact the business strategies and capabilities of the businesses. The periodic waves of IT hype and disillusionment, as created by the IT industry and reflected in the business media, are opportunities for business managers to 'test and learn,' but do not offer the 'answers' to their business problems. Business management and leadership require choices to effectively deploy and use the three basic resources of the firm – its information, people and IT – to improve business performance and execute the 'basics.' That is what effective leadership and management are about.

Key take-aways

■ The biggest challenge in teaching general managers about how IT and information management can add value to their businesses is overcoming the existing management mindset that IT is all about deployment of 'solutions' and that it is 'boring'; in fact IT and information management are tools to aid business performance, not 'answers,' and how they are used matters more than deployment.

■ Effective teaching programs are designed to build the confidence of business managers that they really can manage IT, and extract better business value from IT usage and deployment. The key is to focus on how IT helps executives to manage real business issues.

■ Establishing the validity of the content and credibility of the educator is critical to engaging executives effectively. This requires a combination of real-world examples, relevant research that is clearly linked to business practice and educators that combine academic independence and practitioner experience.

Notes

1 Carr, N. (2004) *Does IT Matter?* Boston: Harvard Business School Press.
2 Most business school academics in the 'IS'or 'IT' field focus on issues related to the role of the IT function in the business and deployment concerns as noted here.
3 Marchand, D.A., Kettinger, W.J. and Rollins, J.D. (2001) *Making the Invisible Visible: How companies win with the right information, people and IT.* New York and London: John Wiley & Sons; and Marchand, D.A., Kettinger W.J. and Rollins, J.D. (2001) *Information Orientation: The Link to Business Performance.* Oxford: Oxford University Press.
4 Marchand, D.A. (2004) Extracting the business value of IT: It is usage, not just deployment that counts! *Journal of Financial Transformation*, Issue 11, pp. 126–27.
5 Brynjolsson, E. and Hitt, L. (2002) Intangible assets: computers and organizational capital. MIT Sloan School of Management, Center for e-Business (working paper).
6 The IO Diagnostic is a trademarked product of enterpriseIQ based in Lausanne, Switzerland, a spin-off of the IMD research project that developed the Information Orientation Maturity Framework. See, Marchand, D.A. et al. *Information Orientation*, op. cit.
7 The IO Diagnostic is a trademarked product of enterpriseIQ based in Lausanne, Switzerland, a spin-off of the IMD research project that developed the Information Orientation Maturity Framework. See, Marchand, D.A., et al. *Information Orientation*, op. cit.
8 Enron, before its collapse, was a very good example of such a company.

9 Marchand, D.A., Kettinger, W.J. and Chung, R. (2003) *Dell's Direct Model: Everything to do with information.* Lausanne, Switzerland: International Institute for Management Development. IMD Case-3–1149 (August 8).

10 Marchand, D.A., Kettinger, W.J. and Chung, R. (2002) *CEMEX: Global Growth Through Superior Information Capabilities.* Lausanne, Switzerland: International Institute for Management Development. IMD Case GM 953 (January 23).

11 Marchand D.A., Panseri P. and Paddack K. (2001) *Managing Information, People and IT to Improve Performance: The Five-Year Journeys of Two Retail Banks.* Lausanne, Switzerland: International Institute for Management Development. IMD Case GM 847 (April 5).

12 The Frito-Lay video was produced by the company in 1994; the Pioneer-Hybred Seed video was produced by the Harvard Business School in 1996.

13 I currently serve as Chairman, founder and President of enterpriseIQ, Lausanne, Switzerland.

14 The IO Diagnostic and Benchmark is a trademarked product of enterpriseIQ in Lausanne, Switzerland. See www.enterpriseiq.com.

15 Marchand, D.A., et al., IMD Dell Case, op. cit.

16 Marchand D.A. (2004) Seeking Global Advantage with Information Management and Technology. *In*: Lane H.W. et al. (eds.) *Handbook of Global Management.* London: Blackwell Publishing, pp. 300–21.

17 Marchand D.A., et al., IMD Two Retail Banks Case, op. cit.

18 Marchand D.A., Kettinger W.J. and Chung R. (2004) *Citigroup's CEEMEA Sales and Trading Unit: Rapid business Improvement Through Effective Use of Information, People and IT.* Lausanne, Switzerland: International Institute for Management Development. IMD Case-3–1306 (June 16).

16

Adapting a case learning script to different purposes: The example of a fierce 'product battle'

Jean-Philippe Deschamps[1]

Summary

This chapter highlights how to effectively adapt a learning script to different program settings. The author draws from the example of *Barco Projection Systems (A): Worldwide Niche Marketing*, a top-selling HBS case. By deconstructing it, he shows us how the case offers a business situation that is valid for different teaching purposes with equally successful results. This example takes you through a broad analysis of the case learning script and the impact on participants when fully engaged.

Good teaching cases are normally conceived and scripted to illustrate a specific business situation and dilemma. They will, typically, describe the context of a company and the challenges to be addressed by management at a particular point in time, given external or internal pressures. Conversations in class will usually focus on the range of options available to managers to address the problematic situation.

With a good case, learning occurs on, at least, three instances:

1 When managers confront each other's perspectives on the issues in the case and argue in favor of or against the proposed solutions, thus discovering a broader range of viewpoints than they might each have initially thought of.

2 When participants hear and reflect on what happened – i.e. what decisions were actually made and what was the outcome – thus drawing lessons from an ex-post rationalization point of view.

3   When the instructor, generalizing from the case, introduces a conceptual framework that will help managers in the class analyze similar situations to the one in the case, which they could face in their company, and choose the right option.

An excellent teaching case has all of the above features, of course, plus three additional characteristics that contribute to a unique learning experience:

1   They tend to raise a broad range of issues, thus allowing several instructors each to use the same case for their own teaching purposes with various audiences and with different learning scripts.

2   They have a script that contains a touch of realistic drama, which encourages participants to empathize with the situation, identifying with the management team featured in the case and stimulating them to formulate the 'appropriate' course of action.

3   They allow the instructor to design a learning script that will capture the imagination of participants, engage the class in the issues at stake and lead them to associate their learning with the 'emotional highs' that occur in the session.

The Harvard Business School case *Barco Projection Systems (A): Worldwide Niche Marketing*[2] meets all these criteria. In spite of its age, it remains a best-selling teaching case; with it, faculty members can consistently deliver a lively session and a great learning experience. It tends also to be remembered by participants – MBA students or executives – long after the program ended, as one of the 'highs' of their program.

To explain how one can build a great learning session around the Barco case, first I will summarize the case, highlighting the dramatic elements in the story. Second, I will outline the aspects of this case that can be used in different program settings and from different perspectives. Indeed, even though the case ends with a set of specific decisions to be made, depending on the functional needs of the instructor and the program theme, different aspects can be explored at the appropriate level of depth. Third, I will present a typical learning script and explain how we can embed the learning into an exciting experience.

The case and the case writer's intent in a nutshell: A high-tech product battle, with company survival at stake

Barco is a small Belgian electronics manufacturer that pioneered the market for professional video projectors. At the time of the case, the company dominated the high-end 'data' and 'graphic' segments of that market. Industrial customers in those segments purchased relatively high-priced, sophisticated projectors for use in demanding applications. These projectors were sold principally through highly qualified 'systems resellers.' In the lower-priced 'video' and 'data' segments of the market, Barco faced competition from several large Japanese manufacturers, notably Sony, the overall market leader. These 'mainstream' segments covered projectors for video entertainment applications and basic computer data projection. They were typically sold through so-called 'box movers,' i.e. dealers providing a lower level of service than 'system dealers.'

In the high-end 'graphic' market – a segment it had created – Barco competed predominantly on the basis of its technological capabilities. Through sheer electronic wizardry, the small Barco was able to:

■ Extract superior picture quality from Sony components than the giant Japanese company could itself obtain; and

■ Be the first to match, with a higher scan rate, the growing graphic display power of the source computers to which its projectors connected.

Barco's customers were accustomed to seeing the company, a recognized technology leader in its industry, at the forefront of innovation, e.g. its projectors established a new standard in scan rate and picture quality. This lasted until Sony unexpectedly unveiled its own high-end 'Super-Data' projector. Sony's projector offered superior performance both in scan rate and in picture quality. Even worse, rumors were circulating that the new Sony projector would be priced much lower than Barco's top line.

This situation has great potential as business drama. To start with, on seeing a demonstration of Sony's new super-projector during a professional show, Barco's management was stunned. In addition, Barco's technicians were flabbergasted by the outstanding picture quality of the 'Super-Data' projector, the result of a new eight-inch tube designed by Sony Components. From a business standpoint, Barco's managers immediately realized that the company stood to lose a considerable part of its sales and profits to

Sony, particularly if rumors about its pricing were true. Indeed, the survival of the business was clearly at stake; this is what creates tension and excitement in class. How could a little 'David' survive the attack of a powerful 'Goliath'?

An intriguing question comes immediately to the mind of the case reader: How did Barco managers fail to anticipate Sony's attack, given the many obvious clues? Namely:

- With Barco's high-end graphic segment growing much faster than Sony's more mainstream segments, a growth-hungry 'predator' like Sony would surely smell a market opportunity.

- Given the strength of Sony's brand association with innovation, the Japanese company's managers were probably not willing to continue to be perceived as a 'technology follower' in projectors.

- Though months earlier Sony components had proposed to sell its new eight-inch tube to Barco, the Belgian company had postponed its use because it was pursuing another project based on a seven-inch tube, Sony's previous technology generation.

The case ends with a crisis meeting of Barco's video projector managers, who must prepare an action plan to respond to Sony's challenge for presentation to the company's board of directors. In essence, the case forces the reader to jump into the shoes of the Barco managers during an emergency. Given the complexity of the industry and the abundance of details, the case creates a particularly uncomfortable situation for a non-prepared reader.

The case writer's intent: Contrast competitive product policies

Barco's teaching note recommends using the case to discuss: 'Issues in the product policy and price dynamics of a technology-based industry.' It continues with a warning:

A very complex case, Barco can be used only after students have a thorough understanding of the fundamentals of new product development. It presents the opportunity to develop student skills in evaluating alternative research and development investment, how to anticipate competitive actions, and how to retain market leadership.[3]

The case does, indeed, require some hand-holding of the participants until they feel comfortable with the case facts and issues. Nonetheless, it has been my experience that, provided it is carefully introduced, the case lends itself to a broader range of learning than indicated in the authors' teaching note, even for participants with limited personal exposure to product strategy or product development issues.

Exploiting the case's richness in different program settings

1 Marketing management course

As claimed by its authors, the Barco case primarily deals with product strategy or policy. However, because it covers both product and pricing decisions – two of the classic four Ps of any marketing strategy – as well as touching upon channel issues (the third P for Place), it fits naturally into a marketing course.

Several aspects of the case are particularly valuable in a marketing class. First, there is the issue of market segmentation, e.g. how has Barco segmented its market and how different is it from Sony's segmentation? Raising this question leads to a whole range of issues which may not be immediately perceived by the class. Most participants argue that Barco's segmentation model is purely technology-driven, that is, it is dictated by an external technological factor: the projector's scan rate. Usually, they understand the rationale behind having created a high-end 'graphic' segment, i.e. to extract a higher price premium in terms of price per kilohertz than in the medium-end 'data' segment. However, very few detect, behind Barco's model, a true customer segmentation approach: Barco's determination to identify and serve 'hard-to-please' customers with demanding applications often goes unrecognized. Stressing that allows the instructor to explain why Barco does not seem to be paying much attention to 'ease of use' as a product attribute, in contrast to its obsession with image quality. The class has to understand that demanding applications require an ability to adjust settings very precisely, something that runs counter to simplicity of installation and operation.

Second, the case can address the concept of 'market niche,' which is often loosely defined. It is directly derived from the segmentation model. Managers can appreciate that, as long as its size remains unattractive to the mainstream players, each industrial application in need of a tailored projector can be considered a market niche. The key learning point emerges from the notion that some of today's niches may actually become tomorrow's mainstream segments. For Barco, the performance standard of the high-end projector is rapidly becoming a mainstream feature.

Discussing Barco's niche strategy leads naturally to the concept of differentiating its 'value proposition,' i.e. what is unique and attractive in Barco's offering as compared to its competitors and at what price. The instructor can also explore the capabilities, both technical and commercial, that a niche player must master to best serve its customers. At this stage, it becomes clear to the class that, in spite of its small size, Barco has been able to prosper thanks to its ability to develop a coherent offering and to align all the elements of its marketing mix – particularly its distribution channels – to serve a well-defined set of unusually demanding customers.

2 Innovation management course

Product strategy is the starting point of any structured innovation effort because it must be translated into technology choices and product development options. The Barco case is, therefore, equally well suited to support a course on innovation and new product development and can illustrate a wide range of issues in product strategy, which I have summarized in Figure 16.1. The diagram will be used as the framework of my session wrap-up.

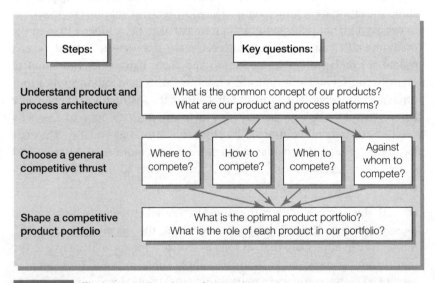

Figure 16.1 The key questions in product strategy

Source: Jean-Philippe Deschamps

The Barco case lends itself to a two-pronged approach. On one hand, the case as written focuses the reader's primary attention on short-term or tactical product decisions, i.e. what should management propose to limit the impact of Sony's attack? On the other hand, behind this lie more fundamental product strategy questions:

■ How does Barco compete effectively against Sony in the long term given the huge difference in resources?

■ Is a high-end niche strategy a viable option in that industry and, if so, under what conditions?

■ What capabilities does Barco need to master in order to sustain a long-term niche strategy?

To exploit the full richness of the case, I like to combine these two perspectives: the short-term tactical response to Sony's attack and the long-term prospect of adopting a technological niche strategy. This requires a solid half-day session of four hours. With a class of seasoned product managers and experienced R&D executives, the session may be extended even further to leave room for a detailed review of long-term strategy issues.

However, given the complexity of the case, two issues must be addressed:

1 How can the instructor quickly engage participants who are unfamiliar with the world of high tech or those who read the case casually (which happens with busy executives)? In other words, how can the instructor avoid a boring fact-unbundling exercise, while making sure participants have grasped the key aspects of a complex case?

2 How can the instructor set the stage in order to emphasize the longer-term context within which tactical product strategy decisions have to be made? In other words, how can the instructor prevent people from rushing into product battle decisions – something they immediately long to do – without having considered the longer-term aspects of the issue?

Designing an exciting learning script

My favorite learning script addresses the above challenges in four parts:

1 Getting attention and understanding the context of the product battle.

2 Challenging participants to come up with a coherent set of responses.

3 Engaging participants to explain their short-term tactical decisions.

4 Reflecting on the longer-term strategy issues.

Act 1: Getting attention and understanding the context of the product battle

The initial task is to help the class grasp the key facts of this complex case. A user-friendly way to achieve that objective is to look at the big picture first, prior to going into the details. To help people absorb it, I write the critical case elements on a sideboard ahead of time; then I refer to them during the discussion until they are understood. This can be done by drawing the three market segments – video, data and graphics – as three distinct columns on the board and then filling the columns with the essential case facts and figures, i.e.:

- Competing products and their characteristics (scan rate and price).
- Market shares of the key competitors by segment.
- Breakdown of market size and growth by segment.
- Breakdown of Barco's unit sales, revenues and margins by segment.

The case offers a marvelous quote from which to start the discussion. A senior Barco manager says: *'All our projections were based on the assumption that Sony would respect our "vision" of the marketplace!'* This sentence, which most participants pick up when reading the case, inevitably triggers giggles and remarks about Barco's naivety or even arrogance. I want, however, to prevent the class from jumping immediately into a judgmental mode – a classic temptation – and so I use that remark to start discussing Barco's vision:

- Its vision of the industry:
  - What makes it tick, i.e. what are its key drivers?
  - How can it be segmented?
- Its vision of itself:
  - What kind of game does it play?
  - What are its core capabilities?
- Its vision of Sony:
  - How does Barco look at Sony as a competitor?
  - What is its apparent game plan and what are its capabilities and strengths?

I then ask the class to look at it from Sony's perspective (i.e. on the industry, on itself, and on Barco), contrasting the companies' visions. Starting with a systematic confrontation of visions is a useful way to build an overview of both the industry and the two competing viewpoints. Participants come to understand what led Barco to develop its vision and they discover:

- The inner logic behind Barco's segmentation model and its chosen basis of competition, in contrast to those of Sony.

- How two business models – the technological niche player and the mainstream volume manufacturer – can coexist in the same industry.

- The fact that Barco, far from being negligent or arrogant, had actually developed an apparently logical scenario as to where Sony should attack them.

- The trap into which Barco fell, i.e. assuming that Sony would continue to play the game in the same way as they had done in the past.

A key additional learning point undoubtedly comes from the observation that competitive intelligence is not only about knowing what competitors are doing, but also understanding how they look at the market and how they think, as this will influence future actions.

At this stage of the discussion, once Barco's and Sony's visions have been clearly articulated on the board, the class should be fully engaged. Participants understand the battle scene and what is at stake for Barco: its sheer survival. The next step is to send them into study groups to devise their response to Sony's challenge. However, before doing so, I want the class to clearly recognize that Barco's pricing and product development responses will depend upon the price level at which Sony introduces its new 'Super-Data' projector.

Act 2: Challenging participants to come up with a coherent set of responses

The group assignment that I use is the one proposed by the case author. It raises three simple, but interconnected questions:

1 At what price would you expect Sony to launch its new projector?

2 What price changes, if any, would you propose on Barco's current products?

3 What product development options would you recommend to Barco as a response?

Participants quickly understand why and how these three questions are interconnected. As I indicated above, the launch price of the new Sony projector will determine whether adjustments in Barco's price are warranted and where its product development process should focus. The case indicates a rumored price range that is wide enough to leave the reader highly uncertain about the future positioning of the 'Super-Data.' This forces everyone to test his/her own interpretation of Sony's vision and intent. If Sony's actual price is on the higher end, then it will threaten only Barco's 'graphic' segment. If, on the other hand, the price is in the lower range, then both Barco's 'data' and 'graphic' segments are dangerously at risk.

Prior to dividing into study groups, I pull out a board with the three development options described in the case, a time line, and the key features of each option. This is done to help the class visualize Barco's product development choices. In addition, I like to heighten the sense of drama – and therefore the motivation of the study groups – by introducing the three options on a 'panic scale,' from the 'no-panic' option 1, to the 'mild-panic' option 2 and the 'wild-panic' option 3.

To encourage study group participants to focus and be concrete, I prefer to define the deliverable output of their study group in terms of three or four numbers:

- The price at which they expect Sony to introduce its new projector, based on what they believe to be Sony's chosen strategic positioning.

- If Barco were to change its prices in response to Sony's challenge, which of course it may choose to avoid, the new prices of the two current Barco projectors.

- The development option they would recommend.

In my experience, participants rarely agree immediately on a common group answer to the three questions in their assignment. But the short time allotted to their group exercise (45 to 60 minutes) forces them to take a position, almost by instinct. As a consequence, they tend to come back on an emotional high, and they are all curious to discover what other groups are recommending.

Act 3: Engaging participants to explain their short-term tactical decisions

To capitalize on the excitement and their curiosity regarding the – usually divergent – conclusions of others in the class, I like to display the answers of all groups on a blackboard. I then launch the discussion by provoking participants into defending their conclusions and their underlying assumptions.

In most cases, predictions of Sony's introductory price span the entire range of rumors. Some groups expect the 'Super-Data' to be priced on the high end – why should Sony relinquish big profit opportunities since they will beat

Barco anyway on a price/performance basis? Others advance the opposite viewpoint, suggesting that Sony will adopt a very low 'predatory' price to kick Barco out of the market. By offering an unbeatable price for superior performance, they argue, Sony can dominate the high-end segment, perhaps alone.

If the class chemistry works well, a lively discussion pits supporters of low prices against advocates of high prices, with the medium-price proponents arguing for an intermediate position. I let the discussion go without too much intervention, simply noting the arguments of each group, all of them valid. This is what makes this case exceptional! Occasionally I fuel the debate by stressing those case facts that support one or the other position.

Next, the discussion on Barco's response (i.e. pricing adjustments), although relevant in an innovation class, tends to be more elaborate in a marketing class. The issue focuses on whether or not to prepare for Sony's market introduction with a pre-emptive price cut on the two Barco projectors under threat. In this discussion, pragmatic proponents of aggressive price cuts – mainly to pacify Barco dealers – debate vigorously against the 'high-end strategy purists,' who reject such a 'defeatist' approach. To extract the class from this binary dilemma, I typically ask for defensive tactics that would increase customer value while keeping prices untouched (e.g. offering free service).

The most passionate discussion, however, often centers on the product development options. Should Barco first launch the 'new' data product already in the works, before pursuing a leapfrog approach on the graphic side (the 'no panic' option)? Or should it delay the 'new' data product launch, developing instead a boosted version of its data projector for the graphic segment with the aim of matching Sony's performance (the 'mild panic' option)? Finally, should it cancel all ongoing projects in order to allocate its resources to a crash program to beat Sony's performance (the 'wild panic' option)?

Because all three options have their pros and cons in terms of benefits and risks, the discussion can become extremely lively. As a consequence, and depending on their management background and risk propensity, participants tend to back their chosen option with great determination:

■ Risk-averse managers and, not surprisingly, managers with an R&D background typically advocate the first option. It would be foolish, they argue, to squander a valuable new product project one month before its planned launch, particularly with customers' orders in hand. Furthermore, confident in the company's ability to leapfrog and beat the new Sony products in a few months' time, they wish to minimize Barco's strategic risk, i.e. of not having anything to exhibit at the upcoming trade show.

■ Pragmatic managers choose the second option as an honorable (if hardly glorious) compromise or escape route. Feeling sufficiently comforted by the limited short-term risks of that option, they accept its modest benefits and longer-term shortcomings, i.e. the risk of damaging its image as the technological leader.

■ In spite of its huge uncertainties, more entrepreneurial and risk-prone managers favor the third option. They are uncompromising about the need for Barco to maintain its technological leadership position at all costs as the only way to secure its long-term viability.

At this stage, with heated opinions erupting on all sides, my role is to keep the discussion orderly and moving – I want to ensure that the participants go beyond their instinctive viewpoints to explore the implications of all three options.

The best way to regain control of the class, when the discussion appears never-ending, is to ask: 'Would you like to hear what happened and what Barco decided?' This question usually triggers a resounding 'Yes!' followed by an eerie silence. The announcement of each choice – that Barco selected the third option, that Sony priced its 'Super-Data' low, etc. – is greeted by hoorays from some, disappointed sighs from others. The ending of the case, in which Barco demonstrates its stunning ability to leapfrog and hence to regain its challenged leadership position, usually leaves the class highly perplexed. Despite the story, speedy and flexible little Davids are seldom expected to beat Goliaths' power, particularly if the latter enjoy Sony's kind of technological resources and brand equity!

At this stage, I typically want to give my interpretation of Sony's and Barco's decisions, supported by a videotaped interview of Barco's Chief Operating Officer. In hindsight, the learning points look obvious: good companies instinctively tend to display a great deal of continuity in their strategy and rely on their core capabilities. Immersed in the heat of their argument, some participants forget that and, obviously, overreact.

Act 4: Reflecting on the longer-term strategy issues

Despite Barco's escape from the trap that Sony had sprung, I like to stress that the company ultimately lost half of its market share to Sony in the year in question. This, combined with the deep economic recession of

1990–1991, nearly bankrupted Barco. Indeed, without a major capital infusion from the Flemish Development Organization, the company would not have survived. This usually sparks an acute awareness in the class of the potential disasters that can result from faulty assumptions regarding competitors' strategies. After a period of intense excitement triggered by the sense of urgency in the case, the class is now ready to pause and reflect on what happened. Why did Barco suddenly take its eyes off the ball? What did management miss? Can we pinpoint a moment in time when the seeds of the drama were planted?

Though this part of the discussion is relatively short, it is essential for achieving the 'ahas' that characterize good cases and engraving the learning experience in the participants' memories. To stimulate their curiosity, I refer to a largely unnoticed exhibit in the case – Barco's product roadmap history – and ask the class to identify a turning point in the company's product development strategy. Some managers notice that, a couple of years prior to Sony's attack, Barco had shifted its product development emphasis to its medium- and low-end lines. That change, triggered by the need to maintain competitiveness in its whole product range, actually led to the neglect of its top-end graphic projector for more than three years.

At this stage, I like the class to imagine a product committee meeting at which these product renewal priorities were discussed. To enable them to visualize the scene more vividly, I ask them to debate as two product managers who are competing for product development resources: the one in charge of data products (the medium line) and the other of graphic projectors (the top line); both would argue for the renewal of their respective products on the basis of different sets of criteria. We then discuss the justifications that each product manager advances to support their desired product decision. Not surprisingly, the evaluation usually leads to a tie because both products actually need to be renewed with equal urgency, but for different strategic reasons: the data line needs to be renewed because it accounts for half of Barco's sales and profits; the graphic line because it is the flagship product and symbol of the company's technological leadership.

Once the class understands that both products score equally in terms of urgency, the next question I raise is: Why did Barco management decide to focus on the data line, a choice that almost killed the business? The class can seldom answer that question. Barco chose to renew its data line, I inform them, principally because it *expected* Sony to attack them in that part of the market! Once they are exposed to that perspective, then the loop with the first part of the session is completed. Barco was so steeped in its own vision of itself and of Sony that it failed to consider any other option than the one *they* had decided would 'make the most sense for Sony' to choose.

That ending of the case discussion usually triggers a number of thought-provoking questions regarding the dangers and merits of strong visions. After this case experience, participants have no difficulty reflecting on their own situation: they have waged a fierce 'product battle' and been forced, under stress, to react to a survival emergency. They have witnessed the dramatic consequences of bad product decisions, and understood what made the company opt for the wrong choice. Hopefully, this will make them better prepared to challenge their own visions and assumptions in future.

Key take-aways

- Effective cases allow for multilevel learning through opinion sharing and discussion, reflection and situation analysis.

- A good case must engage participants with a problem, management team and decisions with which they identify and can feel as their own.

- The learning script can be adapted to different program settings.

- The learning experience intensifies as participants are exposed to new perspectives and outcomes not contemplated before.

- Cases are an even more powerful learning tool when a conceptual framework can be drawn to analyze similar situations.

Notes

1 The author wishes to acknowledge the contribution of Professor Nirmalya Kumar, formerly at IMD, for his contribution on how to make that case an exciting teaching and learning experience.
2 Case prepared by Research Associate Krista McQuade under the supervision of Professor Rowland Moriarty, Harvard Business School, 1991, ref.: 9–591–133. Harvard case material can be ordered by email (custserv@hbsp.harvard.edu), by telephone (+1 800 545 7685), by fax (+1 617 783 7666) or by mail (60 Harvard Way, Boston, MA 02163, USA). Complete information on ordering Harvard HBSP material can also be found at the following webpage: www.hbsp.harvard.edu/b01/en/academic/edu_order-serv.jhtml.
3 Teaching Note for Barco, Harvard Business School, 1991, ref.: 9–591–133.

17

Running effective group assignments

Ralf W. Seifert[1] and Dominique Turpin[2]

Summary

Study groups are an effective and integral part of many teaching sessions, particularly case-based ones. Group work provides participants with increased interest and involvement in the session, by allowing for more in-depth discussion and greater sharing of experience than would be the case in a larger plenary session. Creating the greatest possible diversity in the composition of the groups is key to stimulating this in-group discussion and reflection. However, while group work has the potential to enrich and enhance the quality of learning, not all study group discussions deliver the value-added experience that participants expect. In this chapter, the authors draw on their personal experience of integrating group assignments into larger sessions and offer key insights into what it takes to run a study group effectively, as well as advice and practical tips on what to do to ensure that the group work matches participants' expectations.

Once left on their own, you never know what a group of executives might do. You could find yourself challenged, when attempting to integrate group assignments into a planned session, to stage a simple, decent learning experience, let alone the best possible one! Nonetheless, participants greatly value, and indeed expect, opportunities for parallel in depth discussions and small-group experience sharing, whether for cultural reasons or as a welcome change of pace in longer programs. You have to relinquish control, and then somehow seamlessly integrate the groups back into your session, though you can manage neither the process nor the results directly.

Introduction

As educators, we regularly use study groups, in which the experience and judgment calls of participants are as important as the theoretical knowledge and formal concepts provided by a facilitator. They serve to discuss case studies and to stage business simulations, role playing, negotiation exercises and so on, hence forming an integral part of specific session designs. Usually guided by a simple group assignment and time constraints, they provide an intensive knowledge-sharing experience that requires substantial commitment from all participants.

Most importantly, study groups can significantly enrich the quality of the learning experience by engaging the interest and deepening the involvement of most participants, as they anticipate, carry out, and afterwards discuss a group assignment in a plenary session debriefing. In case study discussions, an effective group assignment can generate far more intense, yet less structured, learning sessions than could occur in a large group setting of 30 to 60 people. However, not every study group delivers on its promise! Unacceptable outcomes, bad group dynamics, and even simple frustration can arise, hindering or stalling the learning experience. Study groups rarely, if ever, work automatically – so watch out!

In this chapter, we present our views on how to run effective study groups as integral parts of case-based sessions. The discussion is placed in the context of long, open-enrollment programs, where participants are drawn from many industries and companies. Specifically, we address the following questions:

1　Why do study groups enrich learning experiences?

2　What does it take to run them effectively?

3　When might study groups fail to deliver on our expectations?

Although the chapter reflects our personal views, these are enriched by many informal conversations and some structured interviews with other IMD faculty members. We conclude with selected lessons learned, drawn from our personal experience as directors of long and intensive open-enrollment programs such as the 10-month Master for Business Administration (MBA), the Program for Executive Development (PED, two modules of five weeks each), and the Mastering Technology Enterprise (MTE) program (three modules of three weeks each).

There are a number of closely related themes that we will not cover explicitly in this chapter, including the idiosyncrasies of managing group dynamics;[3] specialized group assignments, such as simulations and negotiations (please see Chapter 19 of this book on negotiation simulations[4] by Professor Bettina Büchel); and group projects in custom-designed executive programs (please see Chapter 20 of this book on client initiated projects in partnership programs[5] by Professor Robert Collins).

Why do study groups enrich learning experiences?

Why study groups?

Study groups serve a multitude of learning purposes including:

- Helping participants to get to know one another more fully.
- Changing the rhythm of a long session or program.
- Increasing participant involvement, especially of those who prefer to speak up in a smaller group setting for cultural, personal or language-skill reasons.
- Acknowledging the value of the participants' experience, implicitly communicating that they are being taken seriously and that we are building on and incorporating their insights.
- Raising the quality of subsequent discussions by leveraging this sharing of experience and the forming of opinion.
- Providing a test-bed outside the classroom to refine one's thinking, assess other people's insights, and practice collaborating to build a group consensus for later presentation.
- Getting executives to take and formulate a position, individually or as a team.
- Providing time for reflection to think through more complex questions.

The extra dimensions that study groups add are reflected in the feedback from executives, for example:

The study groups enable me to ask basic questions I would not dare to ask in a plenary session. I am a marketing manager and I don't really have a strong background in finance. It can be a bit embarrassing for me to ask so-called naive questions in front of the "experts." In study groups, it's easier to ask a finance colleague for help without making the rest of the class lose their time.

As a Japanese participant, it is difficult for me to make significant contributions in class in a plenary session. It is not really part of my culture to volunteer one's opinion in a big forum. However, I feel more comfortable to speak up in smaller groups when my colleagues ask for my opinion.

The study group is truly an enriching experience for me. When I prepare a case study all by myself, I can normally form an opinion about what the manager in the case should do. However, I can't always be sure that what I am suggesting is right. The study group provides me with an opportunity to hear other colleagues provide different answers and to challenge my hypotheses. It is not rare to find in the study group another participant who has gone through an experience similar to the one described in the case. I can then benefit from another example and get more learning before going into a plenary session and share more.

Indeed, most if not all participants attach significant value to study groups as an integral part of an overall session and program design – if managed correctly.

Different settings for study groups

While study groups serve multiple objectives, they also vary in type in accordance with the learning experience that is desired. For example, study groups are used as: an integral part of case study discussions typically followed by plenary-session debriefings; as standalone negotiation exercises; for business simulations; in role-playing exercises (e.g. in managing conflict); for work on company-specific projects that translate session content into a plan for action; and even for peer consulting on real-life cases faced by participants.

Study groups also represent a powerful means for participants to give and receive feedback. An example of a group dynamics tool used in long executive programs is the 'Desert Survival Exercise,' a group decision-making game that highlights the role of effective group process in the quality of decision outcomes. Participants must first make some individual decisions regarding a particular situation and then decide jointly on what actions to take as a group. For a better learning experience in this context, the participants are videotaped, which allows the exploration of unconscious, as well as conscious, behaviors.

What makes effective study groups (composition, size, mix)

When composing a study group, diversity is crucially important to promote energy and enrich learning with new perspectives. Here, we have the opportunity to 'blend' groups of participants from virtually every sector of industry and geography, ranging from young managers with a few years' experience to board members of leading global corporations. No single business approach or cultural background dominates. However, diversity can also create closed or narrow cliques – we need to pay continuous attention to the composition and management of discussion groups, project teams, working meals, classroom seating, or any other group activity. To gain greatest benefit from group interactions, we typically bring groups together based on four key criteria:

■ **Group Size**: Getting the right size is one of the most important elements of effective learning. A group of less than five participants is unlikely to generate enough discussion and confrontations of ideas. However, with more than seven participants, chaos is likely to result!

■ **Functions and talents**: Mixing skills and experience is likely to generate higher-quality discussions, as many perspectives are introduced. Normally, we avoid putting only accountants or marketers together, as this would limit the perspectives, discussion and ultimately the learning potential. We favor cross-functional learning and communication. A balance of talents is the surest way to maximize learning.

■ **Nationalities**: Similarly, putting people from diverse nationalities together is a good way to ensure diverse views and peer learning.

■ **Group chemistry**: The idea here is to develop a good balance between different personalities (for example, introverts and extraverts; outspoken participants with quieter ones, and so on).

Regardless of the length of the program, we also favor changing the composition of the groups on a regular basis: twice a week for a five-day program; once a week for executive programs; and once a month for our 10-month MBA program. This rotation of participants enables them not only to meet more people and share more insights, but also to experience different 'group chemistries.' Indeed, not every study team works smoothly. Some groups tend to work on a consensus basis, while others degenerate into power struggles, as can occur when an executive attempts to control the approach of the entire group. This diversity usually enhances the learning experience. Relatively small classes and long programs enable program directors to know their participants well, both in terms of personality and as a team member. Through simple observation and participants' feedback, program directors can discern quickly which study groups work better. When personality clashes occur, the program director may, therefore, want to balance the different personalities in a group to promote effectiveness as a team.

Although exploiting diversity is important, we find the process of setting up groups can be both time consuming (from a couple of hours to a couple of days) and dull and so have devised a method of doing so with the 'Team Blender' software described in Chapter 7.

In a case or group assignment, the conclusions of others frequently surprise participants. They may disagree, based on their reading of the material, their own experience, or some direct expertise in a given area. Thus, setting up groups with divergent opinions is key to provoke thought and self-reflection. However, diversity will not automatically boost productivity. We find the following practices can help heterogeneous groups:

1 Encourage groups to define ground rules from the beginning. Although we do not provide direct guidelines on how a group should organize itself (e.g. appoint a rotating chairman), the most effective study groups would often assign roles to the different members of the team: Who will keep time? Summarize key points? Represent the group's position in plenary sessions, etc.

2 Encourage groups to establish a few guiding process principles at the outset (e.g. clarify roles or objectives of the assignment). Also, we promote maximum participation and minimum discipline: anyone frequently disappearing to make phone calls or disappearing for some urgent business matter should be reminded of the loss that their absence costs the group!

3 To avoid confusion, distribute a hardcopy of assignments rather than announcing them verbally. It is important to be crystal clear in your assignments. A written copy will limit the possible misinterpretations of the assignment. However, we still advise facilitators to verbally 'walk through' the assignment at the beginning to ensure that it is well understood and that everyone is on track regarding time and personal involvement.

4 Reserve enough time and space: study groups that meet for less than 45 minutes are rarely effective; similarly, more than 75 minutes for a regular case-related assignment might cause the group to lose momentum, rather than build it. In addition, a 15-minute coffee break (either just before or after a group meeting) often helps to establish that 'group time' does not equal 'break time.' Immediate after-work breaks can also serve effectively as a time buffer and hedge against deadline overruns. A strict starting time for the full-class debriefing is

crucial to avoid delays and drift. Setting and revising time expectations must support the assignment – the shorter the group time, the more structure might be required. Finally, the timing in the course of study-group sessions – i.e. when to send them out – matters. For example, it is better to use groups earlier in afternoon sessions as no one wants to be tied up for long after lunch.

While some of these considerations are rather straightforward, they do help to get the basics right. However, if used mechanically, they won't work magic.

What does it take to run study groups effectively?

To run an effective study group requires the adoption of a process view. It starts prior to study-group formation and doesn't end when we return to the plenary session!

Managing the three stages of the study group process

As we build study groups into the learning script, we normally consider the process in three distinct phases, from a clear assignment to an effective debriefing:

1 Introduction and positioning – before you relinquish control.

2 Group time and monitoring – little to no control.

3 Reconvening and debrief – resuming control.

1 Introduction and positioning

At this point the educator is in control of the process and needs to set the stage for the group work to begin. The first consideration is what the objective of the work will be, both in terms of learning 'take-aways' and the process itself. The learning point goals will be driven by the context of the session (or program) and content – and should be captured in the group assignment discussed below. How participants arrive at these goals is the process objective. We ask two questions as we frame this objective:

■ Does the instructor want the groups to focus on specific aspects of the topic (via consensus building) or explore several different possibilities (via disagreement)?

■ Does the instructor want the participants to struggle through the process alone (the group is fully in control) or to lead them to combine different views into a common perspective or end product (more overt educator guidance and less group control)?

The roles that the instructor and the group take will be driven again by the overall goals of the session and this should be clear from the study group assignment. As you develop this, we find the following guidelines helpful:

■ Be clear in your assignment wording! To ensure good outputs, i.e. those that meet the learning and process objectives, the instructor must clearly communicate the purpose of the exercise (e.g. balancing the pros and cons of different options, looking at the different angles of a problem, exploring in depth the implications of various decision alternatives, taking a stand on a particular course of action, backing up decisions with a series of logical arguments, numbers, facts and so on).

■ Allow sufficient time to explain the group assignment. The instructor must be accessible to clarify any questions the teams may have. But this is not just a passive role. Instructors should actively solicit questions and not just rush the participants out of the classroom. Don't disappear!

■ Encourage the teams to come to a 'shared interpretation' of the group assignment at the beginning of the group time. Bearing in mind that individual participants might have done preparatory work on their own, carefully introducing an extra question (seemingly on the spot) beyond the prepared handouts can help raise the bar and inject added energy. Providing added, more detailed and/or complementary data, such as market shares by segment and price point, can also work well at this stage.

■ Make sure the participants will have the appropriate length of time to deal with their particular assignments: insufficient time will frustrate them, while too much may send the signal that study groups serve as a space filler in the schedule.

■ Set clear expectations about how they should report/present back, if at all. For example, the facilitator may ask the teams to reach a group decision on a particular problem or take a stand on one option among many alternatives. In this particular case, the instructor may instruct the team to come back to class with their selected option, listing their arguments, supporting facts and numbers, and the potential short- and long-term implications of their decisions (for example, its impact on the bottom line, impact on the organization, impact for the other functions of the company, etc.).

▪ Communicate expectations not only on content but also on the delivery format (number of slides) and support limits (transparencies, flip charts, 'no PowerPoint presentation, please!'). In company-specific programs, suggesting participants use posters on the wall enables the group to move around the classroom and illustrate discussions more effectively. Over longer programs, in order to avoid the development of boring routines, we strongly suggest alternating the presentation format. One day without PowerPoint provides relief for everyone!

2 Group time and monitoring

Part of being accessible is being accessible *throughout* the study group period, not just when you send participants off with their assignment. While the instructor has now effectively relinquished control of the session to the groups, he or she should walk around the study group area and be available without being intrusive. However, don't visit too early. You may want the participants to sweat a little first – to experience the difficulty of the problem at hand, before offering valuable guidance or additional information (if the assignment calls for this)!

The monitoring role also involves listening. This provides valuable feedback for the educator in several respects. In the session context, to anticipate the questions and issues that will likely be raised during the debriefing, as well as to inform the choice of groups to call on at the debrief. For example, one group may have developed an option that others have missed, offering the opportunity for them to provide an additional learning. Other groups may offer opportunities to discuss process insights, because they reached their conclusions in a different way to others. Beyond the specific session, the educator who actively listens can find insights that will be useful in future, whether for teaching or research purposes. Every study group period is unique, regardless of whether the assignment is the same, because the individuals that make up the groups bring unique experiences and perspectives that shape the dynamics and ideas generated. There is always something new to take away.

3 Reconvening and debriefing

This is the moment when the instructor retakes control of the session. Proper debriefing of the study groups is an important way to signal to participants that their work is valued. Often, they want to be challenged during the debrief discussions or presentations – their assumptions, use of data, as well as the implications of their recommendations; this is another way to stretch their thinking and to enrich their learning experience.

The appropriate debriefing style depends on the groups and their exercises. For a typical case study debriefing, the educator needs to think through:

- How many groups should present?
- In what particular order?
- Should a particular group be assigned or should the instructor ask for volunteers?

First, it is important to minimize the participants' perception that various instructors are 'always calling on the same groups.' We advise keeping track of which groups present on the day or the session before and then communicating this information with the other instructors on the same program. That way, other groups can be chosen systematically.

Second, to decide the order of presentations in plenary sessions, we ask: 'Which group believes it has a "good" solution?' and then later open the floor to groups with a 'better solution.' If other groups have to present their view on the same problem, we suggest to them that they avoid repetition and instead focus on 'new ideas' as well as 'alternative' recommendations. Another way to avoid this problem is to divide the assignment into complementary questions (group 1 would then present their view on question A, group 2 on question B, and so on).

Third, we prefer the first presentation to set a high bar for the following groups and yet keep the 'best' presentation for the very end, finishing the exercise on another 'high note.' Walking around the study groups just before the end of the study group work usually gives the instructor a quick feel regarding the quality of work that is about to be presented in plenary session.

To accelerate the debriefing process when time is running short (or once a couple of groups have made presentations), you can collect their slides and ask a group member to present directly from their seat. That way, you can control the time, which spurs participants to grant you more attention; hence, interventions by instructors feel less forced as they push the group to move on.

Finally, a couple of tips we have found useful at this stage of the process:

- Keep focused on the discussion within a strict time frame: a spokesperson often has a tendency to monopolize time. The instructor must function as 'timekeeper,' reminding the group representative to stay focused on the essentials. We find that it is most important to ensure that time remains for the audience to question the group.

■ Ask for radically different opinions from the audience in a push for missed points. When possible, use a prepared overview blackboard to capture comparable information (e.g. breakeven estimates or pricing proposals). Then use this overview as a base to (simultaneously) ask groups with opposing views to step forward.

Creating the right environment

At present, we have 113 study rooms at IMD. Each of these rooms is equipped with two networked computers, a white chart board and smart board, as well as standard presentation supplies. Although the rooms represent a major investment in physical facilities, they are dedicated exclusively to the use of study groups. This illustrates the need to create a 'professional' atmosphere within which study groups take place, as we find this sets the appropriate tone for the discussions. Study groups should have their own rooms and supplies, from pens, stickers, transparencies, paper, Post-its and flip charts, to fruit and soft drinks. A directory with educator and support staff contact details should also be available in case the participants need any extra help. 'Details' do matter: they signal that the comfort of the participants is important but also that there is no excuse for delivering poor-quality or unprofessional work!

Adding energy

Study groups are used in many types of session, albeit for different purposes. As a program progresses over several days or weeks, there is the potential for the group work format to become 'stale.' It is, therefore, important for the educator to think through how best to create energy and keep the momentum going in the study groups as the program progresses.

If the educator has not had much contact with the group of participants before, the first thing is to understand how his or her session fits into the overall program, and to talk to colleagues about how they have structured their sessions previously. The aim is to provide a different experience, while at the same time linking it seamlessly to what has gone before and the sessions that are to come. Obviously this is easier for the program director or an educator who has already spent time with the group – the challenge then is to avoid getting into a comfortable routine with the study groups and to keep challenging them. The following points illustrate some options for creating energy and variety:

■ Make sure that the assignment is truly challenging and meaningful.

■ Use cases that 'intrigue' participants.

■ Use the B-case when possible in cases that have multiple parts; provide updates to the class about major events for the companies being studied or the protagonists in the case.

■ Build a store of 'quality' questions and don't be afraid to 'steal with pride' from groups that have furnished these over time.

■ Ask for participant examples that parallel the issues under discussion.

■ Reintegrate points made by the groups back into the discussion.

■ To put pressure on the presenting group, retreat to the back.

■ Introduce time pressure to avoid debates dragging on.

■ Have groups work on/present complementary assignments to enrich plenary discussion. Pitch groups against each other!

■ Introduce some kind of competition and reward, such as T-shirts, drinks, candies. (Our favorite is a 5kg chocolate bar for winning teams – remember we're in Switzerland!)

When might study groups fail to deliver?

Even though it might sound easy, why do study groups sometimes fail miserably to deliver the value expected by either educators or participants? There are a number of potential pitfalls, some of which are easier to deal with than others:

■ The assignment is either not entirely clear or expectations for group output are not. This leads to frustration and a sense of wasted time. We suggest walking around study groups to learn whether this is the case. If so, the instructor needs to acknowledge the problem and then reframe the original objectives, that is, admit that as facilitator he or she can also learn. We sometimes challenge participants to 'help make it work' by giving it their best shot anyhow. We also ask people to share their interpretation of the assignment during debriefing. Another option is to restrict presentations to groups with reasonable outcomes and interpretations in line with the session content. Finally, we talk to the groups outside the classroom setting to better understand where participants differed in their interpretations of the assignment and then revise it and the staging of the group work accordingly.

■ There is a lot of talk in the group, but little concrete learning. To resolve this, we try to give more focus to the assignment questions, e.g. by introducing a rating scale or providing a specific framework to be applied such as SWOT or gap analysis. If a discussion outcome seems too obvious to the groups, we can ask more complex questions to enhance 'experience sharing.' We learn about this both from listening in on new study groups and in subsequent plenary debriefing discussions over time.

■ The integration in the overall session design is non-harmonic, i.e. the study group assignment does not address questions raised earlier in the session. Ideally, this problem is addressed by designing teaching materials to support group work as opposed to 'inventing group assignments after the fact.' For example, case material might be developed to explicitly stage a decision, progress a timeline or demonstrate best-practice questioning transferability to support subsequent study group works. If it becomes evident from listening in on group discussions that the material or process failed to integrate the study-group into the intended flow of the learning script, it is often advisable to acknowledge rather than to ignore the difference in directions as the group reconvenes. The subsequent discussion may then explore issues picked up by the groups by asking explicitly why a certain direction was chosen, thereby drawing in and acknowledging the participants' experience as opposed to artificially forcing a preconceived but flawed process.

■ Lessons learned remain within the group and are not fully communicated to other participants. To resolve this a facilitator may either ask directly 'what else did you discuss?' and/or encourage other participants to question the group's presentation providing lead-ins such as: 'There must/should be more questions for this group,' 'Don't let them off too easy' or 'Is this sufficient, can it be implemented, is it consistent?' These comments are intended to help build peer pressure and to implicitly communicate the facilitator's expectation not being fully met.

■ Groups lack energy and ambition, treating study-group time as 'break time.' To resolve this, we try to schedule separate breaks just before or after a group assignment and provide for a professional atmosphere in our overall facilities. In addition, it can be helpful to start a longer program with group assignments where, from experience or due to their set-up, groups are somewhat likely to miss major points. This can help establish the value of adopting a new perspective, working as a team. Other motivators are the use of B-cases or company visitors to introduce a discovery element and group-based competition to avoid group work being seen as independent from the remainder of the session. Finally, it may help to ask participants upfront if they have previously been taught by the case-method including group assignments and stress their value in terms of experience sharing. A program director may also want to highlight explicitly that it can only work if everybody engages, role playing what they would do as the decision maker or recommend as a consultant given this challenge.

- ■ Group dynamics are dysfunctional. This is probably one of the most difficult challenges for faculty to address. Fortunately, these problems are relatively rare since companies normally promote and select responsible managers to attend executive education programs. A single participant who is repeatedly disrespectful of others, for example regularly arriving late for group sessions or constantly questioning the value of the assignments, is often the cause of the problem. In many instances, the group will take care of the issue by itself. In fact, this kind of incident can be a good test of leadership and group dynamics for the other members of the groups. Nevertheless, the faculty must be sufficiently alert to spot this kind of incident quickly in order to resolve the problem adequately. This is of course a matter of judgment and experience. A one-to-one talk with the participant is often the best way to first understand the root of the problem and then solve it. It may simply be enough to remind the 'troublemaker' of his responsibilities vis-à-vis the rest of the group; however, very occasionally, the participant may be asked to leave if there is no improvement in behavior.

As the examples illustrate, dealing with these kinds of issues requires getting quickly to the root of the problem, not just treating symptoms. While we actively encourage and value diversity for the richness it brings to learning, it also offers one of the bigger hurdles with respect to group dynamics as the following quote from an American female executive suggests:

This has been my worst experience regarding teamwork. It has been a long time since I have felt devalued and subsequently demotivated in a long time. It took all I had to keep myself focused on learning and attempting to try various techniques to help myself.

This executive later related that select senior male executives from other regions and cultural backgrounds failed to acknowledge her contributions to the group. The problem was resolved by sitting down individually with each person of the group together with a respected colleague in organizational behavior that they knew, listening to their respective views of the problem, and providing constructive feedback to the offended female executive.

Another common problem in a multicultural group, is the tendency for the team to delegate the presentation responsibilities to native English speakers. In that case, we recommend that the spokesperson of the group rotate, which allows every participant the opportunity to present in front of the class. Occasionally a participant suggests that the teams be organized by gender. We do not recommend this option, except when there is total consensus in the class to do so because typically it does not reflect the real world and may make other participants uncomfortable.

The problems and solutions outlined above illustrate that managing study groups requires thought, experience and flexibility. Setting the right tone at the outset of programs is critical and needs reinforcement by the program director over time. Ideally, the groups themselves are also employed to raise the level of study-group works as a program progresses, for example, by means of peer feedback rounds at the end of each week concerning team effectiveness.

Finally, using study groups on a daily basis sometimes can lead to a sense of excessive routine. Moving people into groups also takes time, which can lead to deadline difficulties. To avoid these problems, we recommend the use of 'buzz groups' (the name reflects the background noise that results from simultaneous discussions in the classroom). These allow us to more directly harness, or even help to build, group energy in a larger classroom, and as such, offer an effective, time-efficient alternative and/or complement for formal study group assignments – and allow the instructor to maintain better visibility over the group dynamics. Nevertheless, some of the rules for study groups also apply to buzz groups: the assignment has to be clear, the instructor must be available for questions, and a clear sense of direction for discussion is required.

Lessons learned

Leading study groups to perform to their optimum potential can be a significant challenge, especially in long and intensive open-enrolment programs in which the use of study groups can become somewhat of a routine for the participants. As a result, we would like to offer the following final comments:

- Acknowledge any learning that takes place in study groups explicitly and upfront. Independent of the content of the study-group discussion, these groups offer participants practice at formulating their thoughts in a compelling way, negotiating for the attention of others, listening to others, building on points as a team in order to come up with something that no individual could have produced on his or her own!

- Good study-group assignments take time and experience! Anticipate having to revise them early on and in accordance with a group's background.

- The group assignment should not be confused with the desired output in terms of the groups debrief document. It is not a template for a conclusion but rather an introduction and process help. Similarly, the group presentation and discussion should inform and support the overall learning objective for the session rather than equating these elements.

- The first study group in a week-long program should not be too hard: focus should be on fostering group work and exploring group dynamics. Subsequent study-group assignments can be more and more challenging, as the group will have established a reasonable working pattern by this time.

- In longer programs, one needs to continuously raise expectations on study-group output, week by week, to create a healthy competitive pressure among the groups!

- Study-group dynamics differ from encounters in the shared auditorium – this holds for the interaction among participants but also for the faculty interaction with participants and hence can be an added opportunity to engage and encourage participants that have not yet contributed in class.

- Running effective group assignments deserves substantial thought, foresight and flexibility – it may look easy but, in our experience, it is not!

Key take-aways

■ Creating effective study groups requires time and planning in advance: the composition, diversity and size of the group are key in achieving the optimum environment for knowledge sharing to take place.

■ To deliver value, the process (from assignment through to debrief) cannot be left to chance: it must be actively managed.

■ Study-group discussions are just one element of the overall program; the group work must be seen as an integral part of a broader session design.

Notes

1 Professor Seifert has been teaching in a cross-section of various open-enrollment and tailor-made programs. He is the director of the Mastering Technology Enterprise program and the WILD program.

2 Professor Turpin has been the director of the IMD MBA program, the Program for Executive Development and the Managing Marketing Seminar as well as various tailor-made programs for Fujitsu, Matsushita Electric, Itochu, Borealis and Groupe SEB, among others.

3 For more on this topic, see *A Manual for Teamwork* by Professor Preston Bottger, February 2000, Lausanne, IMD. This manual presents guidelines for teams working together on a specific task over a longer time period with regard to airtime and conflict management, stages of team formation, and roles required of team members. In addition, this manual deals with procedures related to teamwork from pre-meeting planning to planning for implementation and gives guidelines for assessing team effectiveness.

4 Chapter 19 of this book considers the successful orchestration of a simulation in terms of planning roles, material and process in detail.

5 Chapter 20 of this book discusses different types of client project works that are an integral part of company-specific programs.

18

Beyond fun and games: Outdoor activities for meaningful leadership development

Gianpiero Petriglieri and Jack Denfeld Wood

Summary

Many managers and academics today view outdoor exercises as simply 'fun and games.' However, framed correctly, outdoor leadership activities provide a uniquely effective method for leadership development. They allow participants to access and explore the deeper determinants of individual, interpersonal and group behavior and can be a springboard for meaningful and long-lasting behavioral learning. To deliver all this, outdoor exercises depend on four key factors: (1) a competent staff of behavioral consultants; (2) participants who are willing to challenge themselves and take responsibility for their own learning; (3) a program design that is sympathetic to learning methods based on emotional experience; and (4) an alignment between the interests of the various major stakeholders.

The use of outdoor problem-solving activities to explore leadership and small-group behavior originated before the Second World War. First introduced over 50 years ago by some of the greatest scholars and skilled practitioners of the applied behavioral sciences, outdoor exercises helped to build the foundation of what we know about leadership, followership and effective teamwork. Notwithstanding this long and solid social scientific tradition, outdoor exercises have become trivialized and overused by unsophisticated 'consultants' and uncritical corporate consumers. As a result, many managers and academics today view outdoor exercises as simply 'fun and games.' They can be, but that is not what we do.

If used properly, outdoor exercises can expose covert and unconscious dynamics in both individuals and groups, providing the raw material for meaningful behavioral learning. This chapter deals with what we mean by 'outdoor activities – if used properly.' After reviewing the kinds of activity currently available, and the history underlying the initial use of such group problem-solving activities, we argue that to properly leverage them, four conditions are necessary:

■ A competent staff of behavioral consultants.

■ Participants who engage actively and assume responsibility for their learning.

■ A hospitable program design.

■ Major stakeholders – participants, sponsoring company, behavioral consultants, and program directors – who understand and are receptive to serious clinical behavioral work.

With these conditions fulfilled, outdoor exercises can function as an extraordinarily practical and uniquely effective method for leadership development.

Outdoor activities: What for?

'Outdoor activities' means different things to different people, and they are used – or misused – according to the different objectives and expectations of those who set them up, facilitate them and buy them. These objectives frequently include team building, motivation, self-esteem, leadership, interpersonal skills, conflict management, creativity, trust building, bonding and so on. Can a few days in the mountains or in the woods really do all this?

Broadly speaking, outdoor activities today fall into four categories, each of which has its own methods and educational philosophy, often implicit and unarticulated. They are:

1 **Incentive seminars:** When companies want to reward their employees, they sometimes contract out for incentive 'seminars.' Similarly, when they hold off-site management programs, they sometimes include outdoor activities as a break from 'real work' – classroom sessions or project work. These activities are intended to provide 'edutainment' (educational entertainment) in a sociable and relaxing environment. The natural background includes alpine mountaintops, tropical islands, country conference centers and more Spartan retreats in forest cabins.

Associated activities include helicopter rides, parasailing, golf games, skiing, football and cooking together. Participants enjoy a light break, a good laugh and a chance to network in an informal setting. Being outdoors together is the main point; the behavioral learning is of secondary importance, if it is considered at all.

2 **Scenic background:** Some companies take their top executives off into the wilderness for a journey, or to an isolated mountain retreat. They believe that the outdoors can prove beneficial as a backdrop for strategic planning and organizational alignment. The scenic background is meant to facilitate the early stages of organizational development and change – pulling senior executives out of their routines, helping them to achieve a 'helicopter view' and to think 'out-of-the-box,' and increasing informal and direct dialogue. Such expeditions aim at strengthening strategy and leadership. However, it is helpful to remember that the strategic endeavor is a largely rational one, while leadership is largely an emotional one; for lasting change, the rational and the emotional need to be integrated, both in the outdoor journey and following it. If there is no follow-up that addresses both dimensions – strategy and leadership – the outdoor activities serve company executives solely as an expensive mini-vacation without their families.

3 **Structured adventures:** Individuals who desire excitement and physical challenge seek 'Outward Bound'-type activities. Such courses involve long hikes, simulated shipwrecks, survival training, rock climbing, rappelling, sailing, camping, scuba diving and the like. While enhancing teamwork, generally these activities challenge the limits of individuals with emotionally stressful, yet hopefully safe, conditions. The main purpose of structured adventures is motivational – the more adrenaline, the better. Promotional brochures describe them as an opportunity for executives to boost morale, feel that they can accomplish more than they thought, and build rock-solid teams. The assumption behind structured adventures is that the newly found camaraderie, team spirit and self-confidence will somehow diffuse into the workplace. Action is emphasized at the expense of reflection. Group facilitation, to the extent that it is employed, is left to mountain guides and sports instructors with limited psychological sophistication, so that the articulation and integration of what one learns during the activities is usually overlooked or done poorly.

4 **Group problem-solving activities:** Outdoor group problem-solving activities have been widely used in management training for over half

a century now. When these activities are used as a part of an incentive seminar, as scenic background, or as a piece of a structured adventure, frankly, their potential is wasted. When these activities are used as they were originally intended, however, they provide individuals with an opportunity for increased self-awareness, understanding how they perceive – and are perceived by – others, and a clearer idea of how they work in groups and how groups work.

A bit of history

Outdoor leadership activities originated within the effort to select and train military officers prior to, and during, the Second World War. The German army had already used outdoor exercises for officer selection between the two World Wars, and the British, Dutch and Americans adopted their methods – the British and Dutch for officer selection, and the Americans for leadership development – subsequent to the War's end.[1] To this day, the basic format of outdoor exercises hasn't changed much. They include situations in which a group confronts a relatively complex task that no individual could complete alone, for example, crossing an obstacle in a limited time using only the equipment provided. While the military origins of these exercises may be misleading, the activities are explicitly designed to eliminate the influence of factors such as physical strength, educational background and gender: Depending on how well – or poorly – they work together as a team, athletes, engineers or musicians have an equal probability of success or failure.

German nobleman Kurt Hahn is generally credited as the creator of adventure training for individual motivational and character-building purposes. Hahn fled Nazi Germany in the 1930s for Scotland, where he created an outdoor activities school to develop students' 'inner resources.' After the outbreak of the War, Hahn moved to Wales, where his second school – Outward Bound – provided one-month courses on marine skills and survival training for British Navy cadets.[2] Subsequently, the target audience expanded to underprivileged inner-city adolescents, offering them a chance to get fresh air and gain confidence. His methods were later exported abroad, and are now used for a range of groups in public and private sector organizations for motivational and personal development purposes.

Around the same time, the British Army established the War Officer Selection Board (WOSB) to address the problem of poor officer selection. Its members included social scientists, who would become a groundbreaking group, and organizational theorists – such men as Wilfred Bion and Eric Trist whose work constitutes the foundation of what we know about the psychology of leadership and teamwork. This multidisciplinary team had found that cadet interviews and school transcripts failed to predict a prospective officer's capacity to understand and manage a military unit. Patriotic speeches, they concluded, did not a good officer make. Convinced that leadership skills needed to be assessed by direct observation of candidates' behavior in groups, the Board soon began to use outdoor problem-solving activities to evaluate leadership potential. One recruit, a young British cadet named Eric Miller – who would later become a world-renowned social scientist, organizational consultant and group dynamics scholar – recounted his experience as follows:

Once in a uniform, I underwent my basic training for about six weeks and was then dispatched to the mysterious two day event called a WOSB. My recollections are fragmentary: being shown a series of fuzzy pictures plus one blank page and told to write stories about them (the Thematic Apperception Test, as I was to learn later); swinging on a rope across a brook; and also being with a group of others inside a tennis court, where various lengths of timber were lying around and we were instructed to escape without touching the wire, supposedly electrified. A few months later I acquired the identity of a junior officer in the Royal Artillery.[3]

What kind of leadership skills was the board looking for? John Rickman, another member of the WOSB, made clear that the Board members' role was to be silent observers, and their primary task was to:

. . . assess the individual's capacity for compassion, because military officers needed to be able to maintain good relations with their own men, whilst promoting aggression towards the enemy.[4]

The Board produced a revolutionary memorandum entitled 'The method of the leaderless group,' which remains a cornerstone in the building of theories about participative leadership and shared accountability.[5] Its findings contradicted the popular stereotype of military leadership as enforcing obedience to formal authority and respect for hierarchy. Instead, it argued, effective leadership required social skills and sensitivity to the emotional life of the group.

Soon after, Rickman, Bion and the others intuited that group activities provided the opportunity to learn about the intimate functioning of groups in general, beyond purely military applications. As Harrison recounts, they soon abandoned their 'passive observer' roles:

. . . by experimenting with ways of intervening to enhance individuals'
understanding of how groups operate and skills in improving them.[6]

These pioneers in the applied behavioral sciences had switched their approach from *silent observation* for assessing an individual's leadership ability, to *intervention and interpretation* as a means to enhance group members' understanding of elusive and covert processes in groups. A more nuanced understanding of group processes, they came to believe, could improve an individual's capacity to exercise leadership. The switch in role from 'observer' to 'interpreter' created the role of 'small group consultant' as well as the discipline of 'process consultation.' It also marked a major evolution in the use of outdoor exercises – from *'assessment'* to *'development.'*

Assessment versus development

The assessment-oriented mentality is deeply entrenched in modern corporate and business school thinking, as reflected in 'competency models' and our obsession with measuring managerial 'performance' via performance evaluations, performance reviews, and pay for performance. This mentality of evaluation and judgment relies on a cognitive-rational lens to capture behaviors, assess them and eventually recommend solutions to improve individual, group and organizational performance.

Most participants – and non-clinically trained group facilitators – spend their time in an outdoor program attempting to *assess* how well the group did in finding and executing a technical solution. For them, the goal remains succeeding at overcoming an obstacle instead of exploring how the group actually behaved in the process. But, let's face it, sponsoring companies do not pay the expensive fees for an outdoor executive development program to have their executives learn how to cross a make-believe minefield using ropes, pipes and planks. Whatever the merits of this cognitive-rational approach to assessment, it fails to recognize the full value of outdoor activities as a method for developing leadership.

The main purpose for the use of outdoor exercises from the perspective of *'assessment'* is evaluation, prescription of 'appropriate' behaviors, and 'transfer of cognitive learning' back to the office work setting.[7] The main purpose of outdoor exercises from the perspective of *'development'* is enhancing an executive's capacity to lead responsibly through the understanding and integration of the rational and emotional factors at work in groups and organizations. From our perspective, the *primary task* of outdoor leadership activities is the development – through personal experience – of awareness and understanding of the exercise of leadership and group dynamics. The goal is not to succeed at any particular exercise; the goal is to accomplish meaningful behavioral learning. This requires a staff team that is competent to work with complex and multi-layered behavioral material.

Getting the most out of outdoor activities

Maximizing the developmental effectiveness of outdoor leadership activities requires: (1) a staff team that is competent to work with complex and multi-layered behavioral material; (2) actively engaged participants who take charge of their learning experience; (3) an appropriate program design; and (4) the buy-in of all major stakeholders.

1 A competent staff of behavioral consultants

Outdoor exercises provide a terrain where the overt, conscious and rational influences of individual and group behavior – and the covert, unconscious and emotional ones – can be brought forward and explored. The exercises recapitulate the essence of group decision making that occurs in all groups and organizations, from the family to the executive committee of a global corporation – behavior we usually don't see, hide behind formalities, dismiss as irrelevant, or flatly avoid looking at. Once these covert patterns are revealed, we have the possibility to understand and influence what happens in virtually any small group setting in which we find ourselves. The contributions of a competent staff of behavioral professionals is essential for shaping the 'raw material' of participants' experience into a solid, meaningful and long-lasting foundation for learning.[8]

Because one actually addresses what is going on 'under the table' instead of pretending things are the way they are 'supposed' to appear, outdoor exercises are arguably more 'real' than 'real' corporate life. A competent staff can enable participants to explore how leadership, followership and teams really work, that is, to sense how decisions are made; to wrestle with the many possible explanations for one's behavior; and to consider how their group deals with authority, boundaries, informal roles and so on.

Rather than forcing our participants into a simple mold – by relying on commercially available models of leadership and personality questionnaires through which they are told how they should view themselves and others – we encourage them to be themselves during their experiences. Together, we figure out what that means and how to work with it.

2 The participants: Attitude, responsibility and risk taking

Many managers approach outdoor leadership activities with some ambivalence about a 'psychological' approach. They often come burdened with an acute sense of being judged, of powerlessness, and of lacking control. Disenchanted with formal authority and feeling isolated and cast adrift, they are looking for help – and they want *tools* to recover control. However, rather than offer managers tools, we are in the business of working with the *instruments* they already have available – themselves.

During the program, managers can learn how they function in their study group as well as how that particular group functions. They might then extrapolate this knowledge to teams 'back home' and even groups in general. But perhaps the most valuable 'take-away' for a manager is the ability to access and understand the deeper determinants of individual, interpersonal and group behavior – to develop a more sensitive and precise 'inner compass.' In other words, they can refine the ability to sense the unseen patterns that operate within social situations, the elusive aspects within others and in oneself, and the courage to trust that information. We work very hard with managers to uncover and to calibrate their capacity to work 'under the surface' – and thus to exercise leadership responsibly.

At the beginning of a program, participants' attitudes tend to fall into one of five general categories: prisoners, tourists, consumers, dedicated students and explorers. Let's examine them one by one:

Prisoners are unwilling conscripts. They have usually been either (a) 'sent' to the leadership program by their boss to get 'fixed' or (b) felt pressured to go for career development reasons. They arrive with all the enthusiasm of someone going to the dentist to have a cavity filled.

Tourists look at leadership education as some kind of vacation. The program is a welcome break from their routine, with its fresh air, good restaurants and pleasant ambience. Expectations regarding their learning experience might be low, but their social expectations are high.

Consumers expect to receive a service. They have paid their fee, consider themselves customers, and look to the program staff as suppliers of that service. They are most comfortable with familiar questionnaires, straightforward theories, lists of bullet points and ready-to-use 'toolkits.'

Dedicated students, at the beginning of the program, are among the most motivated participants. They are enthusiastic about the latest business best-sellers and popular management models. Unfortunately, in their simplicity these models often interfere with their capacity to get in touch with their personal experience in a more genuine way.

Explorers have an orientation to learn, are open to experiment and discover surprises, and actively work to integrate their experiences. However, explorers often represent a serious challenge because, though helpful in a group, their attitude can reinforce the resistance of less enthusiastic group members, rendering group coherence harder to attain.

These are not mutually exclusive categories. With the ebb and flow of the program, attitudes shift. For example, once the initial suspicions of the 'prisoners' are overcome, they can be among the most valuable and straight-forward members of the learning community. On the other hand, 'tourists' can be much more reluctant to join a learning journey where they are asked to reflect on their deeper motives, and 'dedicated students' often shed their initial enthusiasm and reveal a remarkable resistance to learning outside prescriptive models.

We routinely begin a program by asking participants how much they would like to be challenged. More often than not, they understand the question to involve physical challenges. But we mean *psychologically*. What we are saying with the question is that participants have the ultimate authority and responsibility to decide how deeply they want to explore their own behavior. In our experience, faculty cannot challenge groups any further than its members are willing to go – without exception. Regardless of their initial attitude, for a significant learning experience, participants must take individual and collective *responsibility* for how much they are going to put in – and get out of – the opportunity provided. It is also helpful if partici-pants and faculty work collaboratively with a sense of *freedom, curiosity, willingness to take initiative, courage to explore, and willingness to be surprised.*

Optimizing one's learning experience in an outdoor leadership devel-opment program requires authenticity, investment, commitment and *willingness to take some risk.* Eleanor Roosevelt's admonition to 'do one thing every day that scares you' is well suited to this task. The more one steps out of one's comfort zone, the more one learns. Stepping out of one's comfort zone evokes images of bungee-jumping and rappelling off steep cliffs, but the biggest, and most difficult, step is emotional, not physical. Taking emotional risks means allowing oneself to experience, express and explore emotional material that we usually dismiss, prefer to forget, or conceal behind the comfort of our formal organizational roles.

3 Embedded educational design

Outdoor exercises must be embedded within an educational design that is hospitable to learning methods based on emotional experience and reflection upon that experience, i.e. that include some discomfort and ambiguity in addition to readings, lectures and case discussions. They cannot be dropped into a program based exclusively on rational analysis, for example in a finance program – the discrepancy between pedagogical methods would be too abrupt, and the resistance of some participants so high, that leveraging the outdoor learning opportunities would be virtually impossible.

Positioning: In our experience, though the timing factor is of critical importance, it is often disregarded. When outdoor activities take place too early, participants lack the time to build a relationship of trust among themselves; when too late, participants can't shift from working with their 'heads' to working with their 'hearts.' However, timed and framed properly, outdoor leadership activities contribute significantly to a culture of experimentation and openness within a class. In a two-week program, the outdoor activities work best if placed in the middle weekend. In longer programs, they work best if they are positioned relatively early – ideally, between the first and second week in a three-to ten-week program, and between the second and third week in a year-long MBA.

Program flow: Outdoor activities work best when some pre-program preparation and several quasi-theoretical sessions enhance participants' readiness for the experience. The program segment containing the outdoor activities requires a *minimum* of three full days. Anything less is too little to establish a space of trust to do meaningful work. This central segment usually opens with an *initial contracting session*, which is critical for participant groups to transition into the outdoor activities. Without a thorough contracting session, questions of 'assessment' and 'confidentiality' remain unresolved, and contaminate subsequent learning. *Individual coaching sessions* close this part of the program. The faculty switches role to that of individual coach, helping individual participants to articulate their learning and to think about its potential applications to personal and professional life. One or two more classroom sessions after the activities help participants consolidate their learning and integrate it in the context of their family and work life.[9]

4 Alignment of major stakeholders

When a company approaches a business school wishing to include leadership development into an executive program, who are the major stakeholders? So far, we have mentioned two, the individual participants and the staff of behavioral consultants. There are at least two others: the company that sponsors the participants, and the faculty member who has the responsibility for the client relationship and the overall program design – the program director. All these major stakeholders – participants, program staff, sponsoring company and program director – need to understand, or are at least be receptive to, serious behavioral work. This is not always the case.

Customer or client?

Some participants and their sponsoring organizations – and occasionally some program directors – consider leadership faculty to be a 'supplier.' But a *customer relationship* is not a *client relationship*. Customers can pretty much ask for, and expect to get, services as they wish them to be delivered. Your ice cream vendor, your florist and perhaps even your tailor will make your ice cream cone, your bouquet or your business suit to your specifications – adding the extras you want to have, tailoring things to your wishes. Even if you demand an ice cream cone with pickles, honey and broccoli, or a flower arrangement that does not match in color and fragrance, a 'supplier' will meet your wishes – 'the customer is always right.' This is not always the case in a client relationship.

A professional client relationship does not simply involve wish fulfillment – you go to lawyers, surgeons or therapists with different expectations than those you demand from your ice cream vendor, your florist or your tailor. While your tailor might make any style suit you desire, your surgeon should not excise any organ you demand to have removed! Of course, the professional should be sensitive to your preferences, involve you in decisions concerning diagnosis and intervention, and consider your individual needs. But a professional must reconcile the obligation to each client with the standards of his or her profession. There are practical and ethical limits governing professional behavior, and it is usually the professional who is best aware of where those limits are, not the client. If the client is unwilling to accept a professional opinion, it is the responsibility of the professional to decline to perform the service and to refer the client elsewhere. If a corporate client wants outdoor activities for purposes other than the leadership development of their executives, there is a potential for mismatched expectations and a strained relationship.

The sponsoring company

Corporate clients occasionally view outdoor exercises as a tool to manage employees – a speedy way to remove barriers to change, instill desired workplace behaviors, motivate employees, create a culture of openness, trust, collaboration and so on – all ultimately with the purpose of increasing organizational productivity. An enthusiastic sales manager of a multinational corporation captured this practical attitude towards outdoor activities as follows:

When you've got people that are not in a trusting and supportive environment, a fair amount of their energies, both conscious and subconscious, are put into defending where they are. They're worrying about what the other person is going to do to outpace them or stab them in the back. But once they develop support and trust, all the energy and time they put into defending themselves is freed up to focus on business.[10]

What you're doing when you participate in one of these programs is developing a bonding in three or four days that could take place in three or four years . . . in the workplace, given the low frequency of contact and natural barriers to openness and trust that occur in the business environment.[11]

While networking and collegial 'bonding' can be indirect outcomes of the experience, leadership development should be the central goal. However, when the real agenda is hidden – for example, to indoctrinate and motivate disenchanted employees in the midst of a downsizing – it often backfires, increasing distrust and alienation.[12]

Leadership programs must complement a larger organizational development strategy.[13] Done correctly, they encourage independent thinking, self-reflection and a disinclination to do what one is told without good reasons; to develop creative and talented leaders, companies must nurture a supporting environment for innovative and even irreverent approaches once the program is over.

The program director

If the program directors are experienced in outdoor exercises, the program can proceed smoothly. However, if they are unfamiliar with the nuances of such work, they usually ask us to 'do some outdoor stuff.' Even if in effect they are 'subcontracting' the leadership work, these program directors must understand their pivotal influence: they are the key liaison between the client company and the participants in class, and their attitude towards behavioral work is critically important.

Program directors need to work closely with the outdoor exercise faculty from the outset, in particular if they lack a background in the behavioral approach. That way, they will be able to optimize and integrate the various design requirements, harmonize the messages that will be passed to the company representatives and to the participants, and minimize the likelihood that their influence interferes inadvertently with the learning process. Program directors must convey clearly – to company representatives, participants and non-clinical program faculty – that they understand and support the serious nature of outdoor activities in learning for leadership.

Program directors can undermine outdoor exercises in several ways. One way is by diminishing the seriousness of behavioral work. For example, trying to pack a day of 'fun and games' on the school's lawn in front of everyone, or giving the impression that outdoor activities are an amusing interlude in an otherwise 'serious' program. Another way is by failing to understand that some discomfort is an inevitable part of behavioral learning, and an attempt to minimize discomfort is counterproductive for that learning. When a program director colludes with participants who wish to avoid the inevitable discomfort of serious behavioral learning, they undercut the work of the behavioral staff, make the class unmanageable, and put at serious risk the integrity of the learning process as well as their own program. We have seen well designed and delivered leadership programs harmed because anxiety drove the program directors to insist on sitting in on confidential debriefing sessions, chatting with participants during the outdoor day, and commiserating with participants at the bar every night. This is not helpful.

On the other hand, program directors can learn to foster participant openness and commitment to behavioral learning with simple, supportive remarks to the class in the opening sessions – that the outdoor leadership activities represent a change of pace from the classroom and a different sort of challenge; that it is a switch from purely intellectual work to intellectual and emotional work together, rather than merely one from 'work to play.' Sometimes, if a program director is not leading the outdoor activities and lacks an understanding of the behavioral approach, it is best if they surrender control. As one of our colleagues advised: 'Leave it to the behavioral staff, stay away until it's over, and don't look at the middle part – you'd get too nervous.'

Companies can always hire vendors who conduct amateurish outdoor leadership exercises – selling 'fun and games' and filling any request. But meaningful leadership development using outdoor activities is something entirely different: it requires professionalism and an alignment of educational design, participants, staff and key representatives of both the client organization and non-clinical program faculty. When all these stakeholders share an understanding of the requirements of serious outdoor leadership development programs, and are committed to their success, the learning opportunity provided is a unique and not easily available one.

Key take-aways

■ The *primary task* of outdoor leadership activities is the development – through personal experience – of awareness and understanding of the exercise of leadership and group dynamics.

■ Outdoor group problem-solving activities can enhance an individual's capacity to lead responsibly – through the understanding and integration of the rational and emotional factors at work in groups.

■ Participants have the ultimate responsibility in deciding the extent to which they wish to push the exploration of their own behavior – the more they step out of their comfort zone, the more they learn.

■ To maximize the learning opportunity, outdoor exercises must be positioned in the context of an overall program that is conducive to learning from personal experience.

■ Contributions from skilled behavioral professionals are critical in transforming the 'raw material' of the participants' experience into long-lasting learning.

Notes

1 Ritchie, R.V. (1974) *Years of the Tiger*. Squadron Officer School, Air University, Maxwell AFB, AL., pp. 67–69.

2 Wagner, R.J., Baldwin, T.T. and Roland C.C. (1991) Outdoor Training: Revolution or fad? *Training and Development Journal*, 45 (3), pp. 50–57.

3 Miller, E.J. (1993) *From Dependency to Autonomy: Studies in organization and change*. London: Free Association Books, pp. ix–x.

4 Harrison, T. (2000) *Bion, Rickman Foulkes and the Northfield experiments*. London: Jessica Kingsley, p. 91.

5 Research and Training Centre (1944) Part 2 –The Method of the Leaderless Group *In*: R.T.C. Memorandum No 5, *The Work of the Military Testing Officer at a War Office Selection Board* (OCTUs) Reg RTC/Inf/2 S.H. Foulkes Papers, Wellcome Institute for the History of Medicine: CMAC: PP/ SH /1.11.1.

6 Harrison, T. (2000) op. cit., p. 92.

7 Meyer, J.P. (2003) Four territories of experience: A developmental action inquiry

approach to outdoor-adventure experiential learning. *Academy of Management Learning and Education,* 2 (4), pp. 353–363.

8 We have discussed in detail the differences among 'coaches', 'counsellors', 'group facilitators' and clinically trained 'behavioral consultants' in Chapter 12 of this book.

9 For an extensive discussion of program philosophy, design and individual sessions content see Chapter 26 in this book, 'Fundamentals for a world-class leadership program.'

10 Gall, A.L. (1987) You can take the manager out of the woods, but . . . *Training and Development Journal,* 41 (3), pp. 54–8.

11 Gall A.L. (1987) op. cit., p. 56.

12 Miller, E.J. (1999) Dependency, Alienation, or Partnership? The changing relatedness of the individual to the enterprise. *In*: French, R. and Vince, R. *Group Relations, Management and Organization.* Oxford: Oxford University Press, pp. 98–111.

13 Ready, D.A. and Conger, J.A. (2003) Why leadership development efforts fail. *MIT Sloan Management Review,* Spring Issue, pp. 83–88.

19

Negotiation simulations: A dynamic learning tool

Bettina Büchel

Summary

Management simulations can be the basis of a powerful learning script, as illustrated in this chapter by a negotiation simulation. The simulation requires participants to take the role of negotiators in a bid to win a telecommunication license; it lasts around one and a half days. The example highlights the mechanisms through which non-computerized simulations create experiential environments, where personal development and behavioral change can occur. They replicate 'real world' situations in which participants are stimulated emotionally and intellectually by the setting, as well as the pressures and the emotions that induce real world-like responses. While the learning process develops throughout the exercise, it achieves the greatest momentum in the reflection phase, when participants are debriefed and asked to assess the meaning of their individual and collective decisions and behaviors.

In effective management simulations individuals are forced to come up with fast responses in real time and at times are forced to change their normal behavior. The games range from single-concept experiential exercises to complete company simulations. They can also offer a wide range in technological sophistication, from the complete absence of electronic devices to fully computerized scenarios. In spite of these variations, the common goal is to create a practical environment that simplifies and creates a given situation, while reflecting reality accurately enough to induce real-world-like reactions by participants.

In this chapter, we focus on non-computerized, complex behavioral simulations, where the emphasis is on the development of interpersonal skills and behavioral learning, unlike the computerized games that tend to focus on strategic management issues. Behavioral simulations are based on the experiential learning method, in which the level of complexity is determined by the number of participants and decision variables in play. The game setting requires the participant to be involved in a personally meaningful activity, to which he or she can apply previously acquired knowledge. As he or she commits to the simulation, the participant can experience a sense of personal accomplishment or failure depending on the results.

The successful application of behavioral simulations depends on three aspects:

1 Inputs and team selection.

2 The learning process.

3 The expected outputs.

By walking through a negotiation simulation, Egypt Telecom[1], I will analyze the input factors, the learning process and the outputs. I will also draw conclusions regarding simulations as a learning tool.

Negotiating a consortium and bidding for a cellular telephone license: Egypt Telecom

Negotiation skills are part of the 'core of the manager's job,' but in our experience many who are called upon to negotiate miss opportunities or leave 'money on the table.' Given the nature of negotiations – they occur in real time, in emotionally charged situations, and across a range of contexts – they lend themselves to learning through simulation.

Positioning the simulation in context

The illustrated negotiation simulation normally follows input sessions that have allowed participants to apply negotiation skills in short exercises. Participants are then introduced to the negotiation scenario. Each participant joins one of seven teams, either representing a company forming one of the two consortia (Mobinil or Misrtel) – each represented by an equipment supplier, a local company and a telecom operator – or Telecom Egypt. The goal of the negotiation is to successfully form a consortium that wins a competitive bid awarded by Telecom Egypt (see Figure 19.1). This negotiation simulation was replicated based on public information about Mobinil's bid to purchase EMTS, Egypt's mobile telephone company, in

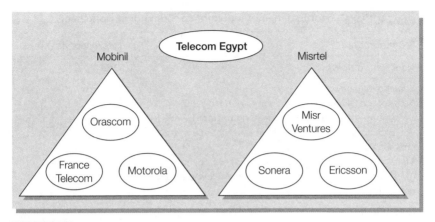

Figure 19.1 Negotiation set-up

1998. (Although in reality there was only one consortium bidding for the license, the case was adapted to have two consortia competing for the license.) To kick off the exercise, participants are asked: Which bid – if either – will Telecom Egypt accept for the existing network?

Developing the negotiation

At the beginning of the exercise, all participants are informed about the context in which the negotiation takes place, including country risks, the telecommunication industry, cultural norms within Egypt as well as ways to evaluate a cellular license according to regulations. Once they divide into teams, participants are asked to think about their Best Alternative to a Negotiated Agreement (BATNA), their bottom line and their desired target goals – all concepts that were introduced in prior negotiation sessions. During the briefing, the teams must understand that their goal is to find an agreement that their company will approve while getting a deal that they themselves want to implement. Within the different teams, participants discuss a negotiating position and craft a timeline for the entire process.

Because participants must negotiate a consortium agreement between three parties – a telecom operator, an equipment supplier and a local company – they need to make key decisions about ownership structure, capital contributions, number of board positions and CEO, dividend policy, termination and deadlock resolution. This leads to the development of a consortium memorandum of understanding (see Table 19.1).

Table 19.1 Consortium memorandum of understanding worksheet

Team number:	Representing:
Negotiation point	Offer

Shareholding structure
Percentage ownership of the joint venture: What percentage of the venture does each partner own? Do you plan to allow for government participation in the shareholding of the company?
Management fees: Do any of the partners or the government receive management fees? How are they calculated?

Capital contributions
Cash: What would be the total capital contribution of each affiliate in consideration for its shares made in cash?
Non-cash: What additional (if any) non-cash capital contribution will be made in the form of equipment contracts?
Technical ownership: Does the equipment manufacturer contribute by the base stations, etc. in exchange for equity in the joint venture? Or does the equipment manufacturer sell the equipment to the venture?

Corporate matters
Number of board positions for each partner: How many board positions are designated for each partner? Who will be nominated as Chairman of the Board?
Control of management positions: Who will be nominated as a CEO? Will the venture retain the existing CEO?
Responsibilities of each partner: Who will fill the key management positions? Which partner will have operating responsibility for the venture? Which partner will have financial responsibility for the venture? Who will be nominated as Finance Director? What other responsibilities will be established?
Working relationships: What working relationships will be established to communicate among the partners?

Dividend policy
Dividend payout: What percentage of company profits or cash flow will be paid to shareholders as dividends? On what base will these dividends be calculated?

Termination
Circumstances for termination: What is your exit strategy? What are the conditions that may cause the venture to dissolve?

Table 19.1 continued	
Team number:	*Representing:*
Negotiation point	*Offer*
Deadlock *Events triggering deadlock*: What events or positions within your company, your negotiating team, or partners will cause you to walk away from this deal?	
Employees *Number of expatriates*: How many expatriates will be used to staff the operation? Will they be permanent employees or will they be phased out over time, replaced by Egyptian employees? *Maintain jobs for existing employees*: Will the existing 300 EMTS employees be retained in the company or will they be released? *Training provisions for local workforce*: How will new local staff be trained? Will they be trained in operating the new equipment, thus improving their technological skill levels?	

The process requires a financial analysis, in which members of the consortium have to calculate the net present value of their bid for a cellular telephone license in Egypt. This value is based on assumptions about the percentage of the population using mobile telephones, airtime minutes per subscriber per year, average tariff per minute, monthly access fees, connection charges, corporate tax rates, management fees and discount rates.

Two rounds of 'official negotiations' between the two consortia and Telecom Egypt create opportunities to adapt the original offers from the consortia. At the end of the process, the consortia hand in a signed copy of the 'last and final offer' to Telecom Egypt, which then chooses a preferred bid. Although there are some fixed points in the exercise's timetable, the rest of the interactions and dynamics, i.e. working out the meeting times between the teams, is driven by the participants.

The entire process lasts approximately one and a half days. There are three deadlines given to the participants – the submission of the memorandum of understanding outlining the agreement between the partners in each consortium; two formal rounds of negotiations between Telecom Egypt and the consortia; and the submission of the last and final offer. These deadlines are designed to create tension among participants and teams. However, if the participants fail to show enough drive or energy, faculty has the option of sending memos from the CEO of each company directing the teams to address their original goals, in order to enhance the urgency.

During the negotiations, faculty act as facilitators and may videotape the participants. To make the session more effective, the video clips are used during the debriefing session to highlight successful and unsuccessful negotiating tactics. Prior to the announcement of who wins the bid, the negotiation is 'debriefed,' i.e. analyzed and discussed regarding what negotiation behavior was effective or ineffective. Telecom Egypt then awards the license to one of the consortia and presents its rationale. To wrap up the whole exercise, faculty usually share with the participants what actually happened in this particular case and describe how Mobinil has evolved since 1998; this anchors the simulation to a sense of reality, adding to its credibility.

Orchestrating the use of simulations

The orchestration of a simulation requires detailed planning of the roles, materials and process. Every party involved in the negotiation plays a distinct part that has to be clearly communicated ahead of time. There are five key points to consider to successfully orchestrate the session:

1 Clearly define the role of participants

It is essential to accurately define the role of participants, as they will be asked to negotiate on behalf of one of seven parties involved in the negotiation. Participant allocation to each company requires careful thought about the diversity of perspectives and skills. Each team representing one of the seven parties needs to have at least one person with adequate financial skills. We have found that teams ranging from two to four participants worked optimally as each individual could participate while at the same time generating useful, alternative opinions within the group; this is consistent with existing research.

Because each team's briefing papers are designed to create conflict between the parties within the consortia, critical and often emotionally tense moments tend to occur in the early phase of the negotiation as each party presents their company position. For example, Orascom and France Telecom both want to control the Mobinil consortium. The degree of conflict that emerges depends on the interpretation of 'control' by the individuals involved. In two instances we observed, discussions were so heated that the parties no longer trusted each other and walked out.

Additional conflict can arise if confidential information from one team is discovered by the other.

Even though the underlying information and set-up are the same, as role playing unfolds each individual interprets them in light of their personal views and style, which renders each negotiation simulation unique and unrepeatable. Table 19.2 shows the different outcomes that we have found with the same simulation and the same briefing.

Table 19.2 Outcome of past negotiations

	Mobinil	Misrtel	Mobinil	Misrtel	Mobinil	Misrtel
License Fee	$1.2 billion	$1.35 billion	$1.0 billion	$1.1 billion	$780 million	$775 million
Length	15	15	15	20	15	15
Ownership	Gov 5% O 40% FT 40% M 15%	Each partner 1/3	O 20% FT 60% M 20%	S 51% M 49%	O 40% FT 40% M 20%	M 30% S 49% E 21%
Dividends	20%	25%	40%	5%	2%	10%
Mgt Fee	$1.2 m Oras	3% split by part.	5% of rev. for FT	5% of rev. by part.	3% of rev.	None
Coverage	90% in 2000	98% in 2002	99% in 3 years	80% in 5 years	96% in 18 months	95% in 7 years
Price	0.18	0.16	0.18	0.15–0.25	0.16	0.17
Technology ownership	Mobinil	Misrtel	Mobinil	Misrtel	Not stated	Misrtel
Maintain jobs	yes	yes	yes	yes	yes	yes
Third license	no	no	no	no	yes	yes
Tax holiday	yes	yes	yes	yes	5 years	5 years

2 Communicate the role of the instructor

The role of the instructor is highly important prior to the start of the negotiation as well as at the debriefing, but he or she is less active during the exercise. At the start, the instructor needs to provide a learning framework and familiarize the participants with the task ahead; it is crucial to engage participants, in effect getting their commitment to the roles they have been assigned. During the negotiations, faculty act as coaches, but they do not intervene as the process unfolds. After negotiations are concluded, faculty may either debrief the participants or facilitate the debriefing within the consortia. The debriefing is the most important part of the learning and we will address it in more detail in the following paragraphs.

3 Ensure a user-friendly and safe environment

To support the process methodologically and convey a sense of reality, we have created for this simulation a 'Negoc' website; it allows participants to email each other, to access documents related to the bidding process, and to work from an established financial spreadsheet valuing the deal. In addition, 'Negoc' contains web links to background information on the country, the companies and the industry. Our support staff are also familiar with the documentation and help the participants when they have questions, particularly related to the financial valuation contained in the spreadsheet. Although the spreadsheet reduces the number of assumptions to be made, uncertainties remain that are similar to real-life negotiations of consortia. For those participants with limited financial skills, their lack of knowledge frustrates them at first; however, as they come to understand it, their contributions to the process turn into a source of pride.

In addition, it is important to create a safe environment. Participants must understand that the purpose of the simulation is to help develop negotiation skills rather than to 'win' or appear 'good.' To do so, it has to be clear to the participants that there can be no real-life career penalties to pay, no matter how 'unsuccessful' the outcome of the negotiation may be, even when senior executives from their firms are observing the exercise. In this way, they become more engaged and willing to participate and experiment.

4 Devote time to debriefing

While the exercise itself entails some learning, the reflection phases are the most important part of the learning process. Throughout the process, feedback must be carefully structured in order to contribute to the learning process. At each chronological phase of the experience, the class must examine the results of participants' actions, linking them with their performance by constantly asking 'What worked and what did not work?' This is the most important part of the learning process. In some cases, faculty intervene in the middle of the process to ask participants to take a step back and reflect upon what has happened; this helps participants to dissect explicit issues and learn throughout the simulation. We have found that participants learn more when they receive positive input from their mistakes. Yet periodic reflection phases throughout the process are not sufficient to fully ensure a successful post-experience debriefing. There are two models of debriefing that we have used.

In the first model, the teams themselves are asked to review the videotapes that were recorded during their negotiations in order to deepen their own understanding of team interaction, leadership behavior and negotiation tactics, as well as providing each other with feedback on specific individual behaviors observed. They are asked to focus on how to most effectively build high-performing teams; deal with differences of opinion; influence others; present well-conceived ideas and strategies; harness creativity; build negotiation skills; and provide leadership. While the learning objectives are crucial, an element of fun is also inserted to ensure emotional engagement – we ask each participant to choose a video clip of himself to illustrate their behavior and to draw a 'picture metaphor' of their team. Once they have analyzed their interactions, participants choose two to three people with whom they worked the most to provide feedback, focusing on behavioral strengths and improvement opportunities. When we introduce participants to the feedback phase, we ask them to use concrete examples from the negotiation, to be constructive, and to discuss potential consequences of the observed behaviors. In this particular set-up, the role of the faculty member is to observe.

In the second model, the debriefing is conducted by faculty. Rather than simply sharing their views of what was observed, the faculty encourages and facilitates a discussion on the process. The main objective of the debriefing session is to understand what happened during the negotiation process in order to determine what was effective or ineffective and what each individual can learn about his/her own behavior. To enhance the flow of the discussion, the facilitator may ask questions to each group, such as:

■ When did you come together for the first time?

■ What was the mood in the room? Warm, formal, tense?

■ What was the initial perception of where power was concentrated? Why?

■ How did you split up the roles and responsibilities?

■ How did you approach the negotiations with Telecom Egypt?

■ Did you step back and do mini-debriefings after each interaction to see how it worked and why?

Please refer to Table 19.3 for a more complete list of questions.

In this model, extensively used in open programs, the debriefing entails a group discussion plus time for individual reflection on their own behavior. The session ends with the following questions:

■ What would I do the same next time?

■ What would I do differently?

■ What are my main take-aways?

Table 19.3 Useful questions to facilitate the debriefing

During the process:

■ Did you have a plan?

■ Did you know your Best, Walkaway and BATNA?

■ Was there a difference between the groups?

Early in the process:

■ What was the climate like in the first 5 minutes of the formal negotiation?

■ Did you exhibit information-seeking or information-presenting behavior?

■ Did you explicitly state your position? (Broad goals, big picture or details right away)

■ Did you make use of open-ended questions and check understanding?

■ How was your information-sharing behavior?

■ Was building a relationship and trust important?

■ Was there an agreement on structure and format?

■ Were there irritators in the negotiation?

■ Did you find an agreement on common ground and agreement on open issues?

■ Did you adapt your plan?

■ Did you avoid deadlocks?

■ Did you summarize and when?

What participants learn in the simulation is associated with its emotional impact as well as the 'harder' learning about specific skills and ideas. This is promoted by the environment, which must feel safe and non-threatening, and the feedback, which helps the participants to understand their experience more deeply. Generally, participants reflect positively on their experience. As one said: 'This is an excellent negotiation exercise as it provides ample opportunity to learn the various aspects of leadership and negotiation from the theory lessons.'

5 Ensure emotional impact

Certain factors in the game can influence its emotional impact, such as its complexity, its realism and its entertainment value. Greater complexity challenges participants to deal with ambiguity and uncertainty as the variables interlink, rendering early conclusions to the negotiation extremely difficult and creating time pressure. While this causes stress and frustration, it also increases the emotional 'highs' and 'lows.' In the early development and initial uses of the simulation, the time allocated to the process requires careful adjustment.

Furthermore, when participants understand that the simulation is based on an event that actually happened, they more easily associate their own outcome with reality. Finally, setting up creative support greatly enhances the entertainment value of the exercise. Websites, dedicated rooms, snacks during stress periods and other logistics can help to increase the level of engagement of participants.

Group compatibility, group dynamics and group negotiation – learning in a team environment – also influence the experience. While skills can be distributed across the teams, faculty can rarely guarantee interpersonal compatibility – group dynamics cannot be fully controlled. Nonetheless, high levels of conflict add to the challenges, enhancing the learning process in spite of a potentially 'painful experience.' We have sometimes observed that a team excludes an individual from the negotiation because that person is deemed 'incompetent.' In addition, the negotiation simulation requires team learning to take place, in contrast to individual learning: by fleshing out each other's understanding of the issues and sharing information, teams can achieve more rapid progress and/or better outcomes. However, certain group pathologies can also develop, such as the refusal to acknowledge alternative points of view or 'groupthink,' which may lead to rigid negotiating positions and responses. Because many real-life negotiations are multilateral (e.g. joint venture negotiations that involve multiple players), it is important to recognize when splitting roles may be useful and when discussions within the team may lead to novel responses. Finally, when groups have members with extensive previous negotiation experience, they are almost automatically placed in the role of 'chief' negotiator. While this may improve the outcome for the group, the other, less experienced negotiators may actually learn less.

Conclusion

Case studies are more likely to result in single-loop learning and to foster the ability to solve structured, well-defined problems. In contrast, simulations are more likely to lead to double-loop learning[2] and to promote the ability to solve less-structured problems. This suggests that management development should include simulations to enrich the participant's learning. Simulations enable participants to identify and learn about the impact of their individual behavior. More importantly, they help overcome two traditional challenges for management education: (1) the transfer of knowledge on proven techniques, and (2) the application of proven techniques in a situation close to 'real life.'

Key take-aways

- Simulations promote participants' ability to deal with unstructured problems.

- Involving participants in a personally meaningful activity ensures emotional engagement.

- Replicating real-life environments and situations facilitates real-life responses.

- Debriefing drives key learning through participants' assessment of their thinking processes plus the implications of their decisions and actions.

Notes

1 See the following IMD case series for more information: IMD–3–0986 to IMD-3–0999, Negotiating for a Cellular Telephone License in Egypt (series).
2 For more on the concept of double-loop learning please see Argyris, C. (1977) Double Loop Learning in Organizations. *Harvard Business Review*, September–October, pp. 115–124; and Argyris, C. and Schan, D.N. (1978) *Organizational Learning A Theory of Action Perspective*. Reading, MA: Addison-Wesley.

20

Client and participant initiated projects to facilitate the transfer of learning to the working environment

Robert S. Collins

Summary

When properly scripted, client and participant initiated projects are very effective in facilitating the transfer of learning to the working environment.

This chapter describes three different approaches to projects that are undertaken as part of company-specific programs. These are either participant initiated, involving a group consensus or an individual project champion, or company initiated, involving a board-level champion.

Projects have both substantive (task/solution orientation) and developmental (knowledge/skills orientation) objectives. On the substantive side, projects result in potential solutions to company-specific issues with members of the project team committed to the implementation of their recommendations. On the developmental side, team members' learning is enhanced through the application of frameworks, ideas and concepts discussed during the program.

This chapter focuses specifically on projects undertaken by participants as part of one- to two-week company-specific programs. Typically such programs involve a target group of executives comprising some 200–400 people and, as a result, are offered on a number of occasions over a two- to three-year period. Each individual program involves between 25 and 40 executives from the same company, who undertake a developmental experience that is focused on issues of importance to that particular company. While the participant group is diverse in terms of function, nationality and country of origin, its affinity lies within its company/organizational identity and the program objectives themselves. The projects discussed here are carried out in teams of five to seven persons.

The first challenge is the manner in which project topics are selected. Three different models are described:

1 Participant initiated – group consensus
Here the project team itself defines a project topic.

2 Participant initiated – project champion
Here the project topic has been selected from input provided by the participants in advance of the program. The program director selects five to six projects with the participants who proposed each of the chosen topics assuming the role of project champion.

3 Client initiated – board champion
In this instance members of the board of the company sponsoring the program select projects. The topics are of immediate concern to the board as they address current business issues and as such have singular visibility within the organization.

Consideration is given to the way in which project work is integrated into the program, and the manner in which it is facilitated by the program faculty. The benefits and challenges associated with each approach are discussed, with emphasis being placed on how the challenges might be addressed. As shown in Figure 20.1, it is suggested that in making the transition from the group consensus model to the board champion model, the projects have increased visibility and potentially greater pay-off to the sponsoring organization. However, these are associated with increased complexity, challenges and risks.

Group consensus projects

Project teams work on business challenges defined through group consensus. This model can be used in a one-week program. The deliverable is a presentation (12–15 slides) of some 20 minutes duration to be delivered on the final day of the program. Each project presentation is followed by a 10-minute question and answer period involving senior executives from the sponsoring organization. Once all projects have been presented, the invited executives provide summary remarks and engage the participant audience in an 'open forum' discussion.

	Client consensus	Pre-program set-up	Support material	On-site group activity	Facilitation	Executive audience
Group consensus				X	X	X
Project champion		X	X	X	X	X
Board champion	X	X	X	X	X	X

Greater complexity and increased risk →

BUT

Increased visibility and greater pay-off

Figure 20.1 Models for project selection

Assuming a Sunday evening start and a Friday closure, the allocation of time to the project experience is as follows:

Day 1	Issue discovery/sharing	1.5 hrs
Day 2	Issue prioritization/selection	1.5 hrs
Days 3–5	Content elaboration and presentation preparation	9.0 hrs
Day 6	Presentation/feedback (plenary)	4.0 hrs
	Total	**16.0 hrs**

Topic selection

After a briefing in plenary during which the projects are introduced and deliverables defined, participants break into their pre-assigned project teams to begin the process of topic selection.

To be selected, projects must meet the following criteria:

- Be consistent with and support the overall program objectives.
- Focus on a relevant business issue of current importance to the sponsoring company.
- Be of compelling interest to the members of the project team; each should feel they have a stake in the outcome.
- Leverage the capabilities and experience of the team members and be 'doable' in the time allocated.
- Go beyond recommendations and include plans for implementation together with designated responsibilities and a time line.

The process for topic selection using a 'Post-it' note exercise is described in Table 20.1.

Table 20.1 The 'Post-it' process for choosing a project topic

This exercise can facilitate the choice of a project topic through:

1 Establishing a priority topic in a timely fashion.

2 Helping team members focus on such a topic.

3 Helping clarify the topic and build consensus.

4 Allowing all team members to express their points of view.

Ground rules

1 All contributions are on 'Post-its.'

2 All team members contribute.

3 Rituals are important: follow the process step-by-step.

4 No evaluations are allowed – no one should criticize another team member's contribution as potential topics are described.

Process

1 In your project rooms, and working in silence, each member of the team writes down a potential topic on a Post-it together with a short statement justifying its importance. Each team member can contribute up to three topics.

2 Each Post-it is placed on the left-hand side of the white board.

3 One member of the team reads each Post-it aloud. Other members of the team can ask the author of the Post-it questions for clarification. Based on the questions, the author may rephrase the topic and/or justification of its importance. The Post-it is then placed on the right-hand side of the white board. All Post-its are processed in this fashion.

4 Team members personally assess the contributions. Each member places a small check mark in the lower right-hand corner of a Post-it that he or she considers to be an issue/topic to be considered. Post-its with two check marks should not be marked again. When all team members have completed their selection, all Post-its with less than two check marks can be removed.

5 As a team, consider the remaining Post-its. Again, working silently, group Post-its with similar messages or affinity together. Avoid groups of more than three Post-its. Some Post-its may not fit in any one group. Leave these as 'lone wolves!'

6 For groups of two to three Post-its, reformulate the issue/justification capturing the essence of the original author's intentions on another Post-it. Place this Post-it above the group of two to three.

7 Discuss and prioritize the groups together with the 'lone wolves.' From the perspective of the team as a whole, which topic most effectively meets the criteria for project topic selection?

This approach is particularly useful in ensuring the choice of a project topic in a timely fashion as well as in clarifying the topic and building group consensus around it.

Project work facilitation

The program director and one additional member of the faculty team assume responsibility for group facilitation. The focus of facilitation shifts from topic selection to content elaboration to presentation preparation as the week progresses. Faculty should be prepared to intervene in the event that a group finds difficulty in reaching consensus on a topic. The progress of the group should be carefully monitored. Typically the selection process goes smoothly; however, on rare occasions difficulties can arise. Usually these become self-evident before the end of the first team meeting. Faculty should be prepared to assist team members in resolving their difficulties by the end of the second day, thereby keeping the team on schedule.

In elaborating the structure and content of the presentation given the constraints of time, participants have found it useful to structure the presentation as follows:

- What is the topic/issue?
- Why is it important?
- What needs to be done?
- How can we implement our recommendations?

A 'story board approach' is then used to elaborate the content. In developing the short presentation in the form of a cartoon or comic strip, participants first consider the key messages to be developed in each slide. The key messages, when read in sequence, essentially 'tell the story' and summarize the overall presentation. The key messages are the acid test to ensure that the presentation is concise, consistent, coherent and compelling. As team members will inevitably use a division of labor approach to develop the presentation, the story board – prominently displayed on a wall in the project group room – enhances communication between them.

Challenges and benefits

The primary challenge in the use of this model is avoiding 'the lowest common denominator' effect where the topic is acceptable to all team members but has no teeth and delivers no bottom-line result. Thus it is vital that the faculty stress and monitor the application of the criteria in the selection of a topic right from the outset. Furthermore, they should be alert to any group process difficulties that a specific project team might be experiencing during its first meeting and be prepared to intervene.

The presence of senior executives from the sponsoring organization for the presentations and indeed the program kick-off does impact the choice of topic. The ideal is for the CEO, on opening night, to stress the credibility of the project experience, its value to the organization and the importance of topic selection. The fact that he or she together with a number of colleagues will be present for the presentations on the final day is further testimony to the internal viability of the projects and the value placed on them by the organization.

In successive offerings of the program, the CEO has the opportunity to refer to prior projects and the extent to which project recommendations have not only been implemented within the organization, but also the way in which such implementation has occurred.

Monitoring project implementation over an extended period of time indicates that significant numbers of project recommendations have been accepted and implemented in a timely fashion within sponsoring organizations. Furthermore, either teams have been mandated en bloc to lead the change initiative within the organization or designated individuals from the team have been appointed as project leaders to spearhead the change within their respective areas of responsibility.

Project champion projects

This model has some similarities to the group consensus model described earlier. It too can be used in a one-week program. The deliverable is, once again, a presentation (12–15 slides) of some 20 minutes duration to be delivered on the final day of the program. Each project presentation is followed by a 10-minute question and answer period. The final session is attended by a senior executive or executives from the sponsoring organization. Upon completion of the project presentations, the invited executives engage the participants in an 'open forum' discussion.

In this instance, the allocation of time to the project experience is as follows:

Day 1	Introduction of project by project champion	1.5 hrs
Days 2–5	Content elaboration and presentation preparation	10.5 hrs
Day 6	Presentation/feedback (plenary)	4.0 hrs
	Total	**16.0 hrs**

Because the project topics have been selected before the program begins, more time can be allocated to content elaboration during the program itself. The differences between the models lie in the manner in which the topic is selected and the nature of facilitation both before and during the program.

Topic selection

The criteria for topic selection applied to the consensus model are relevant to the personal champion model. However, it is in their application that the differences arise. A generic approach to topic selection is as follows: prior to the beginning of the program, participants are invited to describe their chosen project, managerial challenges involved and to justify why it might be an appropriate topic for a team of participants to address during the program. The program director then selects the requisite number of projects and works with designated 'project champions' and IMD support services, where appropriate, to ensure that the necessary reference materials are available to the team from the outset.

The approach is best described using a specific program as an example. In this instance the program participants were from a professional services firm. The program was designed to enhance their skills in evaluating client companies from a business perspective. This involved the application of industry, competitive and client company analysis, the identification and assessment of strategic opportunities available to the client company and how the company might direct its business over a three- to five-year time horizon.

Four weeks in advance of the program and using the *Learning@IMD* platform designed specifically for the program, participants are invited to respond to a project questionnaire. This describes the project exercise in the context of the program learning objectives. Furthermore, it solicits input regarding a major client and its business, the industry it competes in, and its major competitors. Participants are asked to describe the challenges facing the client and the nature of the client service relationship. In a sense, the participants are in competition with one another. Project champions will have the benefit of five to six of their peers collaborating with them on developing a better under-standing of their client's business and competitive environment. A short list of prospective projects is prepared and shared with IMD's Information Center (IC). This is critical since IC personnel prepare the electronic databases containing pertinent information on the relevant industry, client and competitors used by each project team. It is necessary to ensure that adequate information is available in the public domain to support the project work.

The next step is for the program director to contact the prospective project champions directly. Each is asked to prepare a briefing for the team from internally available documents. This should highlight critical aspects of the client's business and the client service relationship. Time is also devoted to discussing the role of the project champion with the emphasis being placed on the need to facilitate the work of the team rather than being a project director.

Project work facilitation

Again the program director and one additional member of the faculty assume responsibility for group facilitation. Once the project champion has briefed his or her team on the opening night the focus shifts immediately to structuring and elaborating the content of the presentation. The 'story board approach' is invaluable in this regard. The facilitators should also be alert to group dynamics and be ready to assist in effecting appropriate and supportive behaviors.

Challenges and benefits

The primary challenge in the use of this model is to ensure that the client company and industry chosen are of interest to the prospective project team and allow for the effective application of the framework, ideas and concepts discussed during the program. A telephone conversation between the program director and potential project champion allows for an assessment of the existing client relationship that should be one of reasonably long standing. Avoid choosing projects where the client is a recent 'win' or indeed a 'target' since in both instances the participant will have had little or no exposure to client senior management.

It is also critical to ensure that the project champion understands his or her role. In some instances this needs to be repeated and reinforced for it is necessary to avoid the perception of inequity between participants. Project team members can and do take umbrage with a project champion that acts not as project facilitator but as a project director. The project champion must be willing to prepare and share the briefing documentation. An effective briefing is the quid pro quo for the engagement and commitment of the other team members.

It is important to have a contingency plan in the event that a project champion drops out at the last minute. The program director can substitute for the project champion directly or, *in extremis*, resort to the use of client and industry data that have been used in a previous program.

The presence of a senior executive/partner at the closing presentations is indispensable. Indeed, unless this condition is fulfilled, experience suggests that the effectiveness of the personal champion model is jeopardized. There is need for a credible sounding board against which to test the rigor of analysis and practicality of recommendations.

The benefits of the personal champion model rest in the practicality of the approach when focusing on current issues of immediate relevance to the participant group and the reinforcement of learning through the active involvement of senior executives from the firm.

Board champion projects

This model has some similarities to the project champion model, and again is suitable for use in a one-week program. The deliverable is, as in previous instances, a presentation (12–15 slides) of some 20 minutes duration to be delivered on the final day of the program, to be followed by a 10-minute question and answer session. Representatives of the sponsoring organi-zation's executive board, or indeed the executive board as a whole, attend the final session and engage the participants in an 'open forum' on completion of the presentations.

In this instance the allocation of time to the project experience is as follows:

Day 1	Introduction to project exercise and project team assignments	1.5 hrs
Days 2–5	Content elaboration and presentation preparation	10.5 hrs
Day 6	Presentation/feedback (plenary)	4.0 hrs
	Total	**16.0 hrs**

During the initial team meeting, participants are provided with a dossier of project-specific materials derived from company sources as well as an electronic database built by staff from IMD's Information Center (IC). These databases contain project-specific information in the public domain.

Topic selection

Topic selection is an iterative procedure and involves collaboration between the program director, the client company's representative (typically the program champion within the client company) and members of the executive board.

The goal is to identify five to six projects which are of current concern to the board and which meet the following criteria:

- Are consistent with and support the overall program objectives.
- Are of compelling interest to members of the project team. Each should feel they have a stake in the outcome.
- Are 'doable' in the time allocated.
- Can move beyond recommendations and include plans for implementation along with designated responsibilities and a time line.

In discussing prospective topics with a member of the executive board, it is useful to have the structure of the final presentation in mind, i.e.:

- What is the topic/issue?
- Why is it important?
- What needs to be done?
- How can the recommendations be implemented?

Given the time available, the topics need to be unambiguously defined. Broader issues of interest to the board member typically need to be reduced in scope and defined as a topic that is action focused. For example, a board member may be concerned with the wider issues of brand strategy. However, a topic could realistically focus on 'implementing our brand strategy in country X.'

Project topics can also be derived from an understanding of a board member's personal 'hot buttons,' namely visible, pressing issues that need to be addressed in a timely fashion. Projects can provide tangible results in such instances.

Project work facilitation

In this instance significant facilitation takes place prior to the beginning of the program. This involves preparation of project-specific material necessary to support the participant team and the selection of the teams themselves.

Project-specific material

Typically the board member's staff will be in a position to provide materials pertinent to the project. While the goal is to avoid 'reinventing the wheel,' there is a concomitant need to ensure that the documentation provided for the participants represents 'the critical few rather than the trivial many.'

Also the program director needs to provide appropriate specifications to the IC for preparing the electronic databases if required.

Choosing the project teams

The diversity of participants on any given program is a great benefit in bringing new perspectives and ideas to project issues. So teams are selected to maximize heterogeneity, although it is important to include at least one individual in each team who is likely to have some experience related directly to the project. On the other hand, maximizing the number of 'experts' assigned to each project team is assiduously avoided. The objective is for the participants to grapple with issues with which they are likely to be relatively unfamiliar. The programs have a general management rather than functional management orientation.

In selecting the team, some attention is paid to potential group dynamics and personal chemistry. While testing instruments are not administered, reliance is placed on the opinion of the client program champion who invariably knows many of the participants. Some 'rules of thumb' are applied. For example, in programs where several country management teams are in attendance, a superior and subordinate would not be assigned to the same project team.

Project facilitation during the program is as described under the project champion model, above; however, greater emphasis is placed on the facilitation of the group process with a specific faculty member assigned to this role.

Challenges and benefits

Experience is such that clarity in the project definition and provision of appropriate support material cannot be overemphasized. Inevitably this means working closely with the board member and his or her staff prior to the program.

On the opening night, the presence of the CEO or a member of the executive board is indispensable. The ideal is for the CEO to stress the credibility of the project experience and its value to the organization. Other than for the first offering of the program, reference can be made to prior projects and their implementation records and successes. Additionally, what can be learned from failure? What projects didn't get implemented and why?

The project experience can be adversely affected by a dysfunctional group process. This can be reduced through collaboration with the client's program champion in assigning individuals to the project team, but it may not be eliminated. Hence it is necessary to monitor group dynamics from the outset and to have faculty with group process facilitation skills present.

There is a need to address 'the fear of failure.' On the first occasion this model was used, the participants, rather than relishing the opportunity to grapple with issues of immediate relevance to the board and subsequently present their recommendations and implementation plans, felt intimidated by the experience. The perception was that the project exercise was, in a sense, evaluative, with inevitable downside consequences. Subsequent efforts made to clarify the scope of the projects and the positioning of the projects within the program as a whole, as well as managing expectations of both participants and board members alike, prevented any reoccurrence. Clearly sensitivities are heightened on those occasions when there is a transition to a new CEO or a rotation of members of the board.

The benefits of this approach can be objectively assessed in terms of the number and speed with which board champion projects have been implemented. Teams have been invited to board meetings to present their recommendations and then mandated to implement them. Others have been seconded to task forces.

Key take-aways

■ Moving from a group consensus to a board champion approach, projects increase in visibility within the organization and have a potentially greater pay-off, but there is a trade-off insofar as the design, development and delivery of the project experience increases in complexity and risk as the move is made.

■ This complexity and the management of downside risk is reflected in the challenges that the program directors face in managing the project development process, particularly the interface with the client, assuring the availability of project-related material and in the facilitation of the projects themselves.

21

Entrepreneurship at the core: The MBA and EMBA start-up projects experiences

Benoît Leleux and Jim Pulcrano

Summary

Entrepreneurship should be a core element of the learning experience, not left on the fringes of the curriculum but rather brought into the mainstream. To operate effectively, today's managers need a good understanding of the issues surrounding the entrepreneurial phenomenon. The most effective way for participants to gain that knowledge is by investing time and effort in a real start-up project. This allows them to compare theory with day-to-day reality and, more importantly, to learn how to manage the complexities of the real world. The authors illustrate the benefits of this approach with a case study of a start-up project that formed part of the IMD MBA program in 2003.

Whereas many might be all too happy to limit entrepreneurship to an elective for would-be entrepreneurs, since they are a breed that never really fitted into MBA programs anyway, we believe it should be a core focus of the educational experience. Below, we review the rationale for incorporating entrepreneurship deeply into the curriculum, how it helps solve some of the dilemmas at graduate schools of business, and finally some insights on both MBA and Executive MBA start-up projects at IMD.

Shaking the tree

To make entrepreneurship a core focus, you have to rethink from the inside out the roles for, and approaches used to teach entrepreneurship within management programs. That means debunking some traditional fallacies about the world of entrepreneurship, dispelling misunderstandings about the field and its potential contributions. Consider these seven popular truths, fallacies and misunderstandings from the 'Hall of Shame.'

1 If they sign up for an MBA, they are probably not entrepreneurs

Let's face it, MBA programs are primarily positioned as graduate programs for future corporate managers rather than entrepreneurs. Not a single one, not even Babson College's acclaimed entrepreneurship program, would ever claim to target 'future entrepreneurs.' At best, most programs provide an entrepreneurial gloss over a solid core of managerial skills and abilities. According to the common view, pure entrepreneurs are too busy launching new companies and would never bother to take time off for an academic program. This attitude, and not some self-selection, explains why the vast majority of MBA students are probably not entrepreneurs.

And that in turn explains the traditional business school approach to the discipline: because entrepreneurship interests only a small proportion of the students it should be offered only as an elective. But is this a proper definition of the field, or just a convenient minimalist treatment that avoids bringing it into the mainstream, where it would compete for airtime and credits with more established disciplines? Are we missing out on a whole array of contributions, such as an understanding of how to nurture new ideas, or how to get the most from renegade, innovative teams or how to best source-in new technologies from outside the corporation?

2 If it matters, there must be a simple model for it

A former Dean of a well-known business school best described the second fallacy. When asked by a journalist how they managed to create such an extraordinary depository of knowledge, his response was stupefyingly simple: 'We recruit the best and brightest students, milk them dry of what they know, and then send them off to new horizons, retaining the knowledge . . .' Most observers have been shocked by the 'conformism' drummed into students by typical MBA programs. Not only do they all end up talking the same generic language, but also it seems they all view the world through the very same models. How do very bright, independent thinkers end up so homogeneously molded into a standard format? Is there anything we can do to retain the freshness of their thinking, and their ability to develop solutions outside the scope of existing management models? Perhaps an understanding of how entrepreneurs thrive in nonconformist situations will help our MBAs become less willing to accept simple models.

3 The world is a gigantic case study

Case studies can be wonderful 'reality tests' that allow students to confront the complexity of business situations and decisions. Nonetheless, however rich these teaching cases may be, they cannot come close to the true complexity of the real world. Similarly, cases often fail to capture the dynamic nature of industries, where every decision will generate an immediate and often drastic response from competitors; or where the long-term impact of a decision can significantly reduce the spectrum of future opportunities or even the company's ability to respond. How do you make sure these critical dimensions are incorporated into the knowledge base? How can live, truly unpredictable situations be put in front of our MBA students for resolution in real time?

4 Entrepreneurs are born, not made

Genetic science has never been much help to the field of entrepreneurship – intense research over 30 years has failed to identify a single trait unique to entrepreneurs. They are not 'risk lovers,' but instead are as risk averse as the population at large. While they may believe that they can control the risk inherent in entrepreneurial situations more than others, they certainly are not masochists! Once this fallacy is put to rest, the real question becomes: Can you really teach entrepreneurship? Our response is always the same: We cannot force anyone to become an entrepreneur, but we can certainly make people feel more comfortable with the fact that this is just another career path and that they can learn the skills needed.

5 Entrepreneurship is just about handling chaos

Too often we find that students and colleagues regard entrepreneurship and discipline as polar opposites, and since discipline is the order of the day in corporations, why would anyone need to understand a day in the life of an entrepreneur? Too often, when an MBA is asked why he or she didn't do an assignment in a rigorous or disciplined manner the flippant response is 'I was trying to be entrepreneurial.' Some of the most rigorous and disciplined managers and teams we've worked with are in start-ups. This stands to reason when one considers the lack of resources available. Is there a way to get students to understand the benefits of an environment lacking in resources, and bring that rigor into their work, wherever it is?

6 Entrepreneurship is just about understanding venture capital

If one looks through the literature most often assigned to MBA students in entrepreneurship courses, it is dominated by text on the venture funding process. While absolutely necessary, it's far from the whole picture. How do we help students to see the intensity of the people side of a start-up, where the psychological ups and downs form a sine wave of high frequency and large amplitude? What tools do we have to show them the difficulty of late-night gut decisions when you're 'betting the company'?

7 Entrepreneurship as a subject doesn't really exist. It is just an integration mechanism

For most of its existence, entrepreneurship as an academic discipline carefully avoided having to provide a formal definition of itself. A young field, the reasoning went, needed as much breathing room as possible to find its place in the academic world. A definition, many feared, would somehow restrict a dynamic and emerging discipline. This allowed people to give their own meanings to the word. Interestingly, the best definition of entrepreneurship was also one of the earliest: Joseph Schumpeter, the famed Viennese economist, defined 'the entrepreneur' as someone who destroys the existing economic order by introducing new products and services, by creating new forms of organizations, or by exploiting new raw materials, or by providing innovative combinations in these areas. For Schumpeter, this was 'creative destruction,' which was often accompanied by the formation of new businesses, though not necessarily.

Following in the footsteps of Schumpeter, we define entrepreneurship as the creation and pursuit of opportunities regardless of the size and resources currently controlled by the company. Simply put, the entrepreneurial process includes all the functions, activities and actions associated with perceiving opportunities and creating (or mobilizing) resources and organizations to pursue them.[1] But isn't that exactly how each academic discipline claims its intellectual territory? Isn't marketing about identifying and/or creating markets and defining the channels to reach the customers? Isn't finance about funding the growth of companies? Isn't operations research about organizing operations to efficiently capture opportunities?

In the definition, we carefully avoid any reference to size or ownership. Entrepreneurship is *not* about small businesses, nor can it be equated solely with family businesses. Most small and/or family-run firms are utterly non-entrepreneurial in their ways and means, i.e. they are not actively searching for growth and value creation. On the other hand, we believe that any entre-preneur is a 'family business problem' waiting to happen. While this may sound facetious, it highlights some common misunderstandings in the field that led to its isolation.

Start-up projects in the Executive MBA

The IMD Executive MBA is designed for high-level, high-potential managers, averaging 17 years of experience and 40 years of age, wishing to get their MBA, but wanting to stay in their current jobs.

In 1998, as we were designing IMD's EMBA program, we wondered how to help our students, corporate executives, understand the way that entrepre-neurs nurture products from a vision to profitability; we called this 'the idea-to-wealth path.' We had already decided to run a one-week total immersion module in Silicon Valley, but we were grappling with how to get beyond voyeurism, that is, visiting and observing entrepreneurs like exotic zoo creatures. We had discussed the idea of having the EMBA students write a business plan on a fictitious company, but then in a conversation with prominent Silicon Valley venture capitalist Jos Henckens we hit on the idea of having the participants work closely with a real high-tech start-up, and then pitching that start-up to real venture capitalists. As Jos said, *'It'll make it a lot more interesting to me to be involved, and probably to your students as well.'*

Our work begins when we select the start-ups. IMD runs a 'business plan' competition across Switzerland and the nearby areas in France and Germany every autumn, looking for early-stage companies that fit our criteria: (1) with a chance of succeeding, (2) while targeting a huge market, (3) with an openness to learn something from working with our EMBAs, (4) in a product area that would interest Silicon Valley investors and (5) in an exciting area for the participants. For a class of 70 EMBA students, we choose four start-ups; three teams work with each of the four ventures.

The first contact between the EMBAs and the entrepreneurs is a 15-minute pitch by the start-up to the entire class in January, trying to convince each and every participant to work with their company (the participants are permitted to choose which start-up they want to work with). It's basically the same exercise the EMBAs will go through months later with potential investors in Silicon Valley.

Between March and September, each EMBA team tries to understand their start-up. First and foremost, they are attempting to get into the minds of the entrepreneurs – to understand why they are doing this, the origin of their idea, how they chose their colleagues, the ups and downs thus far, and so on. To guide the EMBAs we give them a template, 'the entrepreneur's worksheet,' with a series of questions that help them look beyond the company and the product, to the people behind it. We find this worksheet to be a necessary tool, as the EMBAs tend to approach the start-up as a project to be completed, and often need to be prompted to get into the seemingly tangential issues that can make the difference between success and failure in the start-up team.

In addition to this worksheet, the EMBAs have several other deliverables with hard due dates. The first one is their work plan, laying out how the team intends to work with their start-up: who will take what roles, what means or technology they will use to collaborate, how the work is split up and the self-imposed milestones they will work to. The second is a document meant to start moving them towards their Silicon Valley expedition, both literally and figuratively: (a) identification of a existing or potential competitor or client located in Silicon Valley and (b) a simple Porter Five Forces analysis of their start-up's industry. Finally, just before arrival in California, the students submit their team's entrepreneurship worksheet and an elevator pitch for their company.

This period, from March to September, is challenging for everyone. First, there is the geographic distance between the participants in each team[2] as well as from their start-up. Second, though they have differing objectives and time constraints, they must somehow function as a team. Third, while very interested in the EMBA work, the start-ups are also distracted by the hundreds of high-priority tasks and emergencies they must deal with, normally without the required resources to do so. Finally, there is the mindset gap between the entrepreneurs and the typical EMBA participant. Successful completion of the assignment requires overcoming all four of these barriers.

In September, upon arrival on Sunday morning in California, the class learns the details of the remainder of their assignment: take whatever they have done so far, combine it with what they will learn during their week in the Valley, and by the end of the week fashion a 15-minute pitch that *they* will make on behalf of the start-up to a small group of Silicon Valley venture capitalists and angel investors. Most EMBAs accept this as being just a great challenge: *'Why not? We've worked with this start-up for three and a half months, so let's see if we're good enough to get a positive reaction from a tight-fisted VC.'* A few even think it will be simple: *'Just another PowerPoint presentation. How is this different from anything else I've done in my high-pressure corporate career?'*

And then there are those who say it's not possible, that they have been tasked with a challenge that can only embarrass them, the start-up and IMD. They insist that the pitch should somehow be delayed. But when asked, 'Would a real entrepreneur simply say no to an opportunity to pitch his company to potential investors? Would he say that he'd rather come back at a later date when his pitch is perfect?' the EMBAs invariably see the pitch through the eyes of the entrepreneur – an opportunity not to be passed up!

This week is also an opportunity to get to know their entrepreneurs even better, face to face. One member of each start-up company is embedded into the class for the duration of the week, acting as a resource and a sounding board all week long for the EMBAs, while they themselves learn and look for business opportunities in Silicon Valley.

Through the week, we see the EMBAs work on their pitches as they talk to the Silicon Valley people they encounter. When they visit start-ups, they are listening critically to how the founder pitches his firm to them. They ask targeted questions to understand how they raised money and built their teams. They try to understand the questions that VCs typically ask start-ups. They talk to established companies about their acquisitions of, and investments in, start-ups. They push hard to understand how intellectual property is treated strategically in a high-tech start-up (and is not just left as a side issue for lawyers). They talk with HR experts about what it's like to work in a high-speed, intense environment. And all the while their pitch is evolving. Pre-breakfast and late-evening team meetings advance the pitch. Drafts are repeatedly tried and then torn up. Tensions rise in some teams. Excitement in others. And the stress level for everyone is high.

On Friday morning each team gets their time alone in a small room with two or three professionals who have seen hundreds, if not thousands, of pitches. A 15-minute pitch followed by 10 minutes of rapid, laser-fire questions. These VCs and angels are not there simply to help IMD; they are also there because they think, just maybe, one of these Swiss start-ups might be worth looking at more closely. So, they are asking tough questions. They don't care that the presenters are EMBA participants, and not real entrepreneurs – they want to know if this company is worth another five minutes of their time. Their questions show it.

Then, for most, it's over. Afterwards some describe it as a life-changing experience. Others talk of how, for the first time, they understand the thrill of entrepreneurship. Still others talk about how they developed as a team over the last few days. All are looking for feedback on how to do it better the next time, even if that next time is just a PowerPoint pitch to their own management.

This is the only assignment of the EMBA program that is not evaluated by IMD. The faculty does not grade it, though we do provide feedback if asked. Our belief is that the EMBAs get their 'grade' from the feedback of the VCs, a far better evaluation than any academics could provide.

Entrepreneurship at the core: The MBA start-up projects

The ethos underpinning the MBA start-up projects mirrors that of the EMBA projects, although they are run differently. By defining entrepreneurship as the process of pursuing opportunities regardless of size, ownership or the resources under control, we put it at the center of the educational mission – it belongs neither on the fringe of business education for the future general manager, nor is its relevance limited strictly to future independent entrepreneurs. We believe that no manager today can operate properly in a corporate environment without a solid understanding of the entrepreneurial phenomenon, i.e. the 'hows and whats' of entrepreneurial undertakings and innovation. Whether directly in charge of new ventures or as a supervisor of corporate entrepreneurs, senior managers in tomorrow's firms must understand and master the unusual challenges associated with creativity and innovation.

How can such mastery be acquired? Many business schools conduct 'business plan competitions,' which are usually tied to a course in new venture creation or business plans. These events often serve as powerful reminders of the fact that most graduate students are not entrepreneurs; while they may cook up some 'pro-forma' business plans for a grade, they are little more than classroom exercises – any real investor can sense the students' lack of commitment, the formulaic analyses (most are forced to fit it within a standard academic calendar of semesters or trimesters), and the simple futility of the effort. In the end, virtually none of the claimed benefits of the exercise are achieved: students are frustrated by such an incomplete and fictitious exercise, in which they interacted with others as uncommitted to the project as they are. So why force students to manufacture 'opportunities' when most do not have any to offer and are only perfunctorily committed to them? Why waste months in this process while missing out on the most interesting parts of the exercise, that is, the actual development of business models to capture the unseen opportunities and then their implementation?

As with the EMBA projects, in our view, the most effective way for participants to meaningfully learn about entrepreneurial processes is to 'live the start-up experience,' i.e. to actually spend time and effort within an entrepreneur's team and project. Following the success of the EMBA experience, start-up projects became part of the core curriculum of the IMD MBA program in 2002, irrespective of whether participants intend to actually start a *de novo* new venture. The principal purpose of these hands-on projects is for MBA students to experience the specific challenges facing entrepreneurs and then to develop the capability to act as venture boosters. It is not (necessarily) to transform them into entrepreneurs, but to engender a direct and pragmatic understanding of the issues surrounding the entrepreneurial phenomenon. With this intimate knowledge, these MBAs will be able to operate more efficiently in entrepreneurial environments and more effectively deal with internal/external start-ups.

Organization

A few months before the start of the MBA and EMBA programs, as explained earlier, regional high-tech start-ups are recruited through the 'IMD Business Plan Competition.' While the EMBA program selects four ventures, for the MBAs we seek to recruit 15–16 start-ups each year, out of a pool of submissions that has numbered as high as 60. Start-ups selected to work with the MBAs obtain, free of charge, the 'use' of a group of six students to develop/ polish an entrepreneurial business plan, for either 'start-up' or 'growth.' The following criteria are used to select the ventures:

- Exciting projects, with which students will easily connect.
- A dedicated start-up team, willing and able to work with the students.
- Enough elements in place (funding, etc.) to ensure that the company will still be active nine months later (the projects are selected in December and the student projects last from January to June).
- A broad diversity of situations, which enables students to exchange insights across MBA start-up projects. Projects may be at the seed level, at start-up level (with teams and proof-of-concept), and some already in sales/revenue positive mode.

Mandate

During the first week of the MBA program, the students are introduced to 'their' start-up, with a simple mandate: **add value**. This mandate is so simple that it truly baffles them. First, they have to **identify the problems** faced by the start-up company. If they ask us, our response is always the same: 'I don't know what the problems are, but believe us, those are start-ups and they are here for a reason! They have many problems, and it is your mandate to identify them, sort out symptoms from real problems, and prioritize them.' Second, they have to **create solutions** for these problems, for which pre-packaged formulas are unlikely to work. Third, they have to **credibly deliver these solutions to the entrepreneurs** to ensure proper implementation. These start-up projects are *not* consulting assignments but hands-on operational projects, with implementation plans.

The MBA start-up teams are expected to spend the equivalent of six hours per week on their start-up project over the course of the integrated core module of the MBA (January to May); with an average of six participants per team, this represents a total of some 600 man-hours. While some time has been built into the program schedule for this, students also have to make room for the start-up project, usually on evenings and weekends. The student teams provide the start-ups with the support they need to move their project forward significantly, including:

■ Providing methodologies and frameworks.

■ Investigating alternative outpacing strategies.

■ Developing a precise customer-value proposition and its supporting elements.

■ Analyzing business models for specific next steps: entry strategies, marketing approaches, growth plans and so on.

Each project is coached by a faculty member whose role is to:

■ Ensure that the student team understands the needs of, and delivers value to, the start-up.

■ Communicate with the start-up before, during and after the MBA team intervention as a reality check for relevance and understanding.

■ Assess, with the start-up, the effectiveness of the student team in delivering value to them.

MBA start-up projects: The true deliverables

In addition to the obvious project deliverables outlined in the previous section, the MBA start-up projects generate unexpected dividends for the program as a whole and for the participants. They include reality checks, influencing the attitude to life of the students, a demystification of the process, and genuine aid for the start-up.

Instantaneous reality checks

The start-up projects are real-life situations that run in parallel with the core modules of the MBA program, including one module with an 'entrepreneurship toolkit.' These real-life situations are ideal for testing models presented in the classroom, and these tests inevitably point out the limitations of theoretical models. Students learn that the models can be a guide, but are not an end in themselves. They realize that they will need problem-specific solutions, and that is a path we encourage them to take.

The right attitude to life

Start-ups offer ever-evolving, dynamic settings in which humility comes naturally. This is the ideal cure for a traditional 'MBA students attitude': their growing belief that they can solve any problem, that they are all-powerful. The start-up experience usually cuts them down to size and they emerge with a more balanced attitude towards the real world. Not only do they lack pre-packaged solutions for every problem, but also they may simply fail to solve some; they are not superhuman.

Many MBAs at an early stage of their project can be heard criticizing 'their' entrepreneur for being disorganized, or not understanding certain business fundamentals, or for being a dreamer. Through the process of the project the students develop a high level of respect for the entrepreneurs. At the end, one MBA remarked, *'What did I learn? What these guys do is hard work. I never imagined the intensity of their world. This is not for me!'*

Demystifying the entrepreneurial process

Traditional MBA business plan competitions do little to expose the deeper mechanics of the entrepreneurial process. This is the 'blind leading the one-eyed' syndrome, or 'preaching to the converted': because each party to the business plan is equally untrained, no one is really equipped to be critical and realistic. The end-of-program 'presentations' do nothing to provide the participants with any realistic experience of the entrepreneurial process as a whole, for which the business plan development is, at best, the least critical phase.

In contrast, the start-up projects put students in the trenches, alongside real entrepreneurs with their failings, real products and their limitations, real markets and uncertainties. There are neither conceptual escape hatches nor modeling shortcuts: issues have to be dealt with on the ground as they come up. There is nothing elegant or sexy about a start-up – it is the single-minded pursuit of an opportunity with whatever it takes to make it flourish and grow. This is not 'lawn tennis at Wimbledon' but 'mud rugby at Lansdowne Road.' In our view, only this close interaction with a real entrepreneurial team rowing against all elements provides the proper understanding of the entrepreneurial process. Writing a business plan merely serves to formalize this deep understanding of the process: it is an end, but the journey to that end is what is of real importance.

Helping the entrepreneurial community

For a start-up company, perpetually short on time and money, this short burst of outside help and perspective can be manna from heaven. In addition, many venture capital invitees, who are there to witness the final deliverables of the projects, turn into key future start-up project suppliers for IMD. They too see the potential of these projects (or lack thereof) to 'fix' promising ventures with defects or shortcomings. These pre-screened deals, selected by venture capitalists to receive the 'treatment,' are real-world credible: the entrepreneurs understand quickly that this may be the key that unlocks their next round of financing!

An MBA start-up project case study: ABMI

December 2003. Lausanne, Switzerland. Claudio Lucchesi, founder and CEO of Advanced Biomedical Intelligence (ABMI), excitedly picked up his phone. The *Wall Street Journal* had chosen ABMI to receive its top award for technological innovation in Europe, and since then the phone had been ringing non-stop. Friends, local journalists and venture capitalists all wanted to know more about his business.

Lucchesi pressed his ear to the receiver, but he was only half-listening. He could not help reflecting on the last few months. The road to success had been bumpy indeed. Having worked for three years to create a device to provide real-time monitoring of the tiny particles that clog brain arteries and trigger strokes, he knew he could add value to the medical field. However, at the end of 2002 when ABMI was formed, he still felt uncertain about his business model and had little idea of how the market would respond to his concept.

To address these gaps in his knowledge, he had decided in 2002 to bring in the services of an MBA start-up team through the IMD Business Plan Competition. Without their help, would he have gone that far that fast?

ABMI – revolutionizing stroke care

Strokes are caused by particles that block the normal flow of blood to the brain. The culprit is usually a blood clot (or embolus) that has formed in an artery and traveled to the brain. Wandering clots can also emerge because of atrial fibrillation – a disorder in which the heart's upper chambers quiver rather than beat normally. Consequently, some blood pools in the heart and clots; if a clot migrates to the brain, it can trigger a stroke. Some 700,000 Americans and 600,000 Europeans suffer a new or recurrent stroke each year. In the US, 170,000 lives are lost to the disease annually, making it the third-largest killer after heart attack and cancer.

If doctors could monitor the distribution of blood in the brain in the days immediately following the emergence of symptoms, they would be able to better treat stroke patients. Similar real-time data would also be useful during cardiovascular surgery, when surgical debris increases the risk of stroke. Doctors commonly use three types of diagnostic tool. First, Computed Tomography Scan (CAT scan) employs radiation to produce a picture of the brain that indicates the location of the stroke and the extent of brain injury. Unfortunately, CAT scan images are so crude that up to 30 percent of their results can be misinterpreted. Second, Magnetic Resonance Imaging (MRI) generates sharper images and can diagnose smaller, deeper injuries. However, injuries take up to six hours to show up and MRI is poorly suited to patients with ferromagnetic fragments or those suffering from claustrophobia. Moreover, MRI equipment is unavailable in most hospitals. Third, blood flow tests are usually conducted with Doppler ultrasound, an established technology in cardiology. Doppler devices bounce ultrasound waves off a patient's brain; if a blood clot is present, the intensity of the signal briefly increases, alerting the doctor. Unfortunately, this technology can neither distinguish between gaseous blood clots, essentially harmless bubbles of gas, and the life-threatening solids, nor measure their size.

The company

ABMI was attempting to create the next generation Doppler ultrasound, which would be designed to provide doctors with more accurate readings. A spin-off from Lausanne University, it originated with a three-year CHF 800,000 joint-research project with the two main hospitals in the area. On 31 January 2003, Theoretical Physics Professors Giovanni Dietler and Claudio Lucchesi, with Claudio's wife Fabienne, incorporated the company. To launch their venture, the founders invested CHF 100,000; subsequently, they received seed funds and financial support from a number of public and private sources.

Finding resources at little or no cost with the support of Lausanne University, Lucchesi kept the company's 'burn rate' very low, around CHF 2,500 per month, which covered salaries and rent. As of December 2003, he did not receive a salary. The CHF 500,000 Swiss Booster start-up program funding covered all other costs, including the salary of the three employees developing the hardware and software.

ABMI technology

ABMI was developing a pulsed-wave transcranial Doppler, or TCD (see Appendix 21.1 for a description of ABMI's technology). This technology used several 'windows' into the skull (from the temple, orbit and back of the neck) to study intracranial vessels at various depths and locations. In order to provide a better solution than existing products in the TCD market, Lucchesi focused his efforts on: (1) differentiating between signals from solid and gaseous emboli and (2) estimating the size of the embolus.

The MBA start-up project

Lucchesi met his six-student team in late-January 2003 at IMD. He had very high expectations. Having supplied a copy of his business plan a few weeks earlier, he was eager to find out how these business-trained minds could help him. From the MBA team's perspective, the meeting was more about clarification. Two members of the team recalled:

The business plan was quite long, but did not address some of the business basics. For example, the potential market size was covered with only a few lines of text and there was no evidence of where the market numbers came from. It also did not address where the real opportunity was. In fact, it was not clear as to whether the market needed his product.

As a medical doctor, I could not figure out from the plan how ABMI's products would actually improve my medical practice. There was a lot of scientific lingo, which my non-medically trained teammates could not understand. I was eager to learn from Claudio during the first meeting why he thought his product would make an impact in the market. Initially, it really was not clear.

The meeting ran very long. After the usual casual talk, the MBA team launched a barrage of questions, putting Lucchesi on the defensive. He responded that once they understood the technology, they would see things his way. He invited the MBA team to his laboratory for a detailed demonstration. With hindsight, one of the team members elaborated on what went wrong during this first meeting:

We had been trained to question everything and to come on strong, just like in class. However, this approach was not helpful with an entrepreneur. It's different than in the corporate world where you can throw out ideas and have your colleagues shoot them down. Here, shooting down Claudio's ideas was the same as shooting down his life's work! We did not consider his feelings enough.

Rethinking the communication

The MBA team decided that, because their 'six-on-one' approach to communication would put Lucchesi on the defensive, they'd better improve on it as soon as possible. Jeanette Ng, a lawyer who was accustomed to working with delicate situations, was chosen to be the sole point of contact with Lucchesi.

We needed someone who was good at disarming people. Jeanette had that special way of making people feel comfortable. Her seven years of doing legal M&A work had trained her to use her calm and embracing voice in a very effective manner.

The team then went to the University of Lausanne to visit Lucchesi's laboratory. Only two members of the team, both medical doctors, were able to fully appreciate the complexities of ABMI's working model (Figure 21.1). Nevertheless, the visit proved helpful to everyone. They were able to get a sense of what was going on. As one team member put it:

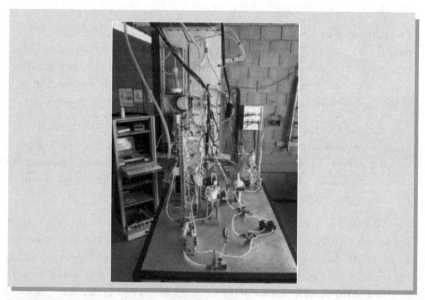

Figure 21.1 ABMI's working model

The passion and excitement really shone through when Claudio demonstrated the product. I think all of us began to take the start-up idea and concept much more seriously when we were able to see the work that he had done in the last three years. There was a greater sense of appreciation from that time.

Getting the pulse of the market

After a number of in-depth interviews with ABMI's management team, the team understood that they had to survey the marketplace. The first step was to develop a questionnaire. Lucchesi was reluctant, because he worried not only about confidentiality, that someone might steal his idea, but also that the respondents – his potential customers – would be put off. After some effort, the team convinced him that the survey would provide invaluable information. (The two medical doctors on the team explained to Lucchesi that doctors received surveys all the time and answered them as part of their obligation to the medical field.) In March the 16-question survey was sent to almost 800 neurologists, radiologists, cardiologists and cardiac surgeons in Switzerland. It was accompanied with a short cover letter, signed by one of the physicians on the MBA team; he was chosen because he was Swiss and might be known by some of the recipients of the survey, which added credibility to the initiative. Given its previous experience with surveys in the pharmaceutical industry, the team estimated that a return rate above 4 percent could be considered a success.

The team eventually received 46 completed surveys, a 6 per cent return rate; two-thirds of the respondents were neurologists, the most important target group. Explained Alexander, who because of his medical background had been chosen to present the results to Lucchesi:

Let me start off by saying that the survey results are promising. It shows a lot of room to capitalize on additional opportunities in the market. Overall, customer needs are not fully met. Although you identified portability as a key differentiator, it does not seem to be the case, probably because existing products are already either portable or can be moved easily or that the patients are stationary . . .

User friendliness still needs to be improved. Regarding ABMI's technology, there seems to be a need to improve emboli differentiation versus artifacts or solid versus gas. Service and upgrades represent another area where customer needs are not met yet.

The further the questionnaire debriefing session advanced, the more painful it proved to be for Lucchesi. There were a few times when he was ready to object, but these results came from the marketplace. It was difficult to argue with them. After having initially taken the feedback as a personal criticism, he finally digested the results and their implications for his business system. He would have to deliver a better product and more service than he had initially planned.

A competitive marketplace

The survey also revealed that the transcranial Doppler market was more crowded than expected. Conventional Doppler ultrasound machines, normally used in neurology, in fact also performed transcranial diagnoses. Most important, ABMI learned that larger players, such as Siemens and Philips, were entering the competition; they already occupied a large part of the market. Another important finding indicated the extent to which ABMI's core product might compete with the products already available on the market. Participants first rated 11 identified needs in order of importance and then assessed how these needs were currently met. The difference between the two answers identified 'potential gaps,' which demonstrated the need for improvement in the market; however, the ABMI product enjoyed no single area of particular strength. In order to make a significant impact in the market, the company would have to go beyond the single-technology attribute, offering not only superior technology but also other improved features, such as user friendliness, regular upgrades and so on. Another key finding pertained to the purchasing decision process: the department chief approved products for the hospital. In addition, the principal sources of information for physicians were medical journals and congresses, which meant that ABMI would have to engage in clinical trials and attend important medical congresses.

Shared benefits

Impressed with their work, Lucchesi said:

I loved this team. I admired their spirit, their dedication, their kindness and their smartness. This was the case for all people in the team. No joke, no false flattery. The market and client expectation survey was the most rewarding aspect of the project.

Capitalizing on their insights, Lucchesi redirected his development efforts. Later on, ABMI won some of the most prestigious technology and innovation awards. In addition to the *Wall Street Journal* Award that recognized his technology as standing at the forefront of medical research, he also won CTI funding (the Swiss Commission for Technology and Innovation).

The CTI award was CHF 1.2 million (US$800,000) that provided funding and manpower to further boost the R&D efforts. He continued:

Now venture capitalists are calling me up, the local press is after me, it's a bit of hype – I need to keep cool!

For their part, IMD's MBA start-up team found the experience highly rewarding. Although none of the six team members joined a start-up or launched their own venture, they all took away some invaluable insights. As two of them explained:

Unlike some of the others on the team, I had never worked with a start-up before; nor had I worked with someone so passionate about an idea. Working with Claudio allowed me to gain insight into the massive complexities that are involved with bringing a scientific idea to the market. The team-building skills and on-the-fly project management skills that I was able to hone during the project are invaluable.

I have worked with many start-ups in the past, but none of them were in the medical field. Seeing how Claudio was able to tackle the challenges of intellectual property rights, clinical trials, and research and development was enlightening. You can't learn this kind of stuff in a textbook or a case study. I'm joining the medical technology field after graduation and I am sure this experience will give me one edge up on my colleagues.

Nonetheless, three of the six team members joined either pharmaceutical or medical device companies after their MBA graduation. When told about the MBA venture team's post-IMD job plans, Claudio declared, 'Maybe I can do some good business with them at their companies!'

Conclusions

With seven years of hindsight, we can certainly say that the use of start-ups in the MBA and EMBA programs has been successful. After their experience working with entrepreneurs we see that the students are more comfortable with ideas, people and teams that do not fit the norm. They have developed respect for those who do not take the typical corporate path, and tried to bring some of those 'entrepreneurial best practices' into their own mode of working. They are more willing to give space to the innovators they work with, but also understand that the skills, frameworks and tools they have learned in their MBA have value in the start-up world. And last but not least, they have a deeper understanding of the many barriers to success along the idea-to-wealth path, as well as the joy in surmounting those barriers.

Key take-aways

- Today's managers need an understanding of entrepreneurship: how to start and develop businesses, stimulate and run growth initiatives; in brief, the 'idea-to-wealth' path.

- Working with real start-ups is the best way of learning about entrepreneurship; business plan competitions, tied to a classroom course, are not realistic enough.

- Involvement in an evolving start-up project offers participants a unique opportunity to develop customized analytical frameworks, as well as to investigate alternative development strategies, a precise customer-value proposition, entry strategies, marketing approaches, venture capital pitches and so on.

- Start-ups provide the challenge of ongoing, dynamic environments which require not only business issues but also psychological and team issues to be dealt with in real time.

Notes

1   Bygrave, W. (1997) The Entrepreneurial Process. *In: The Portable MBA in Entrepreneurship.* New York: John Wiley & Sons.
2   They are not on campus during this time, because the EMBA uses a number of distance learning modules.

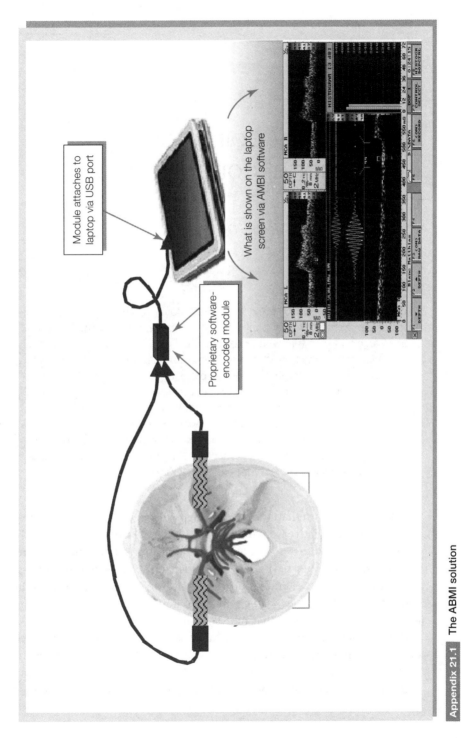

Module attaches to laptop via USB port

What is shown on the laptop screen via AMBI software

Proprietary software-encoded module

Appendix 21.1 The ABMI solution

22

Learning by doing through international consulting projects

Z. Jan Kubes and Mopesola Ogunsulire

Summary

International consulting projects (ICPs) move MBAs from classroom discussion to the practical application of management concepts, theories and frameworks on real-world projects within different organizations. It is action learning in the purest sense of the word. This chapter describes the pre-launch project activities, how the projects are launched, the organization of the project teams, the first client meeting and letter of agreement, the presentations to the client and the four phases of the projects themselves: industry analysis, company analysis, issue analysis and development of recommendations. It concludes with a discussion of the initial implementation of the recommendations in the company itself and a case study of a successful project that has had tangible business impact.

At IMD, the MBA international consulting projects (ICPs) are the way in which participants move from the artificial glass bowl environment of study groups and case studies to the practical application of the management theory with which they have been bombarded in the preceding six months. While the cases studies and group work help to ground their learning in context, the ICP is *action learning* in the purest sense of the word as the groups immediately apply that new learning and skills to real-life projects within different organizations. The MBAs *learn by doing* what they have until then only practiced within the relatively risk-free environment of study groups and class discussion. In the process, they develop the managerial skills and attitudes they will require as future business leaders.

Participants learn to exercise judgment as they start to realize that real-life problems do not always conform to the neat frameworks and models encountered in management theory. During the projects, they practice the judicious application of theory to practical problems, learning to take what is useful and applicable, and gaining the courage and confidence to discard what is not. Finally, as illustrated in Figure 22.1, the ICPs also focus on developing skills that cannot be easily taught in the classroom, such as the formulation of hypotheses, information gathering and real-life implementation skills. The projects extend the participants' skills beyond case studies at either end from recommending to implementing, and before analysis, into information gathering.

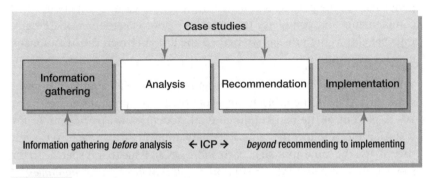

Figure 22.1   Core skills developed through projects

This chapter draws on experience gathered from more than 350 projects carried out at IMD over the past 25 years.

ICP teaching philosophy and approach

The international consulting project as an effective learning tool

The pedagogy of the consulting projects links directly to the four phases of learning outlined in Chapter 1 of this book. As discussed, the individual learning process is fluid and non-linear because every person has a unique set of experiences and knowledge. However, for learning to become embedded and to be applied in practice, learners generally need to go through the four phases of learning: challenge, as the person is exposed to new information and ways of doing things; investigate, where analysis is undertaken to understand the nature of the challenge and possible ways of addressing it; construct, which involves exploring how the potential solutions and learning can be applied; and change, a reflection on what the learning means for the person's beliefs and behavior going forward. Because the ICPs address all the stages of this learning process, their impact on the learning of the MBA participants can be considerable.

The philosophy and approach of the international consulting projects

The IMD MBA projects aim to benefit everyone involved; the corporate sponsors, the MBA participants and the school. Sponsors benefit by receiving specific recommendations to improve their company's economic performance. The participants benefit from a rich learning experience that complements and completes the program's prior classroom work. Finally, IMD benefits as the projects strengthen the links between the institute and its business community.

While many business schools offer MBA projects, not all approach it in the same way. At IMD, the projects are a core part of the program, representing 20–25 percent of the curriculum, and all students must participate in the ICP. All projects follow the same systematic four-phase approach. Yet, while they all use the same approach, each addresses an issue that is specific to the sponsoring company. IMD insists on the *involvement* and *commitment* of the sponsor's top management, including the chief executive officer. Involvement requires that the company's senior officers and decision makers attend three formal presentations, and make the required decisions at the end of phases two and three. Commitment means that the project is officially announced to the company's staff, that the project team is given access to all necessary information, and that the company assigns appropriate members of top management to work closely with the team. Finally, faculty members are actively involved. Senior members of faculty, with experience in either a line function or consulting, direct the project. They also take part in all formal, and informal, discussions with the corporate sponsors and personally supervise and guide the work of the teams, while leaving the project management entirely to the participants.

This distinctive approach to MBA consulting projects is possible because IMD's MBA students are older, and more experienced and mature, than in many other schools. All business schools teach management techniques and skills for problem solving. But in addition to these, IMD MBA participants bring significant and relevant experience to bear on client issues since they are already proven managers in their fields. ICP teams are carefully

" We avoided going ahead with a wrong strategy. **"**
Penti Hätälä, Vice President Business Development, Nokia-Maillefer

" We have been consistently impressed with the analytical contribution, enthusiasm and determination of the students. Their recommendations are well-received, and as a rule, implemented. **"**
Lou Hughes, President, General Motors Europe

selected to balance the interests and learning of the participants with the skills and experience needed on the project.

The approach has paid dividends. The ICPs remain one of the most successful elements of the MBA program, as illustrated by three key points:

■ Many sponsoring companies become repeat clients; by 2003, more than half of the 200 sponsoring companies had become repeat sponsors.

■ In addition, more than half of all sponsors had granted a voluntary bonus.

■ In a survey of past sponsors, the majority of companies indicated that they had benefited considerably in some way from the work carried out by ICP teams.[1]

The project framework: What, when, who and how?

At one time, the projects were launched with a presentation titled 'Putting It All Together' – it was a good title for that is what the consulting projects do. They merge the strategy, marketing, finance and so on that the participants have learned in the first half of the program, as is seen from a quick overview of the four project phases.

Phase 1: Industry analysis. In phase one, the MBAs develop an in-depth understanding of the client's industry, drawing on the techniques of industry analysis and strategy to which they have been introduced during the program. Their analysis starts with a definition and overview of the industry. They continue by identifying the business system and analyzing the competition and, finally, they describe the generic strategies and key success factors required within that industry.

Phase 2: Company analysis. Using financial analysis techniques, and elements of marketing, operations, human resources and so on, the participants analyze the company's performance in the light of the key success factors identified in phase one and its stated objectives and development plans.

Phase 3: Issue analysis. The teams now carry out an in-depth analysis of an issue, or problem, identified in phase 2. They develop strategic or operational options and evaluate each of these based on criteria agreed with the company. Finally, they make actionable recommendations based on their analysis, including a short- and medium-term action plan.

Phase 4: Implementation. In general, the teams are not present for the full implementation period. However, at the end of the project, they assist client executives in launching the short-term program, and develop a monitoring system so that top management can follow the implementation and introduce corrective action if necessary.

So far we have considered the 'What?' and the 'When?' of the projects, and in the following sections we will take a closer look at the detail of each phase. Equally important are the 'Who?' and the 'How?' With regard to the 'Who?' each project involves specific players (see Figure 22.2), as shown below:

The *project director* guides and directs the work of the team. He also manages client expectations, ensures communication between the team and sponsor remains clear and that IMD's commitment to the client is met.

The *sponsor* company commissions the project, gives it the full commitment of its top management and is responsible for

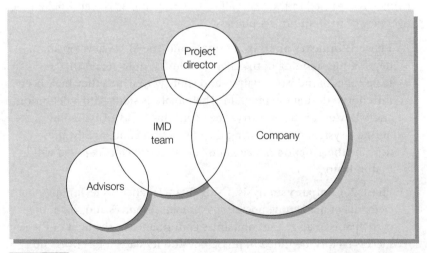

Figure 22.2 Key project players

implementation. During the project, the sponsor grants the team all necessary access to information and key personnel.

Other *advisors* among IMD faculty may be consulted to develop or confirm hypotheses, for information leads, contacts, experimenting with ideas and communication.

Ultimately, the *project team* is responsible for the planning, coordination and execution of the project.

For the 'How?' of the ICP, we shall now describe in detail the execution of the project – from the administrative set-up at the beginning to the project's impact and implementation at the company.

Execution of the ICPs

Step 1: Pre-launch project activities

While the 'official' start of the projects is the session in which the ICP projects director[2] introduces participants to the project, it actually starts some time before then when the teams are put together by the projects director. In April, the year's consulting projects are presented to the MBA participants, with some indication of each project's scope. The students then express their preferences and the projects director forms the project teams based on these preferences, and the skills or experience needed on the project. Subsequently, the team meets with the client company's executives to agree on the project focus. This is then incorporated in a letter of agreement signed by all parties involved.

Step 2: Launching the projects

After the summer break comes the official launch. The participants are shown how to start and administer the projects, and taught the framework of the ICP. Confidentiality and integrity are paramount on the project, and a failure to respect either of those results in immediate dismissal from the MBA program. In addition, participants may fail the program if on the project:

■ They are unable to apply management tools in project-related problem solving.

■ They display a lack of collegiality.

■ They are repeatedly absent during project work periods beyond those approved by the project director.

■ They do not respect deadlines, miss key client meetings or do both.

As he launches the projects, the projects director highlights two issues common to all teams, and which will determine the success of each project: team effectiveness and analytical approach.

Team effectiveness

By mid-year, the MBAs will have worked in several different teams and learned effective group processes. Now, they are reminded of the five stages of project team effectiveness which they will already have experienced several times before: forming, storming, norming, performing and, finally, mourning.[3] They know, therefore, that their teams can, and must, be well managed to be highly effective.

Analytical approach

Participants are encouraged to think strategically, to use common sense or 'street smarts' and to use their previous experience to infer the key issues on the project based on similar situations they have seen before. In his presentation, the projects director stresses the need to exercise judgment in carrying out their analyses, and also outlines the recommended analytical approach.

The teams begin the analytical process by developing an initial hypothesis that will inform the basic conclusions (see Figure 22.3). This approach

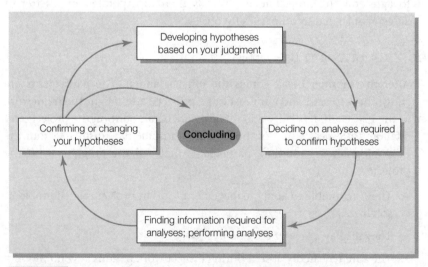

Figure 22.3   Analytical approach should follow five-step sequence

focuses the study directly on specific areas, thus limiting the amount of data gathering, the most time-consuming part of the exercise. It also forces the team to think in terms of what the critical messages of the presentation will ultimately try to convey to the client.

For example, during industry analysis, the dynamics of the business system players are identified. Some hypotheses that might be developed about these dynamics are:

- Distributors hold a high bargaining power, which supports forward integration.
- Buyers are very well informed and price sensitive, which eventually affects marketing approach.

The analytical process then attempts to confirm or otherwise disprove these hypotheses. But the teams' analysis does not stop with the confirmation process. They go further to test the sensitivity of the data supporting the hypothesis by changing one or more of the variables that form the under-lying conclusion.

The results from the analyses are communicated through a visual presentation using the *storybook method*. This is standard for phases 1 and 2, and can sometimes even be used to prepare a work plan for each of these phases.

So, the participants have been introduced to the what, when, who and how of the assignment: an important step in mapping out the steps of the problem-solving process. The MBAs now understand the overall project approach, distinct study phases and analytical approach, and expected end products. Next they organize the project teams, and identify and allocate available resources.

Step 3: Organizing the project team

Ultimately each team will be evaluated on how they handled the operational and administrative project tasks. Both are essential to its success, and the teams must, therefore, decide early on who will be responsible for what. The following roles are assigned among the team members:

1 A **group coordinator/leader**, who coordinates and leads team activities, assigns jobs and takes the final decision in case of disagreements within the group.

2 A **faculty and client contact** who acts as the link between the team and faculty and also between the client and the team.

3   The **treasurer** prepares budgets, accounts for expenditure, sends invoices to the client and reimburses group members. He and the logistics manager are the *only* team members who can operate the project's bank account – both are joint signatories to the account. The treasurer must ensure that there is a positive balance in the account at all times, and that all payments are made on time.

4   An **information manager** who manages all the information activities: from identifying sources of relevant information, storing and retrieval to dissemination. He or she also ensures that all information is returned to the sponsor, and IMD's Information Center, at the end of the project.

5   The **visual and written communication manager** controls the development of the presentation storyboard and the preparation of visual and written reports. In addition, he or she coordinates, and obtains materials for slide production.

6   A **logistics manager** to control the timetable, and movements, of the team. He or she also prepares agenda for meetings, makes reservations for traveling team members, reserves table(s) at the school's restaurant for lunches with clients, reserves rooms for presentations and checks the availability of equipment for the presentations.

The ICP is the longest period in which MBA participants work in the same team. This is essential because they must develop a 'specialization' in the client's business, and build up the team's credibility with the client and his staff. Such an extended period of working together heightens the need to develop a 'positive team atmosphere' of trust, understanding and cooperation. As the project progresses, the team must juggle and accommodate one another's needs – job interviews, family affairs or occasional moods. Therefore, it becomes critical that each one contributes positively to the team's work by setting an example to the others in terms of commitment, motivation and readiness to help.

With the various roles defined and allocated, the team is now ready to move on to the next step in the ICP – setting the stage for the project through initial contact with the client.

Step 4: Setting the stage for the project

Before starting to work on phase 1, each team sets the stage for the project in an initial meeting with the client, followed by the ICP letter of agreement. Both of these are completed by the end of June, and before the students leave for the summer break, as mentioned earlier.

Initial client meeting

This is the first meeting between the project team and the client and is generally held at the school to give the client an opportunity to get to know IMD. At this stage, the client already understands, and has agreed, the concept, approach and conditions of the consulting project. So the meeting is to:

1 Introduce the team members to the client.

2 Introduce the client's business to the team.

3 Agree on project procedures – money, presentation dates, travel and lodging arrangements.

4 Identify sources of information for the first-phase study.

At the meeting, each team member introduces himself and gives some detail about his past education and business experience. The client then introduces his company to the team: sometimes through a formal presentation, or simply by responding to team members' questions. By the end of the meeting, the team should have clear answers to the following questions:

- What is the client's business?

- If the company operates in several areas, which business(es) should the team study?

- What will be the geographical scope of the project – national, regional or global?

- Who are the company's main suppliers, customers and competitors in the related business(es)?

With a common understanding of project objectives and scope, the client and the team now determine specific administrative guidelines for the assignment. This covers the following:

- Who will be the project team's contact in the sponsor's organization?

- Who should the team contact for the financial aspects of the project, i.e. requests for advances, approval of expenses, billing and so on?

- What will be the dates, times and places of client presentations, preferably for all phases?

Finally, the team uses the client's knowledge of his business to identify sources of information for the first-phase study. These might include industry experts, government branches and trade magazines. Furthermore, the team requests names and locations of major industry players, suppliers, manufacturers, distributors and so on.

ICP letter of agreement

After the meeting, the project team sends the client a letter of agreement to confirm what they have discussed. The letter reviews the principles, approach, timing and administrative framework for the project, it confirms the client's agreement to sponsor the project, and later it becomes a planning and reference tool for the team during the project. At a minimum, the letter will restate the project objectives, and the school's commitment to confidentiality.[4] It will also outline the specific steps in each phase, set out the administrative arrangements in full (in particular with regard to finances) and also request the client's active participation in the project. The completed letter is sent in duplicate to the client for his signature in agreement, together with résumés for the team members, a budget for phase 1 and a pro forma invoice for an advance: it is signed, and dated, by the entire team and the project director.

Step 5: Phase 1 – industry analysis (understanding the key factors for success and defining the criteria to evaluate the company)

In this phase, the project team develops a common understanding of the overall scope and nature of the sponsor's industry. They position the industry within the economy and determine its chief macroeconomic characteristics and trends: growth, key stages, industry profit and loss, balance sheet and so on. The team analyzes the major product groups within the industry and determines past and likely future trends and developments. Then they draw up competitive profiles of major industry players and, finally, define the sponsor's own position in the industry and in its national market.

The industry analysis follows three steps: industry definition and overview, outline of the business system and competitive analysis and, lastly, identification of generic strategies and key success factors. To begin, the team defines the industry in terms of size, segments and potential growth. Then they outline the key activities performed in transforming raw materials into a finished product for the end-user, i.e. the business system (see Figure 22.4).

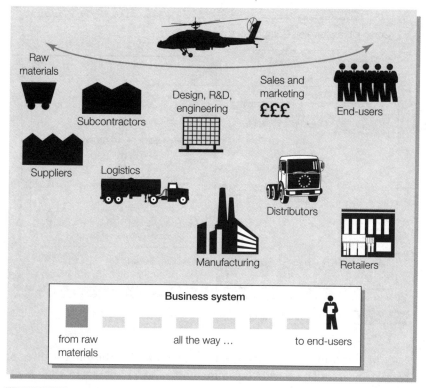

Raw materials

Subcontractors

Design, R&D, engineering

Sales and marketing
£££

End-users

Suppliers

Logistics

Distributors

Manufacturing

Retailers

Business system

from raw materials

all the way …

to end-users

Figure 22.4   Business system outline

From this, they can compare (for different products or services) the production cost versus its value as perceived by the buyer or end-user.

The next step is to map out the competitive landscape. With input from the client, the team selects several industry players and carries out a competitive analysis of these companies. They assess each company's financial performance, geographic focus, products and integration and draw up a series of profiles (see Figure 22.5), which also outline the competitive strategy pursued.

Finally, the team defines the optimum strategy to follow in each target market, or segment – covering product or service offering, activities required, geography and timing (speed of implementation).

Subsequently, the project team shifts their focus to the sponsor company. They define the positioning of the client's products (or services) in each of its main markets, and the generic strategies and the key success factors for

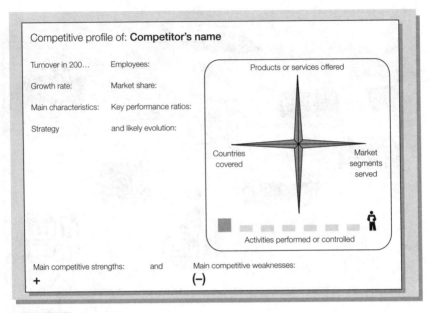

Figure 22.5 Competitor profiling

each of those markets. These are then presented to the project director, revised in accordance with his comments, and presented to the client's executives.

Note that the purpose of the industry analysis is not to explain the industry to the client; they already know it well. Rather, it is to establish the team's credibility with the client. At this stage the client may be dubious about the level of contribution that the team can make to his business. After all, the team knows nothing of his business while he has probably been in it for some time. The team's main task at the end of phase 1, is therefore, to show the client that they have achieved a good understanding of his industry, its environment, its dynamics and the viable strategies available and what it takes to succeed in each of those strategies. The client will only accept the team's recommendations for improvement if he is convinced that the team understands his business at least as well as he does. Nevertheless, this high-level analysis sometimes helps the client himself view his own industry from a more strategic perspective, and exposes him to an additional, sometimes different, insight into the sector.

During phase 1, the team works independently and there is little involvement required from the client. As they will get most of their information from sources external to the company, there is limited interaction between the team and the client's personnel. Accordingly, the team will communicate infrequently with the client, and their main aim is to gain credibility with the company. But as the project progresses and the interaction between the team and the client's management increases, the team's communication effort changes. They begin by gaining credibility, continue by cooperating with the client and end by building a consensus and commitment around agreed upon recommendations.

Step 6: Phase 2 – company analysis (identifying strengths and improvement opportunities and defining the key issues for further examination)

In phase 2, the team's challenge is to demonstrate that they have gained a good understanding of the company: its objectives, its philosophy, its operations and the main issues confronting its management. This calls for a change in the frequency and quality of the team's communication effort as the analysis relies more on sources within the company. The team spends much of its time at the company, observing its operations and holding discussions with the company's personnel. They also meet with suppliers, distributors and customers.

> **❝ On one project, we found that the former owners had succeeded in selling us a 'phantom' company; all the figures had been manipulated and were false. Despite the best efforts of the MBA ICP team, the company could not be saved and went bust! ❞**
> *Urs Wüthrich,*
> *Consultant,*
> *J. Friisberg Robertson*
> *& Partners AG*

The team's main objective in phase 2 is to assess the performance and future of the sponsor company in light of the key success factors identified in phase 1, and its stated objectives and plans, and to identify issues for phase 3 analysis. Among other things, the analysis in phase 2 will benchmark the client's key performance ratios against industry and peer standards, and determine the adequacy of its actual organization, management systems, skills and style. Based on this, the team summarizes the company's strengths and improvement opportunities, and diagnoses key issues of concern for top management consideration. The results are sometimes surprising.

Company analysis starts with an overview of the organization covering its activities, size, growth, results, the business idea pursued and a preview of critical areas. The team continues with a financial review that consists of a DuPont analysis, ratio analysis, assessment of the company's investing and financing, and concludes with an overall evaluation of its financial performance.

Following this, they proceed with a product, market and functional analysis. The product-market analysis scores the client's product line, market segments and channels against other players and thus determines its competitive position. The functional analysis assesses the company's research and development (R&D), operations, marketing, sales, finance, personnel and other critical areas. Finally, the team examines the company's structure and processes.

With a thorough understanding of the company now, the team produces a synthesis of improvements, or opportunities to be explored, to support the client's business idea. This may cover all critical areas with an impact on the business system, suggest ways of improving the flow of goods and information, or give other specific proposals for improvement. These proposals are given in order of priority, and the team suggests issue(s) to be studied in greater detail. As before, the results are first presented to the project director, revised in accordance with any comments, and finally presented to the client's executives.

Step 7: Phase 3 – issue analysis and recommendations (developing recommendations)

By now, the team has gained some credibility with the client and they begin a cooperative effort to single out which, out of those presented in phase 2, are the main issues confronting the sponsor's management team. The team will then develop viable alternatives for solving one or more of these.

With the main issues now identified, the team carries out further fieldwork, if necessary, to prepare an in-depth analysis of the issue or problem. They also develop strategic, or operational, options and evaluate these in light of agreed criteria to recommend solutions that 'fit' the company's resources and objectives. Their recommendations also include a short- and medium-term action plan.

At this stage, the project team increasingly interacts with the client's management, and the level of involvement between the company's personnel and the team, therefore, calls for maximum communications effort.

Step 8: Phase 4 – launching of implementation (going for tangible economic Improvements)

> **❝ At Cristalería Espanola, after the third phase presentation, the CEO Jean-Marie Descarpentries said to us: 'Gentlemen, your presentation was good. Now please convince my managers to implement it.' He then left, and we spent much of the night doing so! ❞**
> *Urs Wüthrich, MBA 1981*

Of all the phases, this is the most variable in terms of the team's involvement and project results. During this period, the project team is to assist the executives responsible for implementation in launching the short-term programs. They will also sometimes develop a monitoring system to ensure that top management can follow the implementation and introduce corrective action if required. However, results vary from the team's simply delivering an action plan and outline monitoring system, to the sponsor's hiring the entire project team to implement a plan.

In phase 4, the communications effort is geared towards building consensus and commitment around a corrective action. All communication is aimed at effecting a change in the client's strategy, operations or organization. To do this, they must develop a consensus among the top management that such a change is viable and have them commit to act along the lines recommended by the team. It is at this stage that the project team capitalizes on the credibility they have built up in earlier phases, to get top managers to agree on recommendations and an action plan.

A final word on communication: another aspect of interaction with the client is that of educating him and his top management. This is not as pretentious as it might sound, because through good analysis and synthesis of information, the project team can help the client see many aspects of his business in a new way. Furthermore, through the analytical process, the client is exposed to many useful analytical tools that may be new to him.

In general, there are no official presentations during the final phase. Nonetheless, it is important that the team and client discuss the overall results of the assignment before the end of the project period. The MBA participants also prepare a final report for the project director.

Learning process

As can be seen from the preceding discussion, the team constantly experiences the first three steps of the learning process as they execute the project. From the outset, they are confronted with *challenge* in the form of building team effectiveness, developing relationships and trust in the client company, and getting to grips with new analytical tools while applying them with confidence in new areas. As the project stage is set, more new information is uncovered and hypotheses need to be built.

The first three phases of the project, industry analysis, company analysis and issue analysis and recommendations provide a rich environment for iterations between the *investigate* and *construct* stages of learning. During each of the analyses, information openness is a prerequisite as the MBAs uncover information that may confirm, but sometimes confounds, their starting hypotheses. They may, therefore, be forced to rethink those hypotheses, which fuels further exploration and encourages them to remain open to new ideas and information, and the possibility of changing the hypotheses if necessary. As they test out their hypotheses, and synthesize conclusions and recommendations, the teams gain confidence in identifying the key issues, and learn to test their own ideas both in terms of intellectual rigor and practicality for implementation within the client company.

The learning loop is successfully closed during the final project completion stage as the teams debrief with one another, and the project director, on the implementation of the project. These reflections underpin the *change* step in learning, consolidating and making explicit the ways in which each individual's learning from the project can be integrated into new ways of thinking and behaviors for the future. In addition, the debrief captures the lessons learned on each project so that they can be carried forward to future students.

Money matters

Efficient administration is essential for the smooth running of the project, and is the responsibility of the project team who must plan, coordinate and execute the assignment. The MBA participants plan all activities involved in the study, organize the timetable of events, and budget and monitor all expenses for the project. They also coordinate one another's activities and those of all other participating parties to the project.

Each team prepares an expenses budget before each phase, with an advance request to the client. Expenses must be incurred within the company's guidelines; however, the first rule of expenses for all the teams is that the bigger expenses, such as air travel, are paid by the company. Otherwise, the team follows company guidelines when incurring expenses within budget (e.g. travel or hotel class) or gets approval before going into any major unbudgeted expenses.

Each project team operates its own bank account, to which only the treasurer and logistics manager are signatories. The accounts are opened with a local bank specifically for each project and are closed at the end of the assignment. The treasurer uses a simple accounting system to keep track of the budget, and must provide a report to the project director, and company if required, at the end of each phase. On top of the basic fee of CHF 50,000 for the project, the sponsor can also award a discretionary bonus of CHF 30,000, which goes into the school's MBA scholarship fund. By 2003, more than half of all sponsors had chosen to award bonuses to the school.

Key take-aways

■ The full involvement, and commitment, of the client company's top management is essential to the project's success, including real-world learning for the teams. Both the team and the company should approach the experience as an opportunity to learn and, therefore, remain open to all possibilities as the project progresses.

■ Awareness and application of the development stages in the life of a team enhances project team effectiveness; the team must 'norm' for excellence. This is one of the greatest challenges the students will face, but it is critical if the project is to succeed.

■ It is critical to manage client expectations, especially during phase 1 industry analysis, and here the project director plays a key role.

■ It is as important to finish the project well, as it is to execute it well for real learning and value added to the client. Competing demands for the team's attention must be managed professionally.

■ A project design that allows continuous iteration between the key stages of the learning cycle, including the opportunity for reflection during the debrief, is the key to learning that sticks.

case study

Ironing out the problems at Divelit

Divelit is a Swiss manufacturer of steam irons that first sponsored an IMD consulting project in 1996. Encouraged by the team's performance on the first project, Divelit sponsored a second project the following year. The relationship has continued until now – the company carried out further projects in 2003 and 2004. Clearly, Divelit is a happy customer. So, just what did the MBAs do? ▶

In 1996, Divelit's financial condition was deteriorating on many fronts. The ICP team accurately forecast that if things continued, as before, the company would run out of cash at the beginning of 1997. Their diagnosis highlighted the causes of the deterioration. Lower sales volumes, combined with high fixed costs, were driving profitability down. In addition, rising inventory levels were pushing up working capital and liquidity was growing increasingly tight. The team's phase 3 presentation of the key issues also addressed problems in Divelit's management of its salesforce, and use of its management information systems (MIS).

The team's recommendations for implementation displayed the benefit of having asked the right questions in the previous stages – a key skill not easily taught through classroom studies and case studies. For example, interviews with managers revealed that a huge IT data processing capability had seduced them into suppressing judgment in favor of more and finer information. The team recommended the rationalization of budgeting and reporting to restore judgment to management. They went further and designed weekly and monthly reports that were both clearer and simpler, and that captured the key indicators, such as revenue and cash management, which their earlier analysis had identified as key to improving the company's financial health.

The devil is in the details . . . so the saying goes. Based on a sound under-standing of Divelit's business, the team set out a finely detailed implementation plan to address the other issues that emerged from phase 3. For one of these, the team proposed that Divelit should, in future, monitor the fixed cost to revenue ratio to give an early warning of escalating costs. The proposal contained *specific* threshold levels for that ratio for each of the company's business units for the following two years. It went further and set out corrective actions to be taken should any of those thresholds be breached. Having predicted an impending cash crunch in early 1997, the team set out specific short-term actions that Divelit could take to conserve, and increase, cash over the next 90 days. One of the recommended actions to increase cash was to negotiate with Divelit's bankers: the team provided detailed projections (run with several scenarios) showing the forecast improvement in 1997 based on corrective actions taken by the company.

Recognizing that consensus and commitment would be critical to the success of any implementation plan, the ICP team set out the three target audiences to be won over. These were senior management, internal staff and product demonstrators. External stakeholders to also be persuaded were the company's bankers and its suppliers. To address this, the 'people' aspect of the imple-mentation, the team listed the tangible changes necessary, e.g. changes in organizational structure and personnel/jobs and also the cultural changes to support these. In addition, the team set out the essential elements of a successful communications plan.

> The results? The company adopted several of the recommendations from the project team and survived the crisis. By 2002, Divelit was the market leader, by value, in Switzerland and Germany; number two in the Netherlands and number three in Belgium. 1996 proved to be a turning point for the company – over the next five years, turnover grew by 85 percent while net profits jumped an impressive 466 percent.

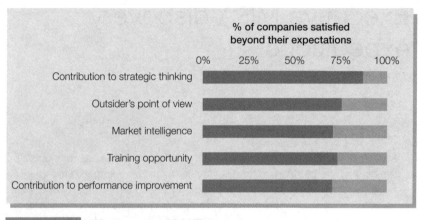

Appendix 22.1   **ICP client survey (1999)**

Notes

1   The response rate for the survey was 80 percent. Please see Appendix 22.1 for further details of the survey.
2   Not to be confused with the individual project director for *each* project. The ICP projects director is the overall manager for *all* the projects. In addition to his overall responsibility for all the projects, he handles the relationship with prospective clients, manages the timing of the projects, and with the MBA program director balances them within the MBA program. Finally, it is his job to 'twist arms' discreetly when required for the smooth running of a project. This faculty member will sometimes also direct an individual project in addition to his general oversight of all projects.
3   Source: inspired by Handy, C. *Understanding Organisations*, London: Penguin, 1999.
4   IMD specifically undertakes that, with regard to any confidential company information given to the team for the project, all such reports and working documents (i) will remain the exclusive property of the sponsoring company, (ii) will not be taken from the company's premises without written permission, and (iii) will not be used for instructional, research or other purposes either inside or outside IMD without the company's prior written permission.

23

Applying theory to new worlds: Executive MBA discovery expeditions

John Walsh

Summary

Participants can learn a great deal when on a discovery expedition, outside the classroom, but learning in this way needs to be managed differently to a typical classroom session or program. You need explicit learning objectives for the trip, beyond exposing the participants to new environments and experiences. Focusing energy through an assignment is critical, as is ensuring dedicated time for reflection on the experiences. Further, planning carefully how the expeditions fit into the overall program script ensures that learning from such trips is effectively integrated with other modules, to ensure lasting effect. Discovery expeditions show participants that they can learn all the time, from everything and everyone around them, not just in a classroom.

As part of the Executive MBA (EMBA), our students take three week-long discovery expeditions to different parts of the world. There are many reasons for asking our participants to learn by immersion in this way:

- With an average age of 38, our participants are older than typical MBA students so hands-on learning is much more suited to their needs and interests.

- The expeditions come at a point in the program when they have covered the theory and now need to apply it in practice.

- The average participant has already had many international job positions and will continue to have in the future. It's critical that they learn how to learn about an economy/country so they can adapt to these new roles quickly and effectively.

■ By immersion in a discovery expedition, our participants appreciate that learning can take place outside the classroom. It makes them more conscious and active learners both during their program and afterwards.

In this chapter, I'll cover how we structure and sequence these expeditions.

When and where?

Discovery expeditions happen at three points in the EMBA program, as illustrated in the program structure overleaf (Figure 23.1). The first trip takes place after ten weeks of classroom study and three months of distance learning. The second expedition takes place four months later, again after a period of distance learning and on-the-job application. The third and final discovery expedition also follows some months of distance learning and application.

The choice of the locations for the discovery expeditions is based on:

■ Covering three diverse regions of the world.

■ Ensuring each expedition is different, not just in terms of the location, but in terms of what the students learn from the trip.

■ By the end of the three expeditions, providing the participants with sufficient experience to construct an immersion program of their own, which would be applicable to them being asked to relocate in their job.

For geographic variety, we pick one location in the Americas, one in Asia and one in Europe. Silicon Valley in the US allows us to explore innovation and technology; Shanghai in China allows us to explore doing business in a developing country; and Dublin, Ireland, provides us with an example of growth through foreign direct investment in a European context. Each of these locations provides its own challenges to the organizers and to the participants. As one compares how we approach each of these locations, there are some differences but many similarities, which I outline below.

Preparing for the expedition

We find it essential to prepare participants in advance of the trip. While some of the participants will have visited some of the locations, very few (and most probably none) have thought about economic and business issues at play there with the necessary depth. To stimulate this thinking and to homogenize the level of knowledge in the class, we require our

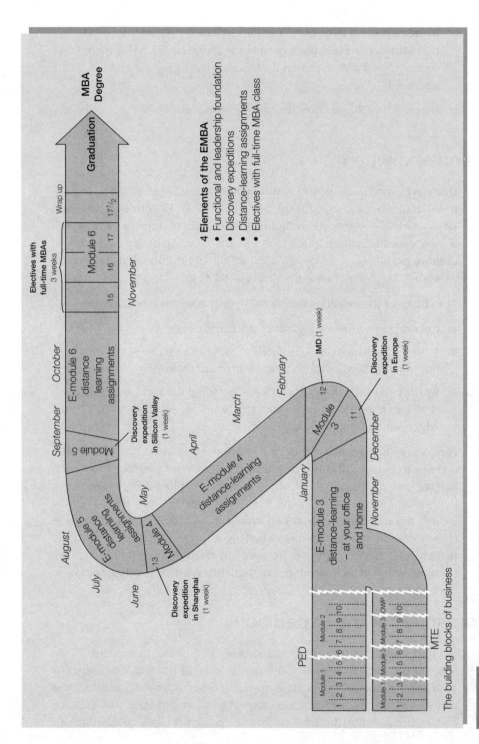

Figure 23.1   The Executive MBA (EMBA) agenda: learning how to learn

participants to spend from 5 to 15 hours on background reading. While this includes articles reflecting the best and most recent thinking on the economic, social, government policy and business issues facing the location, we also ask the participants to round out their knowledge by reading some of the popular press and even seeing some relevant movies. We have a website for the program where participants can exchange thoughts and questions, and where instructors stimulate debate on the topics covered.

To encourage critical thinking we give students an assignment before the trip. In general this requires them to formulate four to five hypotheses based on what they have learned about the location, hypotheses that they could test during their stay – for example, 'Movement of employees between Silicon Valley firms is a critical factor in knowledge transfer' or 'EU expansion will dramatically reduce rather than increase immigration into Ireland as low-paid jobs move eastwards.' These hypotheses may be proven to be true or false ultimately – the objective is to have participants think about what remains uncertain to them after their reading and how to get information that will help them resolve the issue for themselves. We have participants post their hypotheses on the website and engage in debate around them. The goal is to have participants arrive at the location well informed and curious to investigate some hypotheses.

Designing and managing the expedition

It is important to keep in mind the point in the program at which the trip takes place. For example, when we arrive in Dublin and start the discovery expedition, this is the first time that all the participants are together in the same room. It is crucial (more so than in other educational environments) that some time is given to getting to know one another. Not only will they be spending a week together under the same roof (all participants must stay at the same hotel), but also they will be spending an entire year in the same program and repeating this experience twice more.

To maximize the learning, basic ground rules need to be set. For example, no mobile phone conversations and timekeeping must be enforced. It is important that each and every participant is engaged in the discovery expedition as so much learning happens through discussion with other participants.

'Group behavior' takes over very quickly as one unmotivated participant's behavior can spread rapidly throughout the group. This really must be monitored more vigilantly than in classroom settings as spending 24 hours a day together can spread bad behavior quickly.

Each of our discovery expeditions involves an assignment that is appropriate for the location. In each, we create teams and ask them to work on the assignment together. In Ireland we ask groups to role play a foreign multinational company with an investment decision to make. The group is required to give the pros and cons of making the investment in Ireland. In Silicon Valley we ask them to make a pitch to venture capitalists for start-up companies to whom we have introduced the participants in advance. In China we ask the participants to identify and assess a business opportunity.

There are several objectives in designing the assignments. First, the assignment should be a useful lens through which to view the location. We find that having a specific task makes the participants more critical in their thinking and investigation on the trip. However, balance is important and it is key to remind those goal-oriented participants who are likely to focus solely on the assignment that they have a responsibility to learn about the entire location as much as possible. Second, the assignments are an assessment tool and poor performance offers participants an opportunity to learn more by repeating the assignment. Third, we try to make the assignment easier and more structured for the first trip and more difficult and less defined for the last. The aim is to lead participants to a point where, alone, they could do a 'fourth assignment' they may be handed by their company, in which they are relocated to a country with which they are unfamiliar.

The design and flow of the week is unique to each trip and the specific story being investigated: varying from the entrepreneurial spirit and innovation that happens in Silicon Valley (see opposite), to the complications of doing business as a multinational company in China, to the relationship between foreign direct investment and the indigenous economy in Ireland. While the designs do differ, they must fit together in order to reach the goal of leading participants to a point where they can organize such expeditions into 'new worlds' for themselves. So, for example, on later expeditions we give them some responsibility for their own learning, asking them to set up their own meetings for a day.

The entrepreneurial spirit: Meeting a living legend

Reflections on the Silicon Valley discovery expedition 2004

Over lunch we talked with one of the legends of Silicon Valley, Dr Doug Engelbart. The Valley is filled with millionaires with little intellectual capital or emotion invested in their latest, greatest Internet idea or electronic gadget. Doug has spent his career thinking about information technology and the ways in which people can use it to make their lives better. He has been trying to find ways to improve our 'collective IQ,' so that we can better handle the world's increasingly more complex problems.

Back in 1950 Doug decided to dedicate his career and his talents to doing something that would greatly benefit mankind. As he considered what he might do, he realized that most of the world's truly great problems were huge and complex, and could never be solved by a lone genius. He knew that only a collective solution would work. And then he discovered computers. And then what became the Internet. And then he went on to invent the mouse and a few other pieces of key technology that the Internet and our technology-driven lives now rely on. It was a weird and wonderful ride talking with a man who can see into the future.

The activities generally fall into two categories – either all participants are together listening to one speaker they should all hear or they are in smaller groups visiting businesses. Of course, having appropriate speakers is important. So, it goes without saying that representatives from the Communist Party talk to the group in China, venture capitalists talk to them in Silicon Valley, and the Irish government agency responsible for inward investment talks to them in Ireland. This throws up a tricky aspect of designing the trip: the flow of the speakers and the company visits. Should participants visit foreign-owned companies' operations in China before or after they have seen local ones? A similar question is relevant for the Ireland trip. In Silicon Valley, should small start-ups come before or after the more established firms like Intel or HP? It is important that the trip organizer has in mind the learning experience he/she wants the participants to take away, as the sequencing impacts the learning greatly. We place foreign companies after indigenous ones in China as we want participants to have a first-hand appreciation of the challenges foreign companies face prior to visiting them. We do the opposite in Ireland as there, for our purposes, it is more important that the participants assess the nature of and extent to which there is a knowledge transfer from foreign companies to local ones.

Given participants will have different experiences and see different companies, they need the opportunity to share what they observed with their peers. So, at the end of every day we build in time for participants to debrief with others who had a different schedule that day. Then, plenary discussions provide the chance to identify common perspectives as well as areas where there is uncertainty so these can be investigated on a subsequent day.

In designing and managing the expeditions, we have come up against some interesting dilemmas. First, if the logistics do not work there is an impact on the participants' learning. Ironically, participants may have spent an entire week in China hearing foreign businessmen complain about logistics but when the logistics of the trip itself fail – traffic jams, no air conditioning or bad food – they tend *not* to take this as yet more learning about the specific location but as evidence of a poorly organized trip. Like a textbook with misspellings, they discount the experience and their interest in learning diminishes. The dilemma for the organizer is how much to fight against such 'myopia' or to accept it – to insulate participants from the realities of the environment or to expose them fully. It's a delicate issue and we have tended to err on the side of organizing things to the 'nth' degree to make sure they run like clockwork while warning participants that things can go wrong and that they should align their expectations accordingly. When they inevitably do go wrong we use those moments to indicate the realities of doing business in the location and secondly to explore why the participants feel their learning experience is diminished.

A second dilemma deals with the speakers the participants see. Participants will be accustomed to professional executive educators presenting to them and, regardless of what one does as forewarning, they judge other presenters with the same yardstick. Inevitably, some of the people the participants meet will not be great presenters or even communicators. Even the context can impact how speakers are received. Meeting an entrepreneur in a small group of five or six people can be a much more enjoyable experience than seeing him present to a group of 70. Participants will feel they get more out of the trip if they have many interactions in small groups with dynamic speakers. This is not always possible, of course. We point this out and emphasize that powerful content, albeit delivered uninterestingly, can still provide terrific learning. We develop in them the mindset that every experience provides learning, and if they are not learning then they really should be taking a hard look at themselves.

Following up on the expedition

At the end of the discovery expedition it's important to budget time for reflection. We do this in two phases. While the participants are still on site we ask them to capture all they have learned about the location and all they have learned that they could take back to their own 'world,' whether their own country, organization or specific job. This we ask them to do in small groups and report back to all in plenary session. The box below provides some flavor of what these reflections bring to light. Second, we ask participants to perform an 'after-action review' where they articulate how they would have approached the trip differently, given what they now know. That is, how they would have prepared differently in advance of the trip and how they would have interacted with the people they met differently, in order to maximize learning. This second task is important to get participants to improve and take ownership as they go through the series of expeditions.

Selected reflections on the 2004 EMBA discovery expeditions

Dublin, Ireland

In general, people came out of the week feeling they'd learned a lot about Ireland, but more importantly, they felt like they'd learned a lot about how to go about investigating somewhere new. What you can learn by simply asking, how meeting people face to face gives you a much better picture than reading articles, how we come into every situation with biases, and how we have to work to overcome those biases in order not to distort our learning. Here's a quote from one of the participants, who was commenting on the importance of continuing to ask questions and challenge your conclusions: *'I feel like I know a lot more about Ireland than about my own country, where I've never bothered to ask the questions nor to challenge my assumptions.'*

Silicon Valley, USA

Day 5: a day of striking contrasts. We spent the morning at the hotel preparing for the afternoon. A flurry of high-stress preparation as everyone readied his or her presentations and elevator pitches. Lunch was with a living legend, Dr Doug Engelbart (see above). Then the moment of truth arrived. Who does almost every successful entrepreneur have to eventually sell to? Who can pierce through the fog of a PowerPoint faster than any management team? Who can best ask the questions that get to the essence of a great business idea, or the weaknesses in a poorly thought out strategy? Venture capitalists and business angels.

We spent this afternoon pitching four Swiss high-tech start-ups to a group of potential investors. They're the ones with the money, and if you want it, you'd better have a great product, a great team and a huge potential market . . . and know intimately how you're going to pull those three things together to make money for yourself and the investors. And, you'd better know how to communicate all of this to them, quickly, succinctly, and with as few buzzwords as possible. We did our best, pitched, took their questions, asked some of our own, and learned a lot in the process. Next stop: Shanghai.

When the participants are back at home and have had a little more time to reflect on the experience, we have them submit a short document. The nature of the document is dependent on the trip – for example, having been exposed to a multitude of innovative ideas in Silicon Valley, we ask them to document 50 ideas they have seen and to identify one or two that they could apply in their own organization.

Through the course of the program we keep participants informed of events or news from the locations they have visited. For example, if a large multinational announces that it will invest in a new R&D facility in Ireland, we post the announcement on the program website. Through discussion forums on the website the participants can continue to discuss their perspectives on the location and debate different topics. While not obligatory, we find most participants, having spent an intense week learning on location, are motivated to exchange ideas in this way.

Key success factors

There are many ways to approach discovery expeditions and certainly many ways to have a successful one. However, our experience has led us to the following universal truths from the educator's perspective:

- Telling people what they will learn, teaching them and then telling them what they have learned is even more critical on a discovery trip than in the classroom. It's always possible to see more and meet more people or companies on a one-week trip but it is also critical that time is dedicated to reflection and discussion of what has been done. We do this at the end of every day. And we do it at the end of every trip.

■ An assignment is essential. It engages participants at a higher intellectual level than if one isn't required and this is true even for elements of the trip that aren't relevant for the specific assignment at hand.

■ The instructor should have explicit objectives for the trip, over and above exposing the participants to a particular location. Of course, the objectives will help with trade-offs related to content but, moreover, objectives will determine the flow and sequencing of the trip.

■ There should be a reasonable level of variety in how participants spend their time. Clearly an appropriate balance must be found between in-class or in-plenary activities and company visits. In designing a trip one constantly faces this trade-off and our bias is to err on the side of having too little rather than too much in-class time. Perhaps with a younger audience we would view this differently.

■ Finally, if multiple discovery expeditions are part of the program, more difficult expeditions (where process might involve translators or where the content might be more confusing to get to grips with) should be placed later in the program.

Key take-aways

From the participants' perspective, the discovery expeditions are a unique way to really apply what they have been learning. Their feedback tells us:

■ The learning takes on more substance for them personally as they apply it in practice in unfamiliar situations.

■ Cross-cultural awareness increases dramatically.

■ Peer learning is critical; networks are built and strengthened by the shared experiences.

■ Skills and understanding in taking on similar challenges alone (doing business in new worlds) is significantly enhanced.

■ Participants appreciate that the preconceptions they had prior to the expedition may be a barrier to learning.

Learning scripts for programs

24

Scripting a CEO roundtable

Peter Lorange

Summary

A CEO roundtable is a forum where senior executives and business school faculty meet to debate topics that are top-of-mind for CEOs. While such events are short, normally less than a day, if they are well scripted they offer valuable benefits. For senior executives these include new insights into the challenges they are facing, as well as opportunities to build networking relationships with their peers. For the business school, the value too is in building relationships: the active involvement of senior executives contributes to a deeper understanding of the key dilemmas they face. This understanding can then be used to enrich teaching and focus thought leadership to ensure continued relevance to participants' management development needs.

In this chapter we discuss how a CEO roundtable can be organized and run to achieve a number of objectives. These include valuable take-home benefits for the participants and value creation in terms of relationship building for the host organization, as well as value for each keynote speaker who has specific inputs. But first, what exactly is a CEO roundtable? It is a forum where around 75 senior executives – CEOs mostly, but also board chairmen, chief financial officers (CFOs) and others – come together with business school faculty to network, gain insights into the latest management research, and debate the most pressing business issues of the day.

For real learning to take place, participants must be open to change. Thus much of the logic behind the learning script for the CEO roundtable learning session can be traced back to a simple theory put forward by Lewin (1951) and Kolb and Frohman (1968).[1] According to them, first you have to unfreeze the participants' minds so that they are open to new ideas; then you need to change various aspects of substantive views that the participants may hold; and finally you re-freeze the participants' minds around a few select 'must cover points.'

Change is to be interpreted in a special way here. While normally we would focus on change in a given, specific organization, we shall here have many organizations represented through their CEOs at the roundtable. We shall thus focus on change-of-mind for the various CEOs, the objective being to condition them to actively consider the various propositions that are being put forward for implementation in their own companies later.

The chapter is organized around actual experiences from IMD's annual CEO roundtable. It deals with how to achieve a global context, in terms of selecting relevant topics, the diversity of participants and the like; how to create energizing roles to get everyone involved, from the moderator and presenters to all other participants; and how to achieve 'emotional highs' by creating memorable experiences that touch each individual personally.

The design of a CEO roundtable

The roundtable typically starts early one evening and continues until after lunch the following day. The basic outline is as follows:

- Drinks.
- Dinner.
- Informal buffet-style breakfast.
- Faculty-led sessions: this could be three parallel sessions, about 50 minutes each – with presentations and discussions.
- Plenary session: two speeches, about 20 minutes each.
- Panel discussion: three to five panel members, plus moderator, about 25 minutes.
- General debate: about 45 minutes.
- Lunch and summing up.

The idea behind starting the event with a number of social activities is to create an informal network-driven context and help 'unfreeze' the participants. Meeting over a drink and dinner preconditions the participants for networking interaction, by creating a sense of security and preparing them to give and take in a safe context.

The faculty-led sessions the following morning are based on the latest research in thought leadership. Ideally there are a number of parallel sessions – say three – which allows the CEOs to select the topics that they are most interested in and keeps the groups relatively small. The approach is for faculty to present their research interactively, bearing in mind that this makes for a more dynamic learning experience (as Winston Churchill said, 'I'm always ready to learn, although I do not always like being taught'). By encouraging the CEOs to participate, the faculty create a context for these sessions of 'networking in the small.'

For the plenary presentation, two leading CEOs are invited in advance to speak on a prearranged topic for around 20 minutes. This is followed by a panel discussion lasting about 25 minutes, with three to five panelists and a moderator, who raises specific issues with each one. They typically sit in a horseshoe configuration in front of the rest of the group. This panel discussion leads into a general debate with the wider audience for, say, the final 45 minutes. The key is to create a sense of strong, intensive interactivity, in the large. The general purpose of these substance-driven events is to engender a change in perspective in the participants.

The roundtable ends with a social activity, a lunch, which allows further discussions and clarification of key points to take place in smaller, informal groups around the lunch tables. The moderator provides a brief summarizing speech, with the aim of 're-freezing,' providing closure.

Real-world context: topics

It is vital that only a few select topics are chosen as the focus of a given event, partly to capture what is top-of-mind for CEOs at a particular time, and partly to ensure that the roundtable stays focused and does not stray off the point. Examples of such themes include:

■ Restructuring and outsourcing.

■ Governance, and the role of the board.

■ Growth, through internal means as well as through mergers and acquisitions.

■ Top line and bottom line focus, i.e. how to handle key dilemmas, rather than settling on partial answers.

Similarly, it is important that the topics addressed by the keynote speakers are followed up and developed further during the panel discussion and plenary debate.

The faculty-led sessions provide the 'take-home' value for the CEOs in the form of updates on the faculty's latest research, with a focus on truly relevant top management dilemmas. These research-driven topics should reflect thought leadership and are thus entirely different in nature from the plenary topics, the latter being driven more by the experience-based inputs of the senior executives themselves. Examples of faculty topics could be:

- Top management dilemmas.
- Change management.
- Leadership issues.
- Performance measurement.
- Mergers and acquisitions.

It is key, in planning the roundtable, to bring a varied group of participants together in a 'global meeting place,' to achieve eclectic coverage of the various topics and dilemmas under discussion. This means diversity in terms of the countries represented, the companies attending, and the positions of senior executives in the companies. A strong contingent of faculty with a broad range of nationalities and research interests completes the picture.

Energizing roles

It is important to see the CEO roundtable as a network-driven event. The first aspect is to make sure that the networking context allows the participants to 'warm up,' to get closer to each other as colleagues and to prepare them for the intellectual exchange to come. This can perhaps best be achieved through the informal social activities at the beginning of the event.

Broad involvement in the roundtable is essential, particularly in the debates, but also in the smaller groups. This means that the event needs to be designed so that, in principle, all participants get a chance to speak. To facilitate this, plenty of time in the various sessions – both in the large and in the small – needs to be set aside for discussions. Above all, it is key to create an informal atmosphere, thus there should be no press, no faculty research questionnaires – in short, nothing to interfere with the interaction and networking between the CEOs.

Experience has shown that the moderator plays a crucial role, acting as a catalyst throughout the event. He or she must try to ensure that a sense of dynamism prevails and that the overall thread of chosen topics is followed. In this connection, he or she must have prepared beforehand a handful of key questions and issues to reinforce and expand on the points made by the various participants, above all, the keynote speakers – to make sure that the momentum is sustained.

The moderator should be sure to call on as many different CEOs as possible for their inputs. It is critical that the moderator does not let one or a few participants monopolize proceedings. Based on all the inputs, the moderator can also try to draw tentative conclusions, but not impose his or her personal views. There is simply no one right solution to most of the dilemmas handled here!

A key role for the moderator is thus to be a catalyst: keeping the pace, making sure that the CEO roundtable does not slow down, asking questions, drawing conclusions, and bringing in new viewpoints.

When identifying keynote speakers to invite to the event, it is important that they have actually achieved some 'good results' or 'impressive practices' in their company during their tenure. Each should thus be recognized as an authority, someone who has done a good job in the eyes of his or her peers. Clearly, the speakers need to bring out the key issues they have been asked to address based on their experience, ideally choosing what is going on in their own company, but with a broader focus than simply retelling 'war stories.'

In the next part of the proceedings, the panel members who take part in the follow-up roundtable should expand on the speakers' viewpoints, by selectively adding in-depth elaborations or contrasts with their own company experience. They should not, however, duplicate what the speakers have already said. The panel members must thus be established executives, able to speak with authority based on their own performance. Although they should be prepared, they should not come with a pre-written speech. Rather, they should be able to react to particular questions or issues raised in the debate or put to them by the moderator and move the discussion forward.

All the roundtable participants should be given plenty of opportunity to be active, to ask questions, to provide inputs, i.e. to add further depth to the discussion. This is not only the case for the general debate, but also in the smaller discussions, i.e. those led by faculty members. The key here is to be sure that there is enough time and that the atmosphere is sufficiently informal to 'invite' everyone to be active.

Emotional highs

It is important to be able to succeed in creating a network in which all the executives feel that they are bonding with their peers. This bonding should be relaxed, yet intellectually intense. With luck, the bonding will lead to a number of specific contacts that can be activated later, on a one-to-one basis.

In terms of emotional highs it is vital that all participants feel a true sense of having participated, of having been active with a purpose, i.e. giving of their own experience. They must feel that their viewpoints have led to insights for others, i.e. that they have been heard. Similarly, they must leave feeling that they have been able to 'borrow with pride' from others. This sense of active participation is key.

To tap into the emotions, the keynote speakers must truly focus on important dilemmas. The choice of which overall topics to deal with is thus critical. It is also essential to put together a strong panel to allow various viewpoints to be expressed in the panel discussion. Diversity and eclecticism are key here. Throughout the event, the focus should be on cutting-edge dilemmas, rather than on absolute, typically much easier, solutions – or on 'right' or 'wrong' approaches.

The moderator must seek out and encourage dilemma-driven debate points, rather than endorsing a particular solution. Complementary viewpoints are critical for shedding light on dilemmas. The emotional high for the audience will depend on the fact that they have gained deeper insights by being involved, rather than once more passively hearing simple theorizing. The learning comes from the global meeting place context provided by leading executives from various companies, representing different country perspectives and positions.

Practical considerations

It is essential to communicate the dates of the CEO roundtable far in advance – at least a year ahead – so that CEOs can fit it into their busy schedules. Similarly, the keynote speakers and overall topics should be communicated early on – at least six months in advance.

More detailed invitations should be sent out nearer the time, say, three months in advance, followed by reminders. They should name the keynote speakers as well as giving details of the various thought leadership sessions, so that the CEOs can choose which one to attend beforehand. Providing as much information upfront creates a sense of commitment in each CEO, giving him or her a reason to participate.

Immediately after the CEO roundtable a personal letter of thanks should be sent to each participant, mentioning his or her individual contribution specifically. Copies of any presentations and follow-up materials – if the speakers make them available – should accompany the letter. The date and key program topics of the following year's roundtable should also be included. Finally, the follow-up communication should include information on one – or a maximum of two – short IMD programs suitable for a CEO.

Loyalty building: Affinity with the business school

It is key that all the participants, through their active involvement, get a sense of actually contributing to the business school by sharing their views and inputs. Thus, as well as sharing their research insights, the faculty need to listen so that they can pick up on various points to benefit both their follow-on research and their teaching. This openness – and gratefulness – to the participants should be transparent throughout the event. This, in turn, can have a strong loyalty-building effect.

A subsidiary benefit of hosting an event such as a CEO roundtable with such senior executives as participants is that they can become aware of the possibility to provide endowed chairs and participate in furthering thought leadership. By embarking on such a symbiotic relationship, both parties can benefit while contributing to the cutting edge of business learning.

Conclusion

The CEO roundtable can play a major role in creating value. The learning script outlined in the previous paragraphs should give further insights on this. The value must be judged from each participant's point of view, above all in terms of the particular take-homes that the participant leaves with; it must further be judged from the business school's point of view, particularly in terms of the relationships that are created, which might secure future 'business.' Finally, the roundtable should be seen as a memorable event for everyone, providing not only substantial content but also 'social' value in terms of the network-based friendships and bonds that have been established, which can be drawn on later, if necessary. All in all, therefore, the

CEO roundtable must be inspirational and fun – not overprogrammed, not pedestrian, but encapsulating a vision for the future.

Key take-aways

■ Well scripted events, even short ones such as a CEO roundtable, can offer significant benefits for participants in terms of new insights on important topics and networking opportunities; benefits for the host business school include building loyalty and active involvement among senior executives, which offers new insights to drive thought leadership and relevance of future offerings.

■ To ensure the event is valuable, it should focus on topics that are top-of-mind for participants as well as 'social' capital in terms of networking opportunities.

■ Building the informal context that will make participants comfortable engaging in intense debate and opening up to new perspectives is critical upfront; the subsequent role of faculty and executive panels is to stimulate interaction on the key issues, not just present research or experiences to a passive audience – energy and engagement at emotional as well as intellectual level are important to stimulate real learning.

■ Diversity, building a global meeting place of participants with many different perspectives, is important to provide the breadth of perspective that will drive take-home value.

■ Above all, the event must be inspirational and fun, focused on the future.

Notes

1   Kolb, D. and Frohman, A. (1968) An Organization Development Approach to Consulting, *MIT Sloan Management Review*, Fall; Lewin, K. (1951) *Field Theory in Social Science*, New York: Harper.

25

Engaging families in business for insight and action[1]

John Ward

Summary

Family businesses raise unique and often emotional concerns; specific responses need to be developed to address these. Learning techniques range from creating a common base (making participants feel their situation is 'normal') – while at the same time ensuring that a participant's 'uniqueness' is recognized – to establishing a culture of participation and a spirit of sharing. This chapter examines ten elements that form the basis of IMD's family business program to illustrate specific learning approaches that can be used in the practice of family business education.

For the last 17 years IMD has run 'Leading the Family Business.' It is the oldest and longest-running education course for family-owned businesses in the world. More than 800 participants from 500 companies and from 30 countries have passed through this program. Typical company size ranges from $100 to $2000 million in revenues (see Table 25.1).

Our experience indicates:

1 The field of family business education is relatively young. Though family businesses have been around for thousands of years, we have little to teach that is empirically proven.

2 Business-owning families are typically very private, believe that their particular issues are unique, and educational initiatives – or outside interventions of any sort – make them very anxious.

3 Nonetheless, most family businesses are quite normal and face many of the same issues, such as generational succession or the blurring of personal and business issues.

Therein lies the challenge: helping very private people open up to new ideas, see their relevance, and take action. Over the years, we have learned many techniques to meet these challenges.

Table 25.1 Participant profile

Company revenues (€)		Headquarters	
< 100 million	15%	Europe	62%
100–500 million	42%	South America	18%
501–2000 million	34%	Asia	11%
> 2000 million	9%	North America	7%
		Australia	2%
Age of firm (years)		Role in firm	
< 20	10%	Chairman	11%
20–50	39%	CEO	38%
51–100	27%	Senior manager	20%
101–200	22%	Shareholder	18%
>200	2%	Non-family manager	8%
		Advisor/Director	5%

Background

Before discussing the specific approaches we have developed, I would like to mention the common characteristics of family business owners: they tend to be private, somewhat parochial, and protective. Happily, as a result of education and increased access to new ideas, these limitations are disappearing.

Private

Most family businesses are privately owned and proud of it. They view sharing information – for some even revenue size and the ages of leaders – as potential threats to their competitive advantage, which they believe is preserved by their privacy. Others view disclosure of family members' names and ownership positions as risking unwanted publicity. A few worry about the physical security of their family.

Privacy has an additional source. Family businesses feel very close to their entrepreneurial origins, and entrepreneurs by their nature are very private, secretive people. That value is often passed on through the generations of their successors.

Parochial

Almost every family business member believes that his situation is somehow 'different' or unique. After all, they reason, the character and culture of the family business are profoundly affected by the nature of the owning family. It is the same in most families, who rightfully regard themselves as exceptional. 'My situation is surely different' is an expected attitude for first-day participants.

However, if a family feels its situation is unique, why would it register for a family business course? The answer is that they feel a particular concern, one that very deeply affects the welfare of a family member or the harmony of the family. By listening for several days, they hope that somehow, in the maelstrom of information presented, clues to their specific issues will emerge – many even hope to find a single 'magic bullet.'

Protective

As in most business education, family business participants bring an 'action orientation.' What's the take-home value and what can I do with it tomorrow? However, for business families approaching family business issues, the risk-return equation for taking action – even being engaged – has special dimensions.

While the potential upside of proactive efforts is seen as substantial – continuity of the family's heritage, realization of its most deeply felt dreams, a framework to enhance family harmony, clarity on the roles and relationships with loved ones – the downside is also feared as huge. Families worry about reopening emotional wounds or even sparking new conflicts. For example, the avoidance of conflict is a more common concern in family businesses than in a management course on creative strategy or implementing change.

Families also understand and respect the particular challenges of change in an intimate family-based system and the consequences of failing to realize their hopes. In fact, members of a specific family realize that each is watching and listening to the others intently, in and out of the classroom – word choice, an innocent question, and body language provoke immediate and strong reactions.

As a result, most family business participants are unusually reserved and cautious. But the potential impact of their participation in an educational program is extremely positive, perhaps affecting a transformation at the very top of an organization and in the very heart of a sincerely caring family. Of course, each family takes away something different from an educational experience. But ideally, each should take home: (a) an acceptance of their situation as special, though 'normal'; (b) a positive feeling in their attitude towards the future; and (c) an appreciation that they can continue to learn from others. Often, even more is possible, such as the forging of a discreet action plan with broad family support and public commitment.

The opportunities and tactics

Because an education course is so novel and emotional for family business participants – it is usually their first such experience – our program objectives might appear too modest. At IMD, we approach our expectations with two ethical principles: (a) do no harm, particularly in potentially fragile situations, and (b) do all we can to maintain their openness to new learning on the subject. To paraphrase what a participant once said: 'Do you know the definition of a successful family meeting? That there is another one!' Tears of joy and sadness occur regularly in our program. We want participants to leave feeling hopeful and determined.

Our program has ten elements that we attempt to address, each in a continuing variety of ways throughout the program.

- Build a base of common interest.
- Assure attention to particular issues.
- Gain engagement.
- Keep engagement.
- Promote participation.
- Foster sharing.
- Facilitate shared learning.
- Encourage optimism.
- Precipitate action.
- Integrate learning.

A common base

In some business education programs, they start by exploring the diversity of the participants. In 'Leading the Family Business,' we first seek to demonstrate how much the participants have in common, even when the spectrum of national cultures, company size, industry and family structure is very wide. This is the first step in getting them to feel that their situation is 'normal.' Feeling 'normal,' we have found, opens the doors to sharing their experiences rather than guarding their privacy – learning from each other instead of primarily from the professors – as well as to involving themselves as actors rather than spectators. As we've discussed, participants don't usually enter the classroom feeling 'normal.'

To create the common base, we employ the following tactics:

- A pre-arrival survey vividly documents the common interests and perspectives of the participants, illustrating for them that their 'issues' are predictable and virtually universal. Through long evolution and refinement, our survey also supports the theses of the course. Most of the questions in the survey are very descriptive and non-threatening.

- The survey does, however, prompt some ranking of choices in terms of importance. These help us reveal to all the participants that they share a broad number of extremely sensitive concerns.

- We have developed two frameworks that map both the diversity and the shared concerns among the participants. This is invaluable. As we describe these frameworks[2] and ask each participant to 'map' themselves in a group exercise, an immediate (and comforting) sense of empathy emerges, as does a realization that the course will speak to them. Prior to their arrival, of course, we already know where each participant fits into our frameworks and so we can alter the emphasis of the course, if need be, to fit their needs with an advanced understanding of their outlook and concerns; we can also plan how participants will interact during the program.

- Finally, we ask everyone in the course to articulate his/her learning objectives to each other. From many years of experience, we have a good idea of the range that they will cover. We even suggest general objectives that will engage them on our introductory welcome comments. Very predictably, succession is the principal topic. It's a wonderful theme because it expresses a common emotion, yet also includes innumerable specific interpretations that we can build on throughout the course.

On the walls throughout the program we leave the list of objectives, with frequency mentioned, and the two maps, with the names plotted. We can immediately tie theory to participant. The participants are always interpreting whose perspective is saying what in discussions.

Particular interests

From the surveys, mapping and learning objectives, we also learn how participants and their issues are unique. For those with unusual or particularly complicated circumstances, we strive to arrange private meeting times over lunch, on walks, before morning sessions, or on bus trips. We offer custom-tailored advice and counsel, which we also regard as an important learning opportunity for the faculty.

Emotional engagement

Emotional interest is virtually automatic for a family business program. However, it is more challenging to engender a deeper emotional engagement. To do so, the participants must continually 'realize' that we are talking to them, personally.

We start our efforts for emotional engagement in the opening session by pre-assigning seats so as to cluster people who are comfortable situational peers – in age, role and gender. Possible competitors are kept apart, as are family members. We mix people by nationality. In fact, we routinely put patriarchs up front and their children behind them a few rows, lessening parental scrutiny. The patriarchs like that; so, too, do their presumed successors.

Then, we open with a four-generation case study that emotionally engages virtually every participant at some point. The case is chock full of classic family business problems and very real emotions. It's hard not to relate to its humanity and its poignancy.

Our framework maps, described before, are more than identifying maps. As a dynamic picture through time, they illustrate the evolution of roles according to our theory of family businesses. We argue that not only does everyone appear someplace on the map, but they will quite predictably grow into other points in the near future. Each participant then feels a part of the course theory. Our most pleasing comment at the end of the first half-day is, 'You are telling my story as if you were there.'

Continuing engagement

We work to overcome the initial expectation of many that they will find some single insight – the 'magic bullet' – to solve their most conscious concern. We want to benefit from what they can share with others by continuing their engagement, but also provide meaningful value to them and their family and their business.

We build several theories of family business behavior during the course, integrating each family business into them, as far as possible. To demonstrate the theories, we use brief questionnaires (that have been tested over time) to personalize each person's contribution to validating the theories. For example, we relate national culture and orientation to family business issues. As another example, we relate orientation to family issues assumptions in forging a family's family business constitution. If an exception to a theory arises, we immediately attempt to modify or amplify the theory with actual classroom data. While not rigorously scientific, this stimulates new hypotheses as well as engages the participants constantly.

Each theory and each classroom survey is non-judgmental. We do not attempt to prove anyone right or wrong. Instead, we want participants' confidence to grow, which encourages openness and sharing. Normative positions and prescriptions, as will be described later, come from classroom testimonials and best practice cases.

Participation

We strive to immediately establish a culture of participation. At the beginning of the program we match attendees in like-pairs to introduce each other to the full class. In this way, everyone talks in the first hour of the program about someone else from a simple checklist. To further encourage participation, we explain the confidentiality honor code, which to our knowledge has never been violated in over 17 years.

We also use a wide variety of fairly common pedagogical techniques to gain frequent and broad participation. Cases help participation, especially when everyone is asked to take a position. Using role plays can assist this. The illustration of ideas with stories, particularly from the participants who argue for and against commonalities in them, promotes further interaction.

In short, the course should be a dialogue, elaborating and building theories with contributions by the participants. Of course, vigorous participation helps to assure engagement. It also sets the stage for what's especially important in our program – a spirit of sharing, from a group traditionally reluctant to disclose anything.

Sharing

We seek an environment of openness and shared vulnerability, where families recount their foibles and follies, where individuals can examine themselves and, in particular, acknowledge their emotions.

Early recognition of common experiences, fluidly communicated, lubricates a sharing environment, which is further stimulated as the participations project themselves into the cases and stories. An additional spur to sharing occurs when the opening case personalities actually appear in the class, openly describing their mistakes and doubts. When confessing that most of what they learned came from the questions and insights of their classmates, the case personalities greatly enhance the sharing environment. (We have been very fortunate to have very generous and very open role models.)

Reinforcement of the sharing environment is sought throughout the course. Professors constantly interact in private conversations with participants, both to assist them and to search for in-class examples. When found, participants are asked to share the experience with their classmates; most of the time they feel honored to do so. They should also feel free to decline.

Learning from each other

In the hope of generating discussions and sharing of experiences, we actively put small groups together based on a common affinity. They shift naturally to offering advice and counsel to each other. All in all, we attempt to have 25 percent of course time in small common-circumstance groups, starting with a question relevant to class discussion that moves as quickly as possible into sharing personal experiences on issues of particular mutual concern.

We employ a number of techniques. Sometimes we put people in small groups for case activities and for discussion on lecture topics. For lunch, we may assign people to tables and pose open-ended questions, relevant to the issues they face. For example, we may ask a table of board chairmen to discuss the characteristics of their very best board meetings, or what makes board members particularly valuable. During a break, we sometimes ask seniors to explain how their juniors can make better successors, while the juniors are asked how seniors can improve the succession process. At the end of day, similar common-affinity groups also digest their collective thoughts of the day.

Frequently, the relationships developed in these groups become solidified with spontaneous late nights on the town. They can grow into long-term friendships of mutual support, which recall our efforts to uncover how much they shared in common via specific orientation groups.

Optimism

Family business owners, by circumstance and by nature, are a modest and self-critical group. They are quick to deflect praise of their success by crediting it to chance or the efforts of others. They are hard on themselves for their imperfections and frequently hard on each other within their families.

While these qualities are admirable in many ways, we want to raise their expectations of what's possible. Furthermore, we want to temper their instinct of 'what can go wrong' with a sense of hopefulness that things can get better.

We attempt to foster optimism in several ways:

■ Early on, we compliment them on their legitimate achievements and distinction by providing data that proves how unusual their success and longevity are.

■ We offer them many, many success stories and cases and articles. All in all, during our program, they study at least 15 successful business families, which are a lot like them. These would be stories of families who had a problem or problems, took action, and were satisfied with good results.

■ We bring into the classroom actual families who are taking positive action, with good results. We will regularly invite the recent winner of the IMD-Lombard Odier Darier Hentsch 'Distinguished Family Business Award' to visit our program. We also invite a recent participant, who went home and took positive action, to return to the course to tell of their efforts and progress.

The families who do attend our program are predominately open and eager. They represent the small fraction of business-owning families who could, and should, seek education. The compliments are sincere. The positive stories are realistic. The hopefulness we promote is reasonable. That reasonableness, of course, relates to the choice of action steps they take home with them.

Taking action

To assure that learning is later implemented, we focus on two dimensions. First, we help each participant to identify a 'next step' that is both appropriate and feasible, some potentially useful systemic change, starting with very concrete and less threatening suggestions. For some, that means augmenting their board of directors with independent directors or seeking easily described qualifications. For others, it translates into drafting a family employment or dividend policy, for which we can offer samples and templates. Those already secure in basic practices can consider developing a family council, writing an ethical will, or outlining a successor-selection process.

Of course, we don't propose that participant families should necessarily take some critical or highly risky step without good outside counsel. Instead, the family business continuity planning process is eternal, never finished. Our goal, on first meeting, is to pursue a feasible and relevant step that will engender confidence and to prove that progress is possible.

Second, we provide follow-up in several ways. Recently, we have begun to call participants six months after their attendance. In addition, we have started an alumni newsletter for program participants. The newsletter focuses exclusively on what alumni have done once they returned home, plus testimonials of their achievements or lessons learned. Some classes have formed their own online 'chat rooms' for keeping in touch and encouraging and supporting each other; we plan to facilitate and organize that idea in the future. As mentioned, we formally bring to the classroom a program alumnus to tell their own implementation story and offer their 'lessons learned.'

Finally, we ask each family to identify an 'action step' they wish to take after the program. They then share that with their affinity group, which both heightens their commitment to it and provides them with some implementation counsel.

Keep the learning going

Our ideal is to trigger an ongoing learning effort. We hope to encourage this through our alumni newsletter. But our most valuable accomplishment is to leave them with a coherent, integrated theory of family business dynamics and evolution. If so, we have provided them with an adaptable framework with which to observe new examples and synthesize their ideas. (Because family business leaders have a thirst for the stories of others, our framework should help them to crystallize and internalize those new stories.)

We attempt to cement the theoretical framework through an end-of-program case that integrates it all. It is designed to be memorable for both its comprehensiveness and its simplicity. We are fortunate that, as with the opening case, we have a representative of the case family present. They illustrate the ongoing value of the course theory by updating the class on what's happened since. All see the theory working, just as it will for them.

Conclusion

Family business is a highly emotional, private experience. It's also a young and complex field with little to confidently prescribe. An overall science of family business may prove impossible, as the difficulties of integrating family system theory and business system theory appear to demonstrate. Moreover, implementing change in a long-established family system is an intimidating challenge.

The essential ingredients of a successful family business course are: (1) to acknowledge the emotions, (2) to create an open and sharing environment, and (3) to support the participants in the changes they choose to make. To achieve these aims, we help business-owning families to realize that they are in it with others; that they can learn more from each other than from any other source. They develop a reasoned confidence that they can implement change, that they can continue to learn from a network of trusted peers, and that they can influence their family's and their business's destiny.

Key take-aways

■ While business-owning families tend to believe their particular issues are unique, most family businesses face many of the same issues.

■ The challenge in family business education is to help very private people open up to new ideas, see their relevance and take action.

■ Confidentiality is key to creating a spirit of sharing.

■ Active participation ensures engagement, as well as providing the opportunity to reveal a common shared experience among participants.

■ Follow-up helps ensure that learning is translated into implementation and supports participants in the changes they choose to make.

Notes

1 The development and experimentation of the ideas in this article are shared with Professor Joachim Schwass, who was program director of LFB for eight years.
2 One framework groups individuals by their roles and perspectives; the other framework homogenizes all the businesses into generic categories.

26

Fundamentals for a world-class leadership program

Jack Denfeld Wood and Gianpiero Petriglieri

Summary

Meaningful leadership development needs to incorporate emotional and often unconscious aspects of human behavior. This chapter describes a leadership program designed to provide opportunities to learn, in-depth and through personal experience, about the exercise of authority, leadership behavior and team dynamics at individual, interpersonal, group, intergroup and organizational levels. Such a program is not for everyone, and it requires a deep commitment to personal and professional development on the part of individual participants, faculty and sponsoring organization.

There is a significant difference between leadership 'training' programs, whose assumptions derive from an 'engineering' approach, and leadership 'development' programs, whose assumptions derive from a 'clinical' one.[1] The clinical approach invites faculty and participants of a leadership program to collaborate in the creation of a hospitable environment for meaningful and long-lasting learning about the deeper determinants of leadership – an environment suffused by a culture of curiosity and openness rather than one of judgment. In this chapter, we shall focus on the six fundamental elements of a world-class leadership program. They are:

1 A 'potentially' committed group of participants.

2 A solid psychological foundation.

3 A coherent educational framework built upon this foundation.

4 An engaging and interactive experiential program design.

5 A program staff of serious behavioral professionals.

6 A collaborative partnership with the client organization.

Let us examine them one by one.

The participants

The vast majority of participants attending executive education programs are sponsored by their employer. They range in age from their late 20s to their late 50s and have a history of significant achievement in their corporate careers. Professionally, they have been exposed to the challenge of managing and being managed by others. Often, when they arrive, they are facing a moment of personal or professional change – a coming promotion, a change in employer, a change in their family situation, or a mid-life transition.

Corporations typically send participants to leadership programs for one of three reasons: (a) the individual managers have heard the program reputation is good and want to come; (b) they have been identified as 'star performers'; or (c) they are perceived as 'needing help.' The first are being sent as a reward, the second are being sent to be groomed for greater responsibilities, and the third are being sent to get 'fixed.'

The reason one is being sent obviously has a profound influence on a participant's initial attitude towards the program. The final go-ahead is usually made by their bosses in collaboration with the HR department, on the basis (at least officially) of performance reviews, someone else's informal suggestion, or results from a formal assessment center. Those with the most direct experience of a participant's leadership skills – their subordinates – are rarely consulted. For these reasons, a sizable percentage of each class approaches leadership development with some degree of skepticism. We find that in a typical program – between 24 and 90 individuals – participants will learn best if the class is as diverse as possible, both in terms of socio-demographic variables and in terms of attitude towards the program. A balanced mixture of the enthusiastic and the skeptical provides everyone concerned with a richer learning opportunity, because it accurately mirrors the reality of today's organizational life. This flatly contradicts the commonly held assumption that the more homogeneous, open and enthusiastic the class is, the more it will collectively learn.

The psychological foundation

The general assumptions and features of the clinical psychological approach have been presented in an earlier chapter.[2] Our educational methods draw on an eclectic set of perspectives, including depth psychology, transactional analysis, group relations theories, and some methods originated at the NTL and Tavistock Institutes. Together, these perspectives provide a psychological foundation that aims at facilitating the natural flow of human development and integration – and allows the program to embrace intense personal emotion as well as to reveal unconscious processes at work. Unlike adherents of the engineering approach, we do not rely predominantly on a cognitive, rational perspective to 'train' managers in 'defensive routines' that suppress unpleasant thoughts and feelings; we believe these techniques inhibit personal and professional development.

The British psychoanalyst Donald Winnicott found that the best and healthiest human development occurs when we have the possibility to explore and make sense of our experiences within a 'holding environment' – a physical as well as an emotional space – both stimulating and safe enough, where help is available to make sense of, and deal with, the confusion of one's emerging feelings, and where one can extrapolate one's experiences and feelings to similar situations. A holding environment is a space where it is possible to be curious about, and 'play' with, delicate material, without judging or being judged, and without getting overwhelmed or overreacting.[3] The educational framework we provide helps create such a holding environment.

Educational framework: Idiom, symbol and myth

Managers who come to our programs have been working in a 'performance based' social system, probably since kindergarten, and are usually looking for concrete deliverables. Few participants have much familiarity with the concept of the unconscious; many have never voluntarily signed up for a psychologically-oriented seminar; and some can find 'good' reasons to avoid the exploration of unconscious influences in their and others' behavior in favor of a more conventional face-saving and socially acceptable pedagogical approach. Therefore, the principal challenges that faculty face in the early part of a 'clinical' leadership development program are:

- Inviting the unconscious into the room in a non-threatening way.

■ Legitimating, demystifying and depathologizing its manifestations.

■ Establishing its relevance to the clients' *personal* and *professional* situations.

■ Gaining authorization to work with unconscious dynamics in the here and now.

Psychologically speaking, we try to create the conditions where there is a chance for one's 'ego resistance' to the unconscious to soften, and where unconscious forces can be 'enticed' to make themselves heard, seen and felt in a more or less non-threatening way. Four elements that facilitate the effort to make room for emotions and the unconscious in a leadership program are: (a) confidentiality, (b) the use of clear, concise, colloquial language, (c) the importance of symbolic imagery and (d) the integrating function of myth.

Confidentiality

Participants must feel reasonably safe to explore relatively unfamiliar and uncomfortable material, to experiment, and to permit themselves to be clumsy. To do so, both participants and faculty work together to create room that allows this experimentation to take place. Confidentiality is essential. We ensure a clear and explicit confidentiality contract among staff and participants as soon as the program begins. We are not running an assessment centre – we are offering a developmental opportunity. Nothing regarding a manager's behavior is shared with the company that sent them, or with our own organization.

Language and idiom

The language we use has to be comprehensible. 'Psychobabble' and 'biz-speak' simply do not work. The language we use needs to be familiar and relevant to the participants – we have found that plain, colloquial English and familiar idiomatic expressions usually work best.

Symbolic imagery

Symbolic images serve as a pathway to recognize unconscious material and hence play a pivotal role throughout the program. When coupled with plain language, images can guide participants from the familiar into the unfamiliar with economy and effectiveness. Symbolic imagery is the language of the unconscious – of dreams and of fantasy – and we encourage participants to play with the images we at first provide. Later in the program, we invite them to explore the images they create themselves.

Let us give an example. For several years a picture of the Matterhorn mountain has been used in all IMD MBA promotional brochures. The graphic depicts a long, ascending yellow line from left to right that reaches above the Matterhorn, where the word 'leader' appears to hang in mid-air – on top! The yellow line then takes a short plunge down to the right. The alpine image suggests a particular view of leadership, and we ask participants what the metaphor might mean. They answer that a leader climbs the corporate ladder, the path is straight, there are pauses along the way, one makes such an ascent with a team, the team can climb only as fast as the slowest individual, it takes tremendous energy and focus to get there, only one person, the leader,

is visible at the top, it is hard to breathe, there is a precipitous fall, and the line disappears in the mist. Their interpretation almost serves as a warning.

There are countless images that could evoke leadership development. As a

contrast with the mountain, we use an iceberg. When asked for the meaning of the metaphor, managers say that an iceberg is a lonely, broken-off fragment of a larger mass; it floats upon the primal, salt-water ocean; the smaller, visible part is supported by the larger, invisible one; and the part that sunk the *Titanic* was underwater and out of sight. The implications for leading groups and organizations is clear, and implies that it is helpful to develop one's capacity to identify and navigate the covert and emotional aspects of individual and collective behavior so as not to be inadvertently sunk.

Living myths

If the conventional metaphor for managerial success is a linear rise to a mountain summit or hierarchy, ours is a circular one – a journey of 'descent, encounter and ascent' from the safe and familiar to the uncomfortable and unfamiliar and back home again. There is nothing 'new' about this 'hero's journey' – it is timeless – first explicated by psychoanalysts Otto Rank and Carl Jung at the turn of the twentieth century and then popularized by Joseph Campbell in his 1949 classic on the mythology of heroic leadership, *The Hero with a Thousand Faces*. One finds this same journey as a basic theme in myths, fairy tales and stories from every century and every civilization. Campbell describes the journey as follows:

The standard path of the mythological adventure of the hero is a magnification of the formula represented in the rites of passage: Separation-initiation-return: Which might be named the nuclear unit of the monomyth. A hero ventures forth from the world of common day into a region of supernatural wonder: Fabulous forces are there encountered and a decisive victory is won: The hero comes back from this mysterious adventure with the power to bestow boons on his fellow man.[4]

Even the structure of our leadership development programs follows the pattern of the hero's journey. For the participants, the pattern is captured in their departure from home, encounter with the challenges of the program, and return to their families and work. Participants are gently brought into a psychological space where they have the opportunity to cross the boundary between management and leadership – from the rational world of management spreadsheets, annual reports and concrete tools, to the emotional world of leadership mythology, imagery, charisma and inspiration.

Program design

In a program designed to follow the movement of the hero's journey – preparation, departure, fulfillment and return – four distinct phases occur in a typical two-week period:

1 Pre-program *preparation*.
2 An initial *orientation* with the unconscious domain.
3 Outdoor exercises for leadership *experimentation*.
4 *Integration* of the experiences to prepare for the return home.

The pathway leads participants to a threshold between the conscious and rational and the unconscious and emotional and encourages them to descend across that threshold and explore that domain with the faculty and

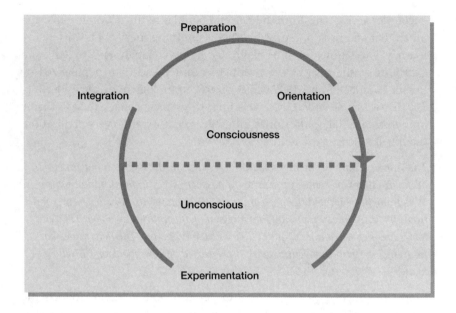

other participants, and then to ascend and integrate the experiences in the final portion of the program.[5]

1   Preparation

The coherence of such a leadership program depends in large part on meticulous preparation that includes assembling the program staff; preliminary staff work on role assignments and session design; negotiation with our own school; preparing the client organization for sending their participants (to be explained below), and preparing the individual participants for the program.

For the participants, preparation consists of reading several psychologically-oriented articles and leadership cases, filling out an application including personal background information for a 'participant handbook' comprising one-page résumés, and writing a 'Personal and Professional Identity Statement' (PPIS) – a confidential 10–15 page in-depth autobiography that invites participants to engage with the theme of their own development in a more personal and meaningful way. For many, the PPIS is the first serious personal reflection in their lives. The discrepancy between their application résumé and the PPIS highlights the fundamental difference between the mask we show others – our *persona* – and who we really are behind that mask – our *self*.

2 Orientation

Study groups

As soon as they arrive, participants are put into a study group of five to eight participants, chosen for maximum diversity by nationality, sex, company, industry, function, managerial experience and so on. This intimate group is the primary 'learning unit' and remains intact for most sessions; attached to it is one principal faculty consultant.

Contracting

One aim of the first part of the program is to establish a 'psychological contract' among faculty and participants, individually and collectively. [6] Faculty and participants articulate their expectations and concerns, and are encouraged to identify what they wish to get out of the program. For meaningful development to occur, individuals must *take personal responsibility* to shape and discover their own learning. While the faculty provides a framework and a learning opportunity, participants determine what they learn, how much they learn, and the pace at which they learn. [7] We have found it helpful if the faculty and participants work with a sense of *freedom, curiosity, willingness to take the initiative, courage to explore, and willingness to be surprised*. Those who take the opportunity seriously, bringing themselves fully into the program and allowing themselves to explore and be surprised, are rewarded with a deeper experience of personal and professional development and a deeper understanding of the unconscious dimensions of leadership – how it *really* works.

Session content

The orientation phase is an introduction for the participants – to the staff, the program material, and the behavioral way of thinking about leadership. In this phase, we attempt to weave metaphor, colloquial language, symbolic imagery and living myth together with more traditional case studies, lectures and behavioral simulations. We use audiovisual media extensively, for example integrating short clips from Hollywood movies into brief lectures to illustrate various learning points, and we videotape the small study group at work. Taken together, these sessions entice participants to explore behavior, give them a preliminary conceptual framework and simple language to do so, and bring them to the fully experiential portion of the program.

3 Experimentation

While experimentation runs throughout the program, the heart of the experience is the outdoor exercises portion. The primary task here is to learn about the exercise of authority, leadership behavior and team dynamics at various 'levels of analysis' – individual, interpersonal, group, inter-group and organizational – using our own experiences in the indoor and outdoor activities.

Outdoor exercises

Groups go through a tightly choreographed series of problem-solving outdoor activities and competitions. It is neither survival school nor 'Outward Bound.' Each exercise is followed by an hour or so debriefing, where the group reflects on its behavior with the aid of their consultant, using a formal debriefing guide designed to systematically explore the covert structure and dynamics of the group.[8]

Participant group retreat and review

Following these outdoor activities, an extensive retreat and video review allow participants to take stock of – and primary responsibility for – their learning without a faculty consultant present. They take time to review the videos and informally discuss how their group works together, exploring key insights on their own.

Classroom presentations

To conclude the experimentation phase, each group presents their experiences to the rest of the class. This offers a multi-faceted learning opportunity. Groups have a chance to articulate their learning thus far and share it with the other groups, ask other groups questions, and experience the residual competitive and less comfortable 'large group' dynamics of a classroom context. Following the presentations, the groups debrief with their faculty consultant regarding the presentations and the events that took place in the larger class.

4 Integration

The final phase of the program focuses primarily on making sense of the participants' experiences. This is accomplished through theoretical frameworks that allow an integration of logic and emotion, thinking and feeling, the rational and irrational, and the conscious and unconscious. We have found that exposure to excessive theoretical materials too early in the learning cycle 'contaminates' the participants' spontaneous experience with alien cognitive structures, and interferes with their intuitive understanding of what is happening.

Structured group feedback exercise

The activity that marks the beginning of this portion of the program is an extensive feedback exercise. Based on their experience with one another, small study group participants prepare and share interpersonal feedback. This exercise is highly appreciated by participants as a way to capitalize on their shared experiences, giving them a tangible collection of others' perspectives on their behavior and preparing them for subsequent sessions as they approach re-entry to their family, friends and jobs.

Understanding and managing individual differences

These sessions explore some of the systemic differences that have been operating covertly and affecting the structure and dynamics of the small study groups, such as culture, ideology, personality and differences in career orientations. Faculty offers theoretical frameworks to enable participants to consolidate and integrate their recent experience.

We normally position more complex theoretical material, such as personality inventories like the Myers-Briggs Type Indicator (MBTI), *after* the outdoor activities rather than before them. To encourage lasting insight and development, we believe it is essential that participants *first* make personal sense of their experience, within their own framework and vocabulary, and only *then* bring in perspectives derived from standard, more technical frameworks. The same reasoning applies for 360° feedback questionnaires.

360° feedback

If we include 360° feedback in the program – with results from a questionnaire completed prior to the program by the participant and his or her supervisor, peers and subordinates – it is best distributed after the outdoor activities are complete. If distributed earlier, survey results tend to hold back participants' mental freedom in the experimentation phase – they naturally focus on the evaluations from their workplace and worry about how to respond to them rather than concentrate on their present learning experience. However, when introduced just prior to the individual coaching at the end of the program, 360° feedback from the workplace can be compared and contrasted with their peer-group feedback, and so is more readily assimilated.

Art atelier and individual coaching

The last day aims to assist participants as they cross back over the threshold into their familiar everyday domain, while honoring their intuitive and emotional experiences from the program. We split the day between a half-day art atelier and a one-on-one coaching session. The combination of these two learning opportunities allows participants to articulate and integrate their experiences from the program – both verbally and artistically – while acknowledging the emotional (less rational) aspects of the experience.

Previously, on the second day of the program, we had provided a 'warm-up' for this session, where participants had a chance to approach the symbolic language of the emotional level through 'play' with finger paints and modeling clay. The objective of this work is to allow participants to get in touch with a dormant part of their creative selves, probably untouched since childhood, and to help them recognize and appreciate non-verbal means of expression as meaningful sources of information. In the final day's art atelier, participants create a painting that expresses their thoughts and feelings in symbol and metaphor – perhaps those that are still difficult to articulate in words – from the program experience.

When not engaged in the symbolic work of the art atelier, participants are preparing for, then involved in, individual sessions with their faculty consultant. The individual coaching sessions aim at maximizing the transfer of their new insights to the 'home situation.' The faculty consultant takes the role of 'individual coach,' enabling the participants to integrate their learning and 'make the link' back to their home and job – thinking through and discussing how they will apply their insights in their personal and professional lives.

Clinical leadership development is not surrogate psychotherapy, although both operate in the same psychological domain and ask similar questions – What am I feeling? What is happening now? Why? What lessons can I draw? Both involve a certain degree of probing and exploring individual and group tensions. It frequently happens, however, that participants find their experiences to be therapeutic in a general sense, and that the program has changed the way they think about themselves and how they lead their lives. This is entirely within the scope of an educational design for leadership development.

Closing dinner

The program ends with a 'reception' and 'exposition' of participant paintings from the art atelier, followed by a formal closing dinner. We encourage senior management from the client organization to attend both the opening and closing of the program, in an effort to serve as a symbolic bridge, respectively 'handing the participants over' and then 'receiving them back.' We have found that holding the closing dinner as a celebration on the last night of the program is much preferable to a luncheon where participants and faculty are preoccupied and distracted with packing, hotel checkout and travel arrangements to return home.

The program staff

Roles

Each faculty member consults to one group throughout the program, but they participate in the management of the program as a whole, sharing a larger responsibility than maximizing their own group's learning. In such a complex program, faculty members take a number of different roles – classroom instructor, consultant to one small group throughout the program, individual coach, and occasionally consultant to various sub-systems. The experience of individual faculty members can be markedly different in each of those roles, as is the participants' perception of them. This is a learning opportunity in and of itself.

Clinical background

It is extremely important that all members of the program staff have the interest and background to work together with the clinical approach, that is, in an authentic and collaborative way – sensitive to covert psychological processes, comfortable with difficult emotional material, and without excessive reliance on prescribed procedure and technique. Our program staff is drawn from a broad range of academic backgrounds, and usually have advanced degrees in the social sciences, clinical psychology or medicine. Regardless of their official academic degree, however, each staff member has had extensive psychological training in individual, group and organizational dynamics. In addition, because past qualifications and experience are not enough, each staff member must be committed to regularly update their personal and professional training and development.

Staff meetings

Frequent, intense and lengthy staff meetings are a central part of the staff's clinical responsibilities. One basic tenet of the clinical approach is not to ask participants to do anything that faculty members are unwilling to do themselves – we need to practice the same authenticity, investment, commitment, risk taking and willingness to explore and reflect upon one's behavior and feelings that we demand from participants. During the staff meetings we discuss what is happening in the participants' groups and the larger 'system,' as well as within the faculty group itself. Such meetings are neither intended to train inexperienced consultants, nor to provide them with therapy, nor to entertain psychology-lovers; instead, they are one of our principal means of guaranteeing the integrity of the learning environment.

The importance of staff meetings is dictated by the perpetual novelty of behavioral work, and encourages an understanding of the uniqueness of each situation and each person in the program. The work is exhilarating as well as stressful, and the staff meetings serve several functions: a 'reality check' to individual faculty from trusted colleagues, an opportunity to release stress, and a way to maintain psychological availability for the participants. In our view, staff groups that avoid frequent and thorough clinical meetings during an experiential leadership program are either incompetent or unprofessional. Even if individual staff members are extraordinarily qualified and experienced, without clinical staff meetings the psychological integrity of the learning process and the program suffer tremendously.

Collaboration of participants and staff

An open and reciprocal collaboration between staff and participants is fundamental for the learning to be optimal. The staff needs to be dependable, without providing either unnecessary reassurance or excessive stress; the former would deter participants from reflecting on their own experience, and the latter would hinder their ability to learn. If the material is provocative enough to challenge them and stretches their boundaries, most participants will engage deeply in the task of learning. However, if the faculty push too little or too much, or if the provocation is out of tune with their deeper needs, participants tend to shut down and give up. Faculty members need to get close enough emotionally to feel with the class members, but remain apart enough to be able to reflect on those feelings and access what might be at work under the surface. Any closer and they risk losing the autonomy of their distinct perspective; any more distant and they risk hiding behind an empty role of 'guru' and jeopardizing their emotional connection with the participants. Ultimately, the staff needs to care deeply about the participants without falling into the trap of 'taking care' of them.

Collaborative partnership with the client organization

In this chapter, we have described the educational framework and program design of a serious leadership development program. However, high-quality leadership development requires more than a professional faculty and a class of committed participants working together. It requires time, space, and the alignment and active engagement of the client organization, the provider of leadership development, the individual managers who will participate, and the program faculty. When any of these four major stakeholders is not on board, trouble is in sight.

Program

Participants fill out detailed evaluation forms at the end of the program. They evaluate every session as well as each faculty member's work as small group consultants on a five-point scale – unacceptable to excellent. In addition to the quantitative assessment, participants have the opportunity to write comments and observations. The *unedited* tabulated results are distributed to all program faculty, the school's president, and the client organization's training or HR representative.

We use the ratings to develop the individual faculty, the staff as a team, and the program as a whole. The numbers and comments are a fairly accurate measure of how well the faculty has managed to make the work relevant to the clients. Participants' ratings are a reliable measure of their feelings about the program. They are not, however, a measure of how much participants have really learned during the program. Nor are they an accurate evaluation of the depth and quality of the behavioral work. It is possible for faculty members to get 'excellent' ratings by colluding with a participant's or a group's desire to be told what to do, to have simple answers, and thus to 'avoid' the difficulties inherent in gaining insight into themselves. By the same token, faculty might earn a 'fair' or 'good' rating and yet have done a superb job in bringing a participant or a group out of their comfort zone, into the space where the emotional fundamentals of leadership can be uncovered and explored, and where serious behavioral learning can occur.

Client objectives

It is essential that the client organization be committed to serious leadership development and that they are also aware of its implications. This kind of program is not simply 'fun and games.' Companies that do not wish their managers to be challenged to examine their real behavior, or companies that do not wish to develop self-aware, independent leaders who are both able and willing to take emotional risks in the service of leading, should probably consider other kinds of programs, perhaps those using exclusively classroom lectures, traditional cases, role plays and motivational speakers.

We believe that the economic temptation to sell as many clinical leadership programs as possible is a mistake. These programs are not for everyone and this must be clearly and honestly communicated. Should client organizations buy a program for which they are unable or unwilling to provide a supportive context for participants upon their return to the workplace, both it and IMD will be poorly served in the long run.

Professionally delivered 'clinical' leadership development, at its best, can foster meaningful and long-lasting behavioral learning – nothing less and nothing more. It is important that individual participants and their sponsoring companies are well aware of what they are bargaining for. This kind of leadership program works best when individual participants have a concrete need and genuine desire to deepen their understanding of leadership and team dynamics, and when their companies reward the pursuit of such learning in two ways: by encouraging managers to develop their self-awareness and leadership skills, and by offering them opportunities to apply those skills at work.

Key take-aways

- Learning about the fundamental determinants of leadership occurs best within a stimulating, yet safe, 'holding environment' where help is available to make sense of one's experiences and feelings.

- Participants' learning is enriched if the study groups are as diverse as possible, both in terms of socio-demographic variables and in terms of attitude towards the program.

- A successful framework for leadership development parallels the mythological 'hero's journey': preparation, departure, experimentation, return and reintegration.

- Outdoor exercises, if tightly choreographed and well debriefed, provide a rich source of experimentation to reflect on how leadership works.

- A combination of structured feedback, experiential group work, questionnaires, artistic expression and individual coaching provides an effective vehicle for integrating personal learning about leadership.

- Competent staff members participate in the management of the program, are present in several roles, and require the same commitment to learning demanded of participants.

- Long and frequent 'clinical staff meetings' are fundamental to maintain the integrity of the learning environment.

- Client organizations need to be well aware of what this kind of leadership program can – and cannot – deliver.

Notes

1   See this book, Chapter 11.
2   They include descriptive and pragmatic use of theories; integration of rational and emotional capacities; familiarity with a range of feelings and behaviors and the development of an attitude of 'reflective spontaneity'; including the unconscious as part of the dialog; participant responsibility for their learning, etc. For a more detailed explanation, see this book, Chapter 11, 'Learning for leadership: The "engineering" and "clinical" approaches.'
3   Winnicott, D.W. (1990) *The Maturational Processes and the Facilitating Environment: Studies in the Theory of Emotional Development*. London: Karnac.
4   Campbell, J. (1994) *The hero with a thousand faces*. London: Fontana Press. Original work published 1949, p. 30.
5   See Appendix to this chapter for a detailed block schedule of a two-week leadership development program.
6   Schein, E.H. (1970) The psychological contract. *In: Organizational Psychology*. 2nd ed. Engelwood Cliffs, NJ: Prentice Hall, pp. 77–79.
7   Miller, E.J. (1989) *The 'Leicester' model: experiential study of group and organizational processes*. Occasional Paper No. 10. London: The Tavistock Institute.
8   See this book, Chapter 18.

	Orientation				Experimentation				Integration		
Day 1	Day 2	Day 3	Day 4	Day 5	Day 6	Day 7	Day 8	Day 9	Day 10	Day 11
Program introduction and guest speaker	Leadership and management	Leadership: Taking the irrational seriously	Introduction to transactional analysis	Outdoor activities	Organizational dynamics in action	Team video review	Team presentations	Managing differences: Structure and dynamics of groups	Managing differences: Career orientation	Individual coaching and art atelier
Interpersonal relations: General manager role play	Group relations: Teamwork and synergy	Inter-group relations: Project	Outdoor activities	Outdoor activities	Personal retreat and reflection	Individual feedback exercise	Managing differences: Personality	360° feedback Results and preparation for coaching	Individual coaching and art atelier	
Contracting session	Diagnostic interview	The value of symbolic expression	Introductory exercise	Organizational dynamics in action					Film and discussion	Closing dinner

Appendix 26.1 Sample leadership program

27

How to build and run long executive education programs

Robert Hooijberg

Summary

Successful implementation of a stimulating and energizing executive program over an extended timeframe requires careful orchestration of the content, as well as the coordination and management of other faculty members. An integrated approach to scheduling is essential to provide variation in the pace and teaching methods to maintain engagement and energy levels; as well as two or three general themes running throughout the program to keep participants focused. This is illustrated with reference to Module Two of IMD's Program for Executive Development and the practical challenges in that context.

How do you create a meaningful learning experience for executives who have an average of 18 years of work experience, 15 years of management experience, and, as a group, extensive international experience? Never easy, this is a particularly challenging task when you have to sustain their engagement for the second five weeks of a ten-week program. In this chapter I will share with you how I structured the Program for Executive Development Module Two (PED II), and how I (try to) manage the faculty, the participants and myself in order to deliver a meaningful learning experience in this context.

Structuring the program

The overall purpose of the PED program is to prepare the participants for general management opportunities. Participants are usually successful functional managers, who need to widen their knowledge of the areas in the business with which they are less familiar as well as learn to think strategically about the overall business. We structure the first PED module (PED I) primarily to address the acquisition of knowledge in the entire range of the functional areas of the business, such as finance, marketing, accounting, IT and supply chain management; in the second module, we focus primarily on the integrative topics of strategy and leadership.

When participants enter PED II, they have already participated in five weeks of PED I. During those first five weeks, they have learned more about business functions with which they have little or no experience, not only with 'real live' cases, but also through reflection on and application of their skills. As such, the program moves beyond just a mental exercise in two main ways: outdoor leadership exercises in the third week and a simulation in the fourth week. When they start the second five-week module, the program focus shifts to thinking about strategies for the company; this requires the participants to take a more abstract view of the company, analyzing the industry in which their company operates and also the demographic and political changes in the world beyond. Participants must then think through business trajectories, business models and strategic options. Finally, they examine how to balance new job demands with their personal lives.

While the first module uses concrete and immediate business problems to stimulate discussion and learning, the second module requires participants to think about the impact of strategic decisions five to ten years into the future as well as the future viability of the company within the changes taking place in the wider business environment. Because most of the participants are action-oriented and prefer to solve concrete issues, they find it very challenging to think about trends and key success factors in their industry; as a result, they tend to turn to what their company *does*, rather than to what it *should do*.

In addition to the shift in the content and focus of PED II, participants find themselves with a different mix of colleagues from the ones they came to know in PED I. This is because the second module begins at different times throughout the year with different participants. Participants tend to congregate with the colleagues from PED I who happen to return with them, because strong friendships and relationships have been built during the first five-week program. The formation of such cliques works against the sharing and exchange of ideas necessary for the success of the program, and so we encourage intense networking in PED II.

General and weekly themes

High energy is absolutely essential – the days are long (every day from 08:30 to 18:00, including Saturday mornings), the work is intense, and a large part of the learning depends on the active and constructive exchange of ideas among the participants themselves. To maintain high energy, we use general themes throughout the program as well as themes for each week. We also orchestrate the final week especially carefully.

The general themes throughout the program are (1) strategy, (2) the general manager toolkit and (3) broadening perspectives. By switching between alternative strategic directions for the company, personal skill development and broader developments outside organizations, the attention of participants remains engaged. The five weekly themes are (a) taking stock of where you are, (b) developing strategic options, (c) growth and global business, (d) developing your vision and (e) implementing change.

With the general themes, participants move 'out-in' from the really big picture through the analysis of the organization to the development of their personal skills. The structure of the weekly themes should follow a corresponding out-in sequence, e.g. teaching industry and company analysis combined with communication skills – there is no point in being able to do great analysis if you cannot communicate this effectively to those who need to know.

High and low energy periods

While the themes help in terms of providing a roadmap and the challenge of moving among three levels of analysis, it is not enough to maintain high energy for five weeks. Given that participants already attended one module that relied on the case method, using more cases, while important, does not tend to motivate them to the same extent that it did in PED I.

The key low energy periods are the Fridays of each week as well as the entire third week. To boost the energy of the participants, we avoid the case method on three of the four Fridays of the program. Instead we spend one Friday on communication skills by placing participants in a wide variety of situations where they must practice and then get feedback in role playing from a real actor. The second Friday is spent in a simulation, where the participants have to manage stakeholder relations amidst an organizational crisis. On the fourth Friday, we ask them to reflect on where they have been in their lives and where they want to go. In addition, we insert shorter role plays, guest speakers and co-teaching every week, adding variety to the learning experience and injecting new energy. In simple terms, these exercises engage not only the mind, but also the body, the heart and perhaps even the spirit, all of which motivate the ongoing effort of participants and continued learning.

The final week

The focus of the last week of the program is on change. This is a special week, both to manage and for the participants. After ten weeks at IMD, the participants are about to re-enter their companies as well as resume their personal lives. Because they want to implement their new ideas and actions, both for themselves personally and for their organizations, they need to address the potential barriers they may encounter. So, the sessions and cases focus on change and that is good, but not enough.

For the last two days of the program, we invite the participants to bring their spouses and partners. We present them with an overview of IMD and PED, ask them to participate in three sessions, and invite them to join us at the closing dinner. This greatly facilitates the transition home as the spouses/partners share in the PED experience, discuss its ideas with their partners, and celebrate the completion of the program together.

The closing dinner is not just a dinner; it is an event that is organized by the participants. As a group, they sing an opera and/or perform skits, songs and game shows between the courses of the meal; they also choose their own master of ceremonies. The official part of the evening closes with a diploma ceremony. However, this evening is not just about fun. It is the final bonding event of the program and an enjoyable way for friends to say goodbye. This ensures that the program ends on an emotional high, appreciating all that they accomplished together, both in learning and in forming personal bonds.

Managing participants

Expectations

Participants and their companies pay a lot in terms of money, time and effort to attend this program. Having already invested in five weeks of the program, they have high expectations regarding the content, process and personal relevance of the material and the faculty.

To manage these expectations, it is crucial to emphasize the value added by the second module of the PED. An important part of this is the presentation of an overarching framework for the PED as a whole (see Figure 27.1). This framework shows that in organizational life we try to balance two paradoxical demands: stability and flexibility, and internal and external focus. These two dimensions create four quadrants that highlight the central task of the general manager. The first module of PED focuses primarily on the bottom two quadrants of managing the internal processes and functions, and managing the people. The second module of PED focuses predominantly on vision and strategy, and adapting to the external environment.

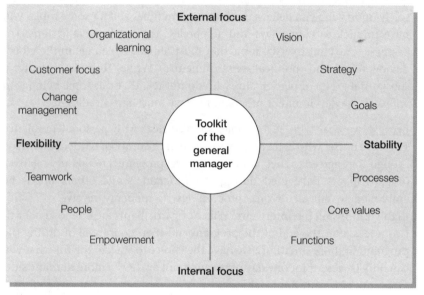

Figure 27.1 Organizing model for PED

We start with this framework at the beginning of the program and refer back to it when necessary. In addition to the presentation of themes for the week and a reiteration of the framework, we begin each week by reviewing what we have done, where we are going, and how it all fits together.

Personal issues and crises

Kurt Vonnegut once wrote that 'Earth would be an engineer's paradise, if it wasn't for the people, the goddamned people, messing up the machinery.'[1] There is also Murphy's law, i.e. 'Everything that can go wrong will go wrong.' It is the same in the PED: there are always things that go wrong no matter how much and how well we plan. We deal with strong personalities, people who are not afraid to say what they like and what they do not like. Even though I have been running the program for two and a half years now, it is still difficult to deal with participants who come up to me and say, 'That session was a complete waste of my time and money!' I respond that I am sorry to hear about their discontent and then ask them why it was a waste and what suggestions they have that might make it more worthwhile.

But, we do not initiate changes on the basis of comments from a single individual. We pay close attention to the feedback of the whole class as well as to what we believe the participants need in order to be well prepared for general management positions. While you cannot run a program based solely upon what you believe is relevant, sometimes and for some topics you have to stick to your views and accept less than stellar evaluations. For example, one controversial topic that must remain is 'change in the global demographic and political environments.' While there is usually a substantial group of participants who do not feel that this topic belongs in an executive development program, here we must agree to disagree.

Because we deal with real people, we also deal with personal problems. There are bosses who demand the presence in the office of participants, even though they agreed to their attendance at the program. Friends and relatives of participants have died during the program, while others might be embroiled in crucial divorce proceedings or suddenly receive offers for highly promising job interviews. Wives of participants are due to give birth two weeks after the end of the program and then go into labor during the program. In those situations, we have the choice to stick to the rule that you can only be absent for one day of the program or show a more humane side. I prefer the humane approach.

Interpersonal relations

Everyone understands that, with 50 to 60 participants, not all will get along with each other. Occasionally, however, people truly despise each other. This comes to me in the form of such requests as 'I refuse to sit next to participant X,' or 'please make sure I am not in the same study group as participant Y,' or 'can't you do something about participant Z's annoying behavior?'

Because we have computer programs that optimize variety in the study groups across the five weeks of the program, we refuse to grant requests regarding study group membership. If necessary, we will speak to both parties concerned and request that they conduct themselves professionally and treat each other with courtesy. Controlling seating in the auditorium, which is also computer generated, is virtually impossible – if participants really do not want to sit next to someone, they simply pick up their name card and take an empty seat. Luckily these instances are rare.

If participants display truly annoying behaviors, as program director, I will both alert the other faculty and talk directly to the individual in private. We expect faculty to manage process issues in their sessions, including 'airtime' of participants. However, it is helpful to alert them to individuals who may prove problematic.

The management of cell phone distractions is more difficult as they are hard to observe. We confront the rare individuals who go too far. For example, we had someone who was on his cell phone all the time. Several participants complained that he was on his cell phone instead of participating in the study group. Personally, he was a friendly and nice person, but his behavior interfered with everyone's learning. I took him aside and told him that if this was not a good time to be attending the program he should come back another time. Though he assured me it was the right time and his behavior improved for one week, it started to deteriorate again, and finally he just disappeared without a word!

Social events

During the five-week program, social events play a key role in maintaining a positive climate as well as creating opportunities for networking. It is a time to relax and to discuss both program and non-program issues. Program administrators are particularly good at picking up significant cues regarding how participants are doing. They serve as our eyes and ears, alerting us to potential issues and allowing us to address these issues one-on-one before they become big problems. Social events also help participants to form strong and lasting bonds, which at times may come under stress due to conflicts in the study groups during the preceding week(s). This is important not only for the program itself but also for relationships after the program. In many cases, these bonds grow into lasting friendships after the program.

Managing faculty

The faculty is the most difficult group to manage throughout all of this. The five-week PED II modules are run four times per year. For each of these four modules, 50 sessions must be scheduled. That translates into 200 sessions each year for this program. The faculty we use for the program are in high demand for other programs and we need them in specific weeks according to the theme for the particular week.

Not only can it be difficult to get faculty members to commit to longer executive programs, but sometimes they are tempted by more interesting opportunities! For example, on one occasion a faculty member announced that he was pulling out four days before he was scheduled to teach. I went to his office to ask why. He informed me that the CEO of a company had invited him to address their board meeting. While I do not want to stand in the way of this kind of opportunity, I had to insist he meet his original commitment to my program.

In addition to scheduling, we work hard to get the faculty to deliver the topic, content and approach that we need at that particular stage of the program. This includes coordinating closely with the program director of Module I. We spend time with colleagues sharing how they fit into the overall program, what has come before them, and what comes after them. We do this so that during their sessions they can refer to the other topics as points of reference, which help participants both to see the overall framework (the 'thread') and to demonstrate to participants that we have an integrated faculty. Of course, our faculty members have their preferred sessions as well as a preferred sequence of delivering them – so to achieve the right approach and order can take a lot of persuasion, cajoling and coaching!

Managing myself

Thinking about these many challenges, on a more personal note, I am reminded how important it is to manage my own emotions and balance my personal and professional life.

When I stay focused on the positive – the constructive participants (the majority), the dedicated faculty (the majority), and my great staff – I can better handle the unpleasant diversions. It is absolutely key to remind myself that overall both participants and faculty are consummate professionals.

The people who come through the program bring a wide variety of experience, knowledge and ideas with them and I learn from them in every session. Over the years, I have learned about the potato starch business, the paper industry, selling yogurt in the German market, ice-cream in Thailand and Chile, ship financing, mining, investment banking, pharmaceuticals, chocolate, oil exploration, helicopter services, internet services and running telecommunications units, to name just a few. I have listened with great interest to people from almost all countries of the world and discovered what it was like going through the currency crisis in Argentina, building businesses in the Cote d'Ivoire and Russia, selling premium paint in Egypt, constructing luxury yachts in the Netherlands, and trading commodities in Japan.

At the same time, I have to be careful not to get caught up in the excitement of the program and forget about my personal life. This means I have to make sure I pay sufficient attention to my wife and children and to my physical well-being. I have to make sure that my five-week programs, four times per year, do not turn into a 20-week disappearance act from home. Most evenings I make sure that I close the program at 18:00 and go home. At least once a week, I bring the children to school. During the program, of course, it is very difficult to avoid working two evenings a week and two Saturday mornings.

Finally, with all the great food sitting around me it is important to both exercise self-discipline and to exercise physically. I always walk back and forth to work, which means I walk about three kilometers per day. In addition, I try to play an hour of tennis each week, usually with some of the participants.

Conclusion

What does it take to successfully run a five-week program four times a year? A clear vision of what you want the participants to achieve is essential, as are having the right faculty and intellectually and emotionally challenging activities that help the participants achieve this vision. Successful implementation of this vision of a great program, however, requires careful management of the faculty, participants and staff. Successful management in turn requires that the program director focuses on the positive, balances his or her personal and professional life, and pays attention to physical fitness. In the end it is the participants – their work and life experiences, perspectives, personalities and attitudes – that make running a program like PED II a wonderful and worthwhile experience.

Key take-aways

- Give participants an overarching framework, showing the value that each session brings to the overall program design.

- Structure the program to take account of, and respond to, potential low energy periods.

- When faculty members are called on to deliver sessions, ensure that the content and approach are coordinated.

- Manage participants and faculty with sensitivity and firmness.

- As program director, manage your emotions and balance your personal and professional life.

Notes

1   Vonnegut, K. (1999) *Player Piano*. New York: Bantam Doubleday Dell Publishing Group; first published 1952.

28

Scripting a top MBA program: Focus on leadership development

Seán Meehan and Janet Shaner

Summary

Designing a top MBA program starts with listening to the customer and sensitivity to the market. Targeting the right participants and building on the strengths of the school are the key ingredients for success. This chapter describes the redesign of IMD's MBA program and its unique features: psychologically-grounded leadership development and four different real-world projects in social responsibility, entrepreneurship, international consulting and network-building.

Over the past 30 years, the IMD MBA has earned a strong reputation for innovation and business relevance. Today it is recognized as one of the world's leading MBA programs and is widely acknowledged to be unique, with innovations responding to the fundamental changes in the business world.

IMD has achieved this position by consistently listening to the needs of the market. Top executives of leading multinational companies tell us clearly: they need leaders, not managers. Leaders with the insight and ability to address issues and problems that are more complex and changing more quickly than ever before. Leaders who understand themselves. Leaders who understand the needs of their organizations and their business environments. Leaders who can build networks between diverse groups of people with different motivations across different cultures. Leaders who can drive change through innovation. Leaders who can move their businesses forward.

The single aim of the IMD MBA program is to develop these leaders.

Each year we limit our program to one class of 90 participants, carefully selected to make up a truly diverse group with complementary skills, nationalities and cultural backgrounds. We keep the class small because this kind of leadership development involves a high degree of personal attention and coaching.

The IMD MBA is a highly intensive 'MBA plus' for people who are driven by the desire to make a difference. Going through this program is like climbing a mountain. Although it is very demanding, both mentally and physically, it is hugely rewarding.

Listen to the customer

In 2002 IMD took the opportunity to critically re-evaluate and redesign our MBA program. Before making any changes, we undertook research to understand the strengths and weaknesses of the design of our existing MBA program. We listened to participants, alumni and recruiters. We gathered input from other IMD faculty. And we analyzed the competition to understand better how to position our offer in an increasingly competitive MBA marketplace. What we found was that the IMD MBA program was an extremely competitive and highly respected MBA program. And that it could be enhanced by implementing the market feedback – by adding elements to develop leaders, not managers, using IMD's 'real world, real learning' approach to create an experience other programs would find difficult to imitate.

Participant and alumni feedback

We started the research by reviewing feedback about the program gathered each year from the participants of that year. In addition, we discussed the program with IMD MBA alumni – who offered insights into what the program meant to their careers and their overall leadership development. We spoke with alumni in focus groups and also asked them to complete a web-based survey questionnaire to determine what they benefited from most in the program, what they would improve and future trends they saw in the business world that MBA graduates should have the skills to address. This survey was sent to approximately 1,000 IMD MBA alumni, and 30 percent of those responded with valuable feedback.

Company/recruiter feedback

With IMD's strong links to business through our learning network and our relationships with corporate recruiters, we spent many hours talking to these clients about the skills they need from MBA graduates. Throughout these interviews, one theme remained consistent. These companies said they need leaders, not managers.

In addition, these companies said that a one-year program is attractive because good, experienced employees are out of the workplace for a shorter period of time, an attractive feature in a world where top talent is difficult to find and where companies need it contributing to the business.

Competitive positioning

IMD assessed the MBA marketplace, which is becoming increasingly competitive with the number of MBA programs increasing and the size of the market decreasing. It also recognized the need to prepare for a time when the US schools would go from a two-year to a one-year model in response to demands from the marketplace.

IMD determined that in this marketplace, it already offered a top notch MBA program. It decided to build on IMD's 'real world, real learning' approach to include four projects required of all participants. The IMD MBA is one of the few MBA programs that can successfully implement this approach because of its small class size and experience in leadership development at all levels of executive development.

Find the right participants

The IMD MBA program is successful because it aligns the needs of the market (both participants and recruiters) with the program it delivers. The success of the program starts with finding the 'right 90' candidates who have demonstrated leadership characteristics and who have the desire to continue on this leadership path to make a difference in the world.

The admissions process has been described as 'world-class' by the AACSB (Association to Advance Collegiate Schools of Business). And participants who have been through the process say that they know the quality of IMD must be good if we devote so much time and care to selecting the participants.

To be admitted to IMD, participants must first submit a written application, consisting of 10 different essay questions, as well as their undergraduate grades, their GMAT score and three letters of recommendation. Two admissions committee members read each application and, based on their assessment, the admissions committee selects 200–250 candidates to interview personally each year. These candidates are selected based on their leadership ability as demonstrated in their application, their previous career or extracurricular achievements and comments by referees.

The interview process consists of an intense day at IMD including a personal interview with a member of the admissions committee, an impromptu presentation designed to test the candidate's abilities to analyze and think under pressure, and a case study presentation led by a professor to simulate the discussion and teamwork required by IMD's classroom methods.

Offers are extended only to those candidates who succeed in the multi-dimensional elements of the interview process, which in our experience are the elements required to succeed in the MBA program and in future leadership roles. In addition, candidates who receive offers must demonstrate a willingness to share their knowledge and experience and to learn from their colleagues because we find that participants learn as much from each other as they do from the faculty. As a result we don't simply select the best 90 individuals. Instead we build a class of the right 90 participants – each of whom contributes something unique.

Typically a successful IMD MBA candidate has had a minimum of 10 man-hours of scrutiny before an offer is extended.

Create a unique program

After selecting the 'right 90' candidates who will benefit from the IMD MBA, we put them through an intense 10-month program in leadership development.

In the increasingly competitive MBA marketplace, success depends on creating a unique program attractive to a specific group of participants. Prospective candidates often ask the question, 'What makes IMD special?' There are five key points that differentiate IMD and that participants say is what makes them select IMD as the right MBA program for their leadership development.

1 Small class size: 90 participants.

2 One-year program.

3 Mature, experienced profile: average age is 30 years and average experience is seven years (80 per cent of the class ranges in age from 28–32).

4 International: each year we have at least 35 nationalities represented in the class and no one nationality is dominant.

5 Real world, real learning approach: four projects that are required of all participants in entrepreneurship, network building, international consulting and social responsibility. These projects are designed to allow participants to apply what they have learned in the classroom and to develop the specific skills necessary for leadership in today's complex world.

The first four of these points defines the demographic profile and the market niche of the IMD MBA program. The last point reinforces the unique approach to leadership development that we offer because of the combination of small class size and deep experience in practically focused leadership development.

Focus on leadership development

The IMD MBA program design has several unique features, notably its leadership stream and the projects in social responsibility, entrepreneurship, network building and international consulting that provide opportunities for participants to apply their leadership skills in real-world situations.

Leadership stream: Personal, team, organization

The leadership stream combines expertise in the leadership development of managers with Jungian psychology. The approach is a 'clinical' rather than an 'engineering' approach.[1] An engineering approach is one where leaders, often CEOs, come into the classroom and give their tips and insights into what made them successful leaders. Participants are supposed to follow their prescriptive tips and apply them to participants' own experiences.

Successful leaders lead from their authentic selves, from their own strengths and weaknesses and from their hearts as well as their minds. A 'clinical' approach to leadership development involves building a deeper understanding of the individual, teams and organizations to understand how a person can combine most successfully his or her own strengths and weaknesses with the needs of the team and organization to successfully lead the organization forward.

Based on this philosophy, the leadership stream focuses on: personal leadership development, team and organizational behavior and organizational leadership. It is complemented by a trip to Bosnia-Herzegovina where participants have an opportunity to understand what it is like to lead in a difficult business environment where business can make a real difference in moving the country forward. This trip is also the focus of the social responsibility project that continues for the duration of the program.

Personal leadership development

Before they even start the MBA program, participants must write a personal inventory statement (PIS). Their assignment is to write about themselves – their strengths and weaknesses, their goals, their failings. And they must rewrite this statement three times from January to June as they grow from their personal and classroom experiences. Participants describe this as a difficult paper and a difficult process. They say, 'I never spent this much time writing about myself.'

In addition, participants have the opportunity to take a 'personal development elective' that includes 20 sessions with a trained psychotherapist – designed to allow the participants to deepen their self-understanding that will allow them to become more effective leaders. Again, participants describe this as one of the most effective parts of the program. They say, 'I would never have had the courage to do this on my own, but it has really helped me to understand myself better and to grow personally.'

Team and organizational behavior

Leaders must understand organizational behavior in order to influence people and accomplish the organization's goals. So participants follow a course on organizational behavior to understand individuals and social systems and how to structure and steer these systems to achieve high organizational performance.

Teams are an integral part of organizations, and MBA participants work in four or five different multicultural teams throughout the year. In these teams, they are under constant pressure from the intensity of the program, the result of which often produces conflict. Early in the year, each study group goes through a series of team-building exercises. An experienced coach assists the team to understand the root causes of conflicts and helps the teams to grow from these to improve their performance.

Organizational leadership

The course in organizational leadership combines the insights about oneself with the needs of the organization to help a participant develop a sense of 'authentic leadership.' The organizational leadership course includes several class sessions with CEOs and leaders from other backgrounds, e.g. military and non-governmental organizations, talking about the challenges they faced and how it inspired them or helped them grow.

Real-world projects

Social responsibility projects: Trip to and project for Bosnia-Herzegovina

The entire class spends one week in Bosnia-Herzegovina (BiH), a European country disrupted by conflict that is trying to get its economy back on track. The objectives are to explore the challenges facing the country and to gain a deeper understanding of situations in which, as a future leader, participants may assume a proactive, broader responsibility. During the week, participants meet with business leaders, government representatives and local people. The experience is much more than a seven-day visit. Preparation starts in the International Political Economy course. It continues through the year as participants develop ideas about their selected class project, for example: how the BiH government could enhance its approach to attracting foreign investment, how it could successfully bid for the Olympic Winter Games of 2014 or how it could build its winter tourism industry. During graduation week, the class presents its findings to IMD and to representatives of BiH.

Entrepreneurship projects: Build skills to drive innovation

Today's leaders need the ability to drive innovation in their companies – be they large or small. In IMD's entrepreneurship projects, participants are divided into teams of five or six and work directly with a local technology-based start-up company to develop a business plan, a marketing plan, a financing plan or whatever other creative input may be necessary to move the business forward. Successful entrepreneurs must be experts in completing projects with limited resources and in convincing the market of the value of its sometimes futuristic ideas. The entrepreneurship projects give participants the opportunity to experience these crucial leadership skills first hand and to stretch their creativity to help the young companies develop innovative solutions to problems.

International consulting projects: Develop and implement corporate strategies

For over 25 years, IMD has included international consulting projects in its program. Participants are again divided into teams of five or six which work directly with the senior management of a company on a project of strategic importance to the company. The projects are divided into four stages: industry analysis, company analysis, problem solving and implementation. They allow participants to apply what they have learned in the classroom to a real company issue – and the teams often develop creative insights and solutions in their analysis and recommendations. Each company must pay a Sfr 50,000 fee to participate and many companies are repeat customers, indicating the value they receive from having a team of highly talented, experienced managers focused on their projects.

Dynamic learning networks: Lead global networks using technology

In today's global world, leaders must be able to build relationships with people they may have never met, from different cultures and across time zones. Technology is a way to help them build relationships and networks with these people, but communicating and leading through the medium of technology requires different skills than face-to-face interactions. IMD created its unique Dynamic Learning Networks project to help participants develop these leadership skills of the future.

In Dynamic Learning Networks, MBA participants create knowledge on a specific topic, led by a faculty member, with a network of participants from IMD's learning network companies and alumni. These participants typically share a passion for the topic and have a familiarity with IMD that creates trust among network members – vital for the success of a network. The network members discuss the topic, generate new research from within their own experiences and contacts and together the network members (both inside and outside IMD) write a 'white paper' about the new knowledge they have created.

Deliver a top-ranked MBA program that meets the needs of the market

The unique leadership development approach of the IMD MBA program has earned its respect in the marketplace and in the rankings among corporate recruiters, potential candidates and alumni. IMD MBA graduates are recognized internationally as highly trained and focused professionals. They are recruited by leading companies for global opportunities with high-level responsibilities. For example, in 2004, graduates accepted diverse opportunities around the globe with an average starting base salary of $121,000 (not including bonuses).

We believe our leadership development approach combined with our one-year program is the way of the future for MBA programs. And we believe that because of our small class size, experienced and international participants and real world, real learning approach, the IMD MBA program is uniquely positioned to deliver on the needs of the market and of our world's future leaders.

Key take-aways

■ The market wants MBA graduates who can not only manage but also lead, because they understand themselves and their environment deeply, know how to work globally and can drive their businesses forward and manage change through innovation.

■ A top MBA program has to use the strengths of the business school and its faculty to develop a unique position in the market that is clearly differentiated from competitors.

■ To develop managers who can lead, the program must put them through real-world, action-based learning experiences; classroom discussion alone is not sufficient.

Notes

1 See Chapter 11 for a discussion of 'engineering' and 'clinical' approaches to leadership development.

29

A proposal to Firm X: IT business consultancy, partnership and appreciation

Andrew Boynton and William Fischer

Summary

To develop a company-specific program, you must script the entire flow of the learning experience, accentuating the activities, roles and key learning points for all participants. Scripting a rich learning experience in words is a challenge, especially if you have to do it in just a few pages. This chapter describes a hypothetical program for a firm attempting to transition its IT services from a technical orientation to a 'professional service' one. This example involves a multi-day learning experience, augmented by six specific learning activities which act as a catalyst to profound change in the mindsets of participating professionals and, ultimately, in their entire organization.

Ever wondered how the program you are attending took shape? The first step is a dialogue between the company and the faculty to investigate what issues the program could potentially address, who needs to be involved and what design principles are most appropriate to the situation. Normally it culminates in a proposal that outlines the program design, which we illustrate here with a hypothetical example. Of course, the proposal may serve as the first of many iterations as the ongoing discussions gain clearer focus. And as we point out in the proposal itself, the workshops will take on a life of their own as the curriculum and group develop together – words in a proposal cannot capture the full richness of the experience:

Dear Jerry,

It was great to meet you last week to discuss your comments on the proposed program design for Firm X. As agreed, please find below a draft proposal outlining how the series of programs could work.

We look forward to your thoughts!

Andy and Bill

Objective of the program

The objective of this proposal is to offer a set of workshops designed to significantly change the mindsets of the IT function within Firm X from an order-fulfiller/service-provider mentality, to a professional service firm ('PSF') mentality; and to simultaneously begin to develop new and complementary expectations regarding IT business consultancy potential within a select group of Firm X clients.

Rationale and philosophy of the program

We live in a world where IT technology and services are changing nearly every aspect of our lives. Yet, too often, within Firm X the in-house IT capabilities are seen in a far less charitable light. Important projects are frequently outsourced to well-known consulting firms, while in-house resources deliver less ambitious projects. This has serious consequences for talent attraction and retention within Firm X's IT function.

We believe that internal IT resources at Firm X are too important to the firm's future to allow this situation to continue. It has been our experience that, in similar situations at other firms, it is vital to develop a different mindset and new capabilities within the IT function. Only then can it reformulate its purpose and future, developing strong and reliable internal IT-related services and support, in order to be seen as the service provider of choice within Firm X. In this way, IT within Firm X becomes an enabler to strategy and transformation, as driven by senior management within the firm.

The best way to begin this process of change, we believe, is to introduce a professional service firm (PSF) approach to the internal IT area within Firm X. This approach stresses both a strategic and a 'professional' way of working, which can position IT resources and IT knowledge professionals as the deliverers of real value to the different business needs within the firm.

To instill the PSF mindset, an effective approach is to develop the concept of internal IT as a 'consulting business within Firm X.' This creates a healthy and inspiring professional responsibility for internal IT's own sustained success. To be clear, we are not proposing that internal IT become a consulting firm in the literal sense of the word. Rather, the PSF mindset and approach are about recognizing that the 'client' (versus a traditional notion of 'user') is central to delivering value within the firm, and that the IT unit of Firm X is competing for management time, attention and resources as an integral participant in the pursuit of the strategic objectives of the company. PSFs are all about delivering technology and/or knowledge to better serve their clients' overall business. The mindset and competencies (e.g. client relationships, listening to clients, managing change) inherent in the PSF approach are a powerful catalyst to transform how IT is presently provided to the 'users' within the Firm X business community.

Our experience suggests that, when the internal IT function managers are encouraged to think of themselves as the CEOs of 'IT, Inc.' within Firm X, they have a far better chance to carry out profound change in what they do, and how they do it. Our experience suggests that internal clients are extremely positive about the resulting improvement in service and knowledge as a result of such changes.

The program and activities described in this proposal are consistent with the PSF transition as described above. Some details to consider: each day will begin promptly at 8:30 and should end between 6:00 and 6:30 p.m. There will be limited reading before the program (several cases) and we will have almost no reading during the week. It may sound 'light,' but it is not. The days will be intense and lively. We demand much from the participants. We cold (surprise) call on individuals constantly, make sure all are engaged in the conversation, and keep a high level of energy going in class. Every lunch is a working lunch. We prefer that they do things together and have fun at night, or (and we recommend a few planned early evening activities) build a professional network, rather than sitting in their rooms alone doing email or reading case material.

Program overview

In order to achieve a high probability of creating 'real' change in the mindset, product and service development and delivery within the IT function at Firm X, we propose three distinct interventions to help propel it forward in a coherent and integrated way:

1 A series of three, six-day workshops [Business Consultancy Program] for IT professionals at managerial levels.

2 Three two-day workshops (spread over time) involving carefully selected groups of IT clients [IT Appreciation Workshops].

3 We also propose a one-day 'cementing' workshop for all of the participants in the Business Consultancy Programs, three months following the last IT Appreciation Workshop.

We will coordinate the content and material of the business consultancy programs along the lines of the objectives and philosophies discussed above. They will be customized for Firm X after we go through a series of development activities, in which we interview key IT managers and selected clients within Firm X. We believe that such a regime of programs and workshops will give Firm X an excellent chance of creating a high-impact mindset change both within the IT function and among its clients in the broader business.

Before we get into detail, it is important to understand how we define a program (or workshop). It is not merely a series of lectures or case studies – we script and design each program as a total experience for the participant. It is flexible so that we can meet the needs and energy levels of the learning group, with continuous and frequent application of the ideas back to the professional interests of the participants and Firm X's strategic interests as well as the role of 'IT, Inc.' within the firm. The total experience is fast paced, with intense dialogue and debate, and involves a variety of media (cases, lectures, simulations, video, etc.) to ensure that the message is both relevant and communicated effectively. The experience will shape the minds of the participants, and the future of IT within Firm X. The series of programs that we propose are, when combined, a catalyst to drive change within Firm X, especially if supported by and aligned with other top management activities.

The IT Business Consultancy Program

Block Schedule A is a prototype of what a six-day program for changing the internal IT function mindset might look like.

Getting started: Sunday evening (Day 1)

We prefer to kick off our program on Sunday evening. We get down to work immediately – by benchmarking the internal IT function against what it means to be a professional service firm. Are they thinking about their work as a portfolio of activities that critically impacts the attraction and retention of talent? How does it affect their brand? How does it affect the resources that they have available to pursue other strategic objectives? Are they thinking about how their clients perceive them – what is their brand? Are they attracting, developing and retaining their talent? Are they thinking strategically? Sunday evening begins the conversation about change that will last the entire week. It also serves as an 'ice-breaker,' where everyone gets a chance to meet almost everyone else – an important step in building a community of IT knowledge-professionals early in the week.

Key learning devices

There are six important learning devices that we will weave through the entire week: volunteer intervention, deep dive, team-teaching (two-in-a-box), learning diaries, buzz-knowledge groups and spatial movement of people. These are discussed below, followed by a day-by-day schedule.

1 **Volunteer intervention**: Each morning (Monday–Friday). At the end of every day, we choose three to four 'volunteers' to provide the class with a stimulating, provocative presentation or activity the following morning that is anchored in Firm X's IT world. During the first hour of the day, we listen and react to it, and then we discuss the ramifications for the professionals in the room or Firm X IT (IT, Inc.). The aim is to have the participants launch each day, and give them the responsibility to do so, in order to pause and reflect on the implications of the material and the conversations for Firm X. The volunteer intervention also serves as an important vehicle to create a team culture in the room, while ensuring that the program stays on track and in tune with the particular group of participants; it allows the group to establish its own personality and generates a feeling of 'ownership' of the week's outcomes.

2 **Deep dive**: This is a particularly important concept that is introduced on Monday afternoon. The deep dive is a team-based approach to managerial solutions that we have created, borrowing from an excellent product and service design firm, IDEO. We teach the deep dive method with a video on Monday afternoon (with other material). By itself, the deep dive is a powerful tool for any PSF firm that is intent on understanding client needs and delivering innovative and effective solutions, be they technical-, managerial- or process-oriented in nature. Any team can use the deep dive to launch a project and get great results, fast. It will be one of the key learning points and take-aways

from the week. Moreover, participants will take away a detailed deep dive user's guide and other materials that will enable them to create their own deep dive teams after the workshop. Throughout the week, we reserve all lunches (Tuesday through Friday) and other selected times for deep dive sessions by teams in the room. During this time, the teams will be asked to translate key managerial take-aways from all the conversations into a prototype design: a model, framework, picture, etc. Therefore, each day, the teams will have intense conversations, create prototype messages (key take-aways), compare prototypes, and apply the concepts to IT in Firm X (IT, Inc.). The deep dive will 'force' participants to carefully consider the application of the ideas and examples from the plenary sessions, and will spawn thoughtful conversations. This is a major element in binding classroom insights with real-world relevance for Firm X.

3   **Team-teaching mode (two-in-a-box)**: During the entire week, Professors Fischer and Boynton will be in class – not only taking turns teaching and leading the discussion, but also interacting both with the class and with each other. Participants call this our 'ping pong' effect and we will stimulate the class, and each other, with provocative comments from the side as the other teaches. In effect, the 'two-in-a-box' approach keeps the energy high, the ideas flowing, and the discussion relevant. It is a major area that differentiates our teaching style, which we have honed over ten years.

4   **Learning diaries**: We will provide each participant with personal learning diaries, to be used several times each day. They are designed to make the implicit learning explicit. This is very important for the individuals in the room. While the deep dive and morning volunteers reinforce group learning, the learning diary ensures that it is up close and personal for each participant. They may spend only 10 minutes a day on the learning diary, but it is another opportunity to engender real-world relevance for each team in the room, as well as to prepare ideas to take back into the team and into Firm X after the program is completed.

5   **Buzz groups, buzz boards and need to know groups**: Frequently (five to six times a day) we will run buzz groups in the room. These are periods of five minutes or so, where the class breaks informally into groups to discuss issues raised in class from a video, or short presentation, etc. Buzz groups are much better than long breakout sessions in separate rooms. (Note: We will use study rooms when teams are applying ideas back to Firm X on select occasions.) Buzz groups are

about moving ideas and boosting energy. From the discussions and cases, it will be clear that sharing ideas is essential! Around the room, we will also place buzz boards, where people can post questions and answers, in order to keep track of ideas, problems and comments. This informal in-class knowledge sharing will go on throughout the week. Starting probably on Tuesday morning, we then will introduce, or the class will suggest, an online 'need to know' option (post class). This is optional, but it can be powerful; it is a simple email device to connect like-minded people to help each other. The programs will create a true community of practice and a habit, and culture, of sharing ideas freely.

6 **Spatial movement of people**: At least twice a day, every person will have their seat moved in the room. The result is that the buzz groups are comprised of different people all the time. Participants will gain different vantage points from their conversations and there is always an element of surprise when people come back in the room! These ingredients combine to create a 'class' and transform it into a team where everyone will interact with everyone else, just in the room alone. Add the deep dive and other team projects, and the week is a powerful team-building experience.

The details of each day

On **Monday (Day 2)**, we look at what it takes to think 'strategically' within a PSF function. The aim of this first day is to provide a framework for the participants to think about the 'competitive terrain' in which they find themselves within Firm X. They should start to think more strategically about the attractiveness or unattractiveness of the choices that they might consider within the IT function (e.g. IT, Inc.). For example, the competitive terrain might cover who Firm X IT is competing with, what the choices driving the clients within the firm are, what different client/customer segments there are, or whether there are critical suppliers to Firm X IT that need to be managed more effectively. After working on a case study from another industry that sets the stage for thinking about terrain, we'll break into groups and apply the framework to the competitive market for IT services within Firm X. We'll then have groups share their learning and analysis with each other to culminate in insights about the terrain in which IT, Inc. (Firm X IT function) is competing within the firm. An important lesson here is that before choices are made about the transformation of IT, Inc. (Firm X IT), the terrain must be analyzed for consistency with the market reality.

On **Monday afternoon** (after the first daily volunteer intervention) we will encourage Firm X IT (IT, Inc.) to become a client-centric operation. Adopting a client-oriented culture is typically one way to strategically build switching costs into a competitive environment, thereby creating a specific competitive advantage over the other rivals in the industry. While everyone wants to be client-centric, at this point in the program we'll look closely (using video-based case material) at several firms who we think are world-class in their client-centric behavior. The idea is 'what can we learn from them and apply to IT within Firm X?' We will examine at least three case studies of firms that won by knowing more about their customers, and then turned that knowledge into value propositions that decisively differentiated themselves from their competition. During the afternoon, we will also introduce the deep dive (see above), which will continue over the whole week.

On **Tuesday morning (Day 3)**, we move from the external terrain and customers of Firm X IT to discuss how participants can effectively analyze the internal organizational terrain for Firm X IT. We spend the morning discussing a case (pre-read case material and video introduced in class) that looks at issues of: managing change, how to understand the internal terrain of a firm's organizational structure, rewards, processes, knowledge-sharing mechanisms, people, etc. We should instill discipline regarding the management of the key levers that Firm X IT has available, in order to become consistent with the external terrain as well as to deliver value to clients in the form of IT services or know-how.

Together, Monday and Tuesday morning provide powerful examples in cases, stimulation via video material, and two simple yet important frameworks to (1) analyze the external and internal organizational terrains and (2) instill a firm knowledge that the client is essential to any PSF or IT, Inc.'s success in delivering value. Strategy is all about choices *and* execution. Monday is about 'how do we think strategically so that the right choices are more obvious?' Tuesday is all about 'what does it take to implement these choices?' This requires an appreciation of the 'internal terrain' and we'll work on a framework which highlights the managerial implications of strategic choice.

After the first of the daily deep dive lunches, **Tuesday afternoon** will focus on change management. 'Effective Change through Negotiation: Introducing IT Enabled Solutions' is largely about managing the people side of things, with an eye to understanding the different interests people have in the success (or failure) of certain projects. By using a video case designed to illustrate IT-driven change, we focus this session on the vital skills of knowing the individual client's interests, effective listening at the interpersonal level, and then formulating a change strategy that is a win-win for everyone involved. The lessons here are powerful. The audience has deeply entrenched technology thinking, characterized by the beliefs that technology is good, that more information is better, and that the more we know, the better will be the results and the easier it will be to obtain managerial buy-in to a plan. The case challenges these beliefs directly and opens up the political, but very real, issues of managing IT projects with an effective PSF mentality.

Wednesday (Day 4), the morning focuses on where IT is used for competitive advantage and when it changes the rules of competition. These insights in themselves can lead to a great discussion. However, the real learning point here comes in a discussion surprise. We will reintroduce the organizational terrain model, but in this context use it very differently. The session centers on an IT system that offered a clear and powerful competitive advantage, but that was rejected because the change process was poorly handled. Through this example, we discuss how to introduce IT systems via change management, which provides participants with the tools and concepts to accomplish that in Firm X and to incorporate it into their new PSF/IT, Inc. mindset. The combination of Tuesday afternoon and Wednesday morning (intentionally split by an evening) is to drive home the insight that an 'effective' IT, Inc. is not just about great technology management. It is also about managing change: from effective negotiation to effective change management in the organization.

Managing client relationships is critical to success as a professional service firm. If it is Firm X IT's function to change their clients' mindset, this must be understood. On **Wednesday afternoon**, we would invite a panel of external consultants, who are presently serving Firm X, to better understand how 'the pros' manage their relationships. This session serves several important purposes. First, the learning is rich and 'real world.' In other words, to build an IT, Inc. mindset based on a PSF mentality, we should bring in great PSF managers. Second, the educational source shifts to other professionals and managers, with whom the participants can closely interact. By mid-week, getting first-hand tips, insights and to-dos and not-to-dos about PSF issues is a welcome change of pace from the high intensity of the sessions up to this point.

On **Wednesday evening** we would pick up the pace and have some fun. We're going into outer space! We use a video of a space mission to examine closely a successful technical team within a large, bureaucratic organization. The objective here is to identify key factors for team success, and to have the opportunity to look, close-up, at what project leadership is all about. This material has been some of the most successful we have used and the focus on teams and leadership are key for an IT, Inc. endeavor. Shown with ample beer, wine and popcorn, the video provides a few hours of relaxation, but also functions as preparation for the next day's discussion. The movie is completed by 8:00 p.m.

On Thursday (Day 5), the morning will kick off with a discussion of the video, that is, the teamwork and leadership they witnessed during the previous evening. No one doubts the importance of teamwork and leadership in the Apollo teams, which leads directly into a team simulation. The group will behave as a team, with a clear goal and challenge to perform in a limited time. In their teamwork, they will have to replicate the effective behaviors they saw and discussed from the video. The combination of the video and the teamwork simulation will drive home how teamwork, leadership and communication must be 'in the DNA' for any effective PSF type firm – and for IT, Inc. as well.

On **Thursday afternoon**, we will have two options to draw from. Flexibility and adaptability – customization – are hallmarks of effective learning experiences. The first option is a video case and discussion about leadership and how to create an effective 'strategy' and differentiation. It covers a firm that crafted an effective strategy and launched it to tremendous success with customers in the marketplace. This case will provide a simple but powerful vehicle to define the strategy of IT, Inc. in Firm X. It will also lead into a discussion of how every participant in the room can be a leader. Leadership can come from every seat! And the importance of a leader effectively communicating and selling a message is key. This material, called *Sudden Impact*, is a powerful learning tool to illustrate a real-world success in dramatic terms.

The second option is to formulate a framework from the video case study of a firm in transformation. The case study is used to provide the framework, which asks fundamental questions that all successful organizations must answer: What business are we in? What do clients really value? What are our capabilities and competencies? Where is the gap in delivering client value? What do we need to do to close the gap? We'll provide the participants with the framework and use a team format, where teams create answers to these questions, compare answers, and then consolidate their learning.

Friday (Day 6). Following the volunteers, for an hour or so we will discuss what it means to be an effective knowledge professional. Every participant in the room is a knowledge professional; their success depends on the ideas they generate, and how well they put those ideas into play in Firm X: within their teams, in IT, Inc. or with clients. This session will raise important issues about being an effective knowledge professional for life – an important personal lesson and common cultural mindset in any great PSF.

Following this opening discussion, we will launch into the final deep dive. At this point, energy will build around the deep dive challenge that has been growing each day during the working lunch – designing a take-away message, which can translate into value back at work. We will now spend several intensive hours to prototype and fine-tune that message, team by team. The work will culminate in presentations of the final prototypes, discussion of the prototypes and closing ceremonies. We recommend a program 'degree,' book and team ceremony to underscore the importance and value of the experience the participants have undergone.

This would conclude the six-day program. Participants should be exhausted, yet exhilarated. The seeds of change will be planted and watered. Mindsets will shift. Follow-up will be valued. A community of different IT professionals will be created.

IT Appreciation Workshop

If this sea change in IT mindset is to work within Firm X, we need to simultaneously begin to inform and modify client expectations. Several weeks after each IT Business Consultancy Program, we will host the first day of the IT Appreciation Workshop, which will work with a carefully-selected client set that is predisposed to Firm X's 'new IT mindset' success. On this first day, we will examine examples of how firms in other industries win on the basis of great IT competencies. The principal idea here is to inform and enthuse the client base of Firm X IT, Inc. Following this, several weeks later, will be a second day in which we'll run a collaborative deep dive, where clients work with Firm X IT personnel to co-develop expectations for the future.

IT Business Consultancy 'Cement' Workshop

Three months after the third set of programs, we propose a one-day workshop where we will reassemble all of the Business Consultancy Program participants to discuss what is working and what is not about the new approach, what best-practices are, what have we learned, and what remains to be done. Learning and applying lessons from the other workshops will enable us to customize in 'real time' the appropriate content and flow for the Cement Workshop.

Ongoing support for building a knowledge community within Firm X

As part of the support for this initiative, we'll help create and participate in an ongoing need-to-know email community that sustains the development of PSF professionalism, the culture and ideas established during the week, and the sharing of expertise and best practices. Firm X will provide the technical support to create and manage the email facility, but the network of professionals from all the programs will come alive in this need-to-know community of practice. This network is an 'issue-pull model,' based on the specific needs of members of the community. To ensure its integrity and usefulness over time, rules of behavior and specific guidelines for using the network should be enforced. The networked community offers Firm X IT a quick response capability, where frontline professionals can instantly share ideas and help each other out. The total expertise from the community is available to all professionals to resolve their biggest issues. We will actively nurture and provide input into this email-enabled community for a period of 12 months following the final program. Of course, a longer-term role in the development of Firm X IT and in the network is possible. This need-to-know community will begin to take shape during the program (Business Consultancy) and it will expand and live on as a rich resource for the knowledge professionals in Firm X IT.

Thank you for considering our proposal. We are confident the combination of experiences will be a powerful change catalyst for Firm X IT. We look forward to working with you to make this a great experience for all your professionals and to meet the needs of senior management in driving Firm X IT forward as an invaluable resource for Firm X and its competitive success.

Key take-aways

■ The creative combination of energizing learning activities with issue-specific content is key to the successful scripting of a company-specific program.

■ Learning activities, especially a variety of team projects that challenge participants to present, synthesize and apply new management approaches, foster energy and involvement.

■ A suite of learning events tailored to different stakeholders, such as customer and supplier programs, follow-up workshops and an e-learning community, is needed for learning to stick in the real world.

30

Company-specific program design: Supporting the roll out of a new corporate strategy

Seán Meehan

Summary

Company-specific programs must be developed according to the individual client's particular strategic needs and learning objectives. In order to achieve this, the development process requires close partnership and ongoing dialogue at all levels of the organization, with a view to identifying the appropriate scope, style and orchestration of the final program. Contribution and buy-in from key decision makers and stakeholders are critical both in terms of ensuring the relevance of the content and in developing learning methods, case material and take-aways that can result in lasting organizational impact. To illustrate the key elements that contribute to successful design and delivery, the author traces the process of company-specific program design from the initial needs analysis, through development, to final implementation using the 'New Horizons' program – designed for Hilti Corporation.

Company-specific programs must be tailored to the specific needs of the client – Hilti Corporation's 'New Horizons' program, run in February/March 1999, was no exception. The company was already extremely successful and had built strong capabilities – supporting the implementation of a new strategy. How could we design a program that would help it improve on what was already good? We were working at the very heart of the company's future, so it was important to take the time to build the right approach, hand in hand with the Hilti executive board. This is the story of how we got there . . .

Program objective: to support the roll out of a new strategy

The company: success ≠ complacency

Since its founding by Martin and Eugen Hilti in 1941, the Hilti Corporation has been a leading supplier of power tools and fasteners to professional customers in the construction and building-maintenance industries. By the mid 1990s, with 14,500 employees in 120 countries, Hilti had become a 'system solutions' provider that emphasized services such as application training, technical literature, comprehensive repair service and environmentally sound product disposal in addition to its high-end tools and consumables. The Hilti direct salesforce, of over 7,000 technical sales representatives, was a key element in delivering the system-solutions proposition. Senior management long believed that this, together with the company's strong emphasis on applications-oriented innovation and superior quality, made Hilti a formidable player. It was well positioned to compete with very strong rivals such as Bosch, Würth and Makita. Nonetheless, in a culture valuing intellect and learning, complacency was never tolerated.

A new strategy creates a development need

Characteristically, in the mid 1990s, the company undertook a strategic review which culminated in the launching of a new corporate strategy, 'Champion 3C,' in 1996. Champion 3C embodied the key strategic imperatives identified by the review: that the 'Customer' is the most important focus of the organization; that Hilti must continue to leverage its technological and marketing 'Competencies'; and that it must 'Concentrate' on those products and markets offering the greatest potential for long-term profitable growth and sustainable leadership. The strategy offered clear, if broad, guidance from the top with detailed implementation being the responsibility of the market organizations and business units. The roll out of the strategy was underpinned by three important tenets: (1) go directly to the customer to develop a comprehensive fact base, listen and respond, and then develop the 'local' implementation; (2) make sure employees understand and support the strategy; (3) accept that mistakes can and will be made. In essence the strategy demanded that Hilti transform itself from an organization that was sales-driven to one that was marketing-driven.[1] The company decided it needed support in achieving this transformation.

Leveraging a well-established relationship

Consistent with Hilti's cultural emphasis on learning and development, the company enjoyed a close relationship with a number of academic institutions, including IMD. It had joined the IMD Learning Network in 1991. Executives from the company had regularly attended programs here, as well as sponsored MBA international consulting projects and actively recruited from the IMD MBA program. In 1996/1997, Peter Killing was writing a strategy and change management case about Hilti's Hong Kong operations. As the case was being finalized with the executive board, they told Killing that they were planning a large program to support the roll out of the new strategy and were considering developing it with IMD.

Program development

Initial needs assessment

Jim Pulcrano, the IMD Corporate Development Director for Switzerland, had been working with Hilti for several years and had a strong rapport with its VP of Corporate Human Resources, Andre Siegenthaler. As they discussed the proposed program, the initial articulation seemed straightforward. Pulcrano recalls:

Hilti wanted to understand and increase its marketing competence while encouraging senior executives to 'look over the horizon.' It would be a New Horizons Workshop.

Pulcrano quickly arranged a meeting with Killing, Siegenthaler and Egbert Appel (a member of the Hilti executive board). Its objective: to better understand Hilti's initial ideas on how IMD might support it. At the meeting, Appel expressed a desire to take a fresh look at marketing from the top down, then cascade the learning throughout the organization. He wanted to create a platform for communication. His preference was for a two- to three-day format, with additional project work. Based on his experience in helping to design many customized programs, Pulcrano wondered whether this would be sufficient to achieve the organizational impact desired. Appel and Siegenthaler agreed to reflect on Pulcrano's challenge and to brainstorm with key executives back at corporate headquarters in Liechtenstein. To provide the opportunity to gain input from more key decision makers (four Executive Board members), they arranged a further meeting there to take place in a few weeks. Given the focus of the potential program, Killing felt a marketing professor should take the lead and asked the author to step in.

Ahead of the discussions, Appel and Siegenthaler identified three areas where they could benefit from external input and guidance:

- Definition: What is marketing at Hilti?
- Process: Review of the marketing process chain using relevant case studies.
- Roles: Review of marketing roles within Hilti using relevant case studies.

They also reached a tentative conclusion that the program should target around 250 Hilti senior executives from the executive board through general managers to product market managers and strategic business unit (SBU) sales managers.

A possible theme and framework emerges

During the visit at Hilti, Meehan and Pulcrano held three two-hour meetings. In the first two, they investigated Hilti's needs in great detail. During the last meeting the whole board was present, which provided an opportunity for IMD to replay what it had learned. During one break, Meehan and Pulcrano reflected on how unusual it was that a company with excellent internal processes, a healthy external orientation, sound sales management and proficient new product development capabilities would be so self-critical. The challenge in supporting Hilti would be to raise a bar that was already set very high.

After the meetings, Meehan outlined his initial vision for the intervention. 'Creating customer value' had emerged as a common theme in the discussions. He suggested it should serve as the 'top-line' focus for the workshops, which would cover the core value creation processes:

- Generating and interpreting customer and competitor data in order to develop a clear definition, and shared understanding, of the Hilti value proposition.
- Understanding that markets are dynamic and analyses and supporting systems should reflect this.
- Communicating these insights so that they become a core competence driving numerous sales, marketing and other processes.

This would involve practical issues such as brand loyalty and a new product introduction process. Meehan went on to suggest a roadmap for the program design, development and delivery. To start, he would interview key executives and formalize a proposal. It was hoped that Hilti would review this and confirm its commitment within a month. Assuming everything was on track, Meehan would then present a course outline by the end of the year that would identify, in blocks of half a day, the topics to be covered and the specific learning objectives for each element. He would also have selected case studies for use during the workshop and, should Hilti require one or more cases of its own, would initiate a custom case-writing process. The document would define the workshop length as five days, with classes consisting of no more than 35 people (to promote teamwork, learning and networking). Based on the initial figures supplied by the company, IMD would be hosting up to seven separate implementations of the workshop with a projected delivery window of 21 months.

As ever, feedback was forthcoming from Hilti. Ten days later they had reverted to say that they were unwilling to make a decision on case studies at that time and that they felt that a one-week program, in seven separate sessions over 21 months, would not sufficiently support the roll out. It would, the company argued, take too long. Their reaction precipitated a crucial dialogue concerning the style and orchestration of the intervention.

The board concluded that, to have the required organizational impact, the program would need to have the character of an important 'event' in the development of Hilti. All key players relevant to the agenda would need to attend. The most senior management, including the board, would attend as full participants, not as observers or experts. The group targeted for participation should ideally go through the program within the shortest possible timeline. This would allow the entire organization to get on the same page quickly and in the event of specific initiatives generated by the program, all would need to agree on the need and approach in a dialogue enriched by shared stimuli, understanding, tools, metaphors and vocabulary.

Drafting a block schedule: Insights from interviews

After agreeing on the broad scope and agenda with the board, an important validation process took place. Meehan and Heather Cairns, IMD's Director of Partnership Programs, conducted twelve 'scoping' interviews with a cross-section of managers who represented the likely types of participant. Some were experienced executives who shared their perspectives on Hilti's strengths and weaknesses (including 'war stories') and some were rising stars in the organization. These were members of the central management team, regional sales directors, product marketing managers, production managers and market (or country) managers. In addition, they sought their views on marketing at Hilti and what they would like the program to contain. Frank and open, these discussions yielded valuable insights into the organization.

In particular, the interviews informed IMD about Hilti's marketing challenges and its competitive environment. They heard a number of marketing success stories, but recognized a gap in the marketing skills of product managers in the market organizations (MOs) relative to marketing managers in the business units (BUs). The role of the proposed workshop – to refocus the organization on marketing – appeared clearly understood and well received. However, interviewees felt the development needs of the product and sales managers were distinct from those of the core group.

Armed with these insights, they produced a formal proposal, describing the objectives of the workshop, initial ideas on form and content, and indicative fees. It also outlined the principal issues IMD had identified from its research and interviews. First, from a marketing point of view, the product manager's role was perceived to be operational rather than strategic. The BU–MO interface also appeared less than optimal. Communication tools were primarily aimed at salesforce incentives rather than brand enhancement. There was also a concern that sales teams tended to focus on the short term, in large part due to the way tools like sales promotions were used. IMD suggested that a more uniformly shared view of the total product portfolio, with a strategic view of priorities, might enhance the sustainability of profits in the sales mix. Finally, because the program should build on existing competencies when possible, they wanted to further examine Hilti's success stories to see where they could be repeated.

A framework of goals emerged from this analysis, including a better understanding of both the competitive environment and the international context in which Hilti was operating, as well as a more comprehensive sharing of information across the organization. In line with these goals, IMD devised the objectives of the program.

Next, Meehan proposed a block schedule outlining the theme of each half-day block. He wished to reflect Hilti's desire to combine external examples with the latest thinking in marketing and with examples of practical relevance to the company. This would be manifested in a learning cycle that incorporated three sequential aspects:

- Concepts – using examples from outside Hilti.
- Application of concepts to Hilti.
- Implications of adopting marketing concepts in Hilti.

IMD would employ a well-proven format of discussion leadership from the 'vehicle' of a non-client case history (usually also non-client industry), as they would prove a 'safe,' non-competitive way to ensure that everyone understood a particular issue without being sidetracked by organizational politics. This did not exclude the use of Hilti examples should they suit the occasion.

The document concluded with a budget for workshop fees and standard terms of business. The former was divided into developmental and delivery costs. IMD wished the document to be viewed as a continuation of the development process. Once Hilti approved its content, IMD would proceed with development and agree delivery dates.

Hilti approved the proposal in December 1997 and then scheduled the workshops within the strategy roll-out plan. In 1998, most of their major market areas would complete their analyses, discuss recommendations, and begin implementation. By 1999, the organization would be ready for the planned intervention. This also gave Meehan ample time to further understand company issues and assemble the faculty delivery team.

Further development

During the first quarter of 1998, Meehan sought out and briefed appropriate faculty members for participation and coordinated the content of the course. Although the team was to be comprised predominantly of marketing faculty, key contributions from professors were integrated in the specialized areas of new product development as well as how to generate and use information across business units and marketing organizations, that is, organization-wide. As faculty members came on board they were introduced to Hilti executives for more direct briefing in their specific areas. As of June 1998, the more detailed content ideas had been validated.

On the Hilti side, Meehan was mobilizing a project coordination team, led by Siegenthaler. They were to select key company personnel for participation and provide input for the optimal configuration of the four workshops. They proposed that one Executive Board member should take an active part in each workshop, on the same basis as other participants, as well as opening and closing the program. The logistics of such an operation had to be taken into consideration: when could managers attend and how could the board team free up five days out of their busy schedules? With regard to the structure of the course, the team decided how best to utilize the time of participants. The way the schedule was panning out, there would be little time for reflection and self-development! There would need to be a 'collective reflection' exercise. Six more stakeholders participated in development interviews. Here, Meehan tried to gauge how participants' attention could be best maintained and what would be the best mix of subject matter. In the end, he tried to balance product-related topics with market-related ones and, for external cases, coverage featuring both large and small enterprises.

During this time, Hilti decided that one 'Hilti case' would be presented, which was developed during 1998. Entitled 'Hilti Corporation: Measuring Customer Satisfaction' and concerning the United Kingdom operation, the case noted how successful Hilti was in gathering customer information and feedback. One of the features of the case was that it included a process in which Hilti knew it had developed a great expertise. By challenging whether the company was in fact interpreting the data fairly and providing the opportunity to critique standard follow-up procedures, the case had the potential to be a symbol for how much further improvement was possible – when a routine process is placed in a more strategic context. This was the way to raise the bar further.

Meanwhile, Meehan presented an Interim Report on Development in June 1998. He had progressed a great deal since his point of first contact a year earlier; he had learned about Hilti's business, its markets, its competencies and its management development needs. He acknowledged the support he had for this initiative, from the executive board to general management, and pointed out that the program was being designed while bearing in mind the very strong management competence that Hilti already enjoyed. The program objectives, as set out in the proposal of the previous November, were further honed to read as follows:

- To enhance Hilti's market orientation.
- To provide a common vocabulary for understanding strategic marketing.
- To provide a toolkit that enables participants to implement strategic marketing.

The list of participants had been pared down to about 182 or four implementation sessions. The cascade approach of re-teaching workshop insights to a wider net of employees remained on the agenda. Meehan described the 'red thread' (key linkages) running through the schedule. First, to set the scene, he would 'push the envelope' regarding common understandings of marketing in the company. The bulk of the course would then deal with specific competencies in strategic marketing that were perceived to be critical to the successful implementation of the Champion 3C strategy. The final day was the time allotted to bring it all together. The proposed sessions were scheduled as shown in Table 30.1.

Table 30.1 Proposed block schedule

Sunday	Monday	Tuesday	Wednesday	Thursday	Friday
	Developing a common framework	Implementing the strategy	Product strategy	Customer bonding	Integrative exercise
Registration and opening	Continuous learning about markets	Implementing the strategy	Product strategy	Advanced tools	Translations

Meehan then went on to break down session topics into purpose and application. The report concluded with revised cost estimates (which were in line with previous calculations) and a description of the next steps. These allowed the Hilti board to validate and agree to work done by IMD to date so that Meehan and the faculty team could proceed with class content and reserving facilities at IMD, plus ensure that a final program could be presented by October 1998.

The New Horizons workshop

Final preview

Months of preparation, interviewing, mobilizing and case research culminated in the final planning document, the 'New Horizons Workshop: Marketing – Preview.' Meehan presented it to the Executive Board in November 1998. In addition to a review of the development process objectives, he walked through the proposed block schedule in detail, providing a preview of learning methods, case material and anticipated take-aways; a supporting document was provided to the board with the case studies to be used as well as faculty biographies.

To begin, Meehan discussed the journey so far from the initial needs analysis in 1997, its development in 1998, to the final plan for the first quarter implementation of 1999. He also reiterated the mandate with which Hilti had charged IMD: IMD was working with a company where a strong sales orientation prevailed; they had the full support of a committed, enthusiastic and talented team. The workshop intended to support and build upon the Champion 3C strategy initiative. Hilti had made it clear from the outset that they wanted to examine competitive strategy and market analysis as well as learn how best to leverage their market-based assets. They wanted to focus on product leadership with a practical application to indicate what to do next.

Meehan continued on to the next section of the brief: the presentation of the block schedule and introduction of faculty members who would teach them. Each implementation would begin and end with a short presentation by the Executive Board member attending the course; he would explain why Hilti was undertaking the program and express his support for the development process and design. A format was created that applied to all sessions whereby the objectives were conveyed, followed by the key insights that IMD intended participants to take from that session. The first session, 'Breaking the Rules,' was scheduled to take place early on Sunday afternoon; it would feature a case study based on Daewoo, which centered on the top-line theme of the program – 'creating customer value.'

This would be immediately followed by the first two of five strategy sessions. Participants would address the issues of marketing planning, the drivers of market size and share, the leveraging of market research, the evaluation of marketing expenditure and the integration of marketing elements. John Walsh was the faculty member responsible and he would employ a simulation exercise as the vehicle for teaching this part of the course. It would involve a process whereby participants formed 'brand management groups' to analyze the current situation based on the information supplied. They then would have to distill the information into meaningful insights and look at alternative courses of action. This meant choosing a brand strategy and following it through the marketing life cycle. Once they made a decision, it would be tested against the computerized simulation, which supplied a market response. Finally, teams had to regroup and amend or monitor further actions.

Following an early morning 'strategy hour,' Monday morning would largely focus on a session entitled 'Understanding Customer Input.' This session would concentrate on using 'Conjoint Analysis' whereby the attractiveness of a product's features could be evaluated in bundles. Hilti had used this technique previously but needed to exploit its potential more. Participants would return after lunch to 'Bonding with Customers,' in which Meehan discussed the CUSAT system used by Hilti to measure CUstomer SATis-faction. Another two-hour strategy session would be scheduled for the evening.

'Competing with Information' would be the title of Tuesday morning's session. Don Marchand would take participants through his study of best practices in building and competing with information capabilities,[2] the benefits of benchmarking and the power of information orientation. That afternoon, participants would learn about building and leveraging the brand via a case study on Ericsson's global brand campaign. Walsh would return to wrap up the strategy portion of the course and then the class would enjoy a well-earned team dinner. However, they would not be allowed to sit back even then! Teams would be asked to formulate issues and questions based on their discussions to date. Jean-Philippe Deschamps would take up the bulk of Thursday's session time with 'Achieving Product Leadership.' He would use the Barco Projection Systems case study[3] to demonstrate the role of technology and product portfolio management in the context of marketing strategy. The day would conclude with a 'master-class' on the BU–MO (business unit–market organization) interface within Hilti, using insights from other companies regarding how to optimize coordination.

A round robin exercise[4] would be scheduled for the final day of the course. Teams would be asked to formulate initial positions on some of the issues expressed at the team dinner on Tuesday. They then would have to visit other groups to get their input. Teams would regroup and revise their own positions to a point where they felt comfortable to 'poster-display' their work, including responses and suggested short-term action plans regarding their chosen issues. This exercise would be a key element of the program, in that it ensured it would end on a 'high.' It would allow some reflection time on how the key issues affected Hilti as well as the individual. Finally, it would give participants a chance to take ownership of their role in trans-forming Hilti from a purely sales to a marketing organization.

Also at that meeting Meehan showed the board the 'Learning Diary.' This was intended for the personal reflection in which each participant would be encouraged to capture, in the form of *aides-mémoire*, the key insights from each section at the end of each day. It was hoped that participants would build on their learning diaries and take the actions they saw as relevant to their roles in Hilti.

Showtime!

After over a year of detailed planning, preparation and research, the first of the sessions took place in February 1999. There were four workshops in all and each group was asked not to confer with the others until all had completed the program. That way, each participant could benefit to the maximum from the course; it also created a certain mystique and buzz about the contents. The program was executed according to plan. Meehan wrapped up proceedings by asking participants to consider the journey upon which they were embarking. He provided feedback by describing the 'obstacles' that participants had mentioned in the program and then described the 'solution' that had been found for each one. This was an ideal way to summarize the key learning points of the course while at the same time focusing on action plans for the future. He went on to compare a number of Hilti's competencies against those of a large database of high-performing companies. It was evident that Hilti had clear strengths – but when benchmarked and in the context of the discussion of the last five days, which included reflections on some of the world's best practitioners in key areas, Hilti could now set their bar for implementation much higher than they might have before.

Organizational impact – learning that sticks

More important than the very high ratings that the participants gave the program was the organizational impact actually achieved. Each participant was chosen because of their critical role in the policy to enhance the market orientation of the company. In a practical sense, participants took away methods, toolkits and vocabulary, all of which helped them to transform the company. In particular the company reflected upon and recognized many opportunities for improvement in the area of competitive sensing. Lessons from every block of the program continued to be applied in the company. Follow-up was encouraged, but not mandated, by the board. The participants were empowered and actively motivated to move the organization forward by proposition, rigorous challenge and debate and, above all, action.

Key lesson in program design 1: Board involvement throughout

The program was conceived and driven by a knowledgeable client, directly by the full Executive Board, rather than by the 'marketing department' or 'human resources.' The highest level of management bought into the program as a strategic necessity. While empowering several other executives to provide input and robust challenge at all stages, board members never took the initiative off their radar. They reviewed, challenged and ultimately approved the program's development at all key milestones. Further, they attended and participated in the workshops because they felt they had something to learn – it had a tremendous impact on the outcome.

Key lesson in program design 2: Real-world context

Some companies might criticize the development process for its length and detail, but it is crucial to achieving a program that is relevant to the company. In Hilti's case, the company perceived that the stakes in its new strategy were high and that it would represent a fundamental departure: transforming its marketing strategy from a sales to a brand orientation entailed business risk and hence it was critical to get it right in every dimension. Thus IMD efforts to meet so many executives, develop new materials and ensure that all faculty understood why their sessions really mattered to Hilti were crucially important. Meehan had access to all levels of the organization and in-depth operational performance data from selected markets and business units. To deliver a relevant program, IMD functioned as both a 'facilitator' and a 'teacher' in four successful week-long discussions about how best to achieve the company's transition. Without a complete immersion in the company needs and culture, developing a program tailored effectively to the company's needs would have been impossible to achieve.

Key lesson in program design 3: Learning community

Great care was taken to ensure that the right people were in attendance at each workshop. A mix of hierarchical levels, geographies and business units – of both large and smaller entities – were blended to provide the maximum opportunity to address the issues scheduled for discussion. None of the four workshops could be characterized as more senior than the other; each had as a participant a board member. The pace was 'hectic': participants worked on campus in Lausanne for approximately 12 hours a day for five days. It was also challenging from an overall scheduling perspective, with all four workshops run in an elapsed timeframe of seven weeks. Participants were asked not to discuss or report back the theme, content, learning points or impact of their session until all four workshops were completed. This alone created quite a 'buzz' within the organization. Following that, however, the organization was ready for a great discussion about 'so what' at the individual, team and company levels. Although hard to replicate in this chapter, it did seem to have a lot of value in terms of building a solid launch platform for implementation.

IMD was happy to be invited to partner with Hilti's Executive Board in the development of a further New Horizons workshop in 2002, this time focusing on change management. The company continues to be an active member of the IMD learning network and has endowed IMD with the Martin Hilti chair in honor of one of the founders.

> ## Key take-aways
>
> ■ The roadmap for design, delivery and implementation should be based on an initial needs assessment carried out in light of the organization's specific strategic objectives.
>
> ■ Involvement from key decision makers and executives will ensure the program's credibility within the organization.
>
> ■ 'Scoping' interviews with other stakeholders are critical to the validation process.
>
> ■ The logistics of scheduling and participant mix must be decided in consultation with the client organization.

Notes

1 Meehan, S. and Baschera, P. (2002) Lessons from Hilti: How Customer and Employee Contact Improves Strategy Implementation, *Business Strategy Review*, 13 (2) p. 32.
2 Please refer to chapter 15, where Don Marchand discusses, 'Teaching general managers about the business value of IT: Making the invisible visible!'
3 Please refer to chapter 16 where Jean-Philippe Deschamps talks further about using this case.
4 Please refer to Chapter 7 for an overview of this type of exercise.

31

Multi-module program scripting: Canon

Vlado Pucik

Summary

The core objective of the program was to accelerate Canon Europe's transition to a pan-European (rather than nationally based) organization. It was designed as a three-module action learning program in which: (1) participants analyzed the competitive environment and suggested possible responses which they evaluated with project work back on the job; (2) identified the supporting organizational competencies required for implementation, again validated back on the job; and (3) developed specific action plans for driving the change process forward.

The scripting process is described from draft 1, to various inputs from inside and outside the firm, the involvement of key stakeholders, and the final draft focused on the European reorganization and the role of the program in the change process. The final script is discussed in most detail: the objectives and principles of the program; the content of each module; the learning activities employed; and the project work between the modules. In a very short period of time, the program helped to nurture a fundamental strategic turnaround.

The principal objective of the Canon Europe Senior Executive Program was to support a transition from a loose federation of semi-independent country-based sales companies to a new unified European organization. In order to implement this massive change Canon had to identify and develop a new generation of pan-European leaders who would identify with the new strategic direction and have the skills to lead in the new environment.

Therefore, the Canon Europe Program was designed with action learning at its core, so the participants could analyze the specific challenges facing Canon in Europe, discuss possible solutions and develop action plans to drive change. The participants came to IMD for input on new concepts and tools, shared and understood each other's problems and challenges and collaborated in order to generate new ideas and create solutions. They went away, tried them out and returned to discuss success or failure and to take on new ideas.

The zoom-in script of three modules looking at the big picture first followed by the organization issues and finally leadership implications, all linked through interim real-time project work, became a core design structure for a number of other programs that followed. IMD provided the all-important safe environment in which to address the more difficult or contentious issues.

Canon Europa in 1999: the change dilemma

Hajime Tsuruoka took the helm at Canon Europe at a time when its sales topped US$7.4 billion – a successful business in anyone's book. Over several decades, the company's model of relatively autonomous national sales organizations had proved a winning formula. But, would this model work in future?

In September 1999 – 100 days after he became CEO, Tsuruoka asked his European presidents:

Gentlemen, is Canon Europe in a critical situation? Can we continue to operate in the way that we have historically or do we have to make some changes?[1]

Tsuruoka dedicated a team of senior managers and engaged two consulting companies to conduct an extensive analysis of Canon's European operations. The analysis revealed that Canon's current organizational and cost structures would not be competitive in the long run since market dynamics were demanding more efficient structures and a new business approach.

If major changes in how Canon does business in Europe were required, then the key challenge would be how should these changes be defined, what would be the specific implementation steps and, most importantly, how to secure buy-in for the changes from a skeptical management team.

Program context

Canon, which can trace its roots back to Japan in 1933, first entered Europe in 1957 when it created Canon Europa S.A. in Geneva, Switzerland. Over the next 10 years, it developed an extensive network of distributors around Europe to sell and service its products and, in 1968, set up a European headquarters, Canon Europa N.V. (CENV) in Amsterdam, The Netherlands. Throughout the 1970s it started replacing its distributors with its own but still highly autonomous sales companies (NSOs). Working in the shadow of the strong NSOs, CENV never really got a foothold as the true head of a European organization. According to Tsuruoka:

Canon Europa until now had functioned as a middleman between Canon Inc. (Japan) and the European national sales organizations. Primary tasks were to consolidate sales results, provide product information, logistic support and encourage a shared direction. In reality the value that Canon Europe added was vague as the majority of the real business was being done at a country level.[2]

Canon Europe's core businesses were divided into two areas: volume and value. The volume business, referred to as a 'box moving' business, was price sensitive and depended on efficient supply chain management for its profits. The value business products comprised office machines. Value products were typically sold with a long-term service contract or other value-added services attached to the sale, depending on customer requirements. Hence, there was a high degree of customization. Sales of Canon goods passed through one of their 13 NSOs or through a network of independent dealers and distributors or, in some cases, through OEM partnerships that the company had developed with companies such as Hewlett-Packard and Danka.

Earlier forays into company reorganization had experienced only a limited success. Tsuruoka's predecessor as Europe CEO had launched Project 2000 in which he attempted to create a pan-European logistics and IT infrastructure. The project finally had to be abandoned due to a lack of knowledge and experience in the organization at the time. It was at that time that Canon first approached IMD with the purpose of designing a course to develop general management skills.

Initial program script

Canon UK's Training and Development Manager was charged with carrying out a due diligence on European business schools with a view to deliver a concept for general executive education to Canon management. IMD presented an initial proposal in September 1998 based on Canon's requirements at that time (see Figure 31.1 for an outline of the process). We met with Canon's human resource management throughout the fall of 1998. Early involvement led to a unique course design and a fluid partnership from the beginning. A proposal with a structure and headings similar to the final course outline was discussed and presented on 1 December that year.

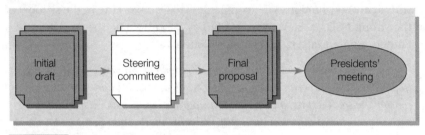

Figure 31.1 The proposal process

There was no European HR organization when the program started. Therefore, a steering committee was formed with a responsibility to review and sponsor the program. Several Canon managers with quasi-European responsibilities and key country presidents joined the team as well as members from Canon's internal task force on European reorganization (see below). I represented IMD. The steering committee helped to identify the initial direction. Subsequent interviews with presidents and senior management, in which they brainstormed issues and possible solutions, revealed a specific set of needs and competency gaps.

Development of the final program script

While these discussions were going on, Tsuruoka set up an investigative team from two consulting companies and Canon senior management members to analyze the company's situation. They presented a number of findings, all pointing to the necessity of building a new pan-European organization:

Company Analysis:

- **Slowing growth rates and eroding gross margins:** Competitive pressure on pricing and market saturation in many segments meant that cost savings had to be achieved elsewhere in order to maintain profit margins.

■ **Weak role of headquarters (CENV)**: Canon needed an HQ to expound a common vision and strategic direction for its European operations.

■ **Inefficient supply chain management**: Canon Europa's decentralized, autonomous structure resulted in a highly fragmented, costly and non-competitive supply chain system.

■ **Changes in distribution**: Transnational wholesalers required consistent pricing, logistics, advertising and promotions across European borders.

■ **Uncoordinated pricing and promotion**: The new euro currency was on its way; the Internet had already led to transparency across borders – Canon NSOs across Europe needed to align their marketing strategies.

Armed with the information presented by the consultant's report, Tsuruoka returned to IMD in order to redefine the scope of the proposed program. He felt that not only did Canon Europa need to look at competency gaps, but it also needed to address the issue of 'Europeanization of the firm' and drastic changes in strategic direction. We responded with a proposal that at first sight resembled the previous script – it would be a program of three one-week modules with project work between each (see Figure 31.2). However, the new script suggested that Canon Europa move the program away from its previous focus on general management development and exploitation of core competencies, towards a more focused agenda that would support Canon's transition from a loose federation of national sales companies to an integrated pan-European organization.

Session topics remained generic but the content changed to reflect the wider implications of Tsuruoka's objectives. More specifically, this would entail:

■ Helping Canon to identify and develop the new organizational capabilities it would need to be a successful pan-European company.

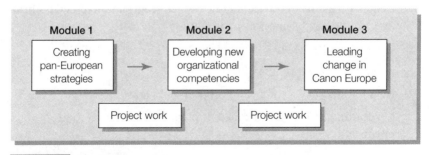

Figure 31.2 Final program script

- The building of a pan-European mindset among key managers in Canon's European subsidiaries.

- Developing practical and implementable change strategies to facilitate the transformation to the new organization.

- Examining the participants' role as leaders of change and team-builders.

- Helping participants to develop personal action plans that encourage them to put new skills and desired behaviors into practice.

- Building people networks across Canon's current organizational boundaries.

The pan-European agenda was not imposed on the participants. Rather, they were asked to analyze the competitive environment by themselves, compare issues across different sales companies, and begin to think about potential solutions. This meant that even those skeptical of the pan-European ideal would be encouraged to participate in the program and be given the opportunity to understand and take part in the direction of Canon Europe's future. Pan-European strategy was referred to more explicitly only as the program developed and as participants started to see the need and the benefit of the new approach.

Program principles

Certain principles were applied to the design of the program in order that key learnings would be applicable to daily Canon life. It was intended to be a highly interactive program that would blur the distinction between classroom learning and daily work responsibilities. All content was chosen keeping the following principles in mind:

- Provide practical concepts and frameworks.

- Help participants to translate these new concepts and frameworks into their day-to-day business responsibilities.

- Bottom-up change but top-down support.

- Add measurable business value.

- Help Canon build strong pan-European networks.

- Key learnings would be cascaded throughout all levels of the organization.

Module 1

The first of the three modules would concentrate on helping the participants to develop a deep understanding of Canon's core businesses, and the ways in which Canon could position itself for industry dominance. It would begin by introducing a set of tools for analyzing the competitive dynamics of industries and markets. Participants would form small groups in order to examine the best practices of companies around the world as benchmarks in strategy development. Subsequent units would address team dynamics and the issues of goal setting and decision making in groups. Participants would refer back to behaviors and reactions in the previous exercise to critique theory in action. The module would culminate by focusing on customer needs and identifying the key success factors for Canon's strategy. At the end of the week, participants would create project action plans that would integrate the key learning points of Module 1. The exact composition of those projects was not outlined at that point but we proposed that they encompass an analysis of the industry dynamics that would determine the success or failure of Canon's approach to the new opportunities.

Module 2

The second module, scheduled to take place some months after the first, proposed to switch the focus from external drivers to the new organizational competencies Canon Europa would have to develop to implement the strategies it had identified in the first module. The first session would present a case study demonstrating how some organizations had built new capabilities quickly to support their strategies. A discussion of the project assignments, completed between modules, would follow. The bulk of the module would focus on areas of competency such as speed, innovation and the use of new distribution channels. Each session would combine faculty presentations with case studies that would benchmark the competencies used by other global organizations to dominate their industries. The final section would explore the possibility of sharing competencies across NSOs and how a pan-European mindset might be promoted among participants and throughout the organization. As was the case in Module 1, this module would end with the allotment of group assignments whereby disparate groups within the organization would have to join forces before the final module in order to devise action plans for translating their business strategies into new organizational competencies.

Module 3

The pan-European mindset alluded to in Module 2 would be expanded upon further in Module 3. Participants would be asked to focus on leading change and the barriers they might encounter while trying to implement it. They would also get a chance to present and discuss their project assignments completed since the previous encounter. The skills and behaviors necessary to successfully lead change would be explored in an effort to identify the most successful leadership models. Participants would be asked to consider their own attributes and how they best interacted with their culturally diverse teams.

We also proposed the creation of a joint IMD/Canon steering committee that would oversee the development and delivery of the program. This committee would also help to communicate the program internally, and act as an internal resource for any questions or clarifications concerning program objectives, content or structure.

Learning activities

The IMD team proposed a variety of activities designed to maintain emotional commitment and energy. These included senior management presentations whereby a senior manager from Canon Europe would open Module 1 and attend the sessions if possible. Participants selected for the program stated that some of their key expectations were 'to learn from others' mistakes, successes and failures.' International case studies would introduce participants to leading concepts in global management that were relevant to their management needs and were based on real business situations. Group work would encourage networking that is essential in building a pan-European identity within Canon Europe. Team-building and coaching exercises would show in a practical way the behaviors and skills necessary to manage teams, while classroom discussions would (aided by faculty) harness the wealth of experience already present in the participant group and direct it towards solution-finding in the face of Canon's current challenges. Of course, the integrated project work would be a learning experience in itself and contribute in a real way to the company's change in direction.

The presidents' meetings

Given the results of the preliminary analysis, and support of the senior executives in Japan, Tsuruoka decided to go ahead with the reorganization in Europe. He also believed in the value of using management development as the tool for change, aligning mindsets and mobilizing the energy of the key people in the organization. In May 1999, he invited all country presidents to a meeting at IMD, the first of the series of presidents' meetings, which took place over the next several years. He wanted to use the opportunity to tell the presidents about his plans for Canon in Europe, sell the idea and receive feedback from them on what they considered to be the key issues. I presented a preview of future Canon senior executive training programs with a focus on creating a pan-European mindset based on the proposal outlined above. Mr Tsuruoka and I began the day by introducing the program in which we explained why everyone was there and what we were trying to achieve. Many of the faculty billed to participate in the final implementation then outlined their plans for the program.

Tsuruoka presented his vision to his European Advisory Board in August 1999 and a month later to all European presidents. There was some dissent among the ranks from those who feared for their positions (the new organization would eliminate the need for powerful country heads) but also from those who believed it was merely change for change's sake – the old model worked well in their view. Subsequent presidents' meetings then concentrated on issues standing in the way of change.

First delivery

Almost immediately after Tsuruoka's presentation to his European presidents, the first of Canon's 150 senior managers arrived at IMD to begin the Canon Europe Senior Executive Program. One country president attended each module in order to host and help participants interpret the strategy. Their presence also lent weight to the objectives of the program and left them exposed to learning and some criticism from their managers. The gaps between modules allowed participants to assimilate the key learnings from relevant sessions and to try them out in practice. Each time the participants got together, they discussed new obstacles to execution of the strategy and further developed solutions.

Value of the projects

The key element of the Canon program was the inter-module projects. Initially, these were intended to be learning experiences with no specific application intended. However, very quickly Canon Europe management came to realize that participants did not want to walk away from the issues after the program was completed – they were committed to seeing them through to implementation.

According to comments from some of the early participants, 'projects were to form the basis of real policy formation in Canon's new structure and this model has continued through to today.' One senior executive explained: 'The relevance for me was the fact that the teams had to work, not being in the same location. It helped the organization to progress on its way towards a truly pan-European company.' The SEP teams, who worked virtually using Canon's and IMD's intranet, proved to be key to the continuous application of the project outputs. Strong relationships were forged and networks created as participants came to the realization that they all had the same problems and issues and had the same objectives in sight. Canon has capitalized on the IMD experience as other teams have been formed to design and execute other projects related to pan-European efforts.

Project definition and team interpretation of tasks were the greatest indicators of a program message well delivered. At the outset, team assignments made no mention of pan-European mindsets or shared services. The scope was broad and asked questions regarding Canon's level of market orientation, or how a 'solutions' business would be introduced. Participants responded by taking on board the learning they had been given and applying it to real-life in Canon. One group benchmarked the company against a database of 400 high-performing companies. During that research they uncovered elements of best practice being used by various NSOs. They concluded that the next step would be to delve further into best practice within the NSOs and apply learnings across the group – a step towards a pan-European mindset. Another group went further down the pan-European route and redefined their assignment to introduce a 'solutions' business in a European rather than local context. When yet another group was asked how they would make the 'volume' business more profitable, they concluded that the economies of scale offered by a European organization was the only way forward.

The projects between Modules 2 and 3 were much more operational in nature. It was clear that all participants had accepted and owned the idea of a pan-European ideal. Now they needed to decide how best to implement it. The first group was asked to expand upon the competitor analysis they began after the first module. They refined their recommendations and outlined how a European headquarters might be empowered. The second group concentrated on why and which shared services should be centralized and in which order of priority. A third group investigated the advantages of a pan-European mindset, outlined the obstacles to its implementation and made recommendations towards how to overcome them.

The project element of the Canon SEP proved pivotal to the success of the program. According to the president of Canon Sweden, 'I believe it changed the mindset to a pan-European one instead of a national one and prepared participants for taking on project work back at home.'

The role of the Canon SEP was to develop a new generation of leaders. It was clear that major strategic change was essential, but the burning question was, who was going to lead it? Canon wanted to ensure that its management had the skills and competencies necessary to carry off the transformation (see Figure 31.3). Canon's needs evolved as the program progressed and we responded to each stage accordingly. Tsuruoka recalls the acceptance of the European mindset as a primary achievement. The focus evolved from 'why change' at the start to 'how to change (and fast)' later on.

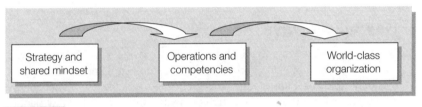

| Strategy and shared mindset | Operations and competencies | World-class organization |

Figure 31.3   **Program benefits and follow-up**

Through the program learning the participants internalized the new pan-European strategy as a clear, logical way forward. IMD provided that opportunity to look at the issues objectively and relate them to the changes in the competitive landscape. Participants left believing that 'if an idea is well-prepared and thought through – almost anything is possible!'

To date, we have delivered seven offerings of the Canon Europa SEP program. Over time the focus of the content has changed from a broad strategic one to a more specific concentration on essential organizational capabilities and leadership competency gaps. Again, the project definition and response has indicated how participants' understanding has evolved. As early as the second implementation, participants designed European business plans on how to launch a wireless network product; they proposed how national differences would be addressed in the introduction of a 'solutions' business; and they discussed how a European Consumer Division would be set up. The Module 2 to 3 projects looked at implementation issues, such as how to share services, or how to create a competitive advantage in a particular sector.

Most of today's senior management team are alumni of the program. Their understanding of Canon and its strategy emanates from the learnings garnered during the program. A clearer understanding of their own needs means that they are well equipped to identify where they might need help in their organization's development. We have also succeeded in creating a learning network within Canon where teams across countries and business unit groups work together to achieve a more streamlined European organization. Many participants cited the opportunity to network as a major raison d'être of the SEP program at IMD. Time away from the pressures of everyday demands allowed executives to reflect and form networks with fellow participants, which continue to flourish today. Five years later, the new Canon Europe has reached record sales revenues and has become the largest business unit among all Canon regions worldwide.

Key take-aways

- Well-scripted company-specific programs provide a highly interactive environment that helps participants to explore, learn and, most importantly, apply new knowledge. This greatly reduces the risk of managers simply 'talking' the new language presented to them and not 'walking' or applying it in their work – for a fraction of an average consultancy fee.

- The Canon Europe CEO, Hajime Tsuruoka, wanted to 'take away the barriers and create an inclusive environment.' Conceptually, IMD did not try to prescribe a strategy; it provided a value-creating learning experience to enhance execution.

- Canon also liked the idea of taking managers out of their usual environment and placing them in a challenging setting that encouraged innovative thought and cooperation among managers from various locations and backgrounds. Tsuruoka says: 'It was an opportunity to listen to how people think, generate ideas and suggestions and a medium to pass on information.'

Notes

1   Govinder, N. and Pucik, V., *Canon Europa (A) and (B)*, Case Study IMD-3-1431–H, 25 May 2004, IMD, Lausanne, Switzerland.
2   Ibid.

32

Developing winning marketing strategies in real time

Adrian Ryans

Summary

This chapter considers the challenges faced by companies in fast-moving global industries when they evaluate market opportunities and develop timely implementation plans. Two company examples illustrate a process and program developed specifically to respond to these strategy issues. As part of the program, participants are asked to evaluate and develop one or two cutting-edge business opportunities, supported by a faculty member who provides the relevant tools and concepts for a ten-step process. It is a disciplined framework within which to structure and capture their discussion and analysis, thereby improving the quality of opportunity assessments and the subsequent marketing plans.

In many fast-moving global businesses, business unit teams need processes to quickly assess the attractiveness of potential market opportunities, and to develop marketing strategies and implementation plans for those most likely to succeed. In high-technology businesses, the issue is more complicated: the knowledge base to assess and develop the opportunity is often distributed among individuals in different functional areas and geographic locations. The composition of the teams also varies from opportunity to opportunity, reflecting the probable customers, the relevant technological expertise, and the appropriate support functions. In addition, many of the people on these teams have technical backgrounds, but have little formal business or marketing training. Many of these individuals have broad responsibilities and it is difficult to get the team members focused on one particular opportunity for any significant period of time before their attention is diverted to some other critical short-term business issue that needs immediate attention.

This chapter focuses on a process and program that were developed for two companies, one in the semiconductor industry and the other in a closely related field. Both were facing challenges in market-opportunity assessments and strategy development. The chapter is based on a composite of their experiences. To address their issues, we designed a development process that involved business unit teams with representatives from all the key stakeholders; they met together for a three to four day session, or two shorter sessions of three days and, six weeks later, two days. All sessions were based on a disciplined process to evaluate market opportunities and then develop winning strategies and implementation plans.

Below, I will describe the challenge that led to the program, the process that was used, how the process was implemented, and how the teams working on the projects captured the discussions and learning points.

The challenge

Companies in fast-moving industries, such as semiconductors, often have a large number of market opportunities, and one of their major challenges is to determine which of these opportunities have sufficient strategic and profit potential to be worth pursuing. If a market looks sufficiently attractive, then the company must decide if it can develop a winning strategy to exploit that opportunity and then an implementation plan that will ensure timely market entry, in an effort to win enough market share to reach (or exceed) its strategic and profitability goals.

While these steps sound straightforward, reality is much more complex. In the last decade or so, both the customer decision-making process and the resource base of many semiconductor suppliers (and related industries) have become geographically highly diverse. It is not uncommon, for example, that a European customer decides to introduce a new product, but rather than design the product itself, it outsources that task to a design center in the United States. Then, if the design goes into production, a contractor in Asia may manufacture the product. This contract manufacturer might in turn have an influence on the choice of component suppliers. Similar situations face the semiconductor suppliers of the subsystems and components. A North American supplier will have sales teams and some marketing resources in all major geographies of the world, and it may have its own design, engineering and manufacturing resources distributed across North

America, Europe and Asia. These market developments, on both the customer and supplier sides, have significantly complicated the processes of assessing market opportunities and designing and implementing winning strategies.

For a particular subsystem or component, rigorous assessment of the market opportunity requires that the supplier pull together a global team, representing marketing, product management, sales, research and development, manufacturing, and perhaps other functions. To benefit from a full interchange of perspectives, it is usually necessary to get the team together for at least one extended face-to-face meeting. During the meeting, the team can work through the analysis process, perhaps completing some parts of it. If the opportunity still looks promising, it should be clear what assumptions need to be verified, what additional information needs to be gathered, and who is to be responsible for what, by when. Ideally, after a reasonable period for this additional data gathering, a second face-to-face meeting would consolidate all the new information and integrate it into the rest of the planning process. However, given the cost and time involved, this is not always feasible, so follow-up meetings sometimes involve video and/or telephone conference calls.

In many companies, the complexity of the business environment hinders the development of efficient and effective planning and decision-making processes. The two companies with whom we were working knew they were not there yet. Top management was dissatisfied with the quality of the assessments and business plans that were being developed: they found them to be based on highly aggregated market data and on the technical aspects of the product with scant regard for customer-buying behavior, the competitive environment, and the company's ability to develop and implement particular marketing strategies. In other words, the analyses tended to be static and failed to adequately reflect the fast-changing nature of the markets in which the company was competing.

They felt that they could benefit from outside help on opportunity assessments and strategy development, but they did not want to 'subcontract' so vital a process out to a consulting firm. What they needed was to improve the effectiveness of their own processes and to enhance the skills of their people to tackle what would only be an increasing number of opportunities. In essence, they needed to be able to ask the right questions, not just receive answers. In addition, by developing an experienced cross-functional team, they might create strategies that better leveraged the resources and capabilities of the total organization. A custom-designed learning experience seemed to offer the best solution, in particular because their teams could work on real current opportunities during the program.

The process: Evaluating market opportunities and developing a winning strategy

The process that was introduced to evaluate the identified market opportunities is shown in Figure 32.1.[1] In practice, this process is modified to reflect the nature of the particular business, and the key issues the company typically faces in developing and implementing winning strategies.

This process formed the core focus of the program. Each step was tackled in turn, with the team undertaking the activity in real time, working on a real opportunity for the company. Each step is briefly outlined below:

1 Identify market opportunities

Here the team segments the relevant market, identifies potential target segments and develops a deep understanding of the needs in each one. The team will also try to quantify the size of the opportunity by market segment.

2 Evaluate market attractiveness of potential target segments

In this step, the team assesses the relevant market forces. Six market forces are reviewed: suppliers, direct competitors, complementors, customers, potential entrants and substitutes. The team will also assess how these market forces are likely to evolve over the planning horizon, and what steps the company might take to shape them to create as profitable a market opportunity as possible for the company.

3 Understand customers

If the market appears potentially profitable, the next step is to deepen the team's understanding of their customers' needs and how they make choices. (By customer, we are referring not only to the immediate customer, but also the downstream members of the market chain, including manufacturers, distributors, value-added resellers and so on.) If the new product represents a discontinuous innovation in some form, it is also useful to look at the product from a diffusion-of-innovation perspective. The work of Geoffrey Moore is particularly relevant in this regard.[2]

4 Assess resources and capabilities

It is also useful to assess the business unit's resources and capabilities, particularly its core capabilities. This is crucial for the development of

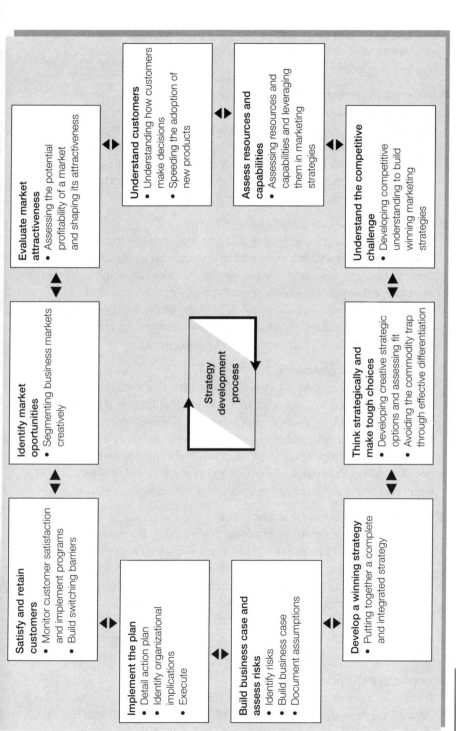

Evaluate market attractiveness
- Assessing the potential profitability of a market and shaping its attractiveness

Understand customers
- Understanding how customers make decisions
- Speeding the adoption of new products

Assess resources and capabilities
- Assessing resources and capabilities and leveraging them in marketing strategies

Understand the competitive challenge
- Developing competitive understanding to build winning marketing strategies

Identify market oportunities
- Segmenting business markets creatively

Strategy development process

Think strategically and make tough choices
- Developing creative strategic options and assessing fit
- Avoiding the commodity trap through effective differentiation

Satisfy and retain customers
- Monitor customer satisfaction and implement programs
- Build switching barriers

Implement the plan
- Detail action plan
- Identify organizational implications
- Execute

Build business case and assess risks
- Identify risks
- Build business case
- Document assumptions

Develop a winning strategy
- Putting together a complete and integrated strategy

Figure 32.1 Building and implementing winning marketing strategies

realistic strategic options that leverage the business unit's resources and capabilities, and, ultimately, for assessing the business unit's ability to win in the opportunity.

5 Understand the competitive challenge

Another critical factor is an assessment of the potential competition that the business unit will face, should it decide to pursue the opportunity. This assessment should attempt to predict future competitive moves, identify areas of competitive vulnerability that could potentially be exploited, as well as to predict competitive reactions to any moves that the business unit might make.

6 Think strategically and make tough choices

At this stage in the process it is useful to review and consolidate the analysis done in the earlier steps and to do some strategic thinking. Is there an opportunity here for some significant value innovation? In any case, at this point the team should develop creative strategic options and evaluate them in terms of fit with the key success factors in the market opportunity and the business unit's skills and resources relative to its potential competitors in the opportunity.

7 Develop a winning strategy

If the market opportunity looks potentially attractive and if the business unit can develop a strategic option that will allow it to capture a good portion of the potential profitability in the opportunity, then the team needs to flesh out the strategy. Here the emphasis should be on providing a complete solution (including training, support, documentation, complementary products or services, etc.) for the target customers and developing a complete and integrated strategy.

8 Build the business case and assess risks

Undoubtedly, early on in the planning process some informal financial analysis was done. At this point, the team needs to do a more formal analysis of the financial case for the opportunity. An integral part of this is the identification and assessment of the risks and the clear documentation of the assumptions underlying the business case. If, and when, the implementation of the strategy proceeds, the careful identification of the assumptions will make it easier to monitor whether the financial results are likely to be achieved.

9 Implement the plan

If the business case is acceptable, then the next step is to lay out a detailed implementation plan. As the plan is laid out, it is useful to clearly identify the organizational units and individuals who will need to carry out certain tasks by specified dates. Then, the plan has to be forcefully executed and the results carefully monitored.

10 Satisfy and retain customers

Once the new product has been successfully launched, the team must focus on customer retention and building barriers to switching. Customer satisfaction also needs to be monitored. If any important sources of dissatisfaction emerge, then new programs may be needed to address them. Such continued intense focus on customers will often reveal additional market opportunities, which will start the whole process over again.

While this 10-step process is described sequentially above, in reality it often turns out to be a highly iterative one, with some of the steps repeated several times as the thinking of the team evolves and is refined.

In order to provide structure for the debates and drive rigor in the evaluations, one or more worksheets were developed for each step of the process to help the team with their analysis. Examples of two of these worksheets are shown in Figure 32.2.

These worksheets helped teams to pull together their discussions and analysis with respect to each of their potential competitors. One set of worksheets would be completed for each of these companies. The worksheets were designed to build on each other where appropriate, so that the knowledge and understanding developed in some of the earlier worksheets were effectively leveraged in the later ones.

The program: Real-time learning and implementation

The program to train the participants on the process was rolled out by business unit. For each session, two current, cutting-edge opportunities were selected for in-depth evaluation. Two teams of five to eight individuals, drawn from the functions and geographies relevant for the two selected opportunities, were chosen to participate in the session. Since some of the opportunities might require technology or products from more than one business unit to provide a complete solution to a customer need, there were often one or more representatives of other business units on the teams.

After a brief introduction on the objectives of the program, usually made by a member of the top management team of the corporation or the head of

Market opportunity:

Name of competitor:

Worksheet 1 – Competitive analysis – Strategy driving forces	
Strategy driving forces	Notes
Goals/objectives (what do you know about this competitor's goals and objectives particularly with respect to the targeted market segment?)	
Assumptions (about itself, about us, and about the industry, etc.)	
Structure (how is the company organized?)	
Staff (backgrounds of key executives, recent hiring activity, etc.)	
Key resources and capabilities	
Systems (e.g. capital budgeting, cost accounting, executive compensation)	
Style (e.g. aggressive, bureaucratic, slow-moving)	
Strategy (target markets, value propositions, 'products', price, channels and marketing communications)	

Name of competitor:

Worksheet 2 – Implications from analysis of strategy driving forces
Major strengths?
Major areas of vulnerability?
Likely future actions?
Can we learn anything from this competitor?
Any other implications for us (perhaps in terms of our strategies or tactics)?

Figure 32.2   Excel® worksheets for capturing team discussions on competitive analysis

the business unit, the 10–step process was outlined in broad terms. Then the program began, in modules organized around each of the steps of the process.

Since some members of the business teams had no formal business training, each step of the process was introduced by the faculty member as a short lecture-discussion that introduced useful tools and concepts. Each module was organized in a similar way with four major components:

- A short lecture-discussion to introduce the module and the relevant concepts and tools. Examples were used to drive home the key messages.

- An introduction of the key tool or tools as implemented in the Excel worksheets. The teams were instructed on how to complete the worksheet, and sometimes a 'best practice' worksheet from an earlier session would be shown as an example.

- Each team then moved to a smaller seminar room, which was their 'home' for most of the workshop. Discussions were usually broad ranging, but the deliverable at the end of each session was the completed Excel worksheet(s) for that module. One of the team members acted as the facilitator.

- After completing the worksheets, each team returned to the main classroom to give a brief presentation of the results of its discussions to the other team using the Excel worksheet(s). Since both teams were drawn largely from the same business unit, this often led to some useful feedback and additional insights.

The total elapsed time for each of the modules varied, but they usually required between two and four hours. Normally, the most time-consuming module was the first one (on market segmentation). The workshops tended to move much quicker if a good market segmentation analysis had been completed prior to the workshop.

To divide the workshop into two parts, a natural place to break was at the sixth step, strategic thinking. In some cases, it was clear by this point that the particular opportunity being analyzed was not attractive and should not be pursued. Should the workshop continue, it would be as an educational exercise rather than a real-life application. Even if the opportunity was judged viable, this was a good point for a break. For starters, there was usually some missing data to be gathered and some assumptions that needed to be verified. In some instances, discussions with potential customers were required, to deepen the understanding of their needs and to get information on their priorities. All of these things take time and it is usually impossible to do some, let alone all, while a workshop is in progress. We, therefore, tend to favor a program design that incorporates the break after the preliminary strategic thinking, as additional questions allow the company to reap benefits from the opportunity assessments in addition to the learning experience itself.

If the workshop is broken into two parts, the second half usually begins with an extensive review of the first six modules in light of the new information that has been gathered by the team in the meantime. If the opportunity still looks worthy of pursuit, then the team can advance methodically through steps 6 to 10, using the same four-step procedure for each of the modules as described before.

Capturing the discussion and learning points

To maintain the energy level and encourage all the participants to actively contribute to the discussion, we project the Excel worksheet on to a wall or screen and ask one of the participants to fill in the worksheet as the discussion unfolds. This makes it very easy for the participants to see exactly what is being recorded and to refine the discussion in real time. By having an Excel workbook with tabs for all of the worksheets, it is very easy for the team to refer back to the notes from an earlier discussion and to update or revise them, if necessary.

The Excel workbook becomes the document of record. If particular topics or issues need additional research or analysis by an individual or a subset of the team, the assignment and due date can be noted in the workbook, and that section filled in as the data or analysis become available.

If, at a later date, a formal business plan must be prepared, the Excel workbook becomes the base source of information and analysis for developing the plan.

Value-added for the client

This program has brought disciplined thinking to the evaluation of market opportunities and the development of marketing strategies and implementation plans into a number of other companies. It has also proved successful in the training of key members of the business unit teams on marketing and business strategy. Since the team members drove the process themselves, they became committed to the outcomes of the process.

One result of the program has been an increased willingness of business units to reject opportunities and focus their energies on the few truly attractive ones, where there is a higher probability of business success. When there was less rigorous analysis of the opportunities, often too many were undertaken – with less than satisfactory results.

The development program also spurred participants to build better and more effective networks with other members of the global business unit team, and with key players in other business units with whom they have to work.

Key take-aways

■ A more rigorous assessment of market opportunities, culling less promising ideas, will lead to a higher probability of business success in the few that are chosen.

■ It is important to train key members of a business unit team on how to apply disciplined thinking to the evaluation of market opportunities and the development of implementation plans.

■ A systematic analytical process, supported by a continually updated document of record such as an Excel workbook with tabs for all the worksheets, is essential for this kind of disciplined thinking.

■ Drawing participants from different functions and geographic areas encourages greater coordination and networking between members of different business units.

■ The process builds strong commitment to any strategies and implementation plans that are developed. The team has a strong sense of ownership.

Notes

1   An early version is described in detail in: Ryans, A., More, R., Barclay, D. and Deutscher, T. (2000) *Winning Market Leadership: Strategic Market Planning for Technology-Driven Businesses.* Toronto: John Wiley & Sons.
2   Moore, G.A. (2002) *Crossing the Chasm.* New York: HarperBusiness.

33

Robust learning from project-based programs

Xavier Gilbert and Rhoda Davidson

Summary

Project work creates an excellent opportunity for executive learning from the construction of new mental patterns. To get the best learning impact from projects, you have to pay special attention to project selection, how the projects are integrated into the program learning script, the composition of the project teams and the roles of the project sponsor and the faculty team. The benefits are not only learning that sticks, but also tangible and relevant business results.

Project work provides a rich experiential context that supports every building block of the learning process. Most importantly project work addresses the fundamental high-level cognitive process of constructing viable mental patterns to deal with a complex business environment (for more on this please see Chapter 13):

- Ensuring strategic focus, simplifying, prioritizing, making choices, the importance of being realistic.

- Undertaking detailed planning, leaving no stone unturned; contrary to the general attitude of hoping for the best.

- Building in systematic follow-up to ensure disciplined execution.

- Actively managing the team and the people involved through: incentives, mobilization, communication, and creating a culture of supportive challenge.

As we discuss how to get the best learning impact from projects it is important to keep in mind that the learning agenda should not be compromised for the sake of project expediency – although we must emphasize that a good learning project must also be a good business project. Using projects to pursue the learning agenda implies that teams should not be told what to do at every step. They need space for some trial and error in defining the project scope and what is the relevant information, for some experimentation as they conceptualize options and for some time spent in discussions that may, at times, seem endless.

All this may make some project sponsors impatient – but learning does take time. The benefits, in terms of cognitive development, reasoning and learning how to learn, are enormous. The managerial capabilities applicable to planning and execution that are developed through action learning are more visible and tangible than those that can be built through cognitive development alone.

In this chapter we describe how to get the best learning impact from projects, by addressing the following challenges:

1 Selecting projects.

2 Integrating projects into a learning script.

3 Putting project teams together.

4 Working with the project sponsors.

5 Selecting a faculty team.

Selecting projects

A good learning project is a good business project

A project is an investment and should be treated as such. Before using a project as a learning initiative, one should ask the obvious question: 'Under normal circumstances, would I put money into this project?' If the answer is no or probably not, this is quite likely not a good project for a learning initiative either. So what makes for a good business project?

First, projects must have **a clear and compelling business purpose**. This can encompass a wide range of business objectives, for example:

■ **Strategy workshops:** Creating a strategy for a business unit.

■ **Turnaround projects:** Refocusing, re-energizing and executing the strategy.

- **Execution projects**: Clarifying the strategic focus and orienting the project around a few execution priorities.
- **Change projects**: Similar to execution projects, but with mobilization and communication playing a major part.
- **New-business projects**: Including a strong element of customer analysis, competition analysis, business system analysis, economic model analysis, these are, in fact, mini strategy workshops.
- **Inwardly focused projects**: Preparing for an imminent environmental change or improving processes; such projects need a compelling business purpose.

Second, projects must be **aligned with strategic priorities**. Clear alignment of projects with the strategy roadmap and the strategic priorities of the company communicate a compelling purpose to the participants, to the sponsors and to the management.

Such alignment also provides an overview structure that supports pattern building, which is a key item in the learning agenda. One powerful way to do this is to define a theme, directly related to a specific strategic priority, for all projects associated with a program. Defining a theme conveys the message that the projects are not just a random set of ideas and provides a rallying point for senior executives and program participants.

A clear purpose plus strategic alignment leads naturally to the third characteristic of a good business project: one that is **expected to deliver tangible and relevant business results**. Projects must deliver actual results. During the program the team should be able to demonstrate the value created by the project, i.e. bottom line impact that can be measured. Good examples of projects with measurable impact might include: cost reduction on specific product lines, introduction of key account management, conversion of innovative ideas to first sales and so on.

Projects that ask for general recommendations should be avoided. Too often these recommendations just end up on a shelf with all the other consultancy reports, gathering dust. In a project where recommendations are an integral part of the output, then a major requirement must be that the recommendations should be very explicit. For example, 'We need to form a joint venture with company X,' rather than 'We should form a joint venture.' The project deliverables should include the quantified upside, detailed action plans, named responsibilities and deadlines. This way, accepting the recommendations is equivalent to pulling the trigger and the plan can be implemented without delay. Sometimes it is helpful to ask the project team to test and evaluate project recommendations through pilot application.

The fourth characteristic of a good business project is that it **must trigger emotional commitment**. Projects must generate adrenaline; managers must want to be part of them because they are a career opportunity, because they are professionally exciting, and/or because they will have a clear positive impact on the company. At the same time, just like any business objective, projects should be 'ambitious, yet achievable,' providing a stretch opportunity relative to the participants' prior knowledge and experience. But they must be achievable. One good way to think seriously about the assignment is to try to do it yourself; if this is something you wish you never had to do, this is probably not a good assignment.

Finally, **projects must have visibility and credibility** and for this top management involvement is required. When the projects have been selected and defined by the executive board of the company, a certain level of visibility through publicity within the organization is helpful. Projects must also be credible: a company that has a tradition of not following up on their execution will have a hard time getting the emotional commitment that supports learning.

The project scope must be clear but challenging

Projects should have a relatively clear project scope with defined boundaries that prescribe what is included in and, perhaps more importantly, what is outside the project scope. The definitions should be tight enough so that the team does not feel that they have to 'boil the ocean' to start the project. Very broad projects will rarely work as learning opportunities because, as in many large corporate projects, the objectives are often unclear.

Once scope is clear, it is important to check that there will also be some challenge for the team. Projects require some inherent complexity that allows the prior knowledge of the team members to be leveraged and stretched within limits, for example:

■ Multidimensionality in some respect such as functions, organization levels or markets, to provide complexity for team members who have had a relatively narrow prior experience.

■ Projects that provide opportunity for looking outside-of-the-box for information and solutions.

■ Some degrees of freedom that provide room for exercising options, for making choices, also increase complexity in ways that support learning.

■ Projects that involve organizing mental patterns and developing overview perspectives are strong vehicles; for example, learning how to identify root problems or how to build an execution roadmap.

However, avoid initiatives that focus on very specific and small areas of the business; these can be interesting for the experts on the team but leave the rest of the group cold. Such projects are often better accomplished by a fit-for-purpose functional team. Similarly, projects where there is already an established formula to do that type of project in the organization will prevent the team members from learning by experimenting.

Finally, projects must provide some opportunity for re-scoping. Expecting the team to adapt the focus of the project as they are building their project roadmap will help them develop capabilities at the cognitive level and at the managerial intervention level (see Chapter 13). Also, the scope of projects often has to be narrowed as the participants realize the size of the detailed planning task. Managers must learn how to segment and prioritize, how to prototype with very few sub-projects, and how to replicate their method-ologies to the next sub-projects on the priority list. This approach is practical and provides the quick-wins that create momentum.

Avoid common pitfalls

Selecting appropriate projects is always a unique experience, as every organization and team has different challenges and agendas. However, there are some common pitfalls that should be avoided if you are to have projects that are relevant and actionable:

■ **Projects that are at a very 'high flying' altitude**: When participants cannot relate to the project scope, they are unlikely to feel committed. Specifically, if the project scope is way above the participants' current positions, they will not feel legitimate in addressing the issue.

■ **Projects with a 'political' agenda**: Projects will not work as learning vehicles if they are known to impinge on someone's territory, or deal with issues that top management is shying away from.

■ **Ideas before their time**: Sometimes executive boards try to establish projects that have little chance of success given the current state of the organization, for example a project to apply the latest management theory. Always question whether the organization is ready for the project.

■ **Organizational redesign or policy writing projects**: These projects should be avoided unless they include demonstrating the validity of the change through its impact on the bottom line.

■ **'Reorganize the company' projects**: Sometimes sponsors try to use project teams to fix everything about the company that frustrates them, offering briefs such as 'streamline work processes.' But this is not the platform to reorganize the company. The better objective is to pinpoint one process that can be reorganized in a tangible and measurable way.

■ **'Change the culture' projects**: While making the company more innovative or more flexible or more customer-focused is a laudable goal, it is not one on which a small group of managers will have much impact. Changes of this nature have to come from the top.

■ **Ritual projects**: Some companies have ready-to-use, one-size-fits-all initiatives, such as 'differentiating commodity products' or 'sharing best practices,' that have never yielded results. These projects are not necessarily bad; they simply carry a legacy of having never been addressed seriously in the past.

Integrating projects into a learning script

The learning script is driven by the program structure within which the projects are integrated. Even good projects fail for two main reasons: poor execution planning and no real will to follow-up. To address this challenge, we recommend a modular learning script to provide a continuous red thread throughout project execution. The first program module covers the planning phase; after the first module, the execution phase takes place, and at the end of the execution phase, a second program module consists of an after-action review.

First module: Mental rehearsal

Planning is akin to mental rehearsal. As discussed in Chapter 13, planning a task uses the same neural connections required for executing the task, so detailed planning will put in place the mental 'wiring' to support execution.

A one-week duration works well for the planning phase and, in fact, it is difficult to prepare a thorough execution plan in less time. The flow of the week belongs to the visible part of the managerial-learning iceberg: the development by the participants of their intervention model. Each step provides a building block towards execution, while at the same time addressing the invisible part of the iceberg: forming viable mental overview patterns to act upon the business context.

The flow of the week is typically as follows:

- Where does our project fit on the strategy roadmap? The purpose is to start from an overview of the project raison d'être.

- What is the scope and what are the deliverables of our project? Here, the aim is to challenge the relevance bandwidth of the participants and to start forming mental patterns linking problems to solutions. A first set of hypotheses is made of what is likely to be within the scope and what is not. These hypotheses may, however, evolve.

- Which tasks need to be completed to produce the deliverables? What? By whom? By when? This phase begins the process of detailing actions, but the path is from the general to the specific, rather than trying to list all details and risking losing sight of the overview. The output is a Gantt chart.

- Do we have the capabilities to execute these tasks? How should the execution plan take into account the development or the absence of these capabilities? Now the team needs to challenge the realism and feasibility of the emerging plan. This will probably lead to re-scoping, prioritizing and focusing.

- Does our project deliver the expected shareholder value? What are the drivers of financial performance? How time-driven is our project? This is again a 'reality test'; it will lead to re-scoping. Identifying the key drivers of performance addresses the fundamental question: what is really critical to make our project succeed?

- Who does what in the core project team? Is individual performance management aligned with the project requirements? The participants begin to see that beyond the plan there is work. This realization started with the Gantt chart that already had names on it. But now is the point of no return, as commitments are made, intellectually and emotionally.

- What is our mobilization and communication plan to execute our project? The question here is how are we going to share our thinking with a wider circle of stakeholders? Who are they? What will get them on board? What are the key points in our thinking, to be communicated?

■ What is our execution follow-up plan? What are the key milestones and review points? This is a further mental rehearsal of execution, focused on the milestones and what we commit to deliver at each one. More adrenaline!

Building these steps into the week will give a timetable that typically looks as follows:

Sunday	Monday	Tuesday	Wednesday	Thursday	Friday
	Task definition	Task definition	Task definition	Task definition	Task definition
	Alignment with the strategy roadmap After-action review	Cascading down to the AAR	Delivering the EVA Identifying the AAR	Developing the mobilization and AAR	Synthesizing the work of the week Developing an execution overview and a project tracker
	Lunch				
	Walk				
	Task definition	Task definition	Task definition	Task definition	Task definition
	Scope and deliverables of the AAR	Capability gap assessment AAR	Team responsibilities Aligning AAR	Developing the follow-up plan AAR	After action review of the week
Program introduction	Dinner				
	Continuation of the work and support exercises				

Each half-day consists of a short session when tasks and deliverables are introduced, a team working session and then a debrief session where the task output is reviewed and discussed. By the end of the week the teams will have developed a number of 'take-homes' that are the key inputs into the execution phase of the project. However, some will be more visible than others:

Visible take-homes	Less visible take-homes
■ A detailed execution plan, with a Gantt chart for operating execution and project tracker for operating follow-up. ■ The project tracker should also include the work remaining to be done to complete the execution plan. ■ A reuseable execution model.	■ A high level of commitment to executing the plan. ■ More self-reliance in applying and stretching prior knowledge and experience, with the ability to redeploy the execution planning methodology to new circumstances. ■ A broader relevance bandwidth when dealing with managerial situations. ■ The ability to develop solid overview patterns to roadmap moving-forward steps to deal with complex business contexts. ■ The ability to leverage discussions to get feedback on, and broaden one's roadmaps through 'supportive challenge' from colleagues; challenging each other while seeking to help each other. ■ The ability to mentally rehearse execution steps moving forward. ■ The ability to revisit one's work to identify improvements.

Execution

Time between modules can vary widely depending on the scope of the projects. Four to ten months are the typical limits. The time needs to be long enough to make sure something is accomplished but short enough that project teams can still remember what happened during the development of the mental pathway in the first module.

While it is the role of the project sponsor to supervise the project team during the action phase of the project, it is also useful for someone from the program faculty to provide a 'follow-up-watcher' coach role, comparable to a 'weight-watcher' coach role. Program faculty is often in a better position than the project sponsor to listen to an honest discussion of how the project is progressing and to offer impartial support.

The most effective way to do this is to hold regular monthly or bimonthly teleconferences or virtual net meetings with the team. To make sure that these meetings can be organized efficiently, it is wise to ask the team to choose a project coordinator who will undertake to fix the dates and the times for the meetings. The team should be asked to submit a written update of their execution tracker before the meeting so that project progress can be discussed effectively. The meetings should then focus on:

▪ Assessing the progress of the team versus the plan; asking the team to identify causes if it is not on track, and what will be done to remedy this.

▪ Gauging whether the team is working effectively together and asking what will be done if it is not.

▪ Determining how the team is working with its sponsor, whether they are working according to the follow-up plan, and again discussing what will be done if it is not.

▪ Asking the team to explain (once again) its execution roadmap, to provide its current overview of progress and current priorities and help the team rethink its overall execution roadmap if it has lost its sense of direction.

Using these types of questions will provide ample scope for discovering how well the project is progressing and how well the team is functioning. During some meetings it may become clear that the project is completely off track and that the sponsor badly needs to intervene. The next step is to raise the red flag to the sponsor and then follow up with the team later to make sure that the situation has improved.

Second module: After-action review

The normal steps of an after-action review will be followed during the second module. The first step is to assess what has been achieved through the project work and to compare it to the execution plan from the first module. Differences between the two should be shown factually.

The second step is to review each key milestone in the execution plan, chronologically: when was it, which activities it involved, and what was achieved it this stage. This leads into the third step, again for each milestone, which involves identifying what was done that led to the successful achievement of tasks and what led to other tasks being unsuccessful. This review could use a grid similar to the one at the end of the execution-planning phase, which focuses on learning and problem resolution 'on the go.' The mindset here is not to look for sources of problems elsewhere, but to identify what the team could have done to prevent, or at least manage, the problems that arose:

■ What was our level of motivation in executing these tasks? How much commitment and conviction did we apply to it? Did we have other priorities that took over?

■ What information did we use in performing these tasks? Was there information that we should have had, but did not? Why had we not considered it? Did we have the right sensors in the right places to get the information we needed to move forward?

■ Did we execute our plan? Was there anything missing in it? Why didn't we put it in? Did we have the mechanisms to adjust the course fast enough? Did we always have an eye on our execution key performance indicators (KPIs)? Typically, the capabilities and communication parts of the execution plan will have been underestimated.

■ How did we work as a project team? Did we stick to our commitment to team discipline, realism and supportive challenge? Or did the team fall apart? When did this happen? Why did it happen?

■ Did we keep, as individuals, an overview of where we were going collectively? Or did we lose sight of our overview roadmap? When did that happen? Why did it happen?

Finally, the fourth step is to agree on what will be done to leverage the execution strengths and to prevent the deficiencies that have been identified in the different areas above. Generally these discussions will center on:

■ Keeping our focus on the essentials, the overview execution roadmap, the key success drivers (KPIs), through personal and team tools. This has an impact both on commitment and on keeping a common sense of direction.

■ More detailed planning with respect to aligning capabilities.

■ More ambitious plan with respect to communication.

■ Much more follow-up discipline with respect to the regular operating reviews and the less frequent, but knowledge sharing, milestone meetings.

■ Insufficient leverage of the project management team, particularly with respect to supportive challenge.

A final key output of project work is that learning from the project can be applied elsewhere in the organization. One way of ensuring that this happens is to make one of the required project outputs a document outlining how the approach used in the project can best be applied again, how best to achieve success and how to avoid any pitfalls. This process also helps the team to be explicit among themselves on what aspects of the project were or were not a success and why.

Full time on project versus part time on project

An important program design choice is whether the project work should be done on a part-time basis during a program, with other sessions being run in parallel with the project work, or whether the project work should be performed on a full-time basis during the program. Our opinion is that full-time work is simply more compelling because it allows undivided commitment to project work with a clear action-learning agenda that builds learning autonomy. Part-time projects encourage skipping over detailed execution planning and lead to an increased risk of project failure.

Some preparatory work will help to hit the ground running

Effective project planning and execution can be enhanced by asking project teams to prepare for the program in a number of ways. The following activities have been used successfully to help teams get up and running fast:

- **Icebreaker exercises:** If team members have never met each other, they can be asked to introduce themselves to their teammates in a virtual environment before the program by answering a series of questions about their careers and their personal lives.

- **Collect information for the project:** While collecting 'just in case' information before the team really knows what it is looking for is not a good cognitive habit, looking at general overview information will provide some familiarization with the issues.

- **Interview experts:** The sponsor may be able to identify experts that the team should interview before the program. This procedure is also helpful in developing some pre-wired brain connections. Experts who share their overview mental patterns, rather than 'how-to' detailed tools, will be much more helpful.

- **Interview customers:** This prior information, on the other hand, is immensely helpful in broadening the relevance bandwidth of participants. Frequently teams start with very little insight into their customers and gaining some knowledge before the program will lead to a much richer project discussion.

■ **Build on knowledge from previous project experience:** If the program has been run previously, then the participants of the upcoming program can be asked to interview one person from the previous program to discover what the manager learned from their project experience and what advice they can give to the new participant embarking on their project.

Putting project teams together

Building up team diversity

Team diversity will ensure rich discussions during which the team members can share their mental patterns and look for overlap zones across them. It is useful for teams to include both experts and non-experts.

Each team should include at least two experts, who know and understand part of the subject matter to be used in the project work. These participants can then act as a point of information for the other team members, bringing everyone up to speed. In explaining their knowledge, the experts are pushed to expand this knowledge to a new context. This in turn increases the experts' own understanding and makes it more applicable. We recommend more than one expert because if there is only one, he or she can very effectively stonewall any new thinking.

It is also important to have non-expert team members who know nothing about parts of the subject matter required for the project. At first sight they may seem like a heavy burden for the team, but they perform a very useful role. Their lack of knowledge means they often ask the obvious questions that go to the heart of the problem. They can see issues in a new, fresh light and may challenge conventional thinking.

Team member assignment also needs to support any overall program goals and create the right mix for the learning agenda. For example, if one program objective is to promote networking and sharing across the company then teams should consist of members from a wide variety of business units and geographies. For the same reasons, carefully mixing MBTI profiles is also helpful. Mixing cognitive styles, for example, will bring together broad-categorizers who help see the whole picture, and narrow-categorizers who leave no stone unturned.

Setting up the participants' expectations

To ensure the required emotional commitment, participants must know why they have been selected to be part of a project team and what are the development expectations. When this has not been addressed, by the sponsor, by their direct boss, or by HR, they will often see their presence as an enormous waste of time.

Participants should also understand that working on the project is as important as their everyday job. So it is critical that the organizational space necessary to work on the project is provided. In particular, the time required to work on projects must have been cleared with their direct bosses. The individual performance objectives of the participants must also be aligned with their expected contributions to the project.

Finally, the expectations of the participants with respect to their attendance at a business school must be clearly set. Participants who expect top-down teaching, or time off, will respond very negatively to projects, so it is helpful to warn them that the focus will be on action learning before they arrive at the program.

Appointing a team leader or not

Appointing a team leader is not the responsibility of the faculty team coaches. This decision must be left to the company and, of course, both options have their advantages and disadvantages.

Some companies have strong views about the need to appoint a project leader for each team. This works well if two criteria are met. First, if the project will continue in the company after the program and the leader will be held accountable for results. Second, if the project leader is appointed for development purposes. Of course, even when these criteria are met, there is no guarantee that the team leader will be respected and actively followed.

Companies may decide not to appoint a leader. Again, this must be a well thought out choice and not made by default. Frequently on executive development programs teams consist of managers of similar grades. Here it is probably better not to officially appoint a project leader. In practice, if the team works effectively, one of two situations arises. Either a team leader will emerge that everyone in the team can respect or at least live with, or alternatively, the team rotates the leadership role at different points in time – a situation commonly found in high-performing teams.

Working with the project sponsors

Choosing the sponsor

Projects absolutely need to have an owner or sponsor within the company who takes a personal interest in making sure that the project will be completed to a high standard and who has a stake in the outcome. The visible commitment of the sponsor adds to the commitment and motivation of the team; it is a measure of the importance of the project. Apathetic sponsors are the kiss of death.

If the program is for senior company executives, then the CEO together with the executive board should choose and sponsor the projects. This sends an appropriate message about the level of importance of the initiatives. If the program is for middle managers, the project sponsors can be senior managers but it is best to choose sponsors who have a real stake in the outcome of the project and who are in a position to free up resources and give expert advice.

Senior HR managers should probably not act as project sponsors. Situations where HR attempts to design and sponsor projects, with only limited line involvement, will generally result in the projects being seen in the business as low priority items. The role of HR is to explain how the initiative fits within the company's people-development plan and to assess the personal development impact of the program over time. HR can contribute to the level of emotional commitment of the participants by making sure that recognition of personal development and development potential is seen as just as important as project results.

Preparing with the sponsor

It is important to make face-to-face or at least telephone contact with the sponsor before the program, both to get a better understanding of the project and to make clear what will be required from him or her during the project process. This provides several benefits, the first of which is hearing about the background to the project from the sponsor's mouth. There are many political issues that he or she might be reluctant to commit to paper but would be happy to talk about on the phone. This conversation will give you the real insight into why the project issue has not been tackled successfully before. It will help you assess the level of complexity of the project and adjust it to a productive learning initiative.

These discussions offer a good point at which to firm up the project deliverables and to confirm that the project is doable. If the sponsor is putting forward an ill-defined project then now is the time to ask him or her to mentally rehearse what the team will do and focus the scope of the project to suit the project timeframe.

You will very quickly be able to determine whether this project is a 'need to have' for the project sponsor. Sometimes it is useful to inquire how he or she came to be the sponsor of the project. Volunteers are clearly more willing than people who feel that they have been delegated 'the black spot.' If the sponsor seems totally unenthused, explore ways for the project definition to be rewritten into something that they can get excited about, even if it means changing the project focus.

Finally, you must discuss the learning agenda with the sponsor. The purpose of this discussion is to agree on the balance between learning and completing the project. Both should be done, of course, but, as discussed before, the project process may not always be exactly what the sponsor expects.

Working with the sponsor

Before the first workshop it is very helpful for the sponsor, the team and the coach to meet together before the project starts. This allows a discussion of the project scope, between the sponsor and the team, in the presence of the coach. At a minimum, the team leader must have met with the sponsor and with the coach.

During the workshop the presence of the sponsors is generally helpful but, of course, they should not be working with the team all the time. It is best if they participate in the short sessions when tasks and deliverables for each half-day are introduced, and in the synthesis discussions and reviews when these tasks are completed. If the sponsor cannot attend the workshop then it is important that he or she is available to speak with the team by phone. This will allow the team to verify certain hypotheses and options, before moving too far down the road with them.

What is risky is the first appearance at the end of the week of a sponsor who has not been sufficiently in the loop throughout the process, who does not exactly know what the team has done during the week. They may, as a result, make rather demotivating comments; for example, sweeping statements on slow progress to people who have just been spending 14 hours a day working on execution; or nitpicking on some minor details with a team trying to communicate in a few minutes the essence of a detailed execution plan.

During the execution phase, the sponsor can play several important roles to support the team:

- **Customer:** The sponsor should help the team fully understand the deliverables that he or she expects and should leave the team under no illusions that results must be delivered and that the team is accountable.

- **Boss:** The sponsor needs to commit to meeting regularly with the whole project team to discuss progress on the project, keep the team on track and to give timely feedback.

- **Challenger:** The sponsor should not be afraid to dig deep into the details and to make sure that no stone is left unturned. Pushing the team to explore the root causes of issues, or to build logical links between problems and solutions, or to keep an overview of the critical issues, can be particularly helpful.

- **Realist:** The sponsor should make sure that the project members' feet are firmly on the ground. If the team seems to be deluding themselves then it is up to the sponsor to speak up and face the brutal facts.

- **Resource provider:** The sponsor's role is to verify that the team has the right resources or capabilities and to help them to obtain them in a timely manner.

- **Roadblock remover:** The sponsor should coach the team on how to remove barriers and where necessary step in himself or herself to offer assistance.

- **Ambassador:** The sponsor promotes the project internally and hopefully deals with outspoken critics.

- **Mediator:** The sponsor needs to quietly work behind the scenes to ensure that the direct bosses of the team members understand the time commitment to the project and that the project deliverables are integrated into their subordinate's performance measures.

The project sponsor needs to be present for the final after-action review of the project. There should be no compromise on this matter. Only sponsors who can commit to being present at the final debriefing need apply for the job. In addition to recognizing project results, this is the time for the sponsor to express his or her appreciation of the learning and personal development that has taken place. Providing specific examples of how team members have developed throughout the project work and singling out exceptional contributions is also important. Finally, saying thank you in the name of the company signals that the efforts were all worth it.

Selecting a faculty team

The team of faculty coaches has to be selected carefully. It is important that they share a common learning philosophy, because this philosophy needs to be reflected in the way project teams are helped to think their way through their project.

A participant-centered learning approach

It should be clear by now that our learning agenda places the learner, rather than the teacher, at the center of the learning process. Academics like to give the answers. In a project context, this is particularly tempting and there are many occasions when the participants will welcome it. However, the coach must accept that he or she is not the center of attention and that demonstrating his or her smartness is not the point; the real point is helping the participants develop new insights. This requires the skill to ask guiding questions. Questioning the team in an open-ended manner about their implicit hypotheses and where they come from, about the problem they are trying to resolve may help them wire the mental patterns that allow a broader perspective.

Even though questions should be open-ended, questioning must be targeted; it is meant to help build solutions-oriented mental patterns for a business context. It requires the ability to spot what needs questioning, which assertions lack business logic, which arguments ignore business constraints, which discussions are unlikely to end with a business-viable outcome.

Working with the teams

The coach will have at heart the success of the project; this is indeed what he or she gets most recognition for. However, it should not be the coach who drives the project to success; it should be the participants themselves.

The challenge for the coach is to make oneself redundant. Thus his or her principal role is not to transmit knowledge, but to assist the participants to construct their own knowledge. This is achieved through two dimensions: one is to design a context that will effectively support this construction.

When doing so, the coach should always ask himself 'What is my desired impact on the learning of the team, on the learning of this participant? How will changing this variable improve the learning?' – and be ready to be wrong and try again differently. The other is through open-ended questioning that leads to responses from the participants and to more open-ended questions. This may create discomfort, annoyance, and more senior participants may attempt to use their authority to stop it, but the coach must explain quietly why this is not a waste of time.

When to intervene in the team's work is a delicate matter, simply because it is helpful to have some sort of a ritual or agreed-upon times for visiting, which legitimizes stepping into the team's thinking. Ideas take time to connect and there is sometimes a lot at stake in reconnecting mental patterns, so the process is not accomplished easily. 'Let's sleep on it' is a good idea that must be taken literally because during sleep, the brain performs some useful housekeeping and allows time for mental brewing. The best that the coach may do to help is to impose deadlines for coming up with some output.

Proposing a break may be the best way to help when the emotional intensity feels overwhelming. Genuinely asking whether this is a good time for a quick update may be a good response to being ignored. A quick around-the-table review of how things are going may provide airtime for dissention and, once this is acknowledged, the team may start moving ahead. Providing specific objectives to be achieved over the next 20 minutes and being back to review may also galvanize fresh momentum in a team at a standstill. And then there are times when intervention is best achieved by walking the talk: rolling up one's sleeves and handholding the team.

A last thought: remember that an experienced acupuncturist uses very few needles. He or she has an overview of what is going on in the body and intervenes selectively.

Key take-aways

■ A good learning project is a good business project that has a clear and compelling business purpose, is aligned with strategic priorities, is expected to deliver tangible business results, triggers emotional commitment and must have visibility and credibility within the company.

■ To avoid poor execution and follow-up, a modular program script is best: a first module on planning the project, followed by on-the-job project execution, and a second program module involving an after-action review of the results.

■ The best project teams have diverse membership, include both issue experts and non-experts, and companies have carefully considered whether there should be a designated project leader or rotating leadership.

■ The project sponsor must be committed and motivated, extensively briefed, and should have contact with the team before the project is launched, as well as during the program workshop, execution phase and after-action review.

■ The faculty coaches have to be carefully selected and share a learning philosophy based on participant-centered learning.

34

From emotions to solutions: Generational transition in family business

Joachim Schwass

Summary

Generational transition in a family business often provokes intense emotions. To deal with the uncertainty and conflict that this creates, families may want to address the issues through an education program. For the education provider, numerous challenges arise, including the heterogeneous nature of the participants; the need to develop rational solutions in response to largely emotionally driven issues; as well as the complex interface between the three levels of family, ownership and management. This chapter shows how to deliver effective learning in this context with a six-step program.

Generational transition, all too often, upsets a fragile and unspoken equilibrium. It confronts the family business stakeholders with a complex set of issues on different but interlinked levels, including family, ownership and management (which may include board members).

As the stakeholders grapple with these issues, a number of questions typically arise, whether before, during or after a generational transition:

- **Family:** Does the next generation share the vision of the outgoing generation regarding its continuing role for the family in the business, that is, does it want to run it like the outgoing generation thinks it should? Does the next generation intend to stay together or sever their family ties?

- **Ownership:** How will ownership in the business be distributed among next-generation family members? What type of ownership strategy will be adopted? Will there be exit opportunities for family members? Will non-family members be invited to invest?

▦ **Management:** Will family members be allowed to assume management responsibilities? If so, under what qualifying conditions? Will non-family management trust a new generation of owners?

Whether out in the open or hidden, these issues create a climate of uncertainty and the potential for conflict, which many families in business want to address through an education program. Their objectives typically are to:

▦ Understand the current situation on both group and individual levels.

▦ Find models and guidelines that might be applied for the identification of options for the future.

▦ Benchmark with other family businesses.

▦ Create a common platform for the family members to decide about next steps.

The educational challenge is multiple:

▦ Provide effective knowledge about the complex interfaces of three distinct disciplines: family, ownership and management.

▦ Shift the emphasis from largely emotionally driven issues to rationally derived solutions.

▦ Educate a group of individuals, who are heterogeneous in terms of age, educational background, activity, career stage, and emotional commitment to the family business.

The challenge is, therefore, to design a company-specific program that addresses the issues the family wants – and needs – to discuss, while providing the required educational input in a way which is relevant and engaging. Below we discuss how we go about this.

The program

While each company-specific program is tailored to the needs and situation facing the business and family, we typically use a six-step approach to guide both program design and delivery. After initial interviews, we carry out an in-depth analysis of the company that serves as a basis to customize the program.

Act 1: Education about the family business system

Typically, families in business operate in a system closed to the outside world. Family and, by extension, issues related to their business, are considered private affairs. Most families consider their case to be unique and different, which represents a crucial hurdle to be overcome.

To get the attention of the participants, it is important to transmit two messages:

1 Family businesses are a complex system.

2 The system is manageable.

We present the family business as a system, which can be analyzed and then changed. The entire logic of our educational program – putting a particular family business situation in context with standardized analytical structures – is based on this insight. Their problems are normal rather than unique.[1] Family participants who accept this experience enormous relief, for they come to realize that they can approach their issues rationally, rather than predominantly as a family member with all the emotional baggage that implies.

The first challenge for participants is to see that the family business system is made up of two very different components: the family and the business. Participants are asked to list the defining criteria of first the family component and then the business component. Typical listings are:

Family	Business
■ Emotions-based and personal.	■ Rationality-based.
■ Egalitarian.	■ Meritocratic.
■ Historically oriented.	■ Future-oriented.
■ 'Socialism'.	■ 'Capitalism'.

The key insight is that the family business system has a built-in potential for conflict because the two components – family versus business – operate according to distinct, if overlapping, sets of logic.

Act 2: Role of the individual in the system

In the second act, we ask participants to identify how they fit into the system as an individual. To do so, we first analyze the seven or more roles of the public corporation. Adding the family component inherent in a family business multiplies these roles, leading to a total of up to 15 different roles (see Figure 34.1 overleaf). By combining the four functions of family, ownership, management and board membership, the family business system is thus seen as more complex, with the innumerable combinations generating potential conflicts.

We explore examples of these conflicts for the individual combining more than one role, including the difficulty to separate and prioritize conflicting objectives as well as the need to clarify and explain this to others. To find a solution to each conflict as it arises, the company needs to balance the issues according to their relevance for family, ownership, management and board membership; this can be done only when the overlapping roles are separated out and approached systematically.

The key insight here is that the creation of boundaries – between the different areas of functional interest – leads to a *structured* understanding of the differing needs, which clarifies them both to the individual who takes (and expresses) a position and the individual receiving this information. The value of this insight for the participants is that what are typically perceived as emotional 'issues' often result from a lack of understanding of overlapping and sometimes conflicting interests and roles. The role model is a crucially important tool to shift from a decision-making process dominated by raw personal emotion to one based more on rationality and clear business concerns.

Act 3: Benchmarking

In this act, we lead the participants through a macro-benchmarking exercise with other family businesses. They are asked to read two multi-generational cases, which are differentiated by the degree of active involvement of the family in the business. Both cases are about recipients of the prestigious annual IMD Distinguished Family Business Award, which gives the cases high credibility both as an educational tool and for benchmarking.

The first case covers the Zegna family business from Italy, where in the fourth generation the family fully owns the business and takes the lead in its management. The second case is the Henkel family business, where in the fourth generation the company is publicly traded with the family exercising voting control, but not being active in management. The rationale for the selection of each case is to: (1) demonstrate the evolution of successful family businesses over several generations, and (2) highlight family roles as they evolve both in terms of ownership and the management levels.

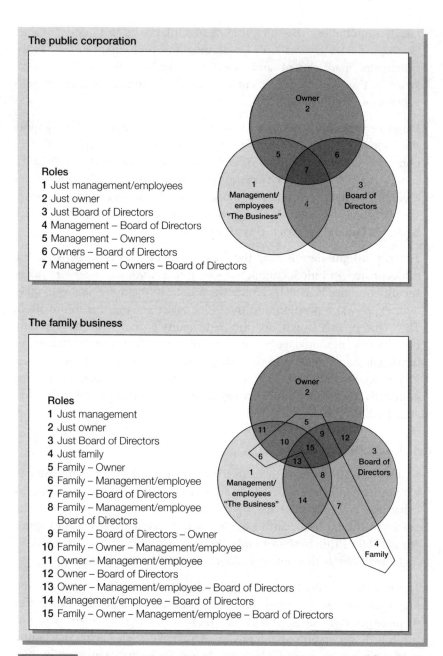

The public corporation

Owner
2

5   6
7
1
Management/
employees   4
"The Business"

3
Board of
Directors

Roles
1 Just management/employees
2 Just owner
3 Just Board of Directors
4 Management – Board of Directors
5 Management – Owners
6 Owners – Board of Directors
7 Management – Owners – Board of Directors

The family business

Owner
2

Roles
1 Just management
2 Just owner
3 Just Board of Directors
4 Just family
5 Family – Owner
6 Family – Management/employee
7 Family – Board of Directors
8 Family – Management/employee
   Board of Directors
9 Family – Board of Directors – Owner
10 Family – Owner – Management/employee
11 Owner – Management/employee
12 Owner – Board of Directors
13 Owner – Management/employee – Board of Directors
14 Management/employee – Board of Directors
15 Family – Owner – Management/employee – Board of Directors

11   5   9   12
10   15
6   13   3
Board of
1   8   Directors
Management/
employees
"The Business"   14   7

4
Family

Figure 34.1 Public corporation versus family business roles

Divided into groups, the participants are asked:

For both Zegna and Henkel, over time, what is the value added by the family to the business, and the value added by the business to the family?

This exercise not only raises the comfort level of the participants as they recognize certain similarities with their own family business, but it forces them to systematically analyze the value exchanged between family and business. This deepens their understanding of why and how these family businesses have successfully mastered several generational transitions.

The conclusions that spring from these cases are that business provides a sense of purpose, beyond the financial contribution to the family, and family provides a value-based vision and stability to the business.

The key insight is that both family and business create value that can be broken down into strategically manageable components.

Act 4: The evolutionary family business model

The two cases on fourth-generation family businesses suggest an evolutionary model[2] for family business generations, with particular emphasis on the cultural dimension:

- **Owner/manager/founding generation**
  'I' culture
- **Sibling/team generation**
  'US' culture
- **Cousin/network generation**
  'US and THEM' culture

We discuss each stage, with emphasis on transition planning, as each stage has different cultural characteristics and needs. Returning to the Zegna and Henkel cases highlights the differences between the stages and how these particular family businesses successfully developed their own strategic plans for the generational transition. The participants are invited to reflect on what they perceive to be the future challenges of both businesses regarding the next generational transition.

The key insight is a systematic understanding of how family businesses can evolve over generations and what elements are required for a strategic planning process that takes the family and the business into the next generation.

Act 5: Where are we?

With the models and benchmarks provided in the first four steps, the participants are now invited to apply these concepts to their own particular situation. They are asked:

For your own family business, over time, what is the value added by the family to the business, and the value added by the business to the family?

Multi-generational breakout groups are formed in order to facilitate intergenerational contacts, the exchange of historic information, and mutual understanding. Ideally, the family is given this assignment at the end of the first day, which creates the opportunity for continuing informal discussion later in the evening. The reporting takes place on the next morning and provides a broad and deep discussion base. Typically, difficult historic events tend to surface and a formal facilitation of the discussion is necessary.

The key task is for the family to apply the structured learning to their own situation. Together, they must systematically analyze their history, thereby gaining a clearer understanding of the current situation on the different interest levels of family, ownership, management and board membership; this provides a platform for the identification of the next steps.

Act 6: What are the next steps?

After summarizing the key lessons from the first five steps, the program concludes with a definition of an action plan for the participant group. Typically, the families understand that the generational transition planning process requires the next generation to explicitly define their own vision for the future of the family business. The younger generation is invited to formalize its vision and to submit it to the senior generation for approval. Educators then explain the components of a 'Program for the Next Generation Vision,' as the program closes.

Conclusion

Family businesses face complex, though common issues, which require both a multidisciplinary approach and multi-level insights.

The six-step company-specific educational program described here provides a unique setting for families to understand the complex system of their family business as well as the models and strategies relevant to them. With these tools, they can apply it to themselves and create a shared vision for the future benefit of family, ownership and management stakeholders. The overall program objective is to give the participants a common platform to develop rational strategies to successfully take their family business into another generation.

Key take-aways

■ The family business system is complex but can be put in context with standardized structures, analyzed, and subsequently influenced.

■ 'De-emotionalization' is key: typically, emotionally perceived conflicts result from a lack of understanding of the conflicting objectives faced by individuals combining multiple roles.

■ Benchmarking against other family businesses deepens participants' understanding as to what these organizations have done to successfully manage their generational transitions.

Notes

1 See Chapter 25 by John L. Ward for further discussion of this topic.
2 This model builds on the Stages Model developed by John L. Ward in Chapter 26.

Appendix

IMD's executive education portfolio

IMD is an independent, executive education institution, funded entirely through its programs, research and partnership activities. Every year, more than 5,500 executives from over 70 countries attend our executive programs. Across a wide range of rankings based on different indices and methodologies, IMD is consistently ranked among the top providers of executive education. For example, *The Wall Street Journal*'s 2004 survey ranked IMD's MBA program No. 1 worldwide, while *BusinessWeek*'s 2003 Executive Education 2003 survey ranked IMD No. 1 in customized programs, No. 1 in Executive MBA programs and No. 2 in open enrolment programs outside the US. Based on the most recent comparison of services, IMD is the third largest executive education school worldwide (*BusinessWeek* Executive Education Survey 2003).

The executive education insights and scripts described in this book represent best practice across our portfolio of executive education offerings, with best practice determined by participant evaluations. This appendix lists the programs in the portfolio which is the underlying database for the book.

IMD offers four distinct types of program: Partnership (in-company) programs, open enrollment (public) programs, degree programs (MBA and Executive MBA) and Learning Network activities such as webcasts, forums and research Discovery Events. For more detail please refer to our website at www.imd.ch.

Partnership (in-company) programs

In-company programs are designed to address the unique learning needs of our corporate partners. In 2004, over 80 companies partnered with IMD to create their own learning experiences through more than 115 programs.

These companies include:

ABB Asea Brown Boveri Ltd

Adecco

Aegon NV

Allianz Group

Bertelsmann AG

BMW Group

Robert Bosch GmbH

Carlsberg AS

Canon Inc

Clariant International Ltd

Coca-Cola Helenic Bottling Company

Credit Suisse Group

DaimlerChrysler AG

Degussa

DuPont de Nemours International

Deloitte

E.ON AG

Ernst & Young

Firmenich SA

Fortis

Fujitsu

Givaudan Fragrances Corporation

Groupe SEB

Henkel KGaa

Hilton International

Hitachi Ltd

F. Hoffmann La Roche Ltd

Holcim Ltd

HSBC Holdings plc

KPMG

Lafarge

Masterfoods

A. P. Möller

Nestlé SA

Philip Morris International

PricewaterhouseCoopers

Royal Philips Electronics

Sara Lee DE

Schindler Management AG

Shell International Petroleum Company Ltd

Siemens

Swiss Reinsurance Company

Telenor Mobil A/S

Tetra Laval Group

TietoEnator Corporation

Toyota Motor Europe

RWE (Thames Water plc)

Unilever

Vodafone Group Services

Wild Group

Wolseley plc

Open enrollment/public programs

IMD offers a wide range of open enrollment programs, centered on strategic leadership and execution. All are aimed at the real needs of practicing business leaders, draw heavily on original learning material developed from IMD research, and target high-potential top to middle managers from global companies. The following programs are offered exclusively by IMD in 2005:

Top Management Forums

- Building High Performance Boards
- Mastering Top Management Dilemmas

General Management Programs

- Breakthrough Program for Senior Executives
- Managing Corporate Resources
- Program for Executive Development

- Mastering Technology Enterprise
- Building on Talent

Orchestrating Winning Performance

Leadership Programs

- Mobilizing People
- High Performance Leadership
- Strategic Leadership for Women
- Work–Life Balance

Execution Capability Programs

- The Booster Program
- Mastering New Challenges
- Business Marketing
- Strategic Finance
- Driving Strategic Innovation
- Leading the Family Business

The following programs are offered in alliance with leading European, US and Asian schools:

- Driving Strategic Innovation (with the MIT Sloan School in Boston, US)
- Strategic Dilemmas (with the MIT Sloan School in Boston, US)
- Mastering Technology Enterprise (with the Swiss Federal Institutes of Technology in Lausanne and Zürich)
- Job of the Chief Executive (with the Singapore Institute of Management and the Asian Association of Management Organizations)

Degree programs

IMD offers the following degree programs exclusively:

- Master of Business Administration
- Executive MBA

IMD Learning Network

IMD maintains a learning partnership with over 140 global companies who drive our research agenda and program design, demanding relevance and challenging innovation. While each company has different strategic and management development needs, they operate at an international level, have a strong market orientation, focus on results and are passionate about understanding how learning can have a positive and tangible impact in an organization. The members of the Learning Network in 2005 are:

Partner Companies

ABB Asea Brown Boveri Ltd
ABN Amro Bank
Accenture
Allianz Group
A. P. Möller
Bertelsmann AG
Boston Consulting Group
BP Plc
BT Group
Caterpillar Inc
Credit Suisse Group
DaimlerChrysler

Deloitte
Dentsu Inc
DSM NV
DuPont de Nemours International
F. Hoffmann La Roche Ltd
Heerema Holding
Henkel KgaA
Holcim Ltd
HSBC Holdings Plc
IBM Europe
ISS A/S
Lend Lease Plc

Masterfoods
Nestlé SA
Nokia Corporation
Novartis
PricewaterhouseCoopers
Royal Philips Electronics
Shell International Petroleum Company Ltd
Swiss Re
Tetra Laval Group
UBS AG
Unilever
Yukos Oil Company
Zürich Financial Services

Business Associates

Adecco SA
Aegon The Netherlands nv
Ajinomoto Co., Inc
Alcoa
Arthur D. Little
Asahi Glass Co., Ltd
ASML Netherlands BV
Assa Abloy AB
Aventis
AVL List GmbH
Ballarpur Industries Limited

Bank Julius Baer
BBVA Banco Bilbao Vizcaya Argentaria
Bekaert Group
Belgacom
BMW Group
Borealis
British American Tobacco
Canon
Carlsberg A/S
Chevron Texaco

Ciba Specialty Chemicals Inc
Clariant International Ltd
CMS Legal Services EEIG
Coca-Cola HBC, S.A
Confederation of Danish Industries
Considium Learning Group
Danfoss AS

Danisco
Danske Bank
Degussa AG
Den Norske Bank
Det Norske Veritas
DEXIA Group
Dubai Internet City
Egon Zehnder
International
EMC
Corporation
Ernst & Young
ETISALAT Emirates
Telecommunications
Firmenich SA
Fortis NV
Fujitsu
Givaudan Fragrances
Corporation
Groupe SEB
Grundfos Group
Hilti AG
Hilton International
Hitachi Ltd
ICI Plc
I.M. Skaugen ASA
International
Finance Corporation
Itochu Corporation
Japan Tobacco
International
Jose de Mello (SGPS)
SA
Jotun A/S

KLM Royal Dutch
Airlines
Kongsberg Gruppen
ASA
KPMG
Lafarge
LEGO Group
Lombard Odier
Darier Hentsch & Cie
Metsaliitto Group
Metso Corporation
MTN Mobile
Telephone Networks
Norske Skogindustrier
ASA
Novo Nordisk A/S
Numico nv
Panasonic Europe Ltd
Philip Morris
International
PubliGroupe
Puig Corporation
Rabobank Group
Randstad Holding nv
Reynolds & Reynolds
Robert Bosch GmbH
Rockwool International
A/S
RPG Enterprises
RWE Group
Sara Lee DE
Saurer AG
Scandinavian Tobacco
Schindler Management
AG

Scottish & Newcastle Plc
Scottish Power Plc
SEB-Skandinaviska
Enskilda Banken
SHARP Corporation
SICPA Group
Siemens
SITA
Skanska AB
Spectris Plc
State Farm Insurance
Statoil ASAJotun A/S
Strauman Holding AG
Telenor
The Dow Chemical
Company
The Wall Street Journal
Europe
The World Bank
TietoEnator Corporation
Toyota Motor Europe
TPG nv
Tupperware
Unaxis Management Ltd
Union Bancaire Privee
Uponor
Vodafone Group
Services Ltd
Wartsila Corporation
Wild Group
Wolseley Plc
WWL-Wallenius
Wilhelmsen Lines AS

Index